Edexcel
Government and Politics for AS

Third Edition

Neil McNaughton

DYNAMIC
L'EARNING

HODDER
EDUCATION
AN HACHETTE UK COMPANY

This material has been endorsed by Edexcel and offers high quality support for the delivery of Edexcel qualifications.

Edexcel endorsement does not mean that this material is essential to achieve any Edexcel qualification, nor does it mean that this is the only suitable material available to support any Edexcel qualification. No endorsed material will be used verbatim in setting any Edexcel examination and any resource lists produced by Edexcel shall include this and other appropriate texts. While this material has been through an Edexcel quality assurance process, all responsibility for the content remains with the publisher.

Copies of official specifications for all Edexcel qualifications may be found on the Edexcel website — www.edexcel.com

Orders: please contact Bookpoint Ltd, 130 Milton Park, Abingdon, Oxon OX14 4SB. Telephone: (44) 01235 827720. Fax: (44) 01235 400454. Lines are open from 9.00–5.00, Monday to Saturday, with a 24 hour message answering service. You can also order through our website www.hoddereducation.co.uk

If you have any comments to make about this, or any of our other titles, please send them to educationenquiries@hodder.co.uk

British Library Cataloguing in Publication Data
A catalogue record for this title is available from the British Library

ISBN: 978 1 444 11327 3

First Edition Published 2006
Second Edition Published 2008
This Edition Published 2010
Impression number   10 9 8 7 6 5 4 3
Year   2014 2013 2012 2011

Copyright © 2010 Neil McNaughton

Hachette UK's policy is to use papers that are natural, renewable and recyclable products and made from wood grown in sustainable forests. The logging and manufacturing processes are expected to conform to the environmental regulations of the country of origin.

Cover photo © Jiri Kabele/iStockphoto.com
Typeset by Servis Filmsetting Ltd, Stockport, Cheshire
Printed and bound in Dubai for Hodder Education, an Hachette UK Company, 338 Euston Road, London NW1 3BH

Contents

Preface to the third edition

The reason for publishing a third edition of this book was, originally, the need to reflect the recent changes that have been made to the Edexcel specification in Government and Politics. In particular, Unit 1 now reflects a changing attitude to the nature of democracy in Britain. Examiners are likely to be less concerned with the state of British political institutions (though they remain important) and more interested in the nature of the relationships between the state and its citizens. This relationship and the nature of the citizenry is often referred to as the *demos*.

There is also a little more emphasis on the distribution of power, not only among institutions, but between people and government – so it is concerned with the evolving role of parties, pressure groups and other social movements, including the new social networks. We must now ask where power is being further dispersed and where it is becoming more concentrated. We also must ask questions about the nature of the disengagement of people from politics that has been taking place over two decades or more. 'Why is this is happening?' and 'What can be done to ameliorate it?' are legitimate lines of inquiry.

In terms of institutions, the new edition reflects growing interest in the changing nature of political institutions and the relationships between them. There is a danger that textbooks can present a static model of politics when the truth is that change has been accelerating since the 1980s. This is partly the result of constitutional reform, which is ongoing, and partly a reflection of the influence of Europe, but perhaps mostly it is the result of a recognition that political institutions today need to be more open and responsive to public moods and demands. The broadcast and electronic social media have brought the public closer to political institutions than ever before. They have, therefore, had to reform themselves.

But a new factor has rendered this new edition essential. That is the aftermath of the general election of 6 May 2010. This has challenged many of our assumptions about the political system. At the time of writing it is impossible to determine whether these changes will be permanent, but they have certainly reshaped the way people think about politics.

The new edition describes the events of 2010, at least up to the creation of the coalition government. It analyses how and why it occurred, and speculates about how government and politics may be changed for ever. It also describes the legacy which that election has left behind. Apart, perhaps, from the judiciary, all Britain's main political institutions have been affected. In addition, it is likely that important constitutional reforms will ensue. Politics in Britain suddenly became 'interesting' again in 2010. Hopefully this edition reflects that development.

Once again I would like to record my thanks to Colin Goodlad and Matthew Sullivan at Hodder Education as well as Viv Church, who has edited the material, for their help, advice and encouragement, especially as there has been relatively little time to produce this new edition. I have also received a great deal of help from my colleague, Anna Rose O'Dwyer at St Paul's School, who updated some of the material.

Neil McNaughton
London, May 2010

Acknowledgements

The author and publishers would like to thank the following for the use of photographs in this volume:

© Library of Congress Prints and Photographs Division, p25; © Christopher Furlong/ Getty Images, p34; © PA Archive/Press Association Images, p58; © Jeff Moore/Empics Entertainment/Press Association Images, p69; © Rex Features, p71; © AP/Press Association Images, p78; © PA Wire/Press Association Images, p82, p88, p99, p104, p107; © Ray Tang / Rex Features, p113; © Rex Features, p143; © PA Archive/Press Association Images, p159; © Andy Butterton/PA Archive/Press Association Images, p162; © US National Archives and Records Administration, p170; © EMPICS Entertainment/ Press Association Images, p200; © PA Archive/ Press Association Images, p205, p222; © PA Wire/Press Association Images, p232, p242, p275, p276; © AP/Press Association Images, p279, p308.

The author and publishers would like to thank the following for the use of copyright material in this volume:

Electoral Reform Society for the tables on p109 and pgs 135-36; Copyright Guardian News & Media Ltd 2006, p318. © Crown copyright material is reproduced with permission of the Controller of HMSO.

Introduction

What is politics?

The linguistic origin of the term *politics* lies in Ancient Greek and is derived from the word *polis*. This referred to the city or state – either is appropriate since classical Greece was divided into a number of small city-states such as Athens and Sparta, each of which was both a city and an independent state. We can hear the legacy of the word *polis* in such terms as 'acropolis' (a city or fortress on a hill) and 'metropolis' (a capital or important city).

Although *politics* derived from the word *polis*, a general term meaning simply 'of the city' or 'of the state', in practice it came to refer to the activity of managing the affairs of the **state**. This is clearly a very narrow definition of what politics is, but it is one that many conservatives in particular might prefer to use. Politics, therefore, could mean simply the business of managing the state in the best way possible, without any ideological content. It might imply little more than protecting the people from internal or external threat and ensuring their general welfare. But such an incomplete definition would be better described by the word **government**. In today's world, 'politics' suggests *conflict* – that is, conflict between ideas, conflict between sections of the community and conflict between individuals.

Often – perhaps too often – political conflict can break out into violence. This may take the form of general disorder and/or terrorist activity (as in Northern Ireland from 1968 to the mid-1990s, or in the Middle East), revolution (as in Russia in 1917) or civil war (China in the 1930s and 1940s, Sudan and Afghanistan more recently). Such violence can be viewed as a *failure* of politics. If conflict cannot be resolved peacefully within political institutions and processes, groups often resort to violence. In Northern Ireland in the 1990s and 2000s, for example,

Key Word

State *The state* is a collective name for the institutions that administer a country. Normally these institutions are non-political and are permanent, such as the civil service, judiciary and law enforcement agencies. *A state*, meanwhile, refers to a country whose government's jurisdiction over a territory is recognised by other states.

Key Word

Government can mean the process of organising the state and giving it political direction. It also refers to the institutions that apply political principles to the running of the state.

successive British governments and leaders sought to persuade political leaders – even those who led extreme groups such as Sinn Fein and the Democratic Unionists – to renounce violence and pursue their goals through conventional, peaceful politics instead. In the event, peaceful politics was finally and happily restored to the province in 2007.

Professor Bernard Crick, in his celebrated work *In Defence of Politics* (4th edn, 1992), summed up the meaning and importance of politics thus: 'Politics arises from accepting the fact of the simultaneous existence of different groups, hence different interests and different traditions, within a territorial unit under a common rule.'

The conflict of ideas

Modern politics would not be politics unless those who take part in it adopt and promote ideas as to how the state should be run and how society should be shaped. When individuals go to the polling station to cast their votes they generally have political ideas in their minds, however mild and unformed these may be, when they vote. The ordinary members of political parties presumably join their party in the first place because they have political ideas and hope to further them through their chosen party. Politicians themselves, whether they be local councillors, MPs or ministers, are continuously involved in promoting political ideas. At all levels of politics, therefore, we see and hear the clash of ideas.

On a grand scale, political ideas become 'ideologies'. An ideology can be defined as a collection of ideas that propose social change and include some 'blueprint' for a future idealised society. These ideas are also based upon one or several specific principles such as equality, common ownership of property or individual liberty. Ideologies are often radical, and so those who support them usually flourish on the extremities of moderate western politics. The

most influential and successful ideologies have included, for example, socialism, fascism, feminism and radical forms of liberalism and nationalism (for now we will not consider conservatism as an ideology, for reasons that will be explored later). When ideologies come into conflict, politics can become extremely volatile. This occurs because ideologically motivated groups tend to have firmly held views and are especially determined to bring about their political goals. It is for this reason that ideological conflict often breaks out into violence, as described above.

On the whole, however, in the stable, well-established 'democracies' of the world, politics remains a moderate, peaceful activity. Most political activists probably wish to create changes in society without proposing any *fundamental* changes. These changes may be based loosely upon ideological thinking, but they may also be viewed as ways of improving the general welfare and security of the people. The table below identifies a number of political ideas that they have emerged in the UK in the early years of the twenty-first century, together with their opposing beliefs.

Contemporary political idea	Opposing view
Britain should retain the pound and not join the single European currency for the foreseeable future.	Britain should join the single European currency.
The people of Britain are overtaxed and therefore the general level of taxation should be reduced.	Taxation is at the appropriate level to support a good standard of public services.
We are losing the war on crime and should adopt a harsher	The UK needs to concentrate more on the causes of crime

Contemporary political idea	Opposing view
attitude towards criminals and criminal behaviour.	and use sentencing to prevent reoffending rather than as mere punishment.
Britain must retain the USA as a close ally and so was right to participate in the war in Iraq to depose Saddam Hussein.	The war in Iraq against Saddam Hussein was unjustified and Britain should concentrate on its relations with the rest of Europe.

How these conflicting ideas are resolved forms the fabric of politics. At every level of politics – the electorate, the media, party members, MPs, peers, ministers and political advisers – such differences have to be ironed out.

The conflict of interests

When we use the term 'interests' we mean sections of the community that have an interest in their own concerns. Various groups may feel they need special protection, that they do not receive their fair share of the national wealth, or are not treated fairly by government. The nature of such groups, or interests, varies considerably. They may be occupational groups, such as firefighters, students or nurses; they may be regional, such as those who live in the countryside, or inhabitants of regions that are economically depressed; they may be representatives of industries such as tobacco manufacturing, brewing or horse-racing. In essence, an 'interest', as far as politics is concerned, is any group that seeks to act to achieve some improvements in its own circumstances.

Interests naturally use the political system and the members of the political community to further their own cause. They sometimes attach themselves to a political party. Trade unions, in particular, have always worked closely with the Labour Party (indeed, Labour actually emerged from the trade union movement at the start of the twentieth century). More recently the Countryside Alliance, which defends the interests of members of rural communities, naturally saw the Conservative Party as its most traditional supporter. In more general terms, interests will use a variety of methods to further their aims. This may involve public demonstrations, media campaigns, influence in Parliament and so on. Their methods will be explored further in Chapter 1.4.

So part of politics is about the clash of such interests. Often their aims conflict with each other and politics is the process of resolving them. Examples of such conflicts are shown below.

Interest groups' aims	Opposing interests
Health groups oppose smoking in public places in the interests of reducing smoking-related diseases.	The tobacco industry naturally opposes such restrictions.
All trade unions in the National Health Service campaign for better wages and working conditions.	Taxpayers resist the extra burden on public finances as they naturally hope to pay less tax or prevent the need for tax increases.
Those who live in the countryside campaign for more state aid for rural transport, local services, farming, etc.	Those who live in cities may resist the idea that they should subsidise rural communities.

So some political activity inevitably involves the resolution of such conflicts of interests.

The struggle for power

Arguably, the desire for power is a natural human characteristic. This is a contentious view and some ideological groups, anarchists in particular, may deny it. However, we need not concern ourselves with psychology or philosophy here. What matters to us in our study of political behaviour is that modern society clearly produces many people who do have a drive to achieve and exercise power. Many will say, of course, that their motives for achieving power are altruistic. They have a desire to improve society in some way and must therefore gain power to be able to do so. Yet some may seek power *for its own sake*. Whichever is true – and perhaps both are true – there can be no doubt that politics is about the struggle for power between individuals and groups.

This struggle takes many forms, some of which are shown below:

● Parties compete against each other for power at European, national, regional and local elections.

● Individuals compete at elections to become representatives in local councils, regional assemblies or the Westminster Parliament itself.

● Individual politicians compete to be appointed to senior positions, either in the government or on the opposition front bench.

● At the very highest level of power, there is a struggle to be prime minister within the governing party.

These struggles for political power are what many of us think of when we use the term 'politics'. This is partly because the media tend to concentrate on such issues when reporting on politics and partly because the struggle for power does, to some extent, reflect the other conflicts we have described. Clearly, which party wins an election will determine to a degree which political ideas become dominant and which interests are more likely to be favoured.

When Margaret Thatcher was elected leader of the Conservative Party in 1975 the policy direction of her party began to change and the nature of British society was ultimately transformed during her premiership in the 1980s. The election to power of the Labour Party in 1997 after 18 years of Conservative government also began to change the balance of power in Britain. Under Thatcher, for example, financial and business interests certainly found themselves considerably more influential, while trade unions lost much of their political impact. Under Labour, after 1997, Britain became more closely integrated within the European Union and the interests of the poor were more favoured.

So, when individuals seek political power, the effects of the outcome can be far reaching. At the same time, however, the struggle for power is, to some extent, merely a reflection of a natural desire of some individuals to gain status and influence.

What is government?

Before we attempt definitions of government and the state, it may be useful to consider a number of concepts that are related to such institutions. In particular, it is important to understand the principles that lie behind the activity of governing.

Legitimacy

Here we are asking the question: what gives any government the *right* to rule? This refers both to the *system* of government – for example, monarchy, single-party rule, parliamentary democracy, etc. – and to the individuals who hold office within the government. It is a difficult question to resolve because it has a number of answers, all of which are plausible.

Key Word

Legitimacy refers to the degree to which the state or its government can be considered to have the right to exercise power. A state or government can be said to be legitimate if it has a valid claim to rule.

There are several possible ways in which **legitimacy** can be claimed.

Tradition is the first option. This suggests that a system of rule is legitimate if it has existed for a long period of time. Traditionalist conservatives will often support this justification on the grounds that government which evolves *naturally* is most acceptable to its people. The best example of this kind of rule is hereditary monarchy. Of course, it is no longer acceptable in most modern societies for such monarchs to govern (the crown heads of such countries as the UK, Sweden and the Netherlands do not govern as such, they are largely figureheads). But there are societies that accept hereditary rule on traditional grounds. Saudi Arabia and the small emirates around the Arabian Gulf, such as Bahrain and Dubai, are prominent examples. As long as such states remain stable and there is an absence of significant opposition, it can be argued that hereditary monarchy is a legitimate form of rule.

Force is a more controversial basis for rule. The argument here is that *any* government, no matter how it is constituted, could be seen as legitimate if it is able to maintain peace and security within a country. This is sometimes described as 'might is right'.

Few of us, however, would accept force as a suitable criterion for legitimacy. This is particularly true if the regime in question is seen as unpleasant, through abuses of human rights, discrimination against minorities and so on. The regime of Saddam Hussein in Iraq, which was removed by force in 2003, was a case in point. Of course, whether the lack of democracy and persecution of ethnic and religious groups in that country was justification for removing the regime is open to question. It is also difficult to establish whether the people of such autocratic regimes consent to be governed by them, even if their methods do not appeal to us. The fact that a government does not respect human rights does not necessarily make it illegitimate. We may wish to judge the current Chinese regime on this basis.

Consent has now become the most important criterion for legitimacy. The principle itself is simple: if a regime enjoys the broad consent of its people, it can be considered to be legitimate. Nevertheless, there are some problems in establishing whether sufficient consent exists. The problems include the following:

- People may have consented in the past, but how do we know they still consent? Do we have to see regular referendums to approve the system of government? Even the most open of democracies do not do this.

- What proportion of the people consent? Is a simple majority enough? Should there be a broader consensus of support?

- How do we know whether the people consent? If turnout at elections is low (for example, in the UK and the USA), does this signify lack of consent to the *system* of government, or does it merely suggest dissatisfaction with the parties and individuals who run the government? Does a lack of open dissent (demonstrations, rioting and so on) signify consent or merely fear among the people?

In practice, of course, we can use general peace and stability as a sign of consent. In the UK there is no significant movement to change the system of parliamentary democracy. We can safely conclude, therefore, that the government is legitimate.

Power, authority and sovereignty

Power

In a general sense, **power** can mean the ability to make other people or groups do what one wants them to do, even if this is against their will. But this is too simple a definition. Clearly we use the term 'power' to signify a whole variety of means by which one individual or institution is able to exert its will over others. In particular we need to consider different *levels* of power. These are set out below.

Coercive power is the strongest form. This can also be described as *force.* Coercion involves the use of physical force, or at least the threat of physical force. In extreme cases, coercion can involve the use of execution, torture, terror and imprisonment of opponents, as has occurred in many totalitarian regimes. Of course, most states do not need to go to such extremes. It is sufficient to reserve the use of force against those who refuse to conform to the laws or who threaten the security of the state itself. In such cases prison is the most common sanction. Indeed, it has been said that 'all states are founded on force'. What this means is that a state must reserve the right to use force in order to ensure security and peace. The law must be enforced and coercion is a key means of enforcement. But the more stable and united the state, the less coercion has to be used.

Political power is perhaps how we generally understand the concept. This is the power exercised by members of the political community, including parties, their leaders and other institutions. Political power includes the ability to persuade, but it normally involves the use of rewards and sanctions. Thus prime ministers in the UK have power because of their use of patronage. Since a prime minister controls the appointment of all ministers and many other senior positions in the apparatus of the state, such as top civil servants and judges, s/he is able

to exercise power. This is particularly true when we consider the way in which the party whips in Parliament are able to control MPs. By making it clear that loyalty to the party line may improve an individual's career prospects, power is effectively being exercised.

The strongest form of political power, however, is that which is granted by Parliament – the ultimate source of all political power in the UK. Thus, government departments, their ministers, devolved government in Scotland and Wales, local authorities and other public bodies have all been granted powers by Acts of Parliament. The powers of the prime minister, meanwhile, have been established largely by tradition or *convention,* as such traditions are often known. This means that a prime minister exercises power simply because everybody in the political community accepts that s/he has the traditional right to do so.

In stable democracies, coercion is not needed to reinforce such political powers. Nearly everybody involved in politics, as well as the electorate at large, understands that certain members of the political system should have such power.

Influence is the weakest form of power. We often use the word 'power' when we really mean influence. Thus it is said that the newspapers have 'power', or that public opinion is powerful, or that trade unions have power within the Labour Party. In each of these cases it is really *influence* that is being referred to. In such examples the press, the people and unions may have some influence over what government and

Parliament do, but they cannot enforce their wishes in any way.

Authority

This is a more difficult term than power. Often the terms **power** and **authority** are used interchangeably. But in politics it is extremely important to distinguish between them. Put simply, authority is the *right* to exercise power, it is not power itself. When we say a teacher exercises authority, for example, what is meant is that he or she has been granted power over the pupils by the head teacher and, more indirectly, by the parents and the wider community. Thus, the source of the authority allows the teacher to exercise power.

In pure democracies all political authority has its source in the people. The situation in Britain, however, is more complex. While it is true that many of those working in the political system exercise power because they have been directly or indirectly elected by the people, this cannot be said of either the prime minister or the monarch. Their sources of authority have been described as *charismatic* or *traditional*. The ruling party, meanwhile, rules because it has won a general election. This is known as *elective* or *rational* authority. The German sociologist Max Weber (1864–1920) clarified the nature of political authority by identifying its nature in three ways:

✔ Key Word

Authority The right to exercise power, rather than the exercise of power itself. Authority is granted to rulers or anyone in power by those over whom power is to be exercised. Without authority, power becomes mere force.

- **Traditional authority**: the right to govern exists because authority has existed over a long period of time. This applies particularly to hereditary monarchies, such as the sheikhdoms of the Middle East. It can be assumed that if the people have allowed such monarchies to exercise power over a long period of time, they are, by implication, consenting to such rule.

- **Charismatic authority**: the term 'charisma' refers to an individual's ability to inspire and persuade and attract a following, by the force of their personality. Here authority is granted simply by acclaim, because the people wish to be governed by a particular leader. Very often charismatic authority is combined with other forms and so increases the quantity of authority, allowing more power to be exercised. We can say, for example, that President John F. Kennedy in the USA enjoyed charismatic authority to add to his elective authority (US presidents are directly elected, so enjoy direct elective authority). Though we may find it unpalatable, it has to be said that fascist leaders such as Hitler and Mussolini also claimed such authority.

- **Legal-rational authority**: this refers to any rational way of granting authority. In practice, in modern democracies, this is always by election. So it can be best described as 'elective authority'. In current politics, elective authority is undoubtedly the most powerful justification for the exercise of power.

If we now turn to an examination of authority within the political system of the UK, we can discover the source of authority of each of the main institutions, as demonstrated in the table on page 8.

Before leaving this subject it is important to note that it can happen that individuals or institutions attempt to exercise more power than their authority warrants. When this occurs we can

Institution	Main source(s) of authority
Parliament	The authority (which is limited) of the House of Lords is **traditional**. The Commons' main source of authority is by **election** and, therefore, the people. However, the fact that Parliament *as a whole* is sovereign has its origins in **tradition**.
The government	Clearly the government's authority is **elective**.
The monarch	Though the power of the monarchy is very limited indeed, the Crown enjoys considerable **traditional** authority.
The prime minister	Much of the PM's authority is **traditional**, but s/he also enjoys indirect **elective** authority in terms of being the leader of the ruling party. Some prime ministers, such as Winston Churchill and Margaret Thatcher, were also said to enjoy **charismatic** authority to reinforce the other two sources.

say they are acting in an *authoritarian* manner. In most cases, however, there will come a time when such authoritarian figures will be brought under control. Certainly some prime ministers have been accused of claiming more power than they have authority to claim. As Margaret Thatcher discovered, when her own party removed her from power in 1990, this is a dangerous practice.

Sovereignty

It is important to avoid a point of potential confusion before examining the meaning of

sovereignty. The monarch of the UK is sometimes described as the 'Sovereign' or even the 'Sovereign Lord'. This appears to indicate that the monarch holds supreme power. While this may have been true up to the seventeenth century, it is clearly no longer the case. The reason this has occurred is that it was certainly true in the past that, historically, the Monarch was indeed the sovereign power. Although the term is no longer valid it is often still used out of tradition. We must, therefore, ignore this anomaly.

Key Word

Sovereignty Ultimate political power and the source of all political authority.

It is useful to divide sovereignty into two main types – legal and political.

Legal sovereignty means the ultimate source of all legal authority. In practice it amounts to the ultimate source of all laws and of all legal power. Although many bodies are granted the authority to exercise power – ministers, local authorities and devolved governments in Scotland and Wales, for example – the ultimate source of that power is Parliament. So we say that Parliament is the legal sovereign. Parliament grants power and sometimes takes it away. Furthermore, all laws in the UK are ultimately determined by Parliament. Parliament either passes laws itself or it grants authority for others to make law. The only exceptions to this lie with the European Union, which has, by various treaties, been granted limited sovereignty in such areas as trade, environment and consumer protection legislation.

Political sovereignty refers to the location of real political power. Instead of thinking only about where legal power lies in theory, political sovereignty allows us to consider who ultimately makes political decisions *in reality*. Thus, at elections, the people are politically sovereign because they decide who will form the next government. Between elections it is more realistic to think of the prime minister and the government as being politically sovereign. Although Parliament is legally sovereign, we know that government invariably controls it. Though Parliament reserves the right to defy the government, most of the time it is government that rules.

State, government and branches of government

As with many political concepts, the terms 'state' and '**government**' can be misunderstood and used as if they have the same meaning. In reality they are very different and should be employed with great care.

The state

If we refer to '*a* state' rather than '*the* state' we mean different things. *A* state is a country, a territory within which sovereignty can be identified and is widely recognised both within the country and abroad. There is no doubt that France, Italy, the USA and Nigeria are 'states'. Other countries recognise them as states and understand who represents their government.

When we say '*the* state', however, we are referring to institutions within the country. *The* state normally refers to the *permanent* collection of institutions that administers a territory. Normally we would include the following within the state:

- the armed forces and the security and intelligence establishment;

- law enforcement agencies, including judges, courts, the police and the prison service;

- the bureaucracy or civil service – these bodies are politically neutral and may stay in office even when political governments change;

- other institutions that may or may not be parts of the permanent apparatus of the state, depending on the arrangements within the country (in the UK, the National Health Service, most educational organisations, the BBC and the Royal Mail are all parts of the state; in the USA, however, health care is largely in the private sector and there is no state-run broadcasting; in France, the railways are part of the state, while in the UK they are not);

- bodies that exist at sub-central level, such as local authorities and devolved administrations.

So, we can make two assertions about the state: first, it is normally politically neutral and, second, it is permanent.

Government

Here we have to include politics in the definition. The term 'government' (without any article) refers to the act of government. In this context, for example, we might say 'government is a complex operation' or 'political parties aim to achieve government'. But when we say '*the* government' we are referring to specific institutions.

The government is a collection of individuals and bodies that are political in nature and that are not permanent. In the UK the government consists of the prime minister, cabinet, junior ministers and political advisers. Should the governing party lose power, all these individuals will cease to be the government and will be replaced by a

Key Word

Government Refers either to the activity of governing or to the institutions that make up the central executive.

new team. Normally we expect the government to give political direction to the state. Indeed, the senior members of the state are usually appointed by members of the government.

MPs, peers and Parliament in general do not fit neatly into either the 'state' or the 'government'. Instead they form the legislature, whose role is to provide consent and accountability to government.

Branches of government

It is customary to divide the activity of government into three branches, as follows:

- **Legislature**: in broad terms this means the law-making body. However, this can be misleading, especially in the UK. Parliament, which is Britain's legislature (known as Congress in the USA, the Chambre de Deputés in France and the Bundestag in Germany), does not normally make law. This is the responsibility of the government. Here in Britain, the legislature is primarily concerned with providing formal consent to proposed laws – an activity known as 'promulgation'. Parliament also has limited powers to amend proposals and may, on rare occasions, reject proposed legislation. Legislatures in other countries sometimes *do* develop their own laws, notably the US Congress, but governments are usually more significant than legislatures in this law-making role.

- **Executive**: the executive branch has three main roles. The first is to develop new legislation and present it before the legislature for approval (this includes identifying the need for new legislation and drafting the laws themselves). The second is to arrange for the implementation of the laws. Finally, the executive runs the state and so administers the country, making decisions when they are needed and organising state-run services.

- **Judiciary**: this refers to the legal system and the judges in particular. Most of the judiciary is not concerned with politics but rather with criminal matters and disputes between individuals and organisations. But at the high levels of the judiciary – in Britain this includes the High Court, Court of Appeal and the Supreme Court – some legal cases involve politics. When there are disputes about the meaning of laws, when citizens' rights are in jeopardy, or when there are disputes concerning the behaviour of the government or the state, the judiciary has political significance. Nevertheless, as we shall see below, judges are expected to adopt a neutral stance, even though they are concerned with political matters.

Freedom and rights

Freedom and rights are difficult concepts, especially since their precise meanings are disputed by proponents of different political ideologies and traditions. We need not concern ourselves at this stage with such controversy, but we do need to attempt to find neutral meanings.

The clearest conception of freedom is perhaps **civil liberties**, also described as **civil rights**. These are rights and freedoms that exist for citizens in their relationship to the state and its laws. Some civil rights are 'positive' in nature, that is they are affirmations of what we are permitted to do by the state. Indeed, such rights will also be enforced by the state, especially the judiciary. These include the following:

- the right to vote;

- the right to form a political party or any other kind of political group;

- the right to form associations such as trade unions, pressure groups, religious groups (freedom of association and freedom of worship);

- the right to express opinions, provided they will not result in breaches of the law (freedom of the press and freedom of speech);

- the right to move freely around the country, to leave and return to the country (freedom of movement).

The other kinds of civil rights or liberties refer to restrictions on the state. That is, the citizen is protected and so enjoys greater freedom. These include:

- the right not to be imprisoned without trial

- the right to a fair trial with legal representation

- the right to privacy and not to have one's home violated by agents of the state.

Most of these rights and freedoms exist to a large extent in modern democratic societies. There may be exceptions in some countries and some rights may be suspended in times of national emergency, such as war or terrorist attack. But, on the whole, democratic states respect our basic rights and freedoms.

If we consider a wider aspect of rights – for example, in the economic and social spheres – there is less clarity and more conflict. These refer to our rights and freedoms with regard to employment, business activity, trade union activity, welfare benefits and the like. In general terms, those who hold liberal or socialist views tend to favour the wide application of such rights and freedoms, while conservatives tend to be less enthusiastic and even oppose some of them. Typical examples of such rights include the following:

- the right to form or join trade unions;

- the right of trade unions to take industrial action in the case of industrial disputes;

- the rights of women and minority groups to equal treatment in employment and in the application of welfare benefits;

- the rights of workers to reasonable and safe working conditions;

- the right to be free from unfair dismissal;

- the right to a decent standard of education and health care (this is a contentious example and in some countries it is not guaranteed);

- the right to a decent pension in old age;

- the right to engage in business enterprise without state interference;

- the right to purchase property.

After centuries of political battles, the majority of these rights and freedoms have now been won for the citizens of most western democracies. Nevertheless they remain the subject of political conflict from time to time. Governments that have become anxious to improve law and order provision and to combat international terrorism, for example, have argued that some individual liberties have to be sacrificed. Should the state be allowed to imprison suspected terrorists without trial in the interests of protecting society, for example? Freedom from imprisonment without a fair trial is, after all, an ancient right and many have fought to protect it.

There remain many countries, too, where human rights and freedoms are not respected. Liberals have therefore turned their attention to campaigning on behalf of the citizens of such countries. But here there remains a difficult dilemma. To what extent should 'liberal' societies tolerate other cultures that do not appear to respect the rights which we hold dear? Do we have a right to intervene? To a large extent this issue remains unresolved.

Tolerance (toleration)

The concept of tolerance did not enter the political arena in Britain in any significant way until the late sixteenth and early seventeenth centuries. But it was not in the arena of worldly politics that tolerance was to become a major philosophical and ethical issue. It was *religious* tolerance, or rather the lack of it, that came to be challenged by the newly emerging liberal philosophy of the seventeenth century. The English philosopher John Locke (1632–1704) argued strongly that the pursuit of religions other than orthodox Anglican Christianity should be tolerated. Nobody, he asserted, has a monopoly on the truth and so there can be no justification for stifling alternative thought and beliefs.

Thus began a long struggle for the tolerance of religious thought. It was not until the creation of the American Constitution in the 1780s and the emancipation of Catholics in England in the nineteenth century that significant political progress was to be seen. Thereafter attention shifted to the more general field of political tolerance. For liberals, any mode of thought and behaviour should be tolerated, as long as their exercise does no harm to others. Conservatives have tended to resist this principle, mainly on the grounds that social order and unity are crucial and are best preserved if excessive variety of belief and thought is discouraged.

Ultimately the liberal argument has prevailed and minorities, especially religions, have achieved widespread legal protection for their activities. Furthermore, the conservative movement has now also accepted tolerance as a necessary feature of modern democracy. So there is no significant political disagreement about toleration. Rather, it is the issue of the *limits* to toleration that still provokes argument. What forms of behaviour *cannot* be tolerated, even in a free society? Some examples of these difficulties are suggested below:

● Should a political party, such as the British National Party, which campaigns on policies that have been widely accused of racism, be allowed to campaign openly?

● Should the publication of material that may be offensive to some though not all people, such as pornography, be freely allowed?

● To what extent should legitimate political demonstrations be allowed to disrupt people's everyday lives by blocking thoroughfares and causing transport closures?

● In the early years of the new twenty-first century, hunting with dogs flared up as a highly contentious issue. The question was asked: should a centuries-old pastime – especially fox hunting – be tolerated even though a majority of the elected House of Commons and the community believed it to be cruel to wild animals?

● Should religious leaders be permitted to make statements that criticise the British 'way of life' and culture, and therefore perhaps promote terrorism?

So, tolerance, and more particularly its limits, is likely to remain the subject of political conflict for the foreseeable future.

Law and order

In 1790 the great conservative thinker Edmund Burke (1729–97) asserted that 'good order is the foundation of all good things'. He was referring especially to the effects of the French Revolution, which had occurred a year earlier. Without order, society will fall apart, just as it had in France, he observed. With order, however, individuals can flourish in an atmosphere of security and stability.

Burke's views formed the foundation of conservatism's stress on the need for stability. Indeed, this is perhaps the most enduring value of the political movement that we call conservatism. Conservatives have always claimed that their guarantee to lay great stress on order stands in contrast to other political ideologies, notably liberalism and socialism – which, they claim, threaten stability.

There is a constant tension in all democratic societies between the basic human need for law and order and the claims of tolerance, freedom and the rights of the individual. For example, to what extent should the law enforcement agencies bend over backwards to protect the rights of suspects in criminal cases, and to what extent should they merely concentrate on securing convictions? Similarly, what rights should householders have to protect their property even if this may result in serious injury or even death to intruders?

Law and order became a major party political issue in the UK during the 1980s when it became apparent that the sharp increase in crime being experienced at that time was not going to diminish. But it is not simply a case of which party has the best law-and-order policies. There is a fundamental question about how far a free society is willing to threaten the individual rights of its citizens to preserve public order and private security. In other words, this is likely to remain an eternal theme.

Equality

This is one of the most difficult words in the vocabulary of political concepts. It has meant very different things to a variety of political movements. It is therefore essential to avoid the temptation of believing that it has any fixed meaning. Equality of outcome refers to the socialist idea that all people should receive equal rewards, but this ideal has never been realised. Nevertheless, it is possible to identify two variations on the theme of equality that have been accepted within mainstream politics. These are the concepts of equal rights and equality of opportunity.

Equal rights

It is now established in western democracies that all citizens are entitled to equal rights. The women's movement of the twentieth century led the way, of course, especially with its demands for voting rights and, later, full political rights for women on an equal basis with men. This has been extended more recently to full legal, political, economic and social rights for such groups as gay people, disabled people and minority ethnic groups. This stems from the notion that all citizens are entitled to the same treatment and that the law should underpin such rights. This does not mean that prejudice and inequality have been eliminated. But the political principle is now well established that the law has a role in attempting to eliminate unequal treatment.

Equality of opportunity

However much we may believe that individuals are naturally unequal in terms of their character, abilities and potential, it is now widely accepted that all citizens should start life with the same opportunities. This means that society should find ways to reduce the advantages and disadvantages that different people have at the time of their birth. A number of practical issues and measures are involved in this process:

- No section of society, such as a hereditary aristocracy, should be born with privileges that are not enjoyed by all.

- No section of the community, such as women, the disabled, followers of a particular religion, gay people or members of minority ethnic groups should be excluded from access to opportunities and choices that the rest of society enjoys.

- The fact that some individuals are born into disadvantaged family situations, especially of poverty and other kinds of deprivation, should not prevent them from achieving their full potential in life. This is mainly achieved through widening and equalising educational opportunity.

● Where a group suffers routine discrimination, that discrimination should be combated and, if possible, eliminated. Failing that, some argue (though many disagree) that positive discrimination should be used, giving these groups an artificial advantage to balance the disadvantage caused by prejudice.

Justice

Of all the political concepts we are considering, justice is perhaps the most difficult and contentious. It is, of course, a term most of us use frequently in everyday conversation and we tend to use it to mean 'fairness'. But it can also be used to denote the successful outcome of a criminal or civil trial. We often speak of 'bringing wrong-doers to justice' or of 'seeing justice done'. Sometimes the phrase 'natural justice' can be heard, referring to some abstract concept of what would be generally considered 'fair', although different people would undoubtedly disagree about what 'natural justice' actually is.

So we are presented with a widely used term, clearly significant in the world of politics, but one that has no clear or agreed meaning. Hence the problems. To tackle these it is advisable to break the term 'justice' into a number of distinct usages. We may then examine each of them in turn.

Natural justice

For some this may imply that nature is a force that has some control over the affairs of mankind, that we could, theoretically, discover some laws of nature that would constitute justice. All we have to do is undertake a rational study of the world and we could discover what natural justice is. The

problem, of course, is that a socialist, communist, liberal, feminist or conservative will undoubtedly discover different conceptions of natural justice. A communist will declare that complete economic and social equality constitutes natural justice, while a liberal or a conservative will claim that inequality is natural. A feminist will be adamant that equality between the sexes is naturally just, while a conservative might counter this by pointing to important biological (and therefore natural) differences between men and women.

Of course, for many, the term 'nature' implies 'God'. In this sense justice becomes a gift granted to us by our creator. Indeed, in societies where religion has become fundamental and all-pervading (for example, some Islamic states), natural or God-given justice can be discovered by careful reference to scriptures and to the teaching of prophets. Jewish people, in particular, refer to the Old Testament of their bible to find important examples of how God has influenced kings and prophets to administer real justice. They refer, for example, to the 'wisdom of Solomon' (who enjoyed a reputation as the wisest of all the kings of Israel) as an important model for how apparently insoluble disputes may be resolved on the basis of 'natural justice'.

Even in the highest levels of the British legal system, judges may find themselves with no known guide as to how to adjudicate in a dispute, no precedents from other countries or from their own past. In such cases they may rule on the basis of natural justice. Here the judges mean what 'normal, everyday folk' would consider to be a just outcome, rather than some philosophical notion of the truth. So, in the end, natural justice must remain a highly subjective concept.

Legal justice and the rule of law

With legal justice we can stand on firmer ground. In western democratic society the principles of legal justice are well established. Important documents such as the American Constitution (1787) and the work of the English nineteenth-century constitutionalist A.V. Dicey (1835–1922) have established certain key elements that are now widely accepted and enforced.

The main principle is that all (adult) citizens of the state are treated equally under the law (also known as procedural justice). This means that the law will be enforced against all on an equal basis and that nobody can be considered to be 'above the law'. This includes members of the government and those who must enforce those laws. Dicey called these concepts the '**rule of law**' and this is an important aspect of legal justice.

It also means that government itself must abide by the laws; it is, in effect, limited by law. Normally it is a country's constitution that sets out the legal limits of government's power. Should a government exceed its legal powers, we would say it is acting *arbitrarily* and *unconstitutionally*; there will be safeguards to ensure that this cannot happen – in truly democratic societies, that is. There is a problem with this principle in the UK. This is because there is no such document as the 'British Constitution'. Therefore, as long as Parliament gives its approval, government can do whatever it likes; there is no constitutional law to constrain it. Fortunately for the principles of the rule of law and legal justice, Parliament has always been robust in preventing governments from overstepping their powers.

Key Word

Rule of law A set of principles asserting that all citizens should be treated equally under the law, including government itself. It also means that every citizen is entitled to due process of law and a fair trial. Overall government should be conducted according to the recognised legal code and the constitution.

Finally, legal justice also implies that every citizen has an equal right to a fair trial if accused of an offence. It must also mean that the judges who try them must be independent of the government. This is, in fact, probably the most common understanding of what justice means. On the whole, it has nothing to do with politics as such, but is simply a long-established right. But it can have political significance in some circumstances. If governments were permitted to imprison individuals without trial there would be a danger they would use that power to silence their opponents and critics. In the past, absolute monarchs and totalitarian regimes have done this. British monarchs were prone to lock people in the Tower of London if they were a threat, while some modern regimes keep thousands of political prisoners in their jails, offering none of them a trial.

Social justice

Different conceptions of social justice lie at the heart of a number of political ideologies. As such it has become a highly contentious term, not least because each ideology that claims it as its own believes that it has a monopoly on what constitutes social justice. In short, therefore, some ideologies claim they are superior because they, and they alone, know what this kind of justice is. Furthermore, justice is often placed on a pedestal (frequently alongside freedom) above all other human aspirations.

Ideas of social justice refer to the way in which goods are distributed within a society. By 'goods' we mean here anything that people find desirable. Of course, income and wealth, and what they can buy, fit into this category. But goods can also mean power, status, privileges, social honour and even freedom itself. Some ideologies believe, as we shall see below, that all these goods should be distributed equally throughout the population. Others, however, assert that there is a natural inequality within mankind so that it must also be natural to expect that goods will be distributed very unevenly, with some enjoying large quantities of them and others being relatively poor.

The clearest approach to this subject is to examine the basic beliefs of some of these ideologies so that we can understand the various usages of the term.

Communism

Karl Marx and Vladimir Lenin, the two main architects of twentieth-century communism, both subscribed to the slogan 'from each according to his ability, to each according to his need'. For them the ultimate destination of human society would be reached when this principle was established. It is an expression of total equality. No one should have significantly more than any other. There was to be equality of wealth as well as social and economic power. This was the only kind of social justice that they would accept. Taking this principle one step further, communists see private property as the root of most inequality. The best way to deal with this, they assert, is to abolish private property altogether.

Fundamentalist socialism

Slightly less radical than communism, fundamentalist socialists also propose economic equality. However, they accept that society requires some incentives to ensure that there will be some who are willing to undertake long periods of education and training and who are prepared to take on stressful and difficult employment. In other words, some jobs should enjoy higher rewards than others. This changes the Marxist slogan shown above to one that is slightly different: 'from each according to his ability, to each according to his contribution.' Here there is room for some inequality since each person's contribution is likely to have a different value to society.

But these two ideas do have one common aspect: they both reject the idea that rewards should be distributed on a 'random' basis. The operation of completely free markets, with no state interference, they argue, is an irrational and unjust way of organising society. Instead they propose a rational way of distributing rewards on the basis of merit rather than market power. Thus the fact that Premier League footballers may earn more in a week than many of their supporters earn in a year is seen as fundamentally unjust by communists and socialists. This is not a comment on the quality and worth of professional footballers, of course (though fans of some unsuccessful teams may argue that it is!), but simply an argument against the completely free market in footballers' wages that creates the apparent 'injustice'.

In practice, this effectively implies that socialists are prepared to tolerate some inequality of wealth and income but would propose that differences should be rather modest. They would also insist that every individual has equal opportunity to aspire to the higher rewards that are on offer.

Liberals

Since liberals place freedom above social justice in their hierarchy of principles, it is clear that, for them, a just society must be one where individuals enjoy extensive liberty. This also means that we must be 'free to be unequal'. Where free markets are allowed to operate, therefore, there will be freedom to move about within the market to seek the highest rewards. For liberals, a society that seeks to *impose* greater equality cannot be just because it will not be free.

Liberals are aware that the 'struggle' to achieve higher rewards, greater wealth, status and power is not a just one if some are born with advantages over others (in the form of wealthy parents, privileged background and so on). They argue, therefore, that a free and unequal society can be just only if there is equality of opportunity for all.

In other words, unjust privileges and social disadvantages should be counteracted by the full availability of good education for all and guarantees of equal treatment to all groups in society.

Libertarians

Also known as extreme neo-liberals, or even anarcho-capitalists, this group has extremely radical ideas about social justice. They propose a society in which all markets – for goods, labour and money   should be completely free, with no state interference whatsoever. They insist that the outcomes of such a free market are always just (provided that individuals act lawfully, that is). They say that, as long as we are all free and have equal chances, we receive rewards that are due to us according to our own efforts. Furthermore, they would reinforce this principle by eliminating all forms of state subsidy to individuals (i.e. no welfare benefits). In this way everyone is treated equally. They argue, therefore, that freedom and social justice can coexist without contradiction.

An overview of government and politics in the UK

Before we examine the various parts of the political system of the United Kingdom, together with the issues associated with them, it will be useful to consider a general overview of how the whole system works.

We can usefully adopt two approaches. One may be described as *linear*, while the other is *pluralist*. We should examine each in turn.

The linear analysis

This views the political system as a production process. First, there are inputs (the raw material of politics). A process then takes place involving various institutions and individuals. This processing converts the inputs into decisions. Finally, the outcomes of the political process emerge in the form of action.

The inputs

- **Demands** are made by different groups in society. These will usually entail the need for action to promote their interests or to protect them from some perceived threat. For example, farmers will campaign for subsidies and price support systems through the Common Agricultural Policy of the European Union; nurses will look for a better deal from the NHS funding pool; home owners will demand tougher action by the law-enforcement system against burglaries. Such demands may be made by pressure groups, media campaigns or from within political parties themselves.

- **Responses** will be required to various problems that may arise. Most commonly, economic action is needed to deal with inflation, unemployment, lack of economic growth or any other such difficulties. If crime begins to rise alarmingly, again a response is needed. Similarly, a rise in homelessness needs a response from the appropriate public bodies. All governments know they will be forced, from time to time, to make decisions to deal with unexpected issues.

- **Ideological** initiatives can promote political action. That is to say, politicians and the parties they represent develop strong political beliefs which they wish to promote when they achieve power. Ideological beliefs concern the more long-term development and character of the country and its society. Conservatives, for example, typically oppose high levels of taxation. When in power, therefore, they will usually attempt to reduce the tax burden. On the other side of the same coin, Labour normally seeks to reduce poverty levels. This may entail higher taxes for the majority in order to pay for measures to help the poor minority. Liberal Democrats prefer to promote personal liberty. They oppose such perceived threats to freedom as the introduction of identity cards or the reduction in the rights of those accused of criminal offences.

● **Crises** obviously create a need for rapid decision making. After the attack on the World Trade Center in New York, for example, and the atrocities in London in the summer of 2005, a whole raft of anti-terrorism measures was suddenly needed. The so-called 'credit crunch' of 2007–08 similarly needed emergency measures to avoid the complete collapse of the world financial structure.

● **Paternalism** also plays a part in creating policy making. This occurs when politicians themselves believe they understand what is best for the country at any particular time. Indeed, the term 'paternalism' suggests that the decision makers claim a superior understanding of issues compared with that of the public at large. The management of the economy, education and health policy, and defence matters are typical examples of such common political behaviour.

The political process

These inputs then have to be processed within the political system. In other words, they are subjected to a *political process*. This involves a variety of individuals and bodies. The main examples are discussed next.

Parties, though of decreasing importance in modern politics, do attempt to have influence over the outcomes. From ordinary members, right up to party leaders, the inputs will be considered and sifted within the parties. Of course, it is here that ideological demands most commonly appear,

as many party members are highly politically aware and motivated.

Political leaders (broadly the so-called 'front benches' of the major parties) are those who ultimately will have to make decisions and be held accountable for those decisions. It is therefore to be expected that they play a major part in processing inputs. The leaders in government are clearly more influential, but opposition party leaders must always prepare alternatives ready for the possibility that they may take power in the future.

Civil servants and political advisers have a dual role. Clearly, they advise political leaders, as we would expect, but it must be emphasised that they are also sometimes called on to make decisions themselves. They are less accountable than elected leaders, but remain highly influential.

Quangos (quasi autonomous national government organisations) and **other committees** play a similar role to that of civil servants. They consider policy options and advise ministers on possible political action.

Parliament also has two main roles. One is to take part in the consideration of political demands. However, on the whole, it does not take the initiative in such matters. When its members debate issues, it is normally under the tight control of political leaders. The House of Lords has become more independent than the Commons, but its power remains limited. The other role is to formalise decisions that have been made elsewhere. When Parliament passes a new Act, or amends or repeals an old one, it is granting formal consent on behalf of the people.

The Cabinet – about 20–25 senior government ministers appointed by the prime minister – now performs the main task of granting the official stamp of government approval on any political decision. The Cabinet cannot make laws, but once it has formally approved a proposal, it is normally the case that the proposal will lead to action. Occasionally the Cabinet does process decisions itself, but its role in this respect has been much eroded in recent decades.

The prime minister is, as one might expect, at the apex of the process. Though s/he has to take account of all the other parts of the political system and can be overruled by Parliament or the Cabinet, it is clear that key decisions are often made in 10 Downing Street. Usually prime ministers gather round them a small 'inner cabinet' of trusted allies to advise them. These, too, are a vital part of the political system.

The outputs

This is somewhat clearer. The outcomes of the political process fall into four main categories.

Legislation obviously refers to new laws that may emerge from Parliament. However, under this heading we should add the possible repeal of old laws and the amendment of existing ones.

Ministerial decisions can often be made without recourse to Parliament. Ministers are granted wide powers to make such decisions as when to go to war (although this is usually in the hands of the prime minister him-or herself), how government expenditure should be distributed, what adjustments need to be made to economic policy (the Chancellor of the Exchequer's responsibility) or what kinds of weapons the armed forces should purchase.

Broad policy may not involve *specific* decisions but does concern the general direction of the government's plans and priorities. In other words, such policy will be converted into action in the future. Typical examples are long-term policies on the economy, foreign affairs, defence, education or transport.

Judicial review is the final stage of the process. It occurs when laws and decisions by government are challenged by citizens or groups of citizens. This may be because laws are unclear, or because there is a suspicion that a public body has exceeded its legal powers. In general such reviews are a 'tidying up' process, ensuring that

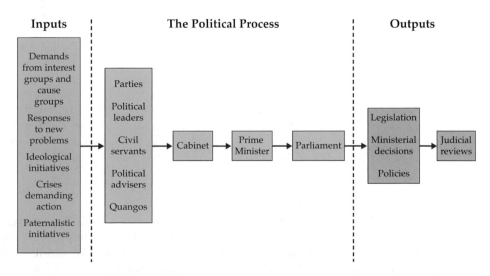

The linear analysis of the UK political process

there is clarity in the laws and that they are being applied properly. If judges in the senior courts reveal serious shortcomings during these reviews, it is for government and Parliament to consider whether new or revised legislation is needed.

The pluralist analysis

This is a more complex and less formal version of the political system. It places a relatively small number of political actors at the centre of the process. These include the prime minister, Cabinet members, some senior political advisers and a number of other influential members of the governing party.

This group is surrounded by a wide variety of organisations that seek to influence them. They will have varying levels of influence, depending on circumstances. The role of the central group of key decision makers is to mediate between competing demands and beliefs, to develop a coherent political programme and to drive their decisions through to decisive action. As we would expect, since the central group comprises party politicians, they will also take into account public opinion and the effects their decisions will have on their party's re-election prospects.

The groups that clamour to gain the ear of the decision makers include the following, most of which we can also see in the linear analysis:

● The wider membership of political parties;

● Pressure groups;

● Parliament (MPs and peers);

● Senior civil servants;

● The media;

● Public opinion;

● Overseas influences including the European Union.

The pluralist analysis suggests that the process is highly informal and does not necessarily follow any set pattern. By contrast, the linear picture

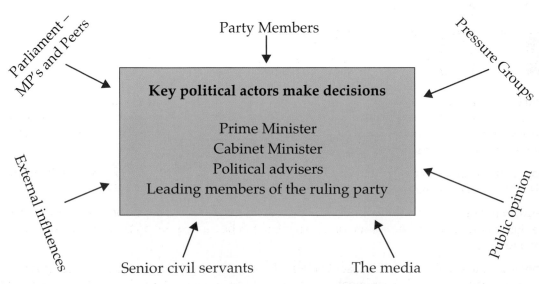

The pluralist analysis of the UK political process

presents a view of the process that is both formal and predictable. However, for the purposes of the student who is new to political study, either analysis can be adopted.

The realities of British politics changed, perhaps for ever, after the general election of May 2010. The events of that day and the weeks and months that followed have had a number of consequences, many of which call into question our assumptions about government and politics.

In particular, these questions can now be asked:

● Is coalition government truly *legitimate*, given that it is an administration for which nobody has voted?

● How is the *authority* of the prime minister affected by his having to deal with two parties and in the knowledge that his party failed to secure a winning majority in the election?

● We now have an additional feature of the 'struggle for power'. Two parties in coalition have to fight for supremacy, even though one is much larger than the other.

● Will the *relationships* between different institutions be significantly affected? How has the *distribution of power* been altered?

● How will *pressure groups* be affected? They must deal with two parties in coalition and may find additional points of access and leverage.

● On a fundamental level we must ask whether the British *two-party system* is now a thing of the past.

● We can also ask whether Britain's ancient and disjointed constitution can cope with the changes now being thrown at it.

● If consensus politics and coalition government endures, does it mean British *democracy* will be strengthened or weakened?

Of course it may be that, in the years to come, coalition politics will prove to be a failure and Britain will return to its tradition of two party, adversarial politics. A number of constitutional reforms may be left behind, but there remains a possibility that May 2010 actually changed very little.

Key concepts in this chapter

State *The state* is a collective name for the institutions that administer a country. Normally these institutions are non-political and are permanent, such as the civil service, judiciary and law enforcement agencies. *A state*, meanwhile, refers to a country whose government's jurisdiction over a territory is recognised by other states.

Government can mean the process of organising the state and giving it political direction. It also refers to the institutions that apply political principles to the running of the state.

Legitimacy refers to the degree to which the state or its government can be considered to have the right to exercise power. A state or government can be said to be legitimate if it has a valid claim to rule.

Consent In the political world consent implies the idea that the people who are to be governed consent to the system of government which has been set up over them. Consent may be explicit, i.e. the people regularly demonstrate that they support the regime, or it may be implicit or tacit. This means it can be assumed or inferred by the fact that the people freely participate in legitimate politics, regularly turn up to vote and that there is a lack of open dissent.

Power The ability of an individual or an institution to force people to do things, whether they wish to or not. The strongest form of power is force or coercion, while the weakest is influence.

Authority The right to exercise power, rather than the exercise of power itself. Authority is granted to rulers or anyone in power by those over whom power is to be exercised. Without authority, power becomes mere force.

Sovereignty Ultimate political power and the source of all political authority.

Government Refers either to the activity of governing or to the institutions that make up the central executive.

Rule of Law A set of principles asserting that all citizens should be treated equally under the law, including government itself. It also means that every citizen is entitled to due process of law and a fair trial. Overall government should be conducted according to the recognised legal code and the constitution.

The concepts of legitimacy (page 4), power (page 6), authority (page 7) and equality (page 13) are particularly relevant to Unit 1. The concepts of sovereignty (page 8), freedom and rights (page 10), law and order (page 12) and justice (page 14) are particularly relevant to Unit 2.

People and Politics

Democracy and political participation

1.1

A definition of democracy

We could spend a great deal of time attempting to develop a watertight definition of **democracy**, but this would not be of great use for a study of this kind. Instead, it is better to define the term in a more straightforward manner. The best approach is to adapt the description of democracy given by nineteenth-century American president Abraham Lincoln and to examine its meaning. This has three parts.

Abraham Lincoln gave us the best-known description of modern democracy

1. **Government of the people.** Here we are straying furthest from Lincoln's definition. We now expect that most of the citizens are able to participate in political activity. This does not merely include standing for elected office or voting in elections, it also means being active in parties or pressure groups, being aware and letting our political views be known. Many people in modern democracies remain politically inactive, but the majority are active, and everyone certainly has the *opportunity* to participate, even if they do not take up that opportunity. We can describe this aspect as *participatory democracy.* It is often claimed that if citizens cease to be active in politics, democracy will wither and die.

2. **Government by the people.** This is a state of affairs where the people themselves make the important decisions that affect them. In effect we could describe this as *direct democracy*, an arrangement that would entail constant use of referendums or direct consultation processes. Government by the people could also describe a circumstance where the government is intensely sensitive to public opinion. In practice this would be virtually direct democracy. All democratic governments consult the people, so this is a useful part of our definition.

3. **Government for the people.** This phrase suggests that whoever governs us does so in the broad interests of the people. In other words,

they are not governing in their *own* interests, nor do they concern themselves only with *one section* of the community. They should take into account, therefore, the interests and needs of *all* sections of society as far as is possible. Since pure direct democracy all the time is not feasible, it is inevitable that government for the people will be carried out by representatives. Thus we speak of *representative democracy* as the most common form. As long as our representatives – MPs, ministers and so on – are accountable to the people, we usually entrust government to them.

Key Word

Democracy A very general description of various political systems that are organised on the basis that government should serve the interests of the people. In liberal democracies it is also expected that citizens should influence decisions or make decisions themselves. It is also expected that government should be accountable, in various ways, to the people.

The importance of democracy

Although there was a brief episode in the history of Ancient Greece when democracy of different kinds flourished in the various city-states of that age, it had a relatively short life as a political system. Even the most direct forms of democracy, where all free citizens gathered regularly to make important decisions, excluded slaves, women and the uneducated. It was, in essence, reserved for the prominent citizens who enjoyed most of the wealth of the city. They were the only people who were considered to be informed enough to vote. Democracy was short-lived in Greece and, once it had disappeared, did not reappear in any recognisable form until the eighteenth century.

Two and a half thousand years later, democracy has established itself as the political system preferred by all economically advanced nations. In the meantime, most peoples had been governed by hereditary monarchs, autocratic rulers, or had effectively not been properly governed at all. It is worth examining why democracy was resurrected after so many centuries in the wilderness. What is it about modern society that seems to make democracy so important? We can identify a number of theories to try to answer this question.

Democracy establishes and protects freedom. Towards the end of the eighteenth century a number of new philosophical and political movements developed. They were largely based on the principle that mankind should be free, both as individuals and collectively as nations. The new democratic spirit was carried forward in particular by the French and the Americans. The French Revolution of 1789 was a bold attempt to free the people from the autocratic rule of the monarchy. For the revolutionaries, the monarchy ruled in the interests only of itself and the aristocracy; it was time the political system took into account the demands of the middle and working classes. If such people were to be truly free, they should also have a place in the new political system.

Similarly, the Americans, during their revolution against British rule, fought to establish freedom for all individuals from the oppressive rule of George III. The constitution that they wrote and approved in 1787 enshrined freedom of the individual in a form of government that could certainly be described as a representative democracy. By ensuring that all citizens could participate and be represented, they believed their newly found freedom would be safe.

Today, democracy continues to ensure that no government can threaten freedom unless it is with the expressed consent of the people. To illustrate this, when the Soviet Union collapsed in 1990 and its satellite states declared their freedom, most of the new governments adopted democratic systems. This process guaranteed that the kind of domination that had occurred during the Cold War could never re-assert itself. The most dramatic demonstration of the power of the new democratic spirit took place in the Ukraine in 2003–04 when it was rumoured that apparently democratic elections had been fixed and that Russia was behind the plot. The people simply took to the streets and stayed there until new, clean elections were held and their chosen government was installed. In this way Ukrainians believed their liberty was assured and the traditional Russian domination could finally be broken.

Democracy protects minorities. If a democracy is to be effective and enduring, the system must take into account the interests and demands of minority groups. Democracy ensures that all groups have access to the political process. It also guarantees that minorities have a free voice and are free from discrimination. Indeed, democracy is sometimes described as a political system where minorities rule. Of course, popular democracy can become little more than government by the majority, and early forms of democracy looked like this. But in the nineteenth century, the liberal philosopher John Stuart Mill (1806–73) described such a circumstance as no more than the *tyranny of the majority*. It is democracy of a sort, but unless the rights and interests of minorities are protected, it does not conform to the modern meaning of the term.

Democracy controls government power. It is a well-established belief that power tends to corrupt those who wield it. If those who govern us are left to their own devices, there is a danger that they will simply claim increasing amounts of power and begin to abuse their position. Therefore, democracy is vital in preventing this. By making governments accountable to the people, by ensuring that they must submit themselves regularly to re-election, and by guaranteeing that they are controlled by elected representatives, the people can feel safe from the corruption of power.

The alternative to democracy is a form of politics where decisions are made without reference to the people, where governments are not accountable to the people and where there are no guarantees that individuals and minorities will be protected.

Democracy encourages popular participation. As it is commonly believed that tyranny can be prevented by ensuring that the people are able freely to participate in politics, democracy is critical in ensuring the prevention of tyranny.

In a free democracy the people have the opportunity to become informed and be directly involved in influencing decision making. A docile and uninformed population is vulnerable to autocratic government. Democracy can prevent such a situation arising, helping to ensure that citizens remain fully involved.

Democracy disperses power more widely. When power become excessively concentrated in the hands of a small number of people or organisations, it is almost inevitable that power is denied to a wider range of the population. This is a severe danger to democratic principles. For example, in many regimes power lies in the hands of a small elite – Burma or China might be appropriate examples of this – or in the hands of those who are economically powerful, such as some small Middle Eastern states or the Sultanate of Brunei. However benevolent such governments may be, it cannot be denied that power has been removed from the vast majority of the population and so democracy will fail to flourish. It should be noted here that some of these elites do *claim* to be democratic on the grounds that they are ruling *on behalf of* the people. For the purposes of this study, however, we can treat this claim as dubious. We should say instead that when power is dispersed widely among people and non-governmental associations in what is called **civil society**, democracy is well served.

Is democracy always appropriate?

So far we have been uncritical of democracy, suggesting that it is a universally 'good thing' to which all societies should aspire. But there may be circumstances in which democracy might not be the most appropriate political system.

We are assuming that the principles that all individuals should be free, that there should be freedom of thought and expression and that all minorities should be respected are shared by all. Certainly it is true that they are firmly established in the USA, in much of Europe and in many other economically developed countries. But there are cultures and societies that do not share these and other democratic principles. In societies that are governed by a strict religious code, for example, there is much less room for alternative belief systems to flourish. There are cultures where the people do not expect or desire personal liberty. In some Islamic states, for instance, most aspects of life are governed by the teachings of the prophet Muhammad, as expressed in the Koran. Muslims in such states expect to be guided in their actions by such teachings. Since Islamic governments view it as their duty to oversee the moral and social principles of the Koran, there can be no reason for them to be democratic in the sense we have described. People do not lament their lack of personal freedom, as they wish to be guided towards the most righteous way of life.

There may also be circumstances in the history of a people when decisive government action is needed. Democracy may well slow down and hinder the decision-making process at a time when speed and purpose are most important. Indeed, even established democracies, such as those in the United Kingdom and the USA, have suspended aspects of their democracy when faced with a major war. In the longer term, some poorer countries may feel that the need for economic development takes precedence over democratic principles. Thus a number of African states, such

as Tanzania and Zambia, introduced one-party systems in order to try to solve their chronic problems in a more effective way.

Having said this, many democrats still insist that democratic principles *cannot* be sacrificed in the name of religion, emergency circumstances or the need for economic development. When it was suggested to Nelson Mandela that democracy and black majority rule in South Africa could lead to the economic decline of his country, he insisted that the people would prefer to be free than to be well fed.

Citizenship and political participation

Citizenship

It is well understood that a citizen is one who enjoys all the rights and privileges that a country can bestow. Since the time of the French Revolution, when the modern concept of **citizenship** was established, the principle of equal rights has always been emphasised. Under absolute monarchies the people were merely seen as *subjects*. In other words, they were expected to

Key Word

Citizenship This term refers to the idea that members of the political community have certain rights with respect to political institutions. It also implies that an individual has the right to live within a particular state and thus enjoy all its rights and benefits. Citizenship implies a certain level of obligation, mainly to obey the law, to give military service in some circumstances, to pay taxes and, arguably, to vote and to engage in some kinds of service to the community.

obey, perform their duties and not question the legitimacy of government.

Once people became citizens of democratic states, however, they had rights and were encouraged to call government to account and exercise their own liberty. But in order to prevent all coherent government being swept away by 'people power' it remains necessary to impose duties upon the citizens. What has happened, therefore, is that the citizens of democracies have both rights and duties (or obligations) and these are balanced against each other. The table below shows the main examples of the citizen's rights and obligations.

Rights	Obligations
<ul><li>To be a resident in the state.</li><li>To vote in free elections.</li><li>To stand for public office.</li><li>To be treated equally under the law.</li><li>To be given a fair trial if accused of a crime.</li><li>To enjoy the modern concept of civil liberties such as freedom of expression, association, movement, religion and thought.</li></ul>	<ul><li>To obey the laws.</li><li>To accept the legitimacy of the properly constituted government.</li><li>To pay taxes.</li><li>Possibly to join the armed forces if there is a need for conscription (compulsory draft).</li></ul>

Political participation

When Tony Blair and his allies developed the New Labour movement in the 1990s, Blair introduced the concept of *active citizenship* as a new kind of obligation that was to be undertaken and that would serve as a price to be paid for a wide range of guaranteed rights. This has also been considered a key part of what is known as **communitarianism**, especially in New Labour circles. Thus

Key Word

Political participation Opportunities for and tendencies of the people to become involved in the political process. At a minimum level this will involve voting, but may also involve active work in political parties or pressure groups. At the highest level it implies standing for public office.

Britain signed up to the European Convention on Human Rights (ECHR) (by passing the Human Rights Act), adopted the European Union (EU) Social Chapter guaranteeing a range of employment rights, and introduced the Freedom of Information Act (FOA), which gave citizens the right to see official documents. But Blair and his supporters were also anxious that citizens should demonstrate a greater commitment to protecting democracy and community life.

Active citizenship had two purposes. First, it was to balance the extension of individual rights that was being undertaken. Second, it was seen as a vital way of preserving and extending a 'community spirit', which, it was felt, had been threatened by excessive levels of individualism and the pursuit of self-interest.

The active citizen is expected to become involved in such activities as:

- making themselves aware of political issues and voting in elections

- becoming actively involved in the promotion of issues in which they are interested – this may be at local or national level and could involve membership of pressure groups

- becoming involved in community action of some kind. Examples include voluntary work among the disadvantaged in the community, helping in environmental projects, Neighbourhood Watch schemes to deter crime and becoming closely involved with one's children's schooling

- joining and being active in a political party (this might apply only to the most active of citizens).

Of course, it was impossible to consider legislation to guarantee such active citizenship. The main way of promoting it, therefore, has been through education. A subject entitled Citizenship has become part of the compulsory national curriculum, so all school pupils will be taught the principles of what it is to be an active and effective citizen.

Despite these initiatives, falling levels of **political participation** have become a major concern to policy makers. The main evidence of lower levels of active participation includes the following:

1. **Turnout** at elections has been falling. The table below, showing general election participation, demonstrates this decline; although there was a small recovery in turnout in 2010, participation in elections remains below the high levels before 1997.

Election year	Turnout
1979	76.0 %
1983	72.7 %
1987	75.3 %
1992	77.7 %
1997	71.4 %
2001	59.4 %
2005	61.3 %
2010	65.2 %

Turnout in local and regional elections has also remained worryingly low.

2. **Party membership** has been declining. The figures for the UK shown below demonstrate this trend.

Year	Membership of all parties	Membership as a % of total electorate
1980	1,693,156	4.12
1989	1,136,723	2.63
1998	840,000	1.92
2006	560,000	1.28
2008	476,000	0.95

Source: 'Party Membership in Europe' by P. Mair and I. van Biezen. In *Party Politics.* Vol 7, No. 1, *Daily Telegraph*, 27 March 2007, House of Commons Library (John Marshall)

Even more dramatic has been the collapse of membership in the British Conservative Party where, traditionally, participation has been very high. Estimated figures are as follows.

1980	1.20 million
1988	0.75 million
1998	0.35 million
2006	0.27 million
2008	0.17 million

(*Note:* Labour Party statistics are less reliable, but there is evidence that membership had fallen to an all-time low by 2007.)

Sources: Mair and van Biezen, as above. *Daily Telegraph*, 27 March 2007, House of Commons Library (John Marshall)

3. A third indication of falling levels of participation comes from a great deal of research material, which suggests that, in general, people identify much less closely with political parties than they used to. This is a process known as **partisan dealignment**. So, not only are considerably fewer people joining political parties, but fewer people are taking any close interest in party politics.

The news for our participatory democracy is not all bad, however. It may be true that much of the electorate has turned away from traditional party involvement, and even from voting, but it seems that pressure group activity has never been higher. Furthermore, rather than relying on parties to represent their concerns, many people are taking direct action themselves. In 1990, hundreds of thousands took to the streets of London to protest against the imposition of the unpopular local poll tax. Their action suc-ceeded in getting the legislation repealed within two years. Similarly, the Countryside Alliance managed to muster up to 300,000 supporters in 2003–04 to demonstrate against the proposed ban on hunting with dogs and over general neglect of rural issues. In 2003, more than 1 million protes-tors made their opposition to the Iraq war of that year clearly known. In 2007, over 1.8 million people signed up to an Internet petition opposing proposals for a road-pricing scheme. This petition was transmitted directly to 10 Downing Street and provoked a major government re-think on the issue.

Membership numbers of some of Britain's leading pressure groups are shown in the table opposite. It is interesting to compare them with party membership statistics shown above.

Thus it can be seen that many millions of citizens are engaged in fundraising, campaigning and undertaking research for thousands of pres-sure groups, all of which are participating fully in the democratic process.

Pressure group	Main concerns	Membership numbers
Countryside Alliance	The interests of those who live in the countryside.	100,000
Royal Society for the Protection of Birds (RSPB)	Protection of bird species and their natural habitats, plus other environmental Issues.	1,000,000+
Friends of the Earth	Various environmental Issues.	200,000
Taxpayers' Alliance	To highlight wastage in public expenditure.	18,000
Liberty	Human rights issues.	5,000

Source: Membership figures are estimates published by the organisations themselves

Discussion topics

Why is there increasing disillusionment with party politics in the UK?

Does this decline matter if there is more participation in 'single issue' politics?

Proposed congestion charges were rejected in referendums in Edinburgh and Manchester

Some recent initiative results were as follows:

US initiatives in 2008		
State(s)	Issue	Outcome
California, Florida, Arizona	Banning civil marriages (effectively gay marriages)	Civil marriages were banned.
South Dakota	A ban on abortions in most circumstances	Initiative rejected and abortions remained legal.
California	Laws providing for humane treatment of farm animals	Passed, forcing such humane treatment.
Michigan	To allow marijuana to be used for medical purposes	Passed.

In November 2010 possibly the most interesting initiative of them all will be held in California when there will be a vote to legalise marijuana for general uses.

We can now review the use of referendums in the UK. The table on page 35 shows the nature and outcome of all major referendums used in Britain's history.

A referendum was held in Northern Ireland in 1973 to decide whether the province should remain in the UK or be united with the Republic of Ireland. Most of the Catholic community boycotted the referendum, so its result became irrelevant.

Although the 1979 referendum of devolution in Scotland produced a 'yes' vote, there was a requirement that at least 40 per cent of the total Scottish electorate (not just those who voted) had to approve. This figure was not achieved, so the proposal was effectively rejected.

Apart from these referendums, two more votes are likely to be held in the future. The first will be on whether Britain should change its electoral system for general elections to the Alternative Vote (AV). This was an agreed policy made by the coalition government that came to power in 2010. The second, more distant prospect is to decide whether Britain should adopt the Euro. As things stood in 2010 this seemed a distant prospect, but it is clear that such a major change would need the expressed consent of the people.

Referendums in the UK					
Year	Location	Question	Yes %	No %	Turnout %
1975	UK	Do you think that the UK should stay in the European Community?	67.2	32.8	64.5
1979	Scotland	Do you want the provisions of the Scotland Act to be put into effect?	51.6	48.4	63.8
1979	Wales	Do you want the provisions of the Wales Act to be put into effect?	20.3	79.7	58.8
1997	Scotland	Do you agree that there should be a Scottish parliament?	74.3	25.7	60.4
1997	Scotland	Do you agree that the Scottish parliament should have tax-varying powers?	63.5	36.5	60.4
1997	Wales	Do you agree that there should be a Welsh assembly?	50.3	49.7	50.1
1998	London	Are you in favour of the government's proposals for a Greater London Authority made up of an elected mayor and a separately elected assembly?	72.0	28.0	34.1
1998	Northern Ireland	Do you support the agreement reached at the multi-party talks on Northern Ireland and set out in Command Paper 3883?	71.7	28.9	81.0
2004	North-East England	Should there be an elected assembly for the North-East region?	22.1	77.9	47.7

Referendums in the UK (continued)					
Year	**Location**	**Question**	**Yes %**	**No %**	**Turnout %**
2002–04	Various (31) localities	Should a community introduce an elected mayor?	11 votes	20 votes	Varied between 10% and 64%
2005	Edinburgh	Should a congestion charge be introduced in the city centre?	25.6	74.4	61.7
2008	Manchester	Should a congestion charge be introduced?	21.2	78.8	53.2

Why were these referendums held?

All the referendums shown above had one factor in common: they were all concerned with important constitutional changes. In other words, they were about proposed changes to the system of government. In the past, constitutional changes have *not* been subjected to popular approval, but the electorate is now considered to be better informed and so insists on being consulted. A further reason for submitting constitutional changes to a referendum is that it has the effect of entrenching the changes. This means that future governments and parliaments will not be able to reverse the changes unless they again consult the people; the changes will thus become permanent.

It is also possible to identify other individual reasons why it was deemed necessary to secure the consent of the people. These are outlined below.

- **The 1975 vote on European Community membership.** The Labour government of the day was itself split on whether Britain should remain a member of the EC. Prime Minister Harold Wilson therefore ordered the referendum to settle the issue and to avoid the collapse of his government. During the campaign ministers were free to oppose the official line that Britain should remain a member. The decisive 'yes' vote ensured the government's survival.

- **The 1979 votes on Scottish and Welsh devolution.** These both failed, partly because the Labour government of the day was less than enthusiastic itself. It was forced to put the issue to the vote by the Liberal Party. Lacking a parliamentary majority, the government relied on the support of a small group of Liberal MPs to survive. The Liberals pushed the devolution issue but were obviously thwarted by the failure to achieve sufficiently large majorities.

- **The 1998 vote to approve of an elected London mayor.** This was going to change the governance of the capital city, so the consent of Londoners was vital. It also implied some increase in taxation, again making consent essential.

- **The 1998 referendum in Northern Ireland on the Good Friday Agreement.** This was a critical vote. After 30 years of inter-community conflict, the agreement held the promise of permanent peace. It was necessary to secure not just a 'yes' vote but a decisive one to ensure that all sections of Northern Ireland were in favour. The 'yes' vote of over 70 per cent was considered good enough.

● **The 2004 referendum in the North-East.** This was really a test run for future referendums in other English regions such as the North-West. The decisive rejection of the proposal led to the government abandoning the policy of setting up more assemblies in the English regions. At least the government could take comfort in the fact that the 'no' vote stopped them introducing a policy that would have proved highly unpopular.

● **Various referendums in localities.** The idea that local communities might have powerful, elected mayors had already been established for London. This was extended to various parts of the country. Between 2001 and 2004, 31 votes were held, of which only 11 were positive. It was considered unacceptable that the central government should impose elected mayors upon communities. In other word, the *local* system of government should be determined by *local* decisions.

● **The congestion charge votes in Edinburgh and Manchester.** This was a difficult decision for local government as there were strong forces on each side of the debate. Environmentalists wanted to see a congestion charge introduced, but the motoring lobby was firmly against. A referendum was therefore convenient. Interestingly, if a congestion charge is considered a tax, we could view this as a vote on a tax issue.

Assessment of referendum use

It has become clear that referendums are here to stay for the foreseeable future. This is not to say, however, that they are necessarily the best way of resolving issues. The next two sections present a balanced view of the use of referendums and are summarised in the table on p 39.

The benefits of referendum use

● It is, of course, the most direct form of democracy. The people's views on a particular question are clearly indicated; there is not the confusion that could be caused if politicians simply *claim* to be representing public opinion. In other words, a referendum helps to make decisions *legitimate* and confirms the principle of *government by consent*.

● If the people have demonstrated their expressed consent, they are more likely to accept the decision. This was especially important in Northern Ireland where the Good Friday Agreement of 1998 could have a chance of success only if it received widespread and *clear* support from most of the community. The 'yes' vote of over 70 per cent was therefore crucial. (The Agreement ran into difficulties later, but the peace did last and a final political settlement was achieved in May 2007.)

● Referendums can prevent governments from making unpopular decisions when a 'no' vote is delivered. This occurred in 2004 when regional government was rejected by the people of North-East England.

● There are occasions when the government and the parties in general are likely to fail to resolve an issue effectively. In 1975, the Labour government, as well as the Conservative opposition, were divided on whether Britain should remain in the European Community. The decisive 'yes' vote resolved this key issue. Similarly, when the Conservative and Liberal Democrat parties were negotiating a coalition arrangement in 2010 there was a problem in that the Conservatives opposed voting reform while the Liberal Democrats were committed to a change. The agreement to hold a referendum effectively shifted the decision away from government and into the hands of the people.

- A referendum effectively entrenches constitutional changes. It protects them from attacks by future governments whose policies may be only short term. In order to reverse a referendum decision, it is widely accepted that a fresh referendum would have to be held. This principle prevents the possibility that a future government would simply dismantle constitutional reforms already made. For example, as the Scots voted for their own parliament in 1997, it would be extremely disruptive if a future Conservative government simply decided to abolish that parliament. Only the Scots will be able to undo what they did in 1997.

The problems of referendum use

- In Ancient Greece the philosopher Plato argued against direct democracy of this kind by suggesting that the people will not respect the decisions that they make themselves. At first sight this seems to make no sense, but further consideration reveals that perhaps Plato had a point. Many people prefer to be led, especially if they can believe that their elected representatives have better judgement than they do. Plato also pointed out that if people make their own laws, they will get used to the idea of simply repealing the same laws when they do not suit them any more. The result would be lack of continuity at best, chaos at worst. In a modern context, Plato's objections can be translated to mean that the excessive use of referendums will lead to a loss of respect for our elected representatives and institutions. It is certainly true that there has been a general loss of confidence in politicians and parties in the modern period, but their replacement by regular referendums might cause the political system to collapse altogether. There are few, if any, political commentators who believe that the people can replace the political system entirely.

- Many issues may be simply too complex for the majority of the people to understand and make a judgement on. We may be better educated than ever, but some political questions remain difficult and technical. For example, issues arising from proposed European Union treaties may well be too complex for popular consideration. The danger of such situations is that the debate will be presented as a few simple, emotional arguments and the true, detailed nature of the issues will be neglected. There are many who feel particularly uneasy about the way in which tabloid newspapers tend to reduce such issues to over-simplistic symbols. In referendum campaigns the tabloids (and, therefore, their owners and editors) may well have a disproportionate influence over the result. Perhaps, many would argue, such matters should be left to our elected representatives under the guidance of experts rather than to the mood swings of newspaper proprietors and their readership.

- Referendum campaigns are expensive operations. There is, therefore, a danger that one side will prevail simply because it has more resources. Although many legal limitations are placed on campaign expenditure, it seems inevitable that money will play a decisive role. It was often suggested, for instance, that the 'yes' campaign in the 1975 European Community referendum spent vastly more money than the opposing side. Most businesses were in favour of membership and they clearly used their wealth to good effect. Furthermore, if the government itself supports one side of the argument, it should give that side a distinct advantage. But we need to be cautious here – government support for one side may prove to be a double-edged sword, as we shall see in the next point.

- There is a danger that people will use a referendum as an opportunity to express their dissatisfaction with the government of the day and ignore the issue in question altogether. The decisive 'no' vote to devolution for the North-East of England in 2004 may well have been the result of such an effect. It would indeed be irrational if Britain adopted the euro or rejected it simply on the basis of whether the government of the day was popular or unpopular. In parts of Europe where referendums are used more often than in the UK, there is evidence that this is a common occurrence.

- Finally, we may turn to perhaps the most serious objection of all. This can be described as the danger of the *tyranny of the majority*. Referendums are, effectively, government by majority. The minority that loses is not taken account of in any way. Elected representatives are able to weigh up the interests of the majority against those of minorities. We expect modern democratic governments to protect minorities. Referendums leave them defenceless. This danger was recognised by liberal philosophers such as John Stuart Mill as long ago as the mid-nineteenth century, when popular democracy was emerging. Most issues, it can be argued, cannot be resolved with a simple 'yes' or 'no' response. Our representatives are in a position to modify decisions to take account of minorities; referendum verdicts cannot do this. If we imagine future referendums on such issues as the level of taxation, euthanasia or abortion, it can be seen how a blunt yes or no may not be the best resolution.

A summary of the arguments concerning referendums	
Arguments for	**Arguments against**
<ul><li>They are the most direct form of democracy.</li><li>People may be more likely to respect and conform to decisions they have made themselves. They represent true government by consent.</li><li>They may prevent governments making unpopular decisions.</li><li>They may resolve issues that cause special problems for government and parties.</li><li>They entrench constitutional change.</li></ul>	<ul><li>They may undermine respect for representative institutions.</li><li>Some issues may be too complex for people to understand.</li><li>They may produce an emotional rather than a rational response.</li><li>Wealthy groups or the tabloid press may influence the result unjustifiably.</li><li>People may use referendums as a verdict on the general popularity of the government rather than on the issue in question.</li><li>They may represent the 'tyranny of the majority'. Minorities may suffer.</li></ul>

Having said that, there are many issues that *do* have only two possible outcomes (such as the European single currency issue). In these cases we may have less fear of the referendum as a political device.

A footnote: the referendums that have not been held

It is interesting to consider some of the referendums that have not been held, but which might

have been. The most controversial issue was the Constitutional Treaty of the European Union. The Conservative Party argued strongly that there should have been a referendum as it was an extensive constitutional change. In the event, the Irish people voted against it in their own referendum and this effectively 'killed' the treaty as it required unanimous approval from all member states. When Britain then signed a second version of the treaty in 2007 (subsequently approved by Parliament and known as the Lisbon Treaty), the

Conservatives had to drop their demands for a popular vote on the grounds that Britain could not cancel a treaty it had already signed.

Earlier the Labour Party had promised a referendum on electoral reform in its 1997 election manifesto, but the government subsequently failed to make good this promise. In 2010, however, the new coalition government committed itself to such a referendum. There is to be a vote in May 2011 on whether to adopt the Alternative Vote for general elections. If the time ever comes when there is a proposal for Britain to adopt the euro, there will have to be a referendum to approve such a momentous change.

Discussion topic

Would a referendum be appropriate and useful in determining the following questions?

- Whether or not to legalise euthanasia.

- Whether to replace petrol and other car taxes with a system of differential road pricing.

- Whether Scotland should have full independence. (Should the whole of the UK be consulted, not just the Scots?)

- Should the UK remain a member of the European Union?

- How should public expenditure be divided between different possible uses?

Representative democracy

The democratic spirit began to spread across Europe and North America between the seventeenth and the nineteenth centuries. But it was not direct democracy that was being proposed. States were larger and more complex than those that had flourished in classical Greece. The idea that

the people should assemble at regular intervals was simply not practical. Perhaps more importantly, however, political philosophers opposed direct democracy on several grounds:

- Most people remained illiterate and ill-educated. Expecting them to reach important political decisions was, therefore, unrealistic.

- There was a widespread fear that minority groups would suffer discrimination at the hands of the majority. The interests of landowners, merchants, manufacturers and entrepreneurs might be swamped by the numerical superiority of the ordinary people. In particular, the property-owning minority might suffer at the hands of the non-property-owning majority.

- In the larger, more complex states of the modern world, it was impractical to expect the people to assemble regularly to exercise their democratic rights.

So a modified form of democracy was seen as desirable. This became *representative* democracy. The mass of the people were to be represented by a minority of office holders. If we concentrate on the British experience of the growth of such democracy, we can identify a number of key developments.

- **1649–53**: Following the execution of King Charles I a number of attempts were made to govern by means of Parliament. However, the system by which MPs were called to Parliament was not democratic and the new representative institution lacked legitimacy. By 1653 parliamentary government had collapsed and was replaced by the autocratic rule of Oliver Cromwell.

- **1688**: In the Glorious (and largely peaceful) Revolution, King James II was replaced by the joint monarchy of William III and his wife, Mary. At the same time the Bill of Rights was agreed between the new monarchy and

Parliament. This effectively transferred sovereignty to Parliament (it declared that all laws required the sanction of Parliament). However, both the Commons and the Lords continued to lack democratic legitimacy.

- **1689**: The great English philosopher John Locke published *Two Treatises of Government*. This highly influential work set out the principles of representative democracy operating within a limited monarchy.

- **1832**: The Great Reform Act introduced a fairer, regular system for the election of MPs. It also widened the franchise to include all of the property-owning middle classes (still a small proportion of the total population). This had the effect of making the House of Commons legitimate and can be treated as the dawn of parliamentary democracy as we understand it today.

- **1830s–1900**: The party system developed over this period. The Conservative Party evolved under Robert Peel (1788–1850) in the 1830s, the Liberals under William Gladstone (1809–98) in the 1870s and Labour was founded in 1900. Increasingly, voting was based on the party affiliation of a candidate rather than on his personal philosophy and qualities. Thus party representation evolved.

- **1884**: The Third Reform Act granted voting rights to most of the male population. The House of Commons could claim even more legitimacy and thus gained superiority over the unelected House of Lords.

- **1928**: In this year the principle of universal adult suffrage was finally established. Virtually all adults, men and women, over the age of 21 were granted the franchise. Britain could now be said to be a true liberal democracy.

- **1945**: The first truly modern election manifesto appeared, published by the Labour Party, which was duly elected with a clear programme of reform, approved by the electorate. The existence of a detailed manifesto, setting out the party's policies, implied that the new government had a mandate to carry out the policies contained in the manifesto. This introduced the representative concept of mandate and manifesto. Since 1945 manifestos have become gradually more detailed and the mandate of the electorate has become clearer.

- **2010**: The first coalition government since 1945 ushered in a new kind of representation. Such a government has no clear mandate but, instead has developed policies that represent a *consensus* of support. These agreed policies are shown in the section entitled 'The British General Election of May 2010' on page 111.

Alongside these specific developments, the nature of **representation**, as it is generally understood, was also evolving. It passed through three main stages.

Burkean representation was expounded by the Whig MP and writer Edmund Burke (who ultimately came to be seen as a conservative) at the end of the eighteenth century. Burke argued that an elected representative should be expected to use his judgement in the best interests of his constituents. He should not be expected merely to follow the instructions of those who have elected him.

Key Word

Representation The *political* idea is that people elect or appoint representatives to make decisions on their behalf rather than making those decisions themselves. On a *social* level it implies that political institutions should have a membership that is broadly a social cross-section of society in general.

Parliamentary representation combines Burke's idea that representatives should be independent-minded with the development of united political parties in the nineteenth century. Here, representatives were expected to strike a balance between their own judgement, the stated policies of their party and the interests of their parliamentary constituents. The middle part of the nineteenth century has often been described as the *'golden age* of the British MP'. This is because representatives in that period retained their independence within the party structure. In so doing they were able to retain real influence over government policy.

Of course, there are still occasions when the party whips are called off and MPs are allowed to vote free of their discipline (so-called 'free votes'). When such situations occur MPs may revert to the Burkean principle – that they should use their own judgement – or will consult their constituents on the issue and follow their wishes. Parliamentary votes on hunting with dogs, abortion laws and public smoking bans are modern examples of such circumstances.

Party delegation evolved during the twentieth century. The parties became increasingly disciplined and monolithic. MPs were subjected to ever greater control by their party leadership. Parliamentary whips became the agents of this discipline so that the age of the independent MP had more or less ended. With a few exceptions MPs toe the party line. In other words, MPs have become largely delegates of their party. Such discipline can be justified on the grounds that the voters typically base their decision on the merits of each party's election manifesto, not on the personal qualities of the candidates. The MP who is elected, therefore, has a moral duty to support the party's manifesto commitments as that is what their constituents voted for. MPs who wish to defy their party's line on an issue are certainly expected to consult their local party members and, ideally, their constituents before doing so.

Student activity

Imagine you are an MP under the following circumstances:

- Your party's last election manifesto carried a commitment to build more wind farms to help to achieve Britain's international commitments to emissions control and anti-climate change measures.

- It is proposed that a large wind farm should be built in your constituency.

- There is a good deal of unemployment in your constituency and the wind farm promises at least 500 new jobs.

- As an individual you prefer the nuclear option for future energy generation.

- There is considerable local opposition to the proposal, though opinion polls say the country as a whole is largely in favour of wind farms and anti-nuclear power stations.

How would you resolve the dilemma and which way would you vote in Parliament?

Parliamentary and representative democracy in the UK

British parliamentary democracy

Representative democracy in the UK is often described as **parliamentary democracy**. This is because Parliament dominates the political system and because representation occurs traditionally through Parliament. The main features of parliamentary democracy, British-style, are as follows.

1. Parliament is the source of all political authority. It is effectively not possible to exercise power without the sanction of Parliament. Even the prime minister, who enjoys many arbitrary prerogative powers inherited from the monarchy, can act only if he enjoys the support of Parliament.

2. The government of the UK has to be drawn from Parliament. Its members must also be members of either the House of Commons or the House of Lords. This ensures that members of the government can be made directly accountable to Parliament.

3. Extending from this second point, it is a fixed principle that government makes itself constantly accountable to Parliament and submits all proposals to Parliament for approval (foreign treaties and actions by the armed forces and intelligence or security services may be excepted in some circumstances). It also means that ministers must report regularly to Parliament on the progress of policies and the results of governmental actions.

4. All citizens are represented by members of Parliament (MPs). This means that their views should be taken into account and their grievances, if possibly justified, should be taken up by MPs for possible redress. It also means that the interests of every constituency in the UK are represented by an MP in the House of Commons.

5. Parliament is normally the guardian of the government's electoral mandate. The governing party has a mandate to put its proposals into action, based on its previous election manifesto (the so-called doctrine of **mandate and manifesto**). Parliament has the task of ensuring that the mandate is not abused and if government seeks to step outside or beyond its mandate, it reserves the right to veto such government action. The House of Lords has become especially active in this particular role. However, when no party wins a clear majority, as occurred in 2010, the doctrine of the mandate is compromised. The role of Parliament then ceases to be guardian of the mandate and instead becomes the supervisor of coalition politics, ensuring that government holds to its original coalition agreement.

6. Parliament is expected, as a whole, to represent the *national* interest. On occasions this may even involve the defeat of the government on a vote, though such occurrences are relatively rare.

So, Parliament stands at the centre of national politics in Britain. In many ways, indeed, it is Parliament that gives government **legitimacy** in Britain (along with elections, of course). A full discussion of the concept of legitimacy can be found in the Introduction to this book. But it is only one aspect of a broader representative democracy, as we shall see below.

Representative democracy in Britain

We may now review the broader state of representation in the UK today. In doing so it is important to appreciate that there is now widespread disillusionment with representative institutions. As we have seen above, party membership has declined dramatically, turnout at elections has fallen markedly and a decreasing number of citizens claim to have any close identification with a political party. Nevertheless there is a wide variety of ways in which people continue to feel represented.

● Each MP represents a constituency. This is also true of Members of the Scottish Parliament, the Welsh and Northern Ireland Assemblies and every local councillor. As such they are expected to represent the interests of the constituency as a whole and their constituents as individuals. Occasionally this may conflict with their party's policy, but there are many occasions when such representatives are able to protect their constituencies and to take up their grievances with members of the government and other public bodies. It is a key part of the democratic system that each individual feels that there is an elected representative who will listen to their problems and injustices and, if appropriate, try to resolve them.

● Both Houses of Parliament are, to some extent, expected to act as a representative cross-section of society as a whole. When debates and committee hearings take place in either House, MPs and peers do express what they believe to be the views and interests of various sections of the community.

Unfortunately neither House of Parliament can claim to be truly socially representative of the nation as a whole. The table below indicates the number of women and minority ethnic groups represented in Parliament, as well as the educational background of MPs following the 2010 election.

Representation in the UK Parliament, May 2010		
House of Commons		
Group	% in the House	% in the whole population
Women	22	51
Ethnic minorities	4	8
University educated	90	31
House of Lords		
Group	% in the House	% in the whole population
Women	21	51
Ethnic minorities	4	8

Sources: House of Commons, House of Lords, Sutton Trust

We can clearly see that Parliament as a whole is far from socially representative. Women and minority ethnic groups are especially under-represented, while those with a university education are over-represented. The fact that three times as many MPs are university educated compared with the rest of the population is perhaps more understandable and desirable. Nevertheless, it is true that various occupational sections of the community are represented in Parliament, especially in the House of Lords. Peers come from a wide variety of backgrounds and thus represent all the main professions (law, medicine, teaching and so on), trade unions, pressure groups, industries and leisure groups. Within the constrictions of party discipline, the interests of these and other groups are represented, to a limited extent. Yet we can see that manual workers are under-represented in the Commons while there is a noticeable bias towards professional backgrounds among MPs.

● All mainstream parties in the UK claim that they represent the whole nation. The days when the Conservative Party represented the middle class and Labour represented the working class are now gone. So representation is now based on party allegiance rather than social class. As we have seen, this is exercised through the principle of mandate and manifesto. Each party manifesto claims to represent the national interest.

● As faith in political parties has declined, people in Britain increasingly feel more represented by pressure groups of various kinds. It is not felt that parties can represent all the interests of all the people at the same time. Pressure groups, however, represent us precisely and accurately. By pursuing the interests of a particular section of society or by promoting a particular cause, pressure groups are seen as more effective vehicles for the demands and views of the electorate today.

● Finally, it can be argued that the media, especially newspapers, represent the general public. Certainly newspaper editors claim they are representing the typical views of their readership. What is more, political leaders pay more attention to the press than was the case in the past. Whether or not newspapers have influence, it is widely believed that they *do*, so the views they express are important.

Direct and representative democracy compared

Representative democracy has a number of distinct advantages over the direct form. Among these are the following:

- Elected representatives may be expected to use superior knowledge, judgement and experience to consider issues more deeply and so avoid over-emotional, hasty conclusions.

- Representatives, especially political parties, are in a position to mediate between the conflicting demands of different groups in society. For example, what are the merits of high petrol taxes to deter its use, reduce emissions and so improve the environment against those groups that wish to see fuel prices as low as possible? Should we allow into the country large numbers of immigrants as a source of cheap labour, or should we restrict immigration in case the country becomes dangerously over-populated with low-income families? These are difficult, controversial issues that require lengthy, sober reflection.

- In a similar way representatives are in a position to protect minorities against the 'tyranny of the majority' as described above. For example, elected representatives may be able to protect the interests of cyclists against the majority who drive cars. Similarly, the cause of tobacco smokers conflicts with the wishes of the majority of non-smokers who want to see the practice restricted. If either issue were resolved by direct democracy, the majority would always prevail.

- The demands of different sections of the community are often incoherent and do not collectively add up to a logical political programme. It is therefore crucial that representative institutions – parties, Parliament and government in particular – 'aggregate' or collate the many demands placed on the political system and convert them into practical, coordinated programmes of action.

Despite these clear advantages of representative institutions, direct democracy has a great deal to commend it. This has become especially true since the 1990s when there has been considerable disillusionment with representative bodies, especially the party leaderships. People are probably better educated and certainly better informed than they have ever been. So they are well placed to make decisions for themselves. It can be observed that an increasing proportion of key political issues is now being resolved either by pressure group activity or through the use of referendums. We can now summarise the primary advantages of each of the two main types of democracy.

Comparison of direct and representative democracy	
Relative advantages of direct democracy	Relative advantages of representative democracy
• It is the purest form of democracy. • It avoids decisions being made by representatives purely in their own interests. • People are becoming increasingly well informed and educated	• Elected representatives may use superior knowledge and judgement. This avoids hasty and emotional decisions made directly by the people. • Representatives and parties are able to mediate between the interests of different sections of society. Direct democracy means the will of the

Comparison of direct and representative democracy (continued)	
Relative advantages of direct democracy	**Relative advantages of representative democracy**
and so can make their own judgements. • When there is disillusionment with representative institutions, people prefer to make decisions for themselves. • Decisions made directly by the people may now carry more authority.	majority always prevails, making minorities very vulnerable. • Issues that involve such conflicting interests require complex solutions. Direct democracy tends to reduce all questions to over-simplified answers. • Demands made directly by the people are often incoherent and illogical. Representative democracy can make better sense of these demands and convert them into practical programmes.

Is Britain a liberal democracy?

If we are to assess whether Britain can be described as a true liberal democracy we need to find a more precise definition of the term than the general word 'democracy'. Different commentators have developed their own definitions of liberal democracy, but the following scheme can act as a summary.

● Government is accountable to the people to ensure that it is attempting to act in their general interests.

● There are free and fair elections.

● There is a peaceful, orderly transfer of power from one government to the next.

● Losing parties accept the democratic legitimacy of winning parties.

● Information is freely available to the citizenry.

● The rights and liberties of citizens are taken into account and protected.

● The powers of government are controlled and limited either by law or by elected institutions or both.

● A variety of beliefs, opinions, cultures and lifestyles is tolerated provided they do not threaten the security and peace of the state.

Others may vary these criteria, but for our purposes they can act as a useful guide.

We can now assess whether Britain lives up to these criteria by looking at each feature in turn.

● **Accountability.** It is true that Parliament forces government to be constantly accountable, requiring ministers to explain and justify their actions and, where necessary, to accept criticism. There is full reporting of proceedings in Parliament and in its committees to ensure citizens are informed. The only word of caution is to say that perhaps Parliament does not have enough time, expertise or technical back-up to undertake this task effectively.

● **Free and fair elections.** Elections in Britain are, by and large, free of corruption, although there have been recent concerns over postal voting. There is an independent Electoral Commission that oversees elections to ensure they are honestly conducted. All adult citizens have the right to vote and stand for office, unless disqualified for justified reasons. However, it could be argued that voting in general elections using the first-past-the-post (FPTP) system is not fair. Many votes are wasted, especially those for smaller parties that have no chance of winning any seats and those cast in 'safe' seats where the outcome is virtually inevitable. Professor David Denver, an expert on elections, has estimated that as many as 80 per cent of votes in a general election are ineffective for these reasons. In practice, therefore, although there is 'one person one vote', votes are of unequal value. The general election voting system is also unfair to all but the main two parties.

- **Legitimacy and the transfer of power.** Britain's record here is excellent. There is a high degree of acceptance of the results of elections, and all mainstream parties accept the full legitimacy of government. There is little or no violence associated with the main political processes.

- **Information.** Britain enjoys a free press and free broadcasting. There is little or no evidence of government attempting to control information coming from the media. The British media are renowned for their investigative work and for their political activism. Citizens are exposed to a wide variety of independent political views. Possibly in matters of warfare and national security, governments have censored and manipulated news, but this is common to all democracies, whether or not it can be justified.

- **Rights and liberties.** Britain has signed up to the European Convention on Human Rights (through the Human Rights Act) and the Social Chapter of the European Union (guaranteeing a variety of employment and other economic rights). However, Parliament retains its sovereignty and therefore the right to set aside such guarantees if it wishes. This means that a number of rights and freedoms have, from time to time, been set aside or suspended, especially in the interests of law and order or national security. As long as Parliament approves, therefore, governments retain control over rights and freedoms. This is a considerably inferior position to most other 'liberal democracies', which generally include entrenched, protected rights against government encroachment.

- **Limited government.** Here Britain has a serious problem. There is no written British Constitution (unlike, e.g., the United States) and therefore no safeguarded set of fundamental laws that set out the limits of government. If Parliament gives its sanction, government can do anything it wishes in Britain. The prerogative, uncontrolled powers of the prime minister in areas of defence, security and governmental procedures are considerable and rarely challenged by Parliament. Having said that, Parliament has a fairly good record of restraining governments when they have attempted to exceed their traditional powers. For example, in 2005 the House of Commons prevented the Government from giving itself the power to imprison terrorist suspects for up to 90 days without trial.

- **Tolerance.** Britain is known and often admired abroad for its tolerant politics and culture. As long as groups have not challenged the legitimacy of government, the laws and the security of the state, they have been allowed to flourish and spread their beliefs and philosophies. However, the recent growing terrorist threat and increased incidence of migration, immigration and asylum seeking have placed such tolerance under considerable strain.

The democratic deficit and democratic renewal

There are three main elements to the issue of whether Britain is suffering from a 'democratic deficit'.

1. The problem of falling *political participation*, which has been described above.

2. The persistence of undemocratic *institutions* within the system of government.

3. The increased *centralisation* of power that is insufficiently accountable within government.

Proposals to rectify these deficiencies are usually described as 'democratic renewal'.

In relation to the first problem – falling participation – solutions are described above in this chapter and largely concern methods to raise voting turnout in general and in particular to engage young people with the democratic process. Solutions to the second issue – undemocratic institutions – largely involve constitutional and parliamentary reform. These are described in units 2.1 and 2.2 respectively. Similarly the problem of over-centralisation is being addressed through the continuing process or devolution and other constitutional reforms. Again these proposals are described in Unit 2.1.

Key concepts in this chapter

Democracy A very general description of various political systems that are organised on the basis that government should serve the interests of the people. In liberal democracies it is also expected that citizens should influence decisions or make decisions themselves. It is also expected that government should be accountable, in various ways, to the people.

Citizenship This term refers to the idea that members of the political community have certain rights with respect to political institutions. It also implies that an individual has the right to live within a particular state and thus also enjoy all its rights and benefits. Citizenship implies a certain level of obligation, mainly to obey the law, to give military service in some circumstances, to pay taxes and, arguably, to vote and to engage in some kinds of service to the community.

Participation Opportunities for and tendencies of the people to become involved in the political process. At a minimum level this will involve voting, but may also involve active work in political parties or pressure groups. At the highest level it implies standing for public office.

Referendum A popular vote where the people are asked to determine an important political or constitutional issue directly.

Representation The *political* idea is that people elect or appoint representatives to make decisions on their behalf rather than making those decisions themselves. On a *social* level, it implies that political institutions should have a membership that is broadly a social cross-section of society in general.

Revision topics and examination questions

Revision topics

● What is meant by democracy?
● What is meant by democratic deficit?
● What is meant by democratic renewal?
● How citizens can participate in politics in the UK
● Nature of direct democracy
● Why referendums have been held
● Arguments for and against referendums
● Nature of representative democracy
● Direct and representative democracy compared
● How citizens are represented in the UK

Short answers (approx. 120 words)

● What is meant by the term 'direct democracy'?
● What is a referendum?
● What is meant by the term 'representative democracy'?
● Outline any THREE ways in which UK citizens can participate in politics.
● In what ways has political participation fallen in the UK?

Medium answers (approx. 250 words)

● Distinguish between direct and representative democracy.
● Under what circumstances have referendums been used in the UK?
● How are citizens represented in the UK political system?
● What is meant by the term 'political participation'?
● What is the nature of Britain's 'democratic deficit'?
● Distinguish between a referendum and an election.

Long answers (approx. 800 words)

● What are the main arguments in favour of the use of referendums?
● What are the arguments against the use of referendums?
● Compare the relative merits of direct and representative democracy.
● In what senses can the UK be described as a democracy?
● Assess the various proposals that have been advanced for democratic renewal in the UK.
● How representative is the UK political system?

Resources and web guide

Books

A contemporary book on current issues is:
P. Ginsberg, *Democracy*, Profile Books, 2008

A good general discussion on issues surrounding democracy can be found in:
A. Heywood, *Politics*, Palgrave Macmillan, 2002.

Or:
B. Crick, *Democracy: A Very Short Introduction*, Oxford University Press, 2002

General contemporary issues in UK democracy can be found in:
S. Weir *et al.*, *Democracy under Blair*, Politicos, 2002.

Useful websites

For information about referendums look at the website of the UK Electoral Commission:
www. electoralcommission.gov.uk
For information on the UK Parliament and devolved parliaments look at:
www.parliament.uk
www.scottish.parliament.uk
www.wales.gov.uk
www.niassembly.gov.uk
The main pressure group concerned with democratic participation is Unlock Democracy:
www.unlockdemocracy.org.uk

Party policies and ideas

1.2

The nature of parties and party government

Features of political parties today

Before describing the nature of political parties today, it is worth establishing a working definition:

> A political party is an organisation that develops a set of political goals and policies, which it seeks to convert into political action by obtaining government office, or a share in government, or by influencing the government of the day. It pursues its goals by mobilising public opinion in its favour, selecting candidates for office, competing at elections and identifying suitable political leaders.

If we now look at each of the elements in our definition we can also develop a useful set of features, to which most parties conform.

- Political parties have to be organised. They need to do this in order to carry out their many functions. A vague and disorganised group of people will find it difficult to create a coherent political programme and will be unable to fight elections successfully. Organisations will tend to be relatively formal, especially among well-established parties. An exception is the British Green Party, which prefers to remain a loose, informal organisation, but, even so, has developed a mechanism for producing election

manifestos and for selecting candidates. New parties, such as the UK Independence Party (UKIP), find organisation difficult at first and this can prevent them making inroads into support for the other parties. Unlike the United States, where small parties can suddenly make an impact (as did Ross Perot's Reform Party in the 1990s) new British parties find it difficult to become quickly established. The problem is partly financial. Wealthy individuals like Perot are able to provide the funding for a new party in the USA. Such benefactors are rare in the UK. Even when a rich individual appears, success is elusive. A large organisation of activists is needed to mobilise public opinion and to fight elections on the ground. In 1997, multi-millionaire James Goldsmith started an anti-EU party, the Referendum Party, with £20 million of funding, but it failed largely because it could not attract enough ordinary members. Indeed, British politics is a graveyard of failed parties, mainly because they were unable to create an effective organisation quickly enough.

- Parties must develop policies and programmes to present to the electorate in order to secure the election of their candidates. Behind such policies usually lies some kind of ideology. This may be relatively weak, as is the case with the Conservatives and the Labour Party since the 1990s, but it remains important for a party to have some sort of 'ideological identity' with which people can identify. This may be little more than, say, *'releasing individuals from the excessive burdens of government'* (a contemporary Conservative slogan) or *'governing on behalf of the many rather than the few'* (Labour). Labour before the mid-1990s, of course, considered itself to be democratic socialist, a far clearer ideological identity. The Liberal Democrats claim to base themselves on the primacy of individual freedom and social justice. There are ideological parties in UK politics, such as the Greens and the ultra-left Respect Party, but these have failed to make a significant electoral impact.

● Large parties have the securing of government office as their primary goal. It is indeed arguable that a party that does seek to become the government – or at least to share government – is not a party at all but rather a pressure group. The reason is clear. There is little point in developing a political programme unless there is a prospect of putting it into practice. Of course, smaller parties like the Liberal Democrats have to be realistic. They are unlikely to win enough seats in the House of Commons to be able to form a majority administration, so their immediate goal has to be to share power with one of the larger parties. From this starting point they may hope to govern alone in the future. The hopes of even smaller parties remain very much further in the future. Their immediate objective may be simply to gain supporters and perhaps win a few seats in Parliament. But even these political minnows may harbour dreams of forming governments in the distant future. All parties must start somewhere.

● If parties are to make progress they must gain public support for their policies. This means they must have strategies for winning such support. They must devote much of their work to presenting their policies, educating the public and engaging in persuasion. This must be carried out on two main levels. One is in the media – successful parties must attract the attention of TV, radio and the press if they are to have any hope of reaching the mass of the people. The other involves more work – this is the slow, gradual building up of support in neighbourhoods, persuading people to attend meetings, to read the party's literature and perhaps even to attend to become active members.

● When a party is in a position to fight elections it must select suitable candidates. Procedures must be put in place for selecting the best – always assuming, that is, that there is competition for such positions. This is normally a local function in the UK as elections are essentially local in nature. Councillors and MPs are expected to represent a locality, so it is logical that they should be selected at a local level.

● The Green Party in the UK has always been reluctant to recognise leaders. It is an intensely democratic party that is highly suspicious of the exercise of political power. But it is an exception. Parties ultimately rely upon successful leadership. Leaders give the party direction and are essential for the mobilisation of public support.

We can now see what features most, if not all, political parties display. There are exceptions – loose political groups that call themselves parties (even some anarchists have described themselves as 'parties'!) – but a modern 'party' is clearly recognisable.

Functions of parties

Making policy. Having identified the main features of political parties and distinguished them from pressure groups, we can summarise the functions of a modern political party.

Perhaps the most recognisable function of a political party is the development of policies and political programmes. This is a role that becomes especially important when a party is in opposition and is seeking to replace the government of the day. Opposition parties are, therefore, in a fundamentally different position to the party in power. When a ruling party controls the government, its leadership *is* the government, there is virtually no distinction between the two. Therefore the policy-making function of the ruling party *is the same as* the policy-making function of the government. It involves not only political leaders but also civil servants, advisory units and committees and private advisers. Of course, the rest of the party – backbench MPs and peers, local activists and ordinary members – have some say through policy conferences and committees, but their role remains very much in the background. Ministers and their advisers make most policy in the ruling party.

In opposition, the leadership of a party is not in such a pre-eminent policy-making position. True, the leadership group will have most influence, the leader especially, but it is when in opposition that the general membership of the party can have most input into policy making. 'Policy' relates to the political objectives of the party – how to run the economy, public services, defence and foreign policy, law and order, social affairs, etc. A political programme is more specific. It describes what priorities the party should have and corresponds generally to what can be achieved in a five-year term of office, or even longer if the party is confident of a sustained period in government.

The policy-formulating function is also sometimes known as *aggregation*. This involves identifying the wide range of demands made on the political system, from the mass of individuals in society as well as many different groups, and then converting these into programmes of action that are consistent and compatible.

Parties claim to have a representative function. As we have seen above, parties have their origins in the representation of social classes. This is a weaker function in contemporary politics because all the main parties argue that they represent the *national* interest and not just the interests of specific classes or groups. So, when we suggest that parties have a representative function, we mean today that they seek to ensure that all groups in society have their interests and demands at least considered by government.

Selecting candidates. Parties spend a great deal of their time and effort selecting candidates for office at all levels. They need to find prospective local councillors, elected mayors in those localities where such a position exists (notably London), members of the devolved assemblies and the Scottish Parliament, candidates for the European Parliament and, most prominently of all, for the Westminster Parliament. This is mostly done at local and regional level, through party committees staffed by activists, though the party leaderships do have some say in which candidates should be chosen. But it is in this role that constituency parties have the greatest part to play.

Identifying leaders. Parties need leaders and in the case of the main parties, this means potential government ministers. They therefore have procedures for identifying political leaders. It is in this area that the established party leaders play a key role. For the ruling party, the prime minister completely controls the appointment of ministers. In opposition parties, the leader will choose a smaller group of 'front bench' spokespersons who form the leadership. But despite the dominance of party leaders in this field, potential leaders cut their teeth to some extent in internal party organisations and committees. The formal organisations of parties give opportunities for members to become 'trained' as leaders.

Organising elections. At election time parties play a critical role. Apart from supplying approved candidates, the party organisations form part of the process of publicising election issues, persuading people to vote and informing

The left–right divide in the UK (continued)				
The economy and related issues				
Left	**Centre-left**	**Centre**	**Centre-right**	**Right**
Redistribution of income to create more economic equality.	Elements from both centre and left.	Pro free trade.	Elements from both centre and right.	Very low levels of taxation.
Strong trade unions, protected rights for workers.		Mild redistribution of income with poverty relief.		Avoidance of excessive government borrowing to stimulate growth.
Protectionism for domestic industries.				Protectionism for domestic industries.
Anti EU.		Pro EU.		Free labour markets with weak protection for workers.
				Anti EU.
Social issues				
Extensive welfare state.		Strong welfare system but targeted at the most needy.		Very limited welfare system targeted at only a small minority.
Tolerance of minorities.		Pro multiculturalism.		
Stress on equal rights.	Elements from both centre and left.	Support for rights balanced against need for security.	Elements from both centre and right.	Anti immigration, asylum seeking and multiculturalism.
Liberal attitude to crime and its remedies.		Mixed liberal and authoritarian attitudes to crime.		Authoritarian attitude to crime.
State is justified in intervening to create social change.		Tolerant attitude on moral issues.		Low tolerance on moral issues.

The left–right divide in the UK (continued)				
Social issues				
		State should facilitate individualism.		Stress on British patriotism. Social change should be natural and organic.

Note: Some policy issues such as environment and foreign affairs do not conform to a left–right analysis.

We can now ask the question: how does this kind of analysis apply to UK parties in 2010? The general picture looks like this.

Labour: Most of the party is now positioned in the centre. There is a small group that may be described simply as 'left', often described as the 'socialist wing' (in the past represented by a faction called the '**Tribune Group**'), and there are some 'left-leaning' MPs who would prefer to be described as centre-left because they do stand somewhat to the left of the leadership without being serious dissidents.

Conservative: Here again the party under David Cameron has moved to the centre, having spent many years on the centre-right. There is still a right-wing faction, represented by an organisation called the **Cornerstone Group**, supported by perhaps 30 or so MPs and some peers. Cornerstone seeks to 'restore traditional conservative values'. On the centre-right stands a group called **Conservative Way Forward**. This faction is dedicated to progress the reforms undertaken under Margaret Thatcher in the 1980s and thereby distinguishes itself from the leadership, albeit without threatening a major revolt. The motto of the Conservative Way Forward is 'Keeping the Spirit of 1979 Alive', demonstrating its desire to keep alive the neo-liberal policies of that era.

Liberal Democrat: The party is difficult to characterise, though centre-left is perhaps the best description. However, there are two distinct factions in the modern party. In 2004 some leading Liberal Democrats published the 'Orange Book', which urged that the party should adopt many of the neo-liberal, free-market policies of the Thatcher period. The Orange Book group is led by David Laws, who became the Conservative–Liberal Democrat coalition's short-lived Chief Secretary to the Treasury. Opposing this right-wing faction is the Beveridge Group (named after William Beveridge, the liberal founder of the welfare state in the 1940s), which is left of centre and supports social democratic policies.

Other parties: The Scottish Nationalists and Plaid Cymru are both centre-left, though their main policy positions concern autonomy for Scotland and Wales respectively. The UK Independence Party stands firmly on the right of British politics, while the British National Party (BNP) is so far right that it lies outside the scheme shown above. There are no significant parties specifically from the far left, with the exception of the Scottish Socialist Party, which has won some seats in the Scottish Parliament. The Green Party has leftward tendencies but is so concentrated on environmental issues that it does not fit neatly into a left–right distinction.

Key Word

Conservatism A state of mind and a political movement that is naturally averse to excessive change and reform. It is sceptical about strongly held political views, prefers the known to the unknown and generally supports the retention of traditional institutions and values.

Key Word

Liberalism A state of political mind or a political movement that places freedom, rights and tolerance high on its scale of values.

Key Word

Socialism A state of mind and a political movement that places such values as equality of opportunity, social justice and collectivism high on its scale of values. It is either opposed to free market capitalism or proposes measures to moderate the undesirable effects of capitalism.

Margaret Thatcher, a leading exponent of New Right policies

conservatism, which came to prominence under the Conservative Party leadership of Margaret Thatcher and which is therefore often described as **Thatcherism**. We must look at these in turn.

Traditional conservatism

Originating in the late part of the eighteenth century, traditional conservatism emerged as a reaction against the newly emerging liberal ideas that were the inspiration behind the revolutions in North America (1776) and France (1789). Conservative thinkers such as Edmund Burke (1729–97) became alarmed at the rise of ideas such as freedom of the individual, tolerance of different political and religious beliefs, representative government and a *laissez-faire* attitude towards economic activity (that is, the state avoiding significant interference in the way in which wealth is distributed in society). Conservatives believed that such a free society,

Similarly, the parties in Northern Ireland defy left–right definitions, though Unionists are broadly centre-right or pure right, while Sinn Fein has strong leftward leanings and the SDLP is centre-left.

Conservative ideas

The task of determining the basic conservative philosophy is complicated by the fact that, since the 1970s, a second, distinctive tradition has emerged. These two very different philosophies are normally described as **traditional conservatism** – the pre-1970s type – and **New Right** with so little control by government, would lead to major social disorder.

Thereafter conservatives have consistently opposed the rise of any new ideology, so, later in the nineteenth century, the rise of **socialism** was opposed. This anti-socialist position remained in place until the 1970s when it reached its height under Margaret Thatcher.

But conservatism is not merely a reaction to any dominant ideology, and it is not simply a political philosophy opposed to change. There are some enduring principles, which are described below.

Human nature

Perhaps the most fundamental conservative value is its belief about basic human nature. In short, this is more pessimistic than the attitude of most other ideologies, notably **liberalism** and **socialism**. The following examples of these beliefs are typical.

- The deepest conservatives take the Roman Catholic view that man is born with 'original sin'. Therefore, he is, and must remain, severely flawed in character. However much he tries, he will be unable to achieve perfection. Ideologies such as socialism and anarchism have argued that mankind can be moulded by a just society into more perfect creatures. Not so, say such conservatives, thus rendering these ideologies impractical and merely utopian. Mankind is driven not by reason but by basic appetites. These include the desire for physical prosperity, for property, for power and for the avoidance of deprivation. This implies that people generally cannot be trusted with government as they will simply use it for their own ends rather than for the welfare of the whole community.

- It is a conservative tradition to see people on the whole as untrustworthy, self-seeking and

generally feckless. This adds up to the clear conclusion that mankind is sorely in need of firm government. This should not be government by dictatorial figures – they may rise to power too easily as people are often led by populist figures. Rather, they need to be governed by benevolent rulers, who should be firm but who have their general interests at heart. As Edmund Burke, the father of English conservatism, observed in the eighteenth century, the relationship between government and the people should be similar to that between a parent and a child. This view is often referred to as *conservative paternalism*.

- It is normal for human beings to think of themselves first; the interests of the rest of society tend to be a secondary consideration. This implies that the state needs to intervene if the pursuit of self-interest is not to take over completely. This has also led to the conservative stress on social unity rather than social conflict.

There are two further practical implications of the conservative view of human nature. The field of law and order is an obvious example. The causes of crime and disorder, conservatives believe, lie with the individual. Indeed, some have argued that they are the product of mankind's inherent sinfulness. This directly opposes the more liberal view that criminal behaviour is the result of economic and social deprivation. The application of these beliefs therefore involves exemplary punishment rather than social remedies.

A second, very different application of this conservative philosophy concerns the nature of government. If there is an excess of popular democracy, the country is likely to be poorly governed. As long ago as the 1870s the great Tory Prime Minister Benjamin Disraeli (1804–81), advocated that conservatives accept the need for universal suffrage, but this did not imply that the people could be completely trusted with government. The conservative view of representation is that governments should not slavishly follow the fluctuating desires and demands of the people, but should use their wise judgement to serve the best interests of the whole community. In a modern context this is reflected in the conservative suspicion of the referendum as a governing mechanism (though the British Conservative Party has supported the use of referendums in some circumstances, such as possible approval for a European Union Constitutional Treaty in 2007 – a typical example of conservative pragmatism).

Order

In the most basic terms it could be said that liberals see mankind's most fundamental need, after food, clothing and shelter, as individual freedom. Socialists and anarchists, meanwhile, stress man's social nature and his preference for the collective rather than the individual pursuit of goals. The conservative view is clear and stands in opposition to these beliefs. It affirms that mankind's most basic need is for order and security.

We can trace this key aspect of conservative philosophy to two English thinkers, Hobbes and Burke. Thomas Hobbes (1588–1679), writing in 1651 shortly after the end of the English civil war, examined mankind's basic predicament. On the one hand, we have a desire to be free and to exercise all our rights. On the other hand, we are intensely competitive and self-seeking. This would, if allowed to flourish, lead to an intolerable situation. Life, he famously argued, would become *solitary, poor, nasty, brutish and short*. In practice, everyone would consider themselves to be in competition with every other person and therefore live in fear of the results of that restless society. Hobbes believed that, faced with such a dilemma, mankind would choose to sacrifice much of its freedom and rights in favour of a secure existence. The only way to assure this was to allow an absolute ruler to govern and so protect us from each other.

Ever since Hobbes, conservatives have preferred strong government and have tended to favour the needs of the community for security above the rights of individuals. We see this philosophy most clearly in the conservative attitude to law and order and reluctance to champion the cause of civil liberties.

Edmund Burke's great work, *Reflections on the Revolution in France,* was written in 1790, one year after the French had dismissed their monarchy and at a time when there was growing hysteria in England in case revolution should cross the Channel. Starting as a vehement criticism of the actions of the revolutionaries, the book turned into a general manual of conservatism. Above all, Burke's *Reflections* is a plea for the preservation of order and gradual reform, rather than the disorder that results from revolutionary change. The French Revolution thus sacrificed order and security for the sake of imposing abstract theories that were premature, unnecessary and not generally supported by the majority of the people. Since Burke, conservatives have always erred on the side of caution and preserving order above promoting 'dubious' new ideas – until Margaret Thatcher, that is.

A clear contemporary example of how the conservative preference for social order over individual rights and freedoms has occurred is the struggle against terrorism. The typical conservative view is that individual rights and freedoms must be sacrificed for the sake of public security in the face of such a desperate challenge.

Tradition and preservation

The conservative preference for the preservation of tradition is related closely to their desire for public order. When we refer to tradition in this context we mean both traditional *institutions,* such as monarchy, established Church and political constitutions, and *values,* such as the preservation of marriage, the importance of the nuclear family, religion and established morality. Here again, it is an attitude that traces itself back to Burke.

The greatest crime of the French revolutionaries, said Burke, was to abandon traditional forms of authority that, according to him anyway, had stood the test of time. This is summarised in his ringing criticism: 'No generation should ever be so rash as to consider itself superior to its predecessors.'

The very fact that values and institutions have survived, argue conservatives in general, is a testament to their quality. Furthermore, they carry the 'accumulated wisdom of the past' and should therefore be respected. In a similar way, traditions bring to an existing society some of the best aspects of past societies. How people thought and behaved in the past can inform current generations. Thus, the nineteenth-century poet and philosopher G.K. Chesterton called tradition the 'democracy of the dead', allowing the wisdom of previous generations to be involved in the activities of current society.

Burke also praised traditions for their ability to provide continuity between the past and the present, claiming that they give a sense of security and help to prevent violent transformations in society. In *Reflections on the Revolution in France* he referred to 'a partnership between those who are living, those who are dead and those who are to be born'.

A typical example concerns monarchy. Elected governments, political ideologies and social change may come and go, but if monarchy endures in its traditional form the people will retain a sense of security and continuity amid the turmoil. Conservatives take a similar view of traditional morality, based around the family. This helps each new generation to hold onto a lasting set of values in an ever-changing world, giving them a sense of security that they can pass on to the next generation.

Allied to their theories of tradition, conservatives also believe that, where institutions and values have proved to be helpful in promoting order and stability in the past, they should be preserved. It is irresponsible, they argue, to reject them

for the sake of ideological principles or new theories. But this is not a recipe for 'no change'. Rather, it is a tendency to conserve what is seen to be good and reform what is proving to be undesirable.

Modern British conservatism has largely ignored the importance of tradition, especially since the 1980s. It has embraced new social theories such as opposition to the dependency culture, and privatisation and economic monetarism, and has attacked some traditional institutions such as the civil service, the Church of England, the legal establishment and the long-standing practices of the financial centre in London. However, we can still see strong support for traditional institutions and values in US and French conservatism, which have proved resistant to 'excessive' social reform.

The organic society and one-nation Toryism

Dating back to the leadership of Disraeli in the 1860s and 1870s, conservatives in the UK have stressed the need to unite the nation and to prevent social conflict. To this end they have stressed the *organic* nature of society. This suggests that the people are part of one single body – the nation – and that they are all interdependent. Even though we may be divided into different social classes, these classes should work together to maintain the welfare of the nation, rather than engage in conflict with each other. Organic society theory also denies the notion that we are merely individuals pursuing our own interests without any regard to the well-being of society as a whole. The strength of this idea has been illustrated by the fact that, when he became Conservative leader in 2005, David Cameron immediately proclaimed himself a 'one-nation conservative', albeit a modern version of the phenomenon.

This does not, however, equate with a socialist vision of society. Conservatives accept that individuals should be able to pursue their own goals increases and making British industry uncompetitive in world markets. In the past, governments had intervened directly to try to control wages and prices (a so-called 'prices and incomes policy', used in the 1960s and 1970s). The New Right was ideologically opposed to such intervention and so attacked the problem from a different angle.

The first measure was to reform trade unions in such a way as to reduce their power. This was achieved by making it more difficult for strikes to be called in support of wage claims (secret ballots on proposed strike action were introduced by law) and making them effectively unlawful if they had a political aim. The unions were also forced to make themselves internally democratic. But above all, the traditional legal immunity of trade unions was removed. This had prevented unions from being sued by businesses that had lost trade and profit as a result of a trade union's actions. The effect of this was to make striking a dangerous practice. A union whose actions caused problems for businesses not directly involved in the strike ran the risk of sustaining orders to pay out heavy financial damages and so face ruin. The result of these reforms was significant reduction in industrial unrest and the destruction of trade union power ever since.

Low taxation

By the early 1980s, levels of income taxes and taxes on business had reached a high level. The justification for this had been that the state was using funds raised through such taxes to create a fair society, to support failing industries and to maintain a high quality of public services. The New Right thinkers, however, insisted that high levels of such direct taxation were a disincentive to enterprise and to hard work. Conversely, reducing taxes on incomes and on business would be an incentive to more entrepreneurial activity, research and development and general investment in economic growth.

To this end, the Thatcher government rapidly reduced levels of income tax, especially on higher-income earners. The top rate of income tax on the very wealthy was reduced from 83 per cent to 60 per cent. By the end of the 1980s the highest rate of tax had been reduced to 40 per cent. At the same time a range of other taxes, including corporation tax on company profits, was reduced. Of course, there was a price to pay and some indirect taxes, especially VAT, were raised to compensate. In the long run, however, it was argued that low taxes would be an incentive to wealth creation. The greater wealth would reduce the need for government spending on welfare while at the same time the 'tax base' would increase, meaning that as people's prosperity rose they would automatically pay more in tax (even though rates were lower).

Dependency culture

The New Right inspiration for a general attack on the use of welfare benefits had its origins in the nineteenth century when a strong political movement, led by the ultra-liberal philosopher Herbert Spencer (1820–1903), had led to opposition to government intervention to alleviate the conditions of the poor. For Spencer, the poor deserved to be where they were because they lacked a work ethic or a sense of enterprise. Therefore the state was not justified in helping them; they should be responsible for their own welfare.

The New Right of the late twentieth century was less dogmatic than Spencer had been, but it shared the same general attitude. Its followers argued that levels of state welfare benefits were too high. They had created a *dependency culture* where many members of society had grown used to depending on state welfare benefits and had no incentive to improve their economic circumstances. Successive generations in some families simply learned to depend on the state in the same way as their parents had done.

During the 1980s and 1990s the levels of state benefits were gradually eroded. Nobody was expected to fall into total poverty (as Spencer had accepted), but lower benefits were certainly seen as an incentive for the unemployed to seek work, for the low paid to seek improvements in their skills and earning power, and for everybody to make better private-pension provision for themselves. Those who chose to remain dependent on state benefits found their standard of living falling significantly.

We can now offer a summary of the distinctions between traditional conservative ideals and the New Right philosophy.

Traditional conservatism	The New Right
• A pessimistic view of human nature • Order • Respect for traditional institutions and values • The organic society and the need to preserve 'one nation' • A pragmatic approach to political action • Stress on individualism • Need to defend the interests of private property • Opposition to ideologies and dogmatic political principles • Empiricism – a stress on the importance of following the lessons of past experience	• Deregulation – the privatisation of industry and the introduction of more competition • Disengagement – reluctance to interfere in the economy or to support failing industry (also known as *laissez-faire* policy) • Opposition to trade union power • Low levels of personal and business taxation as an incentive to wealth creation • Opposition to the dependency culture created by high levels of welfare benefits

Neo-conservatism

The principles of the New Right described above are concerned mostly with economic and welfare issues. Collectively they are often described as **neo-liberalism** because they have much in common with so-called *classical liberalism*, which had flourished in the middle part of the nineteenth century. However, there is more than this to the New Right.

A term developed in the USA in the 1970s and 1980s (and still very prominent in the Republican Party and the new right wing 'Tea Party' movement led by Sarah Palin), neo-conservatism has a number of ideals that have their origins in traditional conservatism, as described above. So, for example, neo-conservatives place a great emphasis on nationalism and patriotism. Sometimes described as *economic patriotism*, this stress on nationalism largely takes the form of insistence that the economic interests of the nation are paramount. Thus British neo-conservatives tend to oppose European integration on the grounds that this does not serve Britain's best interests. They are also sceptical of international free trade, believing that domestic industries should be protected.

A second aspect of neo-conservatism concerns social issues. On crime, neo-conservatives take a very authoritarian stance, seeing severe punishments for criminals as the best form of deterrence. They also believe that modern western society is in moral decline, with excessive permissiveness and tolerance. They therefore propose the restoration of traditional moral values. The 'milder' version of the stress on values mainly concerns the desire for the retention and strengthening of the traditional family unit. A more extreme version proposes an extensive attack on what is seen as 'immorality' and the breakdown of public order.

The extremists are also intolerant of different cultures. They are, as part of this belief, suspicious of immigration and asylum seeking. They see the influx of migrants of various kinds as a threat to traditional British values. Thus multiculturalism as a philosophy is rejected by the neo-conservatives.

So the New Right is often seen as something of a hybrid philosophy. It is neo-liberalism in domestic economic and welfare matters, while it is mostly neo-conservative on social and international affairs.

The policies of the Conservative Party today

The Conservative Party entered a difficult period of its history after 1992. There are a number of reasons why policy-making within the Conservative Party became confused.

Three traumatic election defeats, in 1997, 2001 and 2005, were a unique experience for the party. Before this period they had considered themselves to be the 'natural party of government', a party to which the British people have regularly turned for periods of stability. As a result of these shocks there has been considerable turmoil within the party. Since John Major resigned the party leadership in 1997, there have been four more leaders, a rate of turnover that illustrates the problems in the party.

The division within the party over the appropriate attitude for a conservative to take to the European Union persists. This conflict has been so damaging and overwhelming that the normal task of adopting a winning set of policies was suspended until after the 2005 election. The party had been effectively paralysed by its internal conflict.

Many of the recently successful policies of the Conservative Party, especially of the New Right, have been adopted by the Labour Party since the mid-1990s. This left the Conservative Party with

a dilemma – whether to accept the situation and campaign on the basis that they are more competent than the Labour Party, or whether to adopt a different set of policies to attract the electorate.

Perhaps the most important reason was that there were still two distinctive wings of the party, broadly represented by the traditions described above. The New Right section was certainly stronger, but the rest of the party retained a desire to return to a less dogmatic position and to maintain the 'one-nation' philosophy that seeks to prevent social conflict and to unite the country. The two sides seemed to be incompatible.

Despite this internal division there are a number of policies that remain distinctly conservative and that most members of the party can agree upon.

Less government

The party believes that Britain is over-governed. This includes the over-regulation of business and commerce, excessive interference in people's lives and an over-protective attitude towards the vulnerable in society. The European Union is seen as one of the main culprits in this area.

Reduced taxation when possible

The Conservatives under David Cameron retain the traditional instinct for reducing the overall tax burden. Of course, in the aftermath of the economic recession of 2008–09, Britain had accumulated huge amounts of government debt. Reducing that debt is also a Conservative priority so their desire for tax cuts had to be put on hold. Nevertheless, in the negotiations with the Liberal Democrats after the 2010 election, the leadership did not find it difficult to agree to the proposal for taking all incomes of less than £10,000 out of income tax altogether.

Law and order

Conservatives remain concerned that there are excessive levels of crime and disorder. While they clearly wish to see the main thrust of anti-crime policy in terms of a more authoritarian approach to sentencing and policing (with many more police employed), they also see the causes of crime in terms of the breakdown in family life and too many modern 'liberal' methods in education.

Choice in public services

Conservatives share with the other main parties a desire to retain high-quality public services, especially health and education. However, they argue that individuals do not have enough choice in their experience of the use of these services. They wish to see services arranged so that the public can have a variety of provision available to them, have the means to search out the best services available and even have some financial assistance if they choose to use private-sector health or education. This is sometimes known as a 'voucher' or 'passport' system of public services.

Euro-scepticism

Most conservatives (though not all members of the party) are suspicious of the power and activities of the European Union. Only a minority propose that Britain should withdraw completely, but most agree that there are too many European regulations and that members do not retain enough of their independence within the Union. It remains official policy that Britain should not join the European single currency.

David Cameron's reforms

As we have seen, when David Cameron took over leadership of the Conservative Party in 2005, there was a great deal of internal conflict. The party could not move forward as long as there was so much internal dissension and low morale. Cameron therefore decided to take an enormous risk. This was to 'modernise' and reform policy, taking the party in a completely new direction. He decided there was no future in positioning itself to the right of the Labour Party. Instead, he argued, conservatives should fight Labour for the centre ground.

This meant he had to defeat the New Right and other extreme right-wingers in the party and persuade the rest that his strategy would be successful. By the end of 2007 he had at least achieved the objective of putting together a leadership team that hoped to carry the new policies through to the next general election. Cameron's new philosophy was styled 'social' or 'modern' conservatism, a break from both the New Right and from traditional conservative concerns. Its main features were as follows.

David Cameron sought to modernise the Conservative Party

Big society

Many of Cameron's social policies fall under the general description of 'big society'. In particular the term refers to an aspiration to allow communities to take control of services within their own areas. This includes the right to set up independent 'free schools' (financed by the state but not controlled by local authorities), to elect leading officials in police and health services, and generally to form voluntary associations that will seek to improve neighbourhoods. It also implies less state control in general. This is how Cameron described the concept of 'big society' in an election speech in March 2010:

> 'Big society – that's not just two words. It is a guiding philosophy – a society where the leading force for progress is social responsibility, not state control. It includes a whole set of unifying approaches – breaking state monopolies, allowing charities, social enterprises and companies to provide public services, devolving power down to neighbourhoods, making government more accountable. And it's the thread that runs consistently through our whole policy programme – our plans to reform public services, mend our broken society, and rebuild trust in politics. They are all part of our big society agenda.'

Inclusiveness

It was accepted that significant minorities within Britain were excluded from mainstream society. This was because they were suffering from economic deprivation, were excluded from an attainable range of choices, were discriminated against routinely or had simply had their demands ignored. In a modern version of 'one-nation conservatism' the new conservatism sought to widen opportunities, life chances and equality for all. In practice this meant a full-scale attack on poverty, on discriminatory practices against groups such as women, gay people, disabled people or members of minority ethnic groups and the greater accessibility of services such as education, health, housing and other welfare benefits. This social concern has led to such a movement being described as 'caring conservatism'. Similarly, the term 'social justice' has entered the conservative vocabulary for the first time in the history of the party.

Education

As proof of his desire to see the extension of opportunities to all, Cameron abandoned the traditional support for selective secondary education (effectively grammar schools) in 2007. Instead, he supported Labour's policies to create a wide range of different *types* of secondary schools and colleges, but insisted that all these different types of schooling should be available to all, no matter what their economic, social or educational background. Local communities were also to be given the opportunity to set up their own schools.

Environmentalism

All parties in Britain have taken on board the need for stronger environmental policies to combat climate change, conserve energy and implement emission controls. Cameron, however, wanted the Conservatives to take a lead, rather than simply being followers. He therefore proposed even tougher environmental measures than those suggested by other parties.

Law and order

The traditional hard line taken by Conservatives on crime issues was greatly softened by Cameron's followers. In particular, they proposed measures to combat youth crime that involved fewer custodial sentences. Education was to be a key, but also more enlightened policies on the sentencing and rehabilitation of offenders. However, hardened offenders who refused offers of help to change their lives were to expect longer custodial sentences.

Human rights

Traditionally, conservatives have accepted that sometimes individual rights have to be sacrificed in the interests of law, order and security. For Cameron and his supporters, however, basic human rights are absolute and should be set aside only with great caution. Certainly the new social conservatives stand closer to the liberal position than their traditional predecessors or than Labour.

Taxation and public services

It is a natural conservative instinct to want to cut taxes. However, David Cameron and his chancellor, George Osborne, have asserted that tax cuts cannot be made at the expense of the quality of public services. In other words, they see it as most important that health, education, social services and so on should be protected even if public opinion asserts that taxes should be reduced.

We can now stand back and summarise the various elements in the so-called 'Cameron revolution'.

George Osborne, a close ally of David Cameron

The Cameron revolution		
Policy issue	Traditional conservative position	Cameron's initiative
Social justice	Inequality is natural in a free market system. Welfare support to be reserved only for the most needy.	It is society's responsibility to improve the conditions of those who are deprived and to open up opportunities for them. Nevertheless, claiming welfare benefits is to become more difficult for those unwilling to help themselves.
Taxation	Taxes on incomes and company profits should be kept to a minimum.	Tax levels must be set at a level that can sustain good-quality public services. Tax must not be a disincentive to work.

The Cameron revolution (continued)		
Policy issue	Traditional conservative position	Cameron's initiative
Environment	Though the environment is important, it is not the highest priority. Environmental protection should not over-regulate business and industry.	Environmental protection has the highest priority and is the responsibility of all.
Law and order	Government should take an authoritarian, hard-line approach to crime and offenders.	Attempts should be made to understand better the causes of crime and to deal with them. This needs to be balanced against a tough approach to serious crime.
Role of the state	The role of the state should be limited and the state should not seek to create economic and social change.	The state has a key role to play in increasing opportunities and reducing poverty. Citizens should have more control over the state at local level. There should be less state regulation at local level.
Education	There should be maximum choice and the more able should be offered specialised, selective education.	Education should not single out the more fortunate. Good educational opportunity should be available for all, regardless of circumstance. Communities should have the right to set up their own schools. More academies to be set up.
Rights	Rights and liberties have a lower priority than order and security.	Basic rights and liberties should not be sacrificed for the sake of security.
Political system	Reform should be resisted unless absolutely necessary.	Acceptance of the need to reform the House of Lords, the Commons and to allow the people to decide on electoral reform.

Those who criticise Cameron's reforms – among them many conservatives – say he has moved too far away from conservative principles and traditions. His defenders, however, suggest that he is merely placing his party at the centre ground of British politics. It is in the centre ground, they argue, that conservatism has always stood. He is, they continue, trying to unite the country around a single set of values and priorities, just as Disraeli did in his day. He is, in other words, an updated version of a 'one-nation conservative'.

Discussion topic

Is the Conservative Party today still genuinely 'conservative'?

Socialism and Labour in the UK

Supporters of the British Labour Party have, in the past, often been described as 'socialists'. But in most cases this is misleading. For most of its life – dating back to the end of the eighteenth century – socialism has been a more radical ideology than the one followed by Labour in Britain in the twentieth century. British 'socialism' has certainly been traditionally more moderate than those forms that have flourished in the rest of Europe and elsewhere.

The most radical form of socialism has been Marxism (which has also been described as communism). In fact, Marxism has had relatively little influence on British Labour. Above all, Marxists are revolutionary, desiring the complete destruction of capitalism and the political system that has supported it. Labour has never been revolutionary, but has always argued that its brand of socialism can be achieved through peaceful, parliamentary means. Of almost equal importance is the fact that Labour has always accepted that a limited, regulated form of capitalism is acceptable

and desirable. Marxists and other radical socialists have always insisted that capitalism must be completely destroyed and replaced by forms of common ownership (i.e. by all) of all the means of production, distribution and finance.

Some non-Marxist forms of socialism have been almost equally as radical as communism. Particularly in the nineteenth century, a number of European socialist movements were either revolutionary or radical or both. Such a form of socialism never caught hold in Britain. The one attempt to create such a movement – the Social Democratic Federation in 1884 – soon withered away. Parliamentary candidates representing radical socialist parties have been remarkably unsuccessful. Only the Independent Labour Party (ILP), a radical offshoot of the main Labour Party, has ever won significant representation. The Scottish Socialist Party did win six seats in the Scottish parliamentary election of 2003 and George Galloway's socialist-inspired Respect Party won a Westminster seat in 2005, but these were isolated successes. So British socialism, as represented by the Labour Party, has been remarkably moderate.

The socialist ideas described below can be viewed both in terms of *fundamental* principles and in terms of the way they have been adapted by British Labour.

Core values of British socialism – 'Old' Labour

Class

All but the more moderate socialists have seen social class as a crucial aspect of society. It has been assumed by socialists that most people define their position in society, to some extent, in terms of their social class. This implies that they develop a sense of common interests and common purpose with other members of their class. Marx described this effect as 'class consciousness', but backgrounds. Equality of opportunity therefore demands that such institutions must make themselves more open to a wider social spectrum. Members of the middle classes still seem to have advantages in a number of walks of life, especially university education. The answer that socialists have offered is to break into this cycle of discrimination, either through positive discrimination or by introducing laws and codes of practice that outlaw social discrimination.

Third, the modern Labour Party, along with liberals, has sought to open up more opportunities for a wider section of the community to become involved in business and so secure for themselves a greater share of society's wealth. In other words, one of the ways in which the prosperity of the poorer sections of society can be improved is by allowing them to take part in capitalist enterprises themselves.

Collectivism

The term *collectivism* refers to two main ideas – first, that people usually prefer to achieve goals collectively rather than independently and, second, and more fundamentally, that action taken by people in organised groups is likely to be more effective than merely the sum of many individual actions. These ideas stem from a socialist view of human nature that man is a social animal who will prefer to live in social groups than alone.

Of course, the degree to which society should be organised on the basis of collectivism has varied with different branches of socialism. Marxists and other state socialists have proposed that the centralised state should be the vehicle for collective action in the form of organising all or most production and distribution. Socialists who accept some degree of free-market capitalism have promoted collectivism alongside individualism.

Socialist collectivism, of the kind described above, became very much the norm for socialists throughout Europe after the Second World War. Indeed, the collectivist arrangements that they introduced came to be accepted by non-socialist governments, albeit reluctantly. Three main examples of collectivism, as practised by the British Labour Party, are shown below.

1. In the 1940s, several large British industries were nationalised. These included the railways, coal, steel, electricity, gas and telecommunications. Nationalisation was a collectivist enterprise that had two main purposes. The first was to prevent the industrial muscle of such private industries from exploiting its workers. The second was to ensure that these industries were run in the interests of the whole community, rather than merely for the benefit of their owners. By bringing them under public ownership and state control, the interests of the workers and the whole community could be safeguarded.

2. Labour has always supported trade union power. Having accepted that capitalism will be allowed to flourish, British socialists have agreed that there is an unbalanced relationship between workers and employers. The more radical of the socialists have argued that workers are effectively exploited by capitalist employers. In order to redress this balance to some extent, therefore, Labour has sought to ensure that workers have strong *collective* representation through unions.

3. The welfare state in all its forms is a collective enterprise, organised by the state. Rather than allowing or forcing people to make their own, individual provision for such services as health, education, pensions, housing and insurance against unemployment or poverty, the welfare state does this on their behalf. The welfare state collects funds through taxation and National Insurance contributions and distributes the benefits according to need. Indeed, the welfare state is perhaps the most enduring symbol of Labour's attachment to collectivism.

Common ownership

A feature of socialism that is closely related to collectivism is common ownership of the means of production and distribution. In fact, common ownership is a key form of collectivism. It is perhaps the oldest socialist idea as it pre-dates the onset of capitalism.

Some socialists have claimed that common ownership of property is a Christian principle, pointing to the fact that Christ insisted that his followers pool their resources and shared them out equally. There have also been many movements throughout history – mostly among the poor peasantry – that have demanded the seizure of land and its transfer to a communal system of production. In seventeenth-century England, the Levellers (or Diggers) purchased tracts of land in the south of the country and began to farm collectively, with the equal distribution of its output. But it was the development of capitalism that brought about a more complex set of ideas about the evils of private property and the virtues of common ownership.

As with most socialist principles, there is a great deal of variation in thought in this area. But before looking at common ownership itself, it is useful to consider the variety of reasons why socialists have objected to private property. These have included the following:

● The Earth is given to mankind in general – no individual has a right to claim that any part of it belongs to himself.

● Claiming private property deprives someone else of its use.

● Property gives rise to inequality, especially between those who have and those who lack property.

● Ownership of property, particularly land and capital goods, gives rise to exploitation by property owners of those without property.

By contrast, common ownership can give rise to a number of good outcomes, including the following:

● The possibility of imposing economic equality, as described above.

● Since many socialists see collectivism as natural, it creates, or re-creates, a natural state of society.

● It is possible to direct commonly owned property to serve the interests of the whole community, not just those of fortunate owners of property.

The value of common ownership, along with the evolution of the principles of equality, social justice and collectivism among socialists, has certainly declined in the modern age. The failure of the socialist 'experiments' that were introduced in the USSR, China and much of Eastern Europe during the twentieth century served to destroy faith in the idea of common ownership by the state (on behalf of the people). Socialists have therefore tended to modify their attitude to common ownership, seeing it as a complement to private property rather than a replacement for it.

The Labour Party appeared to have adopted the principle of common ownership when it wrote its first constitution in 1918. Clause 4 of that constitution contained a commitment to:

'secure for the workers by hand or brain the full fruits of their industry and the most equitable distribution thereof that may be possible upon the basis of common ownership of the means of production, distribution and exchange and the best obtainable system of popular administration and control of each industry or service'.

This appeared to be a clear call to nationalise all major industries. In fact, Labour never approached the full implications of the original Clause 4. The nearest it came was the nationalisation of several major industries. Most production, distribution and exchange remained in the private sector.

In recent times Labour has retained some elements of common ownership organised by the state, the welfare state institutions in particular, but has also encouraged free enterprise where this is seen as the best method of wealth creation and distribution. As the twentieth century progressed, however, Labour gradually lost its commitment to common ownership through the state (central and local government), accepting that, in modern society, most individuals prefer to own and control their own private property.

Policies of the Labour Party – 'New Labour'

The Labour Party experienced a huge trauma in the 1980s. It found itself completely divided over how to deal with the challenge of Thatcherism and the New Right. Some of the party believed it should move to a more moderate, centre position in politics. This group lost the internal argument and many of them therefore left the party, forming the Social Democratic Party (SDP) in 1981. Electoral support for Labour fell to a meagre 27.6 per cent of the popular vote in 1983 (only 2 per cent ahead of the SDP–Liberal alliance that was formed for that election). This figure recovered only slightly, to 30.8 per cent, in 1987. Labour had been taken over by a large left-wing faction, led by Michael Foot and Tony Benn, that believed that the correct response to Thatcherism was more, not less, socialism. Unfortunately for them, the electorate did not agree.

The leftward-leaning Labour Party of the mid-1980s was routed at the polls by the Conservatives. There were some, at the time, who believed that the party was doomed for ever. But forces were gathering that were to transform Labour fortunes in the 1990s. Led by Neil Kinnock, who was the party leader through the defeats in 1987 and 1992, a new group of

Tony Blair, one of the founders of New Labour

reformers began to emerge. They understood that there had been a massive change in the nature of British society. Traditional socialist policies were no longer appropriate, they argued. In short, the party needed to find a new direction without abandoning its traditional values. A cohort led by John Smith (party leader from 1992–94), and including such figures as Tony Blair, Gordon Brown, Bryan Gould, Peter Mandelson and Robin Cook, set about creating what has come to be known as the *Third Way*. So great was the proposed change that the party itself came to be known as **New Labour**. It is the policies of the Third Way and of New Labour that have dominated party policy since then.

The expression 'Third Way' refers to the idea that New Labour policies were to be distinct from the one way, which was traditional socialism (as described above) and another way, which was Thatcherism and the New Right. Labour should not pursue traditional socialism because it made the party unelectable. Thatcherism was unacceptable because it flew in the face of the values of the Labour Party. The principles of the Third Way are shown in the table below, contrasted with the two alternatives.

Current Labour policy

For most of its period in office after 1997, Labour followed the principles of the 'Third Way'. Many have argued that it has gradually shifted towards a more 'New Right position' – that is, even further away from its core socialist values – and this is certainly true in some areas of policy. Yet Labour

Key Word

New Labour The name given to the leadership of the Labour Party, later to the party as a whole, which came to prominence in the mid-1990s. New Labour was a moderate version of the old Labour Party and was seen as a combination of liberalism and social democracy.

New Labour and the Third Way			
Policy area	**New Right policy**	**Socialist policy**	**Third Way policy**
Attitude to capitalism	Capitalism should be given a free rein, with as little state interference as possible.	Large-scale industry should be brought under state control. Capitalism should be controlled by the state.	Capitalism should be allowed to flourish but the state should enforce competition and fair trade.
Industrial relations	Trade union power should be minimised.	Trade unions should be powerful to protect the interests of workers.	There should be a limited role for trade unions, but individual workers' rights should be protected by law.
Welfare state and its services	Welfare benefits create a dependency culture and are a disincentive to work and enterprise.	Welfare benefits are a vital way of compensating for disadvantage and of redistributing income from rich to poor.	Welfare benefits should be used as an incentive to work and to take responsibility for one's own prosperity. Their role is not to redistribute income.
	Individuals should be able to choose freely between public and private sector. Maximum choice of services for families.	The welfare state is to be protected. All welfare services should fall under the control of the state.	High-quality public services should be preserved. The private sector should be involved if this improves quality and efficiency.

New Labour and the Third Way (continued)			
Policy area	**New Right policy**	**Socialist policy**	**Third Way policy**
Economic management	State interference in the economy should be minimised. Above all, public sector debt to be avoided and inflation kept under control.	State should interfere extensively in the economy to keep unemployment low. Public sector borrowing acceptable when needed to stimulate the economy.	Similar to the New Right, but public sector borrowing is acceptable if used for investment in public services.
Law and order	An authoritarian position, with punishment to be the main deterrent to crime	Concentration on the causes of crime, especially economic causes	'Tough on crime, tough on the causes of crime' (Blair in 1994). A combination of authoritarian attitudes and tackling social causes of crime
European Union	Highly suspicious, keeping Britain away from close integration. Opposed to single European currency	Anti-European on the whole. Britain probably to relinquish membership. Britain to be free to protect domestic industries from foreign competition.	Britain to remain at the centre of the EU, but retaining its independence. Cautious support for the single currency
Foreign policy	Britain to defend its vital national interests.	As far as possible, Britain to distance itself from international affairs.	Britain to take a leading role in world affairs. 'Ethical foreign policy' designed to help poor countries and to defend human rights
The constitution	Opposed to reform of the constitution on the whole	Radical proposals to democratise institutions, destroy inherited privilege and promote equal rights.	Less radical reform, concentrating on decentralisation of government, mild Lords reform, Human Rights Act

supporters can claim, with some justification, that a number of key values have been preserved and even extended.

A generalised term for Labour's social and economic policies is **communitarianism**. This could be described as a synthesis between the creation of a society where individualism can flourish successfully, with one in which individuals also retain a sense of social responsibility towards the community as a whole. A healthy and prosperous economy, argue New Labour thinkers, does require a great deal of freedom for individuals to undertake their own enterprises and to fend for themselves in the labour market. But, they add, there is a danger that the old socialist benefits of collectivism will be lost, and that the uncontrolled pursuit of self-interest (an idea in neo-liberal thinking that they criticise) threatens the unity of society.

In place of socialist collectivist ideals or the authoritarian, traditional approach of conservatism, New Labour has argued that individual citizens themselves should take responsibility for ensuring the cohesion of society. To this end they should be politically active, should engage in voluntary initiatives to protect and develop their local communities (for example, in the fields of law and order and the environment) and should support voluntary organisations that seek to help the disadvantaged. This adds up to a kind of voluntary, locally based 'socialism'.

The role of the state in communitarianism is different to its role in a socialist-based society. Rather than undertaking the function of maintaining social unity, protecting communities and caring for the disadvantaged *itself*, the state should facilitate individuals and private or voluntary sector organisations that wish to undertake this role. Underpinning such a society, however, is the key role that education has to play. For that reason education as a whole has to be strengthened in order to help individuals to make the most of opportunities available to them, and also to undertake the task of promoting the kind of responsible citizenship that communitarianism demands. Hence Tony Blair's famous declaration in 1996 that his government's priorities would be 'education, education, education'.

We can now look in a little more detail at Labour policies after the party's 2005 election victory.

Anti-poverty

New Labour has largely abandoned the traditional socialist aim of redistributing income to create more economic equality. Instead, the party has adopted an attack on poverty, especially child poverty. This is a priority largely sponsored by Gordon Brown, one of the more socialist-leaning members of New Labour's leading cohort.

While it is accepted that economic inequality is inevitable, Labour also seeks to ensure that everybody who is willing to work, is unable to work through no fault of their own or accepts very poorly paid employment should enjoy a decent standard of living. Families with children especially have been targeted. In practice this meant increases in some welfare payments, such as child benefit, and a system of tax credits that subsidises the income of deserving poorer families, lone parents, the disabled and pensioners. Part of the anti-poverty programme also involved a policy known as *selective universality*. This meant that benefits were being targeted at specific groups in society who are poor through no fault of their own. The real value of benefits that are available to *all*, such as old-age pensioners, was eroded, but large subsidies were available to those most in need.

Economic policy

Here New Labour largely followed New Right principles, with additional methods introduced to control the public finances. Thus, direct taxes were kept at a much lower level than had been normal under Labour in the past, there was a resistance to heavy government borrowing (though this began to creep up from 2003 onwards), inflation was controlled by the independent intervention of the Bank of England Monetary Policy Committee (using interest rates as the control mechanism) and Gordon Brown's 'Golden Rule' was designed to prevent excessive government borrowing unless it was to be used for investment in public services.

Until 2007 the Labour governments' economic management and the policies of former chancellor Gordon Brown were acknowledged, even by Conservatives, as the most successful aspect of the party's administration. From the mid-1990s (suggesting that the improvement actually began under the Conservative government of 1992–97), for at least ten years, the British economy achieved steady growth, low inflation, interest rates and unemployment, and no significant slumps. This was something that had not been achieved through most of the twentieth century.

However, the credit crunch of 2007 and the recession that followed blew Labour economic policies off course. Much of Britain's growth was

Gordon Brown towards the end of his premiership

revealed to have been financed by unsecured, risky credit. The economic recession, therefore, required large adjustments in policy. In particular, the party under Gordon Brown attempted to lead a world movement towards more responsible banking and better control over financial markets.

Welfare services

Labour inherited public services – health, education, policing and public transport in particular – that were seriously run down by long-term lack of investment and low levels of efficiency. Labour adopted a two-pronged attack on these problems. One was to divert large increases in public expenditure (financed partly by the rewards of economic growth, partly from higher taxation) to these services. The other was to attempt to drive up standards. Rising standards were pursued through the use of performance target setting, incentives for success and sanctions for failure.

Education

As we saw above, education formed the central theme in Labour's social policy. Improvements in education have been seen as critical in its policies towards poverty reduction, equality of opportunity, law and order (especially youth offending), communitarianism and long-term economic prosperity.

The most controversial aspect of education policy has been in the field of higher education. Labour governments have adopted a target of creating places in higher education for 50 per cent of each generation of school leavers. While this target itself has been criticised as being unnecessary and ignoring the need for skilled manual labour, it is the funding issue that has caused most problems. The decision to pay for the greater provision of higher education places by levying extra fees (so-called 'top-up fees') on students, thus forcing them to take on high levels of debt and possibly therefore deterring students from less well-off families, was controversial. Socialist-minded left wingers in the Labour Party see such fees as a denial of the principles of the welfare state. Liberals have criticised such funding policy on the grounds that it is unjust and will cause hardship for poorer individuals and families.

Labour is fully committed to the experiment of developing academies (as are the other main parties). Academies are schools set up to replace failing institutions, usually in challenging environments. They enjoy external funding from business, charities or voluntary organisations and lie outside the control of local authorities. They are, therefore, more independent than other schools and so are free to tackle problems in their own way.

In addition, *Surestart*, the provision of pre-school education for problem families, is seen as a key method of improving the education of the next generation of deprived children.

Law and order

Labour's intentions towards law and order issues were based on Tony Blair's assertion in 1994 (when he was shadow home secretary) that the party would follow a policy of 'tough on crime, tough on the causes of crime'. Although at the beginning, in the late 1990s, the government attempted to develop 'joined-up' policies to combat crime (through education, poverty reduction, community work, etc.), especially youth offending policy (which has evolved in a different direction), the party leadership gradually adopted a more authoritarian position on crime. This led to increasingly harsh measures against young offenders – tagging, curfews and the well-known anti-social behaviour orders (ASBOs), as well as persuasion of the judiciary to give out more severe sentences. Not surprisingly, after the 9/11 (2001) attack on New York and the 7/7

(2005) attacks in London, the police and security services were given additional powers to deal with actual and suspected terrorists.

In the early years of the twenty-first century, policy concentrated on increasing police numbers, setting performance targets for forces and the recruitment of ever more community support officers to assist the police and to create a clear, visible policing presence on the streets. The community approach to crime prevention continued, but was a long-term policy. In the short term, Labour shares, with conservatives, an authoritarian approach to crime. Successive home secretaries – Jack Straw, David Blunkett, Charles Clarke and John Reid – moved towards 'tough on crime' positions as opposed to 'tough on the causes of crime'.

Welfare benefits

A number of key groups in society were targeted in Labour's anti-poverty programme. These were poor pensioners (those who rely totally on a state pension), the deserving disabled, lone families and members of families who are working, or seeking work, for low wages. Indeed, targeting welfare is a fundamental social policy. The main device for raising the living standards of these groups was a variety of tax credits, whereby such individuals and families receive additions to their incomes through the tax system.

This policy had three main objectives. First, it targeted benefits more specifically on the most needy. Second, it was a system designed to create *incentives* for those who can to find work and to make it worth their while to take up low-paid employment where there are labour shortages. Third, it was designed to take people out of poverty *permanently* by persuading them to join the workforce and so have no need to rely on the state. As an adjunct to this policy, people were encouraged to make their own private pension provision (the government offers a subsidised scheme) so that they would not need support in old age.

majority. Liberals have traditionally defended the rights of such minorities. The interests of the homosexual community, minority ethnic groups, the disabled and women (who are not, of course, a minority but have been treated as one) have all been championed by liberalism.

Tolerance

Tolerance is a principle that is closely allied to that of freedom. Liberals insist that all forms of expression, belief, thought and lifestyle should be tolerated in a free society. There is a proviso to this. Where the words or deeds of an individual or a group are harmful to the rights and freedom of others, the state is justified in suppressing them.

In the modern, multicultural society of Britain, the liberal support for tolerance has become a key social issue. It has also come under great pressure with the terrorist activities of Irish Republicans and Islamic extremists, suggesting that tolerance might be overplayed. But the liberal principle is clear – that it is for individuals to decide what they believe and what lifestyle they adopt as long as their activities do not affect others adversely.

Equality of opportunity

As we have seen, socialists and many conservatives share this essentially liberal principle. It contains three main aspects. The first is that inherited and undeserved privilege should not be allowed to give an individual or a group an artificial advantage in life. This has meant that liberals have always argued that political power should rest only in the hands of elected representatives and should never be exercised by those who enjoy inherited social privilege. It also implies that people in general should advance in life purely on merit rather than on the basis of social position.

The second is that examples of discrimination against any group must be outlawed. This has been true of the position of women for over a century, but now includes minorities such as those from non-British ethnic backgrounds, gay people, the disabled and even the old.

The third is that no matter what our circumstances of birth, we are all entitled to the same life chances. Liberals therefore champion the cause both of those who are born into deprived circumstances and of various minorities who have traditionally been disadvantaged. As we have seen above, education is seen as the key to this principle.

Social justice

For most of the nineteenth century many liberals saw justice in terms of individual merit. In a free society, they argued, people were responsible for their own prosperity. If they worked hard and showed enterprise they would do well; if they were not prepared to use their initiative they would remain poor. This was seen as a just outcome. But as it became apparent that many were deprived through no fault of their own, liberalism began to adopt a new conception of social justice.

It remains true that a liberal will argue that a free economy is bound to result in inequality of economic outcome. But they now insist that the most dramatic examples of inequality – especially when wealth is seen as the result of market forces rather than deserving effort and enterprise – should be reduced by the state. So liberals have become committed to the reduction of excessive inequality, protection for deprived groups in society and the principle that taxation must always be based on the ability to pay. In other words, they see it as 'just' that the wealthy should be subject to considerably higher tax rates than those who live on more modest means. In this sense liberalism has a great deal in common with socialism.

Welfare

Associated with the liberal/socialist position on social justice is support for state-organised welfare. Indeed, it was governments formed by the Liberal Party under Herbert Asquith and David Lloyd George in the early decades of the twentieth century that introduced the first forms of state-run pensions, housing, health and unemployment insurance schemes. As we have seen above, another liberal, Beveridge, extended these services into the full-scale welfare state we know today.

Liberals support welfare partly because it constitutes social justice, partly because they recognise that the whole community has a responsibility to help those in need, and partly because they believe that everybody is entitled to a reasonable standard of living and prospects of future well-being. In addition, as Beveridge pointed out, the most serious threats to individual freedom were not just government power but also poverty, unemployment, poor health and lack of education.

Constitutionalism and democracy

Liberals are instinctively suspicious of the power of government. They see the power of the state as perhaps the main threat to liberty. At the same time it is a guarantee of freedom that government should be under the democratic control of the people. This has given rise to two practical applications of liberal political thought. One is that governments should be controlled by law. In effect this means a constitution that sets out the powers of the different branches of government and that asserts the limits of governmental power. Constitutions also describe and protect the rights of citizens (civil liberties) against government and between themselves.

The second application requires that government must be highly democratic. This means it must accurately represent the demands and interests of the people, must be fully accountable to

the people and must allow full participation by all citizens on an equal basis. This does not necessarily mean that governments need be 'slaves' to the will of the people (that would be 'direct democracy' which carries dangers of its own), but it certainly implies that government should be open and responsive and that its institutions should fall under the general control of the people.

The policies of the Liberal Democrats

The Liberal Democrat Party was formed in 1988, the result of an amalgamation of the original Liberal Party (which dated back to the nineteenth century) and the very young Social Democratic Party, which had broken away from the Labour Party in 1981. Its policies have always been, therefore, something of a synthesis of core liberal values (as shown above) and social democracy, a very moderate form of socialism.

In 2010 the main Liberal Democrat policies were as follows.

Fair taxation

Three main policies are prominent in this category. First, Liberal Democrats wish to replace council tax with a system of local income tax. As council tax is based on property rather than income, it contains certain anomalies whereby relatively poor families are forced to pay relatively high local taxes while the better off pay proportionally less. A local income tax would be based purely on ability to pay. Second, the party supports the raising of the starting point for paying income tax to £10,000 per year. This takes millions of poorer families out of direct taxation altogether. Third, the party supports the idea of a 50 per cent tax rate on incomes above £100,000 per annum. In the wake of the banking crisis of 2007–09 it has also proposed higher taxes on bonuses paid to employees by financial institutions.

Nick Clegg and Vince Cable, the leading members of the Liberal Democrat party

Economic management

Liberal Democrats have few arguments with the way in which Labour governments have run the economy since 1997. There is a general tendency in the party to believe that more intervention is necessary to ensure greater industrial democracy – more power for employees in principle and to protect some industries that are in decline. But on the whole, Liberal Democrats are included in part of a widespread consensus on an economic policy that sees the state taking a minimum role in management of the economy, leaving control largely to the Bank of England and to a responsible attitude to the public finances by the Treasury.

The welfare state

The Liberal Democrat Party is perhaps now the main defender of the principles of the welfare state in Britain. It argues that services should be given an extremely high priority in public spending decisions. It also insists that quality should be guaranteed for all. Liberal Democrats oppose the Conservative view that there should be more choice for users of public services, on the grounds that the same high-quality services should be available for all so that choice becomes unnecessary. They also oppose the Labour policy of driving up standards through the use of performance targets, incentives and sanctions. Instead they would simply ensure that the welfare state has the necessary resources and allow its natural tendency to want to deliver first-class services to flourish.

Law and order and right

For the majority of Liberal Democrats the most effective way of dealing with criminal behaviour is to concentrate on tackling the *causes* of crime rather than on punishment and sanctions in general. Education is seen to be on the front line of law and order policy, as is the role of other state agencies in supporting families. The excessive use of prison sentences, and the lengthening of sentences in general, is opposed. Liberal Democrats support instead the wider use of 'community-based' and innovative methods of attempting to deal with criminal behaviour.

As we have seen, liberals are firm defenders of the rights of citizens. They see modern law and order policies as a profound threat to civil liberties. The Liberal Democrat Party, therefore, has argued consistently that human rights must not be sacrificed merely in the interests of a firmer position on law and order. This policy has been thrown into greater focus with the increasing pressure on government to take ever more authoritarian powers to deal with the threat of terrorism.

Thus, although the Human Rights Act went a long way to satisfying Liberal Democrats in their pursuit of the defence of human rights, the party still insists that the Act is too weak as it is not binding on Parliament. It now proposes an *entrenched* Bill of Rights that cannot be overturned by Parliament.

Constitutional reform

The programme of reform undertaken by Labour governments after 1997 was supported by Liberal Democrats. However, they criticised Labour on the grounds that the reforms did not go far enough.

As we have seen, they wished to see a stronger Human Rights Act. They also believe that devolution has not gone far enough. *More* power should have been devolved to Scotland, Northern Ireland and Wales, say Liberal Democrats, including full legislative and taxation powers. Liberal Democrats support decentralised government on the grounds that it will be more democratic.

Therefore they support the general weakening of central government and the strengthening of regional and local government institutions.

But the key Liberal Democrat proposal for reform concerns the electoral system. They see 'first past the post' (FPTP) (the current system in general elections) as fundamentally unjust, distorting political representation and granting excessive power to the executive over Parliament. It has to be said, of course, that electoral reform is most supported by Liberal Democrats because they have the most to gain from it. But this also indicates that they are the greatest sufferers in a system that discriminates against smaller parties. Elections at all levels of government, therefore, should be conducted under some form of proportional representation, they argue. This would include elections to a reformed House of Lords. Liberal Democrats are very reluctant to compromise on the second chamber. It must, they argue, be fully elected in the future.

European Union

Liberal Democrats are the most enthusiastic of all the three main parties about the European project. While they agree that its institutions must be made more democratic, they are content to see a good deal of power being transferred to the EU. This is not, however, because they wish to see power centralised in Brussels. On the contrary, Liberal Democrats support a 'Europe of the regions', where most power would be exercised by regional and local government. This would bring government closer to the people and thereby make it more democratic.

Foreign policy

The Labour policy, supported by most Conservatives, of seeing British national interests as largely identical to those of the USA is opposed by Liberal Democrats. In fact, the party 'adversary' models. They can be described in the following way.

Consensus politics refers to a process whereby decision makers seek to find a wide level of general agreement within the political community before attempting to bring forward proposals. This may be a formal process, whereby representatives of all parties are consulted before decisions are reached, or it may be informal, with government adopting only policies that they are confident will enjoy cross-party support.

In recent times there has been a high degree of *formal* consensus on such issues as Northern Ireland policy and anti-terrorism measures. There has also been a good deal of *informal* consensus over the management of the economy.

Consensus politics also refers to periods when it is noticeable that there is little difference between the policies of the parties on a wide range of public policy. It was said for much of the 1950s and 1960s that Britain enjoyed *consensus politics* only because the parties were largely agreed on policies towards the economy, law and order, defence and social policy generally. Indeed, this consensus remained largely intact until the 1980s. Some commentators have spoken since the 1990s of a *post-Thatcher consensus*. This consensus includes agreement on the need to allow free market capitalism to flourish, to maintain responsible financial policies (especially in keeping inflation under control) and to promote

the development of private enterprise. Only the more radical members of the Labour and Liberal Democrat parties question these consensual values.

On the whole, British politicians are uncomfortable with such a form of politics. They much prefer that proposals are subject to critical examination in a process known as 'adversary politics'.

Adversary politics is defined as the situation where there are deep and widespread ideological differences between the mainstream competing political parties who have a realistic chance of gaining power and forming a government. This would cover issues such as economic policy, defence policy and welfare policy. The policy differences are expansive and fundamental.

An example of adversary politics in Britain would be the early 1980s when the Labour Party, led by Michael Foot, advocated nationalisation, unilateral nuclear disarmament and increased welfare provision, while the Conservative Party, led by Margaret Thatcher, advocated privatisation, multilateral nuclear disarmament and reduced welfare.

There may be confusion with **adversarial politics** which is a common feature even in times of consensus politics. For instance, there is often disagreement in an adversarial style in the House of Commons between the PM and the Leader of the official Opposition. This was a feature of the Blair

 Key Word

Consensus politics A circumstance where two or more major political parties broadly agree on most basic policies. In other words, a period when there are few or no major political conflicts. It may also refer to a single issue where different parties agree to support the same policies. This implies a lack of strong ideology in politics.

Key Word

Adversary politics The opposite of consensus. This is a circumstance where political parties are engaged in considerable conflict over political issues. This also implies there are strong ideological conflicts in politics.

years where there were adversarial exchanges but the principles of policy and ideology were not too different between the two main parties.

Even in this hostile environment some consensus politics can take place. As we have seen above, some recent policy areas have been the subject of cross-party agreement, notably over Northern Ireland. For the most part, however, opposition politicians prefer to be free to be as critical as they wish.

We can now review the main policy areas in 2007–08, dividing them between those that enjoyed largely consensus support and those that remained hotly contested. See the table opposite.

Coalition politics

The arrival of coalition government in the UK in May 2010 brought into greater focus the relationship between consensus and adversarial politics. The agreement between the Conservatives and the Liberal Democrats at that time required a good deal of compromise and acceptance that there would remain some issues where the coalition partners would have to 'agree to disagree'. Indeed, there was a national mood at the time that, in the face of a severe economic crisis, a period of consensus politics would be beneficial.

A detailed description of the coalition agreement of May 2010 is shown on pages 111–112. However, the table on the next page shows some of the main elements of that agreement and areas of 'agreement to differ'.

Some consensus issues	Some contested issues
• Responsible management of the economy • Keeping personal taxation relatively low by European standards • The maintenance of largely free markets with relatively little state interference • Preserving the union of England, Scotland, Wales and Northern Ireland • The maintenance of good-quality public services within the basic principles of the welfare state • Support for the system of parliamentary democracy • Reform of the second legislative chamber	• The degree to which the private sector should be involved in the provision of welfare state services • The degree to which law and order policy should concentrate on punishment as opposed to dealing with the social causes of crime • Britain's relationship to the European Union and whether Britain should adopt the single European currency • The degree to which Britain should be open to immigrants and asylum seekers • How much Britain should support US foreign policy

Conservative–Liberal Democratic Agreements	Agreements to differ
<ul><li>There was to be an immediate and radical attack on public expenditure.</li><li>Income tax for the lower income groups should be reduced in stages.</li><li>There was to be reform to the banking sector.</li><li>Welfare benefits were to be reformed to reduce payments to the better off and to deny benefits to those unwilling to work.</li><li>Virtually all schools to be allowed to apply for academy status.</li><li>A referendum to be held to determine whether the Alternative Vote should be adopted for general elections.</li><li>Fixed-term parliaments set at five years.</li><li>The House of Lords to be fully or largely elected.</li><li>Cancellation of the ID card scheme.</li></ul>	<ul><li>Liberal Democrats are in favour of the Alternative Vote system but the Conservatives may oppose it in a referendum campaign.</li><li>Liberal Democrats support the European Convention on Human Rights while the Conservatives would prefer a 'British Bill of Rights'.</li><li>The Conservatives completely rule out British entry into the euro-zone whereas Liberal Democrats believe Britain should join when conditions are favourable.</li><li>Liberal Democrats oppose the renewal of the Trident missile programme while Conservatives support it.</li><li>While Conservatives favour the further development of nuclear energy, Liberal Democrats oppose it.</li></ul>

Key concepts in this chapter

Conservatism A state of mind and a political movement that is naturally averse to excessive change and reform. It is sceptical about strongly held political views, prefers the known to the unknown and generally supports the retention of traditional institutions and values.

Liberalism A state of political mind or a political movement that places freedom, rights and tolerance high on its scale of values.

Socialism A state of mind and a political movement that places such values as equality of opportunity, social justice and collectivism high on its scale of values. It is either opposed to free market capitalism or proposes measures to moderate the effects of capitalism.

Consensus politics A circumstance where two or more major political parties broadly agree on most basic policies. In other words, a period when there are few or no major political conflicts. It may also refer to a single issue where different parties agree to support the same policies.

Adversary politics The opposite of consensus. This is a circumstance where political parties are engaged in considerable conflict over political issues.

Political party An association of people who have similar political philosophies and beliefs. Normally a party will seek power and develop an organisation whose purpose is to fight elections.

Revision topics and examination questions

Revision topics

- Definition of a party
- Features of parties
- Functions of parties
- Democratic role of parties
- Undemocratic features of parties
- Role of parties in political participation
- Nature of party government
- Nature of two-party system
- Nature of conservatism
- Nature of British socialism
- Nature of liberalism
- Current policies of all three parties
- Difference between consensus and adversary politics
- Main policies on which parties agree
- Main policies on which parties disagree

Short answers (approximately 120 words)

- What is a political party?
- Outline THREE features of a political party.
- Outline THREE functions of a political party.
- What is meant by the term 'party government'?

Medium answers (approximately 250 words)

- How do parties encourage political participation?
- In what senses is the UK a two-party system?
- Outline the main policies on which the main UK parties agree.
- Outline the main political issues on which the main UK parties disagree.
- Distinguish between consensus and adversary politics.
- What is meant by 'coalition politics'?

Long answers (approximately 800 words)

- In what ways do parties enhance democracy?
- How, and to what extent, can parties be said to be undemocratic in the UK?
- How far has the current Conservative Party retained basic conservative principles?
- To what extent is Labour still a socialist party?
- How liberal are the beliefs of UK political parties?

● First, that the winning party has authority to put into effect the commitments in its election manifesto (this can be referred to as the 'doctrine of mandate and manifesto'). Of course, when no single party wins a majority, as occurred in May 2010, the doctrine of the electoral mandate is severely damaged. The agreed policies of the coalition have, in a sense, no mandate at all because the electorate does not know in advance which policies would be agreed and adopted.

● Second, that it grants authority to the new government to do whatever it feels necessary to promote the security and welfare of the country. This therefore covers unforeseen events, such as military crises, economic problems, unexpected public demands or any other crisis or emergency. This can be described as the 'doctor's mandate' (which those facing an operation must sign to cover anything the surgeon may find when they open us up). In a sense, the doctor's mandate applies in the circumstances of coalition, as described above.

This is not a blank cheque, of course. Parliament is there to ensure that the government sticks to its manifesto commitments (unless it has good reason to stray from them) and that it does not abuse its doctor's mandate.

Key Word

Electoral mandate Refers to the authority to govern granted to the winning party at an election by the voters. The mandate suggests that the government may implement the measures in its election manifesto. It also implies that the government has authority to use its judgement in dealing with unforeseen circumstances (the 'doctor's mandate').

So, an election is an event with several different functions. It can be added, indeed, that the election campaign also provides an opportunity for the major political issues and philosophies of the day to be subjected to public scrutiny. It has, in a sense, an educative function, informing the public of what alternative programmes of action are available.

Elections to the Scottish Parliament and the Welsh and Northern Ireland Assemblies serve a very similar function to UK-wide general elections, though the issues are on a regional basis. The Northern Ireland Assembly elections have one further function. The overwhelming issue in the province, one that overshadows all other political conflicts, is the question of the status of Northern Ireland in relation to the UK. Thus the election result there tells us much about the strength of feeling on that fundamental issue. If Sinn Fein does well, it indicates growing support for independence from the UK. If the radical loyalists, the Democratic Unionists, gain support, it demonstrates resistance to the demands of the nationalist community. Northern Ireland, in other words, is a separate political system and elections there have their own special meaning.

Finally, turning to local elections, the functions are more limited. The local community is not really electing a 'government' as such. Rather, it is electing a number of councillors to represent them and showing a rather generalised party preference, which is often based more on national than local issues. So local elections tend to be something of an opinion poll on the performance of *national* government, illogical though that may seem. To some extent local parties can determine their own fortunes based on the quality of the services that they provide when in power, but voting usually follows national trends.

Voting in progress

The British electoral system in general elections

How the system works

The main British **electoral system** is properly titled 'simple majorities in single member constituencies'. But this is not how it is generally known. The common description is 'first-past-the-post', usually abbreviated to FPTP. (We will use the expression FPTP from here onwards.)

Key Word

Electoral system A system that converts votes in an election into seats. It may also refer to the process of electing a single leader, such as a president or a mayor.

The features of FPTP are as follows:

● Each constituency returns one Member of Parliament.

● Each party may nominate only one candidate in each constituency.

● Voters have only one vote each. They choose their preferred candidate by means of the proverbial cross on the ballot paper.

● Whichever candidate wins the largest number of votes is declared elected. This is known as gaining a **simple majority** or **plurality**. It is not necessary for a candidate to achieve more than 50 per cent of the votes.

To demonstrate how this plurality, or simple majority system, works, below are the results from the 2010 election in the constituency of Hampstead and Kilburn (London).

Hampstead and Kilburn constituency, 6 May 2010			
Candidate	Party	Votes	% vote
Glenda Jackson	Labour	17,332	32.8
Chris Philp	Conservative	17,290	32.7
Edward Fordham	Lib Dem	16,491	31.2
Bea Campbell	Green	759	1.4
Magnus Nielson	UKIP	408	0.8
Victoria Moore	BNP	328	0.6
Tamsin Omond	Independent	123	0.2
Gene Alcantra	Independent	91	0.2

Glenda Jackson won by a mere 42 votes and was returned with less than one third of the total votes cast. The Conservative and Liberal Democrat candidates came a close second and third, but only Labour won a seat in the Commons. It can also be seen that small parties were completely squeezed out of the contest.

The effects of first-past-the-post

The most striking feature of FPTP is that it discriminates in favour of some parties and against others. It certainly does not award seats in proportion to the total votes cast. If we study the results of recent general elections we can see how FPTP has such effects. The table on page 101 looks at results between 1979 and 2010, showing the advantage given to the winning party and the disadvantages to the third party. The third party was the Liberals in 1979, a union between Liberals and Social Democrats (known as the Alliance) in 1983 and 1987, and the Liberal Democrats since then.

It can be seen that the winning party always won a considerably higher proportion of seats than votes. This was seen at its most stark in 1997 when Labour won 43.3 per cent of the vote but converted this to a landslide 63.4 per cent of the available seats. The opposite effect has occurred for the third party. Most dramatically, the Liberal/Social Democrat Alliance won an impressive 25.4 per cent of the vote in 1983, but this yielded a meagre 23 seats, that is, 3.5 per cent of the total. Indeed, the 1983 election was extraordinary in that Labour, the second party, won only 27.6 per cent of the vote, barely 2 per cent more than the Alliance, yet still obtained 209 seats – 186 more! If we look at 2005 and 2010 we can see that the Liberal Democrat share of the vote rose, from 22 per cent to 23 per cent, but they won fewer seats.

FPTP has also produced several anomalies in modern history.

- In 1951 the Labour Party actually won more total votes than the Conservatives, but the Conservatives won 26 more seats than Labour and formed the next government. Not surprisingly, this brought strong demands within the Labour Party for electoral reform.

- In February 1974 the Conservatives beat Labour by over 200,000 total votes but ended with four fewer seats.

- In 2005, if we look at England alone, the Conservatives won 0.3 per cent more of the votes but were awarded 92 fewer seats than Labour.

The effects of first-past-the-post, 1979–2010								
Year	Winning party	% of vote	No. of seats won	% of seats won	Third party	% of vote	No. of seats won	% of seats won
1979	Cons.	43.9	339	53.4	Liberal	13.8	11	1.7
1983	Cons.	42.4	397	61.1	Alliance	25.4	23	3.5
1987	Cons.	42.3	376	57.8	Alliance	22.6	22	3.4
1992	Cons.	41.9	336	51.6	Lib Dem	17.8	20	3.1
1997	Lab	43.3	418	63.4	Lib Dem	16.7	46	7.0
2001	Lab	40.7	412	62.5	Lib Dem	18.3	52	7.9
2005	Lab	35.2	356	55.1	Lib Dem	22.0	62	9.6
2010	Cons. (minority)	36.1	307	47.2	Lib Dem	23.0	57	8.8

- Meanwhile, in Wales, also in 2005, Labour won 42.7 per cent of the total vote there and 29 seats. Three other parties – Conservatives, Liberal Democrat and Plaid Cymru – put together won 52.4 per cent of the vote but only 10 seats in total.

- Labour won 35.2 per cent of the vote in 2005 and a comfortable majority of 65; the Conservatives won a bigger share in 2010 – of 36.1 per cent – but found themselves in a minority.

So we can say with great certainty that the FPTP electoral system converts votes into parliamentary seats in a totally disproportionate way. Why is this so? The best clue lies in the results of the Hampstead and Kilburn constituency in 2010, shown above. Glenda Jackson scraped home by 42 votes, but she won the seat. This kind of result was replicated up and down the country. Liberal Democrats commonly came a close second or third in constituencies, but they did not win enough to make a serious challenge. Their 23 per cent of the popular vote was simply spread too thinly.

The Liberal Democrat performance in 1992 and 1997 is also instructive. The Liberal Democrat vote actually fell between 1992 and 1997 (from 6 million to 5.2 million), but the number of seats won went up from 20 to 46. What happened was that the Liberal Democrats managed to concentrate their support in a number of 'target' seats by putting more electoral effort into them than into seats they knew they could not win. In other words, they were able to convert their votes into seats *more efficiently*.

One other statistic can help us to illustrate the disproportionality of FPTP. In the table below we divide the number of votes won by each of the three main parties by the number of seats obtained, and get a statistic demonstrating the *average number of votes* needed to elect an MP for each party in 2010.

What this means, effectively, is that a vote for Labour or the Conservatives in 2010 was worth more than three times as much as a vote for the Liberal Democrats. Thus, it could be said that votes in UK general elections are not of equal value.

Conservative	
Total votes (a)	10,738,826
Total seats (b)	307
Average votes per seat won (a divided by b)	34,979
Labour	
Total votes	8,609,527
Total seats	258
Average votes per seat won	33,370
Liberal Democrat	
Total votes	6,836,824
Total seats	57
Average votes per seat won	119,944

Turning to the effect on the formation of governments, FPTP *used to* have one overwhelming result: it nearly always produced an overall majority in the House of Commons for one party. The outcome of the May 2010 election was, therefore, an exception. It remains an open question whether this was a 'one-off' result, an aberration, or whether it represented a permanent change in the effect of FPTP.

Year	Winning party	Overall majority in the Commons
1979	Conservative	43
1983	Conservative	144
1987	Conservative	102
1992	Conservative	21
1997	Labour	179
2001	Labour	167
2005	Labour	65

This meant that it was not necessary to form a coalition government until 2010. All that, however, has now changed.

It is also interesting to compare the *actual* results of the 2010 general election with the results as they *would have been* if the seats had been awarded strictly in line with the proportion of total votes cast for each party. This is shown in the table below. With strictly proportional results, shown in the right-hand column, we can see that the business of forming a decisive government would be extremely difficult. But, of course, each of the parties would be *proportionally* represented in Parliament.

May 2010 general election		
Party	Actual seats won	Seats in proportion to votes cast
Conservative	307	234
Labour	258	189
Liberal Democrat	57	149

We can now summarise the main effects of the FPTP system.

1. There is a strong, unique relationship between a single MP and every constituency.

2. The majority of MPs are elected without securing an overall majority of the votes in their constituency. In other words, more constituents usually vote *against* their MP than *for* them.

3. The system tends to favour the party that is leading in the polls, usually ensuring that a single party will win an overall majority in the House of Commons and so be able to form a government with a clear mandate. However, this is not a certainty.

4. The system favours those parties that are able to concentrate their votes in specific constituencies.

5. It makes it extremely difficult for smaller parties to break into the domination of the two main parties.

6. Votes are not, in effect, of equal value. Votes are more valuable in 'marginal' constituencies where the result is in doubt. Votes for the second and third parties are of less value than votes for the winning party.

7. Votes for very small parties that have no hope of winning any constituencies are virtually completely wasted. Voters who are considering voting for a losing party increasingly tend to vote for their second, not their first choice of party. This is known as *tactical* voting.

8. The House of Commons does not reflect accurately the political balance of the whole electorate.

At this point it will be useful to review the May 2010 election.

The British General Election of 6 May 2010

The general election of May 2010 may well prove to be the most significant poll since 1945. In that year the Labour Party won an overall majority in the House of Commons for the first time in its existence. Effectively that event created the two-party system that was to dominate British politics for the next 65 years. The 2010 election arguably brought the two-party system to an end. Whether Britain will like what it sees of a three-party system remains to be seen, but it is certainly true that the possibility of a new system did emerge in 2010.

Key features of the election

The following headline features can be identified:

● It failed to give one party an overall majority in the House of Commons for the first time since February 1974.

● In terms of the votes cast it was a close election, with the Conservatives winning 36.1 per cent of the national vote, Labour 29 per cent and the Liberal Democrats 23 per cent.

● All three parties were disappointed by the result. The Conservatives failed to win an overall majority despite having been well ahead in opinion polls since 2007. The Liberal Democrats failed to make a significant break-through in terms of their share of the vote. Having enjoyed opinion poll ratings of up to 30 per cent early in the campaign, their support slipped away in the last week of campaigning. They also won fewer seats than in 2005. Labour lost its majority and its share of the national poll fell to its lowest level since 1987. In the event, there was relief for Labour, as they had feared that much of their support was leaking away to the Liberal Democrats. This did not happen.

- Though the introduction of three live televised debates between the three main party leaders seemed to have transformed the election campaign, in the end their impact failed to be converted into significant changes in support for the parties.

- Small parties failed to make a breakthrough. Though the Green Party won its first seat in Brighton Pavilion, it performed poorly elsewhere. The BNP and UKIP did not approach winning any seats, each party typically polling 1,000–2,000 votes, often many fewer.

- There was no significant progress for the nationalist parties in Wales and Scotland.

- There was a stark difference in support for the Conservative Party between England and Scotland. The party won only one seat in Scotland. Indeed, if there were an English Parliament, the Conservatives would have won a spectacular victory. They enjoyed more than 40 per cent of the votes in England and 56 per cent of English constituencies.

- The MPs' expenses scandal of 2009 seemed to have had a negligible effect. For example, former Labour minister Hazel Blears, who had received enormous quantities of bad publicity over her expenses claims, retained her seat easily.

- There were wide variations in the swings from one party to another in different constituencies. In other words, electorates proved to be very volatile in different parts of the country.

- The overall turnout was better than in 2005, rising to 65 per cent. However, this was disappointing for those who are anxious about the state of democracy in Britain. Though there were high turnouts in some constituencies where the contest was close, there was no major recovery in the turnout, despite the fact that it was generally agreed that this was an exciting, close election.

Caroline Lucas (centre), the first Green MP in the Westminster Parliament

The campaign

The beginning of the campaign largely centred upon a narrow range of issues:

- Labour's long-term record in office

- Labour's handling of the credit crunch and economic recession (to what extent were the government to blame?)

- Who had the most effective policies to deal with the perceived excess of immigration into Britain

- Whether to start to tackle the huge budget deficit straight away by making immediate cuts in public expenditure (Conservative) or wait a year while recovery was under way (Labour and Liberal Democrat)

- Gordon Brown's competence

- David Cameron's potential competence

- The extent to which inevitable future tax increases would fall on the rich or the middle classes

- How much political and tax reform there should be

- Who had the best policies to deal with the discredited banking industry.

In the first two weeks of the campaign it appeared that there might be a hung parliament or that the Conservatives would win a narrow overall victory. However, a series of three televised leadership debates transformed the campaign. These debates seemed to have a number of effects:

- Most importantly, Nick Clegg was highly impressive and looked like a credible leader. He was helped by being given equal status with the other two main party leaders in the debate. As a result the opinion polls saw Liberal Democrat support rising to nearly 30 per cent of the electorate polled.

- David Cameron was acknowledged to have performed moderately and his party lost ground in the opinion polls.

- Gordon Brown held his ground and support for Labour held up, albeit at a low level of about 28 per cent of the electorate.

One single event in mid-campaign also had an impact. Following a lively, televised exchange between an elderly Labour supporter and Gordon Brown, where immigration was a key issue, Brown was heard to call the lady a 'bigoted old woman' when he got into his car without realising his microphone was still on. The remarks were broadcast and he was forced to apologise. Brown's already damaged image suffered a further setback, and Labour's fortunes with it.

As polling day approached, the opinion polls increasingly pointed to a hung parliament so that the parties began to discuss openly the possibilities of a coalition government. The Liberal Democrats declared that they were most likely to discuss power sharing first with the largest party after the election, but it was expected they were more likely to join with Labour. Certainly, Liberal Democrat philosophy and policies lay closer to those of Labour than to those of the Conservatives.

The results

An overview

The full results of the national votes were as follows:

The general election of 6 May 2010				
Party	Seats won	No. votes (millions)	% votes	% seats
Conservative	307	10.73	36.1	47.5
Labour	258	8.61	29.0	39.7
Lib Dem.	57	6.84	23.0	8.8
Green	1	0.29	1.0	0.2
Scots. Nats	6	0.49	1.7	0.9
Plaid Cymru	3	0.17	0.6	0.5
DUP	8	0.17	0.6	1.2
Sinn Fein	5	0.17	0.6	0.8
SDLP	3	0.11	0.4	0.5
Alliance	1	0.04	0.1	0.2
Others	1	1.93	6.9	0.2
Total	650	25.69		

Some figures have been rounded up or down.

Clearly we see a hung parliament, with no party able to command an overall majority.

The main features of the result included the following:

● The effect of the first-past-the-post electoral system favoured both the two main parties, but, as usual, discriminated seriously against the Liberal Democrats.

● The Conservative share of the vote rose by only 4 per cent from 2005 while Labour lost 6 per cent of the share. However, even such a large swing between Labour and the Conservatives did not produce a majority government.

● Though the Conservative share of the vote had risen by only 4 per cent since 2005, the party's share of seats won rose from 30.6 per cent in 2005 to 47.4 per cent in 2010. The Conservatives had clearly become more efficient at converting votes into seats. This may have been the result of their heavy emphasis on 'marginal' constituencies.

● The share of the vote won by the two biggest parties was predicted quite accurately by

Margaret Hodge (Labour) easily beat off the challenge of the BNP led by Nick Griffin (both pictured)

opinion polls in the days leading up to the election. However, the polls over-estimated Liberal Democrat support by about 4–5 per cent typically.

- The Liberal Democrats won a slightly larger share of the votes than in 2005, but won five fewer seats.

- The first ever Green candidate won a seat in Brighton Pavilion. However, the Greens failed to make a breakthrough, gaining only 1 per cent of the national vote.

- The two small right-wing parties, UKIP and the BNP, also failed to break through. UKIP won only 3.1 per cent of the total vote and the BNP 1.9 per cent.

- Patterns of voting and seat winning in Wales, Scotland and Northern Ireland had varied very little since 2005.

- Despite high hopes for a significant change in the gender make-up of the Commons, only

143 women were elected, a small increase over 2005.

The result in England

If we isolate the result of the election for English constituencies we can see an interesting outcome:

| The May 2010 election result in England ||
Party	Seats won
Conservative	298
Labour	191
Lib Dem.	43
Green	1
Total	**533**

Therefore, had England been a separate political system altogether the Conservatives would have enjoyed an overall majority of 63 and could have formed a comfortable majority government.

This has important implications for the *West Lothian Question*. This refers to the fact that, since devolution in 1998, a large proportion of government jurisdiction has been split up between Britain's four countries. Particularly, this concerns such issues as health, education, transport and social policy. The West Lothian Question means that matters that affect only England, such as those above, are debated and voted on by MPs from constituencies *outside* England. A possible solution, and one which was being considered by the coalition government after 2010, is to create an 'English Parliament'. This would mean that, when matters affecting only England are being considered, all MPs from Welsh, Scottish or Northern Irish constituencies would be told to withdraw, leaving only MPs representing English constituencies.

This seems straightforward enough until we consider the results of the 2010 election in England, as shown above. Here the Conservatives have an overall majority and could therefore form an 'English government' *without* the support of any other party. This implies that, when English matters are being considered, the coalition would become meaningless. Only matters affecting Britain as a whole, such as the economy, foreign and defence policy and national security, would require a coalition arrangement.

Thus the May 2010 result poses a special problem for those who wish to see an English Parliament to solve the West Lothian Question.

The result in Scotland

There was very little change in the political map of Scotland compared with 2005. The results in the 79 Scottish constituencies were as follows:

Party	Seats won
Labour	41
Conservative	1
Lib Dem.	11
Scottish Nationalist	6
Total	**59**

Therefore, just as the Conservatives have a legitimate claim to govern England, so they do *not* have such legitimacy in Scotland. Labour dominates voting in Scotland and their grip was not loosened in 2010. The case for more Scottish autonomy might be strengthened, and certainly Labour is more sympathetic to extending devolution, but this was not a vote indicating an appetite for full independence.

The result in the regions

Though the majority of English constituencies returned Conservative MPs, the voting strengths of the parties are very regionalised. The results for four regions appear in the table at the top of page 109:

We can see clearly the extent to which the Conservatives dominate the wealthy South-East but are almost eclipsed in the poorer North-East. Liberal Democrats traditionally do well in the South-West but hardly feature in the other regions outside London.

Party	South East (not London)	London	South-West	North-East
Conservative	75	28	36	2
Labour	4	38	4	25
Lib Dem.	4	7	15	2
Green	1	0	0	0
Total	**84**	**73**	**55**	**29**

The implications for electoral reform

Immediately after the election, the Electoral Reform Society, in partnership with the polling organisation ComRes, interviewed a sample of voters and estimated what the election result *would* have been under different systems. They came to the following conclusion:

Results of the election under different electoral systems				
Party	Actual result	AV	AV+	STV
Cons	307	281	275	246
Labour	258	262	234	207
Lib Dem.	57	79	110	162
Others	28	28	31	35

Source: Electoral Reform Society using actual data and ComRes.

Although such research can never be fully accurate, it provides interesting evidence when considering electoral reform. Under the Alternative Vote (AV), on which there is to be a referendum in due course, the result is closer, with the Liberal Democrats gaining some seats, largely at the expense of the Conservatives. AV+, the system favoured by Labour, brings the Liberal Democrats above 100 seats, this time largely at the expense of Labour. The Single Transferable Vote (STV) is the Liberal Democrats' favourite choice. We can understand why, when it produces 162 seats for them. However, it is also the system that produces the most proportional result.

But the most compelling implication is this: one of the main defences of the disproportional first-past-the-post system was that it almost always produced a decisive, majority, single-party government. The May 2010 election failed to do this. Thus the main argument for retaining FPTP is now severely weakened. Supporters may claim that this was a 'one-off' result and things will return to normal, but it now seems likely that AV will be introduced (provided there is a positive vote in the referendum) and that may well 'lock in' the three-party system.

The coalition government

The hung parliament presented major problems. Not least, the potential Labour–Liberal Democrat coalition seemed an unlikely one as the two parties together could not command a majority. The procedures for such a situation had been laid down by Gus O'Donnell, the Cabinet Secretary, Britain's most senior civil servant. He had foreseen such an event and so produced a 'roadmap' for the party leaders to follow. In essence, they did so. The events of the five days after the election were these:

1. On the Friday after the election, Gordon Brown stated he was staying on as prime minister and would seek a coalition with the Liberal Democrats, supported by other 'progressive' MPs such as the nationalists and the new Green MP, Caroline Lucas. This had the potential for an overall majority for a rainbow coalition of progressives of four or five parties.

2. Nick Clegg kept his promise to speak first with the largest party and started negotiating with the Conservatives.

3. Over the weekend following the election, Clegg negotiated with both Labour and the Conservatives.

4. On Monday 10 May, four days after the election, Gordon Brown announced that he would resign as Labour party leader immediately and would relinquish his position as prime minister after a new Labour leader had been elected, probably by late summer.

5. On Tuesday 11 May, talks between Labour and the Liberal Democrats broke down. Brown therefore resigned as prime minister and advised the Queen to ask David Cameron to form a government.

6. On the same day, David Cameron went to Buckingham Palace and was appointed prime minister. Later that day it was formally announced that a Conservative–Liberal Democrat coalition would be formed.

Thus, an orderly transfer of power had taken place, despite the confusing election result.

It took two weeks before the coalition partners produced a full set of agreed policies. This was, effectively, a *post-election manifesto.* It certainly will be used as a means to judge the performance of the coalition. The main elements of the agreement are shown below.

The Coalition Agreement May 2010		
Liberal Democrat compromise	Policy	Conservative compromise
	Civil liberties: Introduction of a Freedom Bill or Great Repeal Bill, which will scrap ID cards, biometric passports and the National Identity register, as well as restrict use of DNA. The Freedom of Information Act will be extended. There will also be safeguards against anti-terror legislation. CCTV will be regulated to reduce its use. A commission will be established to create a British Bill of Rights, which will incorporate the Human Rights Act. Trial by jury will be protected by law.	Instead of abolishing the Human Rights Act for a British Bill of Rights, a new commission for a New Bill of Rights to encompass the European Convention on Human Rights will be set up. The contentious Human Rights Act will be extended, as will the Freedom of Information Act. This is an area where a strong Conservative tradition on security will conflict with Liberal Democrats' traditionally strong stance on civil liberties.
Liberal Democrats have committed not to prepare to join or to join the euro in the life of the parliament. Any Justice & Home Affairs legislation from the EU will only be agreed to on a case by case basis. The British government will not get involved in establishment of a European prosecutor.	**Europe**: There will be a review of a Sovereignty Bill to guarantee parliamentary sovereignty. In addition there will be an amendment of the 1972 Act to ensure any transference of competences to the EU would be subject to a referendum. In addition, Britain will push for the European Parliament's only seat to be in Brussels.	There will not be any repatriation of powers from the EU. There will also be official support for further enlargement of the Union.
The Trident nuclear defences will be maintained, although they will be scrutinised to ensure they represent value for money. There is an acknowledgement that the Liberal Democrats are against a nuclear deterrent for Britain and they will continue to make a case for alternatives.	**Defence**: Britain will maintain a nuclear deterrent. Britain will play a strong role in a non-proliferation treaty review conference. The running costs of the Ministry of Defence will be cut by 25%. The operational costs of Afghanistan will be doubled. There will be a war cabinet to oversee the Afghanistan mission. The Military Covenant to be rebuilt; Britain will work for an international ban on cluster munitions, as well as on an ethical aspect to support for British defence industry jobs.	The strategic pay review will look at value for money from British defence contractors.
Liberal Democrats agreed to start cutting immediately rather than in 2011. They will be allowed to abstain from a vote on recognition of marriage in the tax system.	**Deficit reduction**: £6bn to be cut between 2010 and 2011. This money is to be found through cuts in public spending. There will be cuts to the Child Tax Fund and a reduction of tax credits for higher earners. Increase in capital gains tax. Increase tax-free allowance to £10K.	There are no tax cuts for married couples, the ceiling on inheritance tax has not increased; increase on capital gains tax to 40%. A new flat tax on non-domiciles has been postponed. Increase in tax-free allowance.

Liberal Democrat compromise	Policy	Conservative compromise
There will be no amnesty for illegal immigrants. There will be a cap on the number of non-EU immigrants.	**Immigration:** Annual limit on non-EU migrants admitted to UK. Speeding up of asylum system.	
	Prevention of the deportation of asylum seekers who had to leave their home because of sexual orientation. There will be an end to the detention of children in immigration centres.	
Liberal Democrats did not want to ringfence NHS spending.	**Health:** The government is to protect the National Health Service.	
	Devolution: Increased powers to Wales through a referendum in 2011; review of the Calman proposals for more power to Scotland. Review of Scottish MPs voting on England-only legislation.	
Abstinence from voting on National Planning Statement on the building of new nuclear power stations.	**Energy & Transport:** A new plane tax to be introduced; no new runways at Heathrow, Stansted or Gatwick. A national planning statement for nuclear construction to be submitted to Parliament; a new green investment bank to be created. A high-speed rail network to be built; no new coal-fired power stations will be built without carbon capture and storage capabilities. Increased target for share of energy from renewable sources.	Accept Liberal Democrats will speak against statement.
Some new prisons may be built; review rather than abolition of control orders.	**Crime & Policing:** Police commissioners will be directly elected. Trial by jury will be protected.	No clear increase in sentencing. Anonymity for rape defendants
	Justice: There will be a judicial inquiry into claims of torture of terrorist suspects.	
No freezing of tuition fees.	**Education:** Pupil premium (additional funding for pupils from deprived backgrounds) and expansion of academies programme.	
Free vote.	**Hunting ban repeal.**	No timetable.

Source: compiled by Anna Rose O'Dwyer, St Paul's School

Summary

The May 2010 general election was extraordinary in a number of ways. It produced the first hung parliament for 36 years and resulted in the first coalition government for 65 years. How long the coalition will endure and whether the two-party system will re-assert itself remain to be seen. So, too, does the question of whether the radical political reforms promised by both coalition parties will be realised. Whatever happens, however, no election has had such dramatic results since the 1945 poll swept the Labour Party into single-party government for the first time in its history.

Electoral systems explained

Majority systems

This term describes an electoral system that is designed to try to ensure that the person or party elected enjoys a broad majority of support from the electorate. Of course, if there are only two candidates or parties to choose from, the winner must, by definition, receive a majority of support (except in the highly unlikely event of a tie). However, few elections have only two candidates. **Majority systems**, therefore, normally have two parts. The first part is designed to reduce the contest to only two candidates. The second part is a 'run-off' between the two survivors. As we have said above, in a two-horse race, one must achieve an absolute majority.

Of course, we need to be careful here. Majority systems where there are more than two candidates do not usually produce a winner who enjoys over 50 per cent of the *first choice* support of the electorate. Sometimes they will, but if not, we can say only that the majority support includes the first and second choices of the majority. This is a broad majority of support, rather than a specific absolute majority.

The only major political example of a majority system operating in Britain is that which elects the London mayor. It is known as the **supplementary vote**. A similar system is used to elect the French president every seven years. The figures on page 114 demonstrate the way the most recent elections in London and France worked.

London mayoral election, 2008

Each voter has two votes, a first and second choice. Had one candidate secured more than 50 per cent of the first choices, they would have been elected. Failing that, the top two candidates go to a second round. The second-preference votes on

✔ Key Word

Majority systems Description of electoral systems where the winning candidate is required to win an overall majority, i.e. more than 50 per cent of the votes cast.

Sample STV ballot paper for the 2008 London Mayoral election

Candidate	First-choice votes	Total with second preferences added
Johnson	1,043,761	1,168,738
Livingstone	893,877	1,028,966
Paddick	236,685	
Berry	77,374	
Barnbrook	69,710	
Craig	39,249	
Batten	22,422	
German	16,796	
O'Connor	10,695	
McKenzie	5,389	

all the losing candidates' ballots are added to the top two candidates' totals. One of them must then have a majority over the other. The figures for 2008 are shown in the table above.

So, Boris Johnson was elected with a final majority of 53 per cent over Ken Livingstone's 47 per cent. On the first ballot Johnson was very far from securing an absolute majority. But he picked up 124,977 second-preference votes to secure victory.

French presidential election, 2007

In France, the voters show their second preferences on a separate date, not on the same ballot paper. On the first Sunday ballot, all the candidates stand. A week later a second vote is held (unless one of the candidates secures over 50 per cent of the first vote, in which case they are

elected). In the second ballot, only the top two candidates from the first ballot stand.

The 2007 results in France follow below.

First ballot		
Candidate	Votes (millions)	%
Sarkozy	11.45	31.2
Royal	9.50	25.9
Bayrou	6.82	18.6
Le Pen	3.83	10.4
Besancenot	1.50	4.1
Others (7)	3.62	9.8

Second ballot		
Candidate	Votes (millions)	%
Sarkozy	19.98	53.1
Royal	16.79	46.9
Turnout (both ballots): 84%		

We can see that the conservative candidate, Nicolas Sarkozy, obtained less than a third of the votes on first ballot, but once all the other candidates except Ségolène Royal had been eliminated, he won over enough of the votes previously given to those losing candidates to be able to win an overall majority a week later. It is also interesting to note that the turnout in both ballots was 84 per cent, suggesting that the system certainly attracts plenty of interest among the French voters.

Alternative vote

The most common type of majority system is known as the **Alternative Vote** system, known normally as **AV**. Here voters are given two votes, a first and second choice. If, when the first-choice votes are counted, one of the candidates achieves 50 per cent or more – an absolute majority – they are elected automatically. If none of the candidates achieves this, however, the second-choice votes have to be taken into account. The top two candidates retain their first-choice votes. The other (losing) candidates are eliminated, but not before the second choices on their ballot papers are added to the first-choice votes already won by the two leaders. The final totals for the two leading candidates now must produce an outright winner.

A slightly more complex version of the Alternative Vote is used to elect members of the Australian House of Representatives. In this system, voters may place *all* candidates in order of preference. If no candidate achieves an overall majority on first preferences, the bottom candidate drops out. Their second preferences are then added to the others. If a candidate now has an overall majority, they are elected. If not, the candidate now at the bottom drops out and their second preferences are added to the surviving candidates. The process continues until one candidate has an overall majority. As an example, the results from 2004 for the candidates of one constituency (Melbourne Ports) are shown below.

The 2004 result in the Australian constituency of Melbourne Ports (using AV)		
First-preference results:		
Name	**Votes**	**% votes**
Cameron	958	1.2
Southwick	35,058	42.9

The 2004 result in the Australian constituency of Melbourne Ports (using AV) (continued)		
First-preference results:		
Name	**Votes**	**% votes**
Beale	1,102	1.3
Danby	32,046	39.3
Jackel	444	0.5
Isherwood	146	0.2
Horin	374	0.5
Lewis	11,510	14.1

The results when losing candidates were eliminated and their second preferences redistributed:

Southwick	37,878	46.4
Danby	43,760	53.6*

* Note that Danby was second on first preferences, but won when second preferences were added.

Plurality systems

The term 'plurality' refers to a candidate who wins more votes than any of their opponents, but who does not necessarily achieve an overall majority of more than 50 per cent. This is essentially the way in which the current British electoral system for the Westminster Parliament works, as shown above. Today, plurality systems are relatively uncommon. The UK and the USA are the most prominent examples of its use. In the USA, both the Senate and the House of Representatives use a plurality system.

Plurality, or FPTP, is not particularly controversial in the USA. This is because, in nearly all Senate and House of Representatives contests, there are only two serious candidates. There are no significant third or fourth parties, as in the UK, so effectively every election is contested between just two serious candidates – the Democrat and the Republican. This means that the winner virtually always has an absolute majority – more than 50 per cent – and not just a plurality. It is in the UK, where Liberal Democrats, nationalists and others win significant numbers of votes, that the plurality system throws up many winners who have failed to gain an absolute majority of support in their constituencies.

A full explanation of the UK system is shown on pages 99–103.

Proportional representation

It must be emphasised at the outset that **proportional representation** (we will refer to this as PR from now on) is *not* an electoral system. PR is a description of a *number of different* electoral systems and the effect that they have.

Proportional representation defined

PR is a description of any electoral system that tends to produce institutions that are representative of the people who have elected them. The term *representative* normally refers to the balance of party representation in the institution. However, it can also refer to the *social* make-up of the body – are women, minority ethnic groups, social class and age groups, for example, appropriately represented? If a system is exactly proportional, parties will be represented in accordance with the proportion of the total votes that they win. Under pure PR, if a party wins 40 per cent of the vote it receives 40 per cent of the seats available and so on. Such a system operates today in Israel. Similarly, a system that returned 50 per cent of women members would be socially representative. Nevertheless, it is unlikely that *any* electoral system can be exactly proportional in its result. Therefore we describe any system as PR if it *tends* to produce results that reflect *reasonably* accurately the social and political divisions within the electorate as a whole.

Different kinds of PR systems are examined below.

Single Transferable Vote (STV)

This is possibly the most complex electoral system, but is favoured by many for both its fairness and the amount of choice it gives to voters. It dates from the 1850s, so it has stood the test of time. It is used in local and assembly elections in Northern Ireland and also for local elections in Scotland. It is also the system operating in the Republic of Ireland.

STV works in the following way:

● Constituencies return more than one member each. In Northern Ireland, the normal number is six.

- In order to be elected, a candidate must achieve a 'quota'. The quota is calculated by taking the total votes cast and dividing it by the number of seats plus one (i.e. if there are six seats, the number is seven; the whole result, plus one, is the quota).

- Voters may vote for all the candidates in their own order of preference. They do not have to vote for all candidates, but only the number they wish to select.

- Voters may vote for candidates from different parties and may show a preference between candidates of the same party.

- Candidates who achieve the quota on their first preference are elected. When that happens, their second and subsequent preferences are redistributed among the other candidates.

- When more candidates achieve the quota by adding redistributed votes to their first preferences, their spare votes are also redistributed. This continues until no more candidates can achieve the quota. At this point the votes of the candidates at the bottom of the poll begin to have their subsequent preferences re-distributed.

- When the required number of candidates have achieved the quota, the counting can end.

STV was chosen for Northern Ireland partly because it was the system used over the border in the Republic of Ireland, so it was reasonably familiar, but largely because it fitted the special needs of a community that suffered from a number of serious problems.

Essentially the new electoral system of Northern Ireland, adopted in 1998 under the terms of the Good Friday Agreement, was chosen to achieve a number of objectives. First, it had to reflect the different sections of a very divided society. Second, it was used to prevent the unionist parties winning

an overall majority, which they would have done under FPTP. This was essential as one of the main problems in the history of the province was the so-called abuse of power by the unionist, Protestant majority. Third, there was a strong civil rights movement in Northern Ireland. These campaigners insisted on an electoral system that maximised voter choice. STV was able to achieve all three aims.

List systems

A list system is one where there are no individual candidates. Instead, the voters are offered a choice of political parties. Each party produces a list of candidates. This list is shown on the ballot paper. The voter chooses one of the lists and casts their vote for it. The seats are awarded in proportion to the votes cast for each party. This is the most proportional of all systems and this is its greatest attraction. There are three main variations.

- First, there is the **national list system**, as used in Israel. Each party list covers representation for the whole country.

- Second, there are two **regional list** systems, the most common form in Europe. The country votes in regions, rather than nationally. Regional systems are either **closed** or **open.**

  * With a closed system it is the party leaderships who decide in what order their candidates are elected.

  * In an open system the voters may determine both how many seats each party wins and the order in which candidates are elected.

  * The UK operates a closed regional list system to elect Members of the European Parliament.

List systems normally include a **threshold** system. The threshold is a minimum proportion of the total votes that a party must receive to win any seats at all. In other words, if a party fails to achieve the threshold figure, it is eliminated and its seats distributed among the other parties. The purpose of the threshold is to keep out very small, extremist parties. In Germany, for example, where the similar AMS system was adopted after the Second World War, a high minimum threshold of 5 per cent was adopted to prevent Nazis or communists gaining representation.

How the regional list system works

- The country is divided into regions.

- In each region the parties produce lists of candidates.

- The voters are invited to vote for one of the lists.

- Seats are awarded to each party in exact proportion to the votes cast.

- If a party wins, say, 40 per cent of the total votes, the top 40 per cent of its candidates on the list are elected.

- In some cases, including the UK elections to the European Parliament, a small adjustment is made depending on the performance of parties at the previous election.

- If it is a **closed** system, voters have no influence over which individuals are elected off the list. The order of the list is determined by the party leaderships.

- If it is an **open** system, voters can, if they wish, show a preference for certain candidates on a party list. This will influence which individuals are elected from the lists.

- There is normally a threshold of 1–5 per cent, or minimum proportion of the votes, which a party must win to gain *any* seats.

Additional member systems (AMS)

AMS systems are known as **hybrids** or **mixed**. They are a combination of FPTP with a regional list system. A proportion (which varies from country to country) of the seats is awarded through FPTP. The rest are awarded on a regional list system. This means that every voter has two votes. One is for a constituency candidate in the normal way, the other is from a choice of party lists.

So, some of the elected representatives have a constituency to look after, while others do not. They have been elected from the lists and are free of constituency responsibilities. No real distinction is made between them, though the senior party members tend to be elected from lists rather than in constituencies.

AMS is something of a compromise. It is designed to make a system *partly* proportional, but also preserves the idea of parliamentary constituencies with an MP to represent them. It helps smaller parties, but also favours the larger ones. It achieves two objectives at the same time, preserving the idea of constituencies and a constituency representative, but producing a much more proportional result than FPTP.

How AMS works in Scotland and Wales

- Two-thirds of the seats are elected using FPTP, as for UK general elections.

- The other third of the seats is elected on the basis of closed regional list voting (see above to show how the regional list system works).

- There is an important variation in the regional list part of the vote.

- The variable top-up system adjusts the proportions of votes cast on the list system.

- This is a complex calculation, but, in essence, what happens is the seats awarded from the list system are adjusted to give a more proportional result.

- Parties that do less well in the constituencies (typically Conservatives or Greens) have their proportion of list votes adjusted upwards. Those that do proportionally well under FPTP (typically Labour) have their list votes adjusted downwards.

- The overall effect of variable top-up is to make the total result close to proportional of the total votes cast in both systems.

AV Plus system

We can now begin to see just how many different systems can be devised for the conversion of votes into parliamentary seats. The descriptions above, indeed, show only the main variations. In practice, there are even more variations on these themes.

One such possible variation is known as AV Plus (AV+) a system that is not currently used but which was recommended for general elections for the UK by a Commission led by Lord Jenkins in 1998. The Jenkins Commission recommended that general elections should be held under this system. It is essentially the AMS

Electoral systems summarised			
System	**Examples of use**	**Main features**	**Main effects**
First-past-the-post	UK general elections. US Congress	Plurality in single-member constituencies	Strong constituency–MP link, strong, single-party government
STV	Northern Ireland Assembly, Republic of Ireland	Multi-member constituencies with wide voter choice	Highly proportional result. Many parties gain representation
Closed regional list	European Parliament elections	Voters select a party, not an individual	Highly proportional result. No constituencies
Open regional list	Various in Europe	As above, except that voters influence which individuals are elected	As above
AMS	Germany, Greater London Assembly, Scottish Parliament, Welsh Assembly	A hybrid system of FPTP and regional list with a variable top-up system	More proportional than FPTP, but constituencies are preserved. Small parties do well
Alternative vote	Australian House of Representatives	Voters show two preferences. Guarantees an overall majority for the winner	Helps small parties, but not very small parties

Electoral systems summarised (continued)			
System	**Examples of use**	**Main features**	**Main effects**
AV Plus	Not used, only proposed	Same as AMS except that constituency MPs would be elected by the AV system	Would be very beneficial to small parties, especially Lib Dems
Supplementary vote	London mayor	Used to elect individuals. Voters show two preferences	Guarantees that the winner enjoys an absolute majority
Second ballot majority system	French president	Voters vote twice on successive weeks. Only top two candidates run off in second ballot	Guarantees that the winner enjoys an absolute majority

system, as adopted in Scotland and Wales, except that the constituency MPs would be elected using the Alternative Vote (AV). This would retain constituency MPs, but would give the smaller parties, notably the Liberal Democrats, a much fairer degree of representation. The proposals for electoral reform were ultimately dropped by the Labour government after 1997, but the Jenkins proposal was resurrected in 2010 and became once again Labour's first choice for reform.

The issue of whether Britain should reform its system for general elections is further considered in the next section.

Effects of, and comparisons between, different electoral systems

STV in Northern Ireland

Shown below are the results of the election to the Northern Ireland Assembly in 2007.

Northern Ireland Assembly election 2007				
Party	**Type**	**Seats won**	**% of votes won**	**% of seats**
Democratic Unionist (DUP)	Strong Loyalist	36	30.1	33.3
Ulster Unionist (UUP)	Moderate Loyalist	18	14.9	16.7
Alliance Party	Neutral	7	5.2	6.5
SDLP	Moderate Nationalist	16	15.2	14.8

Northern Ireland Assembly election 2007 (continued)				
Party	Type	Seats won	% of votes won	% of seats
Sinn Fein	Strong Nationalist	28	26.2	25.9
Others	Various	3	8.0	2.8

The figures below are an extract from the results of one constituency, South Antrim, in 2007.

Candidate	Party	1st preference votes	Result	Count
McLaughlin	Sinn Fein	6,313	Elected	1
McCrea	DUP	6,023	Elected	1
Ford	Alliance	5,007	Elected	5
Burnside	UUP	4,507	Elected	7
Clarke	DUP	4,302	Elected	8
Lucas	DUP	2,840	Not elected	8
Burns	SDLP	2,721	Elected	8
Kinahan	UUP	2,391	Not elected	6
McClelland	SDLP	1,526	Not elected	6
Nicholl	UUP	927	Not elected	4
McCartney	UK Unionist	893	Not elected	3
Whitcroft	Green	507	Not elected	3
O'Brien	Conservative	129	Not elected	3
Delaney	Workers' Party	89	Not elected	3

The electoral quota was 5,454. Only McLaughlin and McCrea achieved this on first-preference votes.

Note: the number shown in the 'Count' column refers to how many preferences were counted for each candidate, so, for example, Clarke's, Lucas's and Burns's final totals included some eighth-preference votes.

The following features are important:

- There is a large number and variety of candidates – 14 in total.

- The large parties do not put up more candidates than they expect to be elected.

- The six elected were not the same six who came top of the first-preference votes (Lucas beat Burns on first preferences, but was not elected).

- The candidates at the bottom end of the poll were significant in that some of the lower preferences on their ballots were added to the more popular candidates. In other words, those who supported such candidates as Kinahan or McClelland did have an influence on the overall result through their second, third and subsequent preferences.

- The constituency is clearly very mixed as there was significant support for nationalists and loyalists of various kinds. Candidates from five different parties were elected, which is representative of the fragmented social and political nature of Belfast North. If the election were by FPTP, the DUP might well have won outright, with all the other groups excluded.

We can draw a number of conclusions from this. STV is clearly a very representative system, an example of a highly proportional representation system. The voters have been given a wide choice and their second and subsequent choices are taken into account, not just their first choice.

The overall result was fairly even between the four main parties – DUP, UUP, SDLP and Sinn Fein. This was important for the province as the different political groupings needed to have decent representation. It was expected that they would share power. We can also see that the proportion of seats won was close to the overall proportion of votes, so the system lives up to its description 'proportional representation'.

Of course, such a system would have produced a very indecisive result in a more 'conventional' system. If we require strong, single-party government, STV will not produce it, as these results indicate. If STV were used throughout the UK in general elections we could expect that the three main parties would dominate and that smaller parties such as the Greens or UKIP would also gain a few seats. This would be good for representation, but bad for those who want to see strong government.

It is also clear that STV is a complicated system. Some voters may be confused by the sight of a large ballot paper with many names on it. They may also not understand the result. But the Irish on both sides of the border where STV is used seem reasonably happy with their electoral system, however well or badly they understand it. It is a slow system to count and final results can take several days to be calculated. However, a few days' delay seems a small price to pay for fair representation.

Additional member system in Scotland and Wales

The main results of the election to the Scottish parliament in 2007 are shown on p 123.

A number of interesting features can be seen in these results:

- We can see that, had the election been conducted purely as FPTP, Labour would have won a narrow overall majority, with 37 constituency seats won, with the others adding up to 36.

- However, when the *list* seats were taken into account, especially as they were distributed disproportionately, Labour no longer had a majority. Indeed, no party won an overall majority. The Scottish National Party won most total seats, on 47, with Labour a close second on 46.

Main results of the election to the Scottish Parliament, 2007				
Party	% of votes (constituencies)	Constituencies won	Top-up seats	Total
Labour	32.2	37	9	46
SNP	32.9	21	26	47
Lib Dem	16.2	11	5	16
Conservative	16.6	4	13	17
Green	0.2	0	2	2
Others	1.9	0	1	1

Party total seats won:	Seats	% seats won	% of regional list votes
Labour	46	35.7	29.2
Scottish Nationalist	47	36.4	31.0
Conservative	18	14.0	13.9
Liberal Democrat	17	13.2	11.3
Green	2	1.5	4.0
Others	1	0.8	10.2

- Under FPTP the Conservatives would have been an insignificant party, with only 4 seats won. However, the AMS system secured them a total of 18 seats.

- The Green Party would have won no seats under FPTP, but secured two under AMS.

- Perhaps most importantly, the overall results are quite proportional to votes cast. Labour won 29 per cent of the list votes and over 35 per cent of the seats. The SNP won 31 per cent of the votes and 36 per cent of the seats. The Conservative result was almost exactly proportional, as was the Liberal Democrat outcome.

In Wales, the overall results to the Assembly looked as shown on p 124 in 2007.

As with Scotland, no party won an overall majority. The result was fairly proportional, though Labour's dominance of the constituency voting assured them of a good share of the seats. The system did few favours for the Liberal Democrats and perhaps contributes to their general dislike of the system and preference for STV or the Alternative Vote.

The regional list system in the UK

Used to elect Members of the European Parliament, the regional list system has had the effect of awarding seats broadly in proportion to the votes cast and gives the smaller parties a greater chance of gaining some representation. This can be seen in the results of the UK elections to the European Parliament in 2009.

Results of the Election to the Welsh Assembly, 2007					
Party	Constituencies	Top-up seats	% votes	Total	% seats
Labour	24	2	32.2	26	44.1
Conservative	5	7	22.4	12	20.3
Liberal Democrat	3	3	14.8	6	10.2
Plaid Cymru	7	7	22.4	14	23.7
Others	1	0	8.2	1	1.7

Results of the UK Election to the European Parliament, 2009			
Party	% Votes	Seats Won	% Seats won
Conservative	27.7	26	36.1
UKIP	16.5	13	18.1
Labour	15.7	13	18.1
Lib Dem	13.7	11	15.3
Green	8.6	2	2.8
BNP	6.2	2	2.8
SNP*	2.1	2	2.8
Plaid Cymru*	0.8	1	1.4
Sinn Fein*		1	1.4
Democratic Union**		1	1.4
Others	8.5	0	

* Awarded a disproportionately high number of seats as they are regional parties

** voting figures not shown as STV was used rather than the list system.

So, we can see how much more proportional this system is (even with the adjustments made). Interestingly, UKIP was able to win seats to an assembly of which they do not approve!. But this was justified by the fact that 16 per cent of the electorate wished to express their disapproval of the European Union and their view was given representation. The Greens and the British National Party won seats, as did nationalist parties, but their numbers remain small.

Student activity

Individual students should select one of the electoral systems described above. They should then make a presentation, with appropriate evidence, explaining the possible benefits of introducing that system to UK general elections.

Manifestos and mandates

Before leaving the subject of elections, we need to consider one of the principles of election politics in the UK. This is the 'doctrine of manifesto and mandate'. One of the purposes of an election in the UK is to give the governing party a mandate to govern – that is, to give it elective authority. But the mandate does not give the government *carte blanche*. The authority granted to the government at elections is based very much on the manifesto of the party. This represents the policies of which the electorate has approved.

The mandate is subject to certain conditions. The first is that the government should go beyond its manifesto commitments, or amend them significantly, *only* if it can carry Parliament with it. Indeed, the House of Lords, which is more independent than the Commons, sometimes sees its role as that of guardian of the mandate. The Lords tend to obstruct proposals for which they feel the government has no mandate. The second condition is that the government will be judged by the electorate on its performance against its previous manifesto proposals at the next general election. The third condition is that we expect the government to use its judgement when unforeseen circumstances arise. Again, it is for Parliament to judge the performance of the government in this respect.

Elections therefore provide a triple opportunity for the electorate. First, they can judge between the competing manifestos of the parties. Second, they can deliver their verdict on how well or how badly they feel the outgoing government has delivered its mandate. Third, they can give a fresh mandate to the existing governing party, or give a mandate to a different party.

As we have seen above, however, this doctrine largely depends upon a single party winning an overall majority in the House of Commons. The failure of the electoral system to produce an overall majority in May 2010 compromised the principle of the electoral mandate.

Electoral systems and the party system

Introduction

The **party system** that characterises any democratic state is closely associated with the electoral system that underpins it. It is not necessarily true that the electoral system actually *determines* the party system, but there is no doubt that it is *one* of the determining factors. It is therefore important to study party and electoral systems together.

Before we investigate them individually and together, however, we need to define the two terms

Party systems

A party system describes the typical number of important parties that compete in a political system, the way they relate to each other and the part they play in the formation of governments. Thus we speak of *two-party systems* (for example in the USA), *three-party systems* (Spain) or *multi-party systems* (Italy). This does not mean that the USA has only two parties, or Spain three, but it does mean that the system is *dominated* by two or three parties, while in a multi-party system a significantly large variety of parties have some political influence.

Allied to these descriptions is the question of how governments are typically formed. Many systems are essentially *one-party governments*. This was certainly true of the UK until 2010. Others are typified by coalitions where more than one party shares government, a situation that is extremely common in Europe. Occasionally systems have minority governments, as occurred in the UK in the 1920s (Labour minority government), but these are usually temporary circumstances.

Key Word

Party system Refers to the typical structure of parties within a political system. It describes the normal number of parties that compete effectively. Thus we may speak of two-, three- or multi-party systems. It also refers to the typical party make-up of governments – for example, single-party government, coalitions and so on.

Electoral systems

An electoral system is a method by which votes are converted into seats in the legislature, or sometimes into the election of a single leader such as a president or a mayor. It is connected to the party system in that certain types of electoral system normally (but by no means always) will produce a particular party system. Thus UK and US elections have normally reinforced the two-party system, while German electoral arrangements have produced a three- or four-party result. As we shall see, there is a general rule that the more proportional an electoral system is, the more parties with political significance it will produce. But we need to beware. While there is a close causal link between electoral systems and party systems, it is not a totally predictable relationship.

So, when we consider the possible effects of a reform in the electoral system, we must not assume that we can predict the outcome of such reform. In other words, the party system is determined by a number of different factors, not just the electoral system.

The UK party system

Until the 1980s the UK was undoubtedly a two-party system. This had been broadly true since the 1870s. The term *two-party system* implied a number of realities:

- General elections tended to produce a result that demonstrated the dominance of only two parties – at least in terms of the seats won in the House of Commons. There was a brief period in the 1920s when three parties were effectively competing for power, but this occurred only because the Labour Party was replacing the Liberals as the main opposition to the Conservative Party. As Labour was overtaking the Liberals there was a short-lived three-party system. But it was clear that the

two-party system was reasserting itself very quickly. The table on page 127 showing elections in the UK since 1945 demonstrates the dominance of two parties very clearly.

- While it is true that the dominance of the two parties has begun to subside since 1997, it is still plain to see that it remains the 'normal' situation in the UK.

- It is a less clear question whether Britain is a two-party system in terms of *votes*. Here again, up to the 1980s the two main parties dominated the voting, but since then the third party – now the Liberal Democrats – has gained considerable ground. This is shown in the table on page 128.

These two tables therefore, suggest that Britain remains very much a two-party system in Parliament, but that in terms of popular support it is a *three*-party system.

- Until May 2010 there was a near certainty that the government would be formed by one of the two main parties while the third party would be habitually excluded from power. There had been no coalition government in the UK since 1945 and there was only a brief period – 1976–78 – when a second party had any significant influence on the governing party. At that time, Labour had lost its parliamentary majority and so had to rely on parliamentary support from the Liberals. This was known as the Lib–Lab Pact, but it was not a coalition; rather, it was a formal parliamentary arrangement and it was an exception to the rule.

- These realities were severely shaken in May 2010 when the Liberal Democrats gained a share in governmental power. However, this was not achieved as a result of a large surge in Liberal Democrat support but was the product of an unusual election result in which neither of the main parties was able to dominate.

Two-party dominance in the UK				
Election	Conservative seats	Labour seats	Liberal (or Lib Dem) seats	% of seats won by largest two parties
1945	210	393	12	94.2
1950	298	315	9	98.1
1951	321	295	6	98.6
1955	345	277	6	98.8
1959	365	258	6	98.9
1964	304	317	9	98.6
1966	253	364	12	98.0
1970	330	288	6	98.1
1974 (Feb)	297	301	14	94.2
1974 (Oct)	277	319	13	93.8
1979	339	269	11	95.8
1983	397	209	23	93.3
1987	376	229	22	93.0
1992	336	271	20	93.2
1997	165	418	46	88.4
2001	413	166	52	87.8
2005	198	356	62	85.6
2010	307	258	57	86.9

Now that we have established that Britain has been, until recently, a two-party system but that this status is becoming less certain, we can turn to the electoral system and its possible reform to understand what the likely effects of such change might be. We must also examine the experience of the devolved systems of Scotland, Wales and Northern Ireland for clues as to how *national* reform might unfold.

Election date	% votes won by Labour and Conservatives	% votes won by third party
1979	80.8	13.8
1983	70.0	25.4
1987	75.1	23.2
1992	77.5	18.3
1997	75.5	17.0
2001	72.4	18.3
2005	67.5	22.0
2010	65.1	23.0

Electoral systems

As we have said, an electoral system exists to convert votes into seats in the legislature (we will ignore, for now, systems in the UK that are used to elect mayors). In order to evaluate systems and their effects we must first examine what we are trying to achieve through the electoral system. We will concentrate for now on general elections because it is these that determine who shall govern the country.

So the possible aims of any electoral system *might* include the following:

● To ensure that representation in Parliament accurately reflects the range and strength of political opinion among the voting population.

● To ensure that people will feel they are effectively represented within the political system.

● To ensure that every vote is of equal value.

● To give voters a fair choice in their preferences.

● To ensure that an effective government can emerge from the result of the election.

The problem is that there is no electoral system in the world that can deliver *all* these objectives, except in highly unusual circumstances. A system can produce some of them, but not all. For example, the UK system does tend to produce governments that can rule effectively – that is, they are highly stable once elected – but this is achieved at the expense of a truly representative House of Commons, where the Conservatives and Liberal Democrats are under-represented.

A detailed account of the nature of different electoral systems has already been presented above in this chapter. However, we should remind ourselves of the main alternatives that exist. These are shown in the table below.

Electoral systems – a brief review		
Category	**Electoral system**	**Main characteristics**
Plurality system	First-past-the-post	Single member constituencies. Winners need only a **plurality** of the votes. Distorts results in favour of larger parties. Individuals and parties are often elected on a minority of the votes. Normally produces single-party government.

Electoral systems – a brief review (continued)		
Category	**Electoral system**	**Main characteristics**
Proportional systems	List systems	Are accurately proportional. Tend to produce multi-party systems. Give representation to small parties. Eliminate constituencies.
	Single transferable vote (STV)	Preserves large constituencies. Highly proportional result. Voters have wide choice. Favours small parties.
Mixed system	Additional member system (also known as a mixed-member system)	Gives voters two choices. Preserves constituency representation. Helps small parties. Creates a reasonably proportional result.
Majority systems	Second ballot or alternative vote	Preserves constituencies. Gives voters a second choice. Favours small parties but not very small parties.

Key Word

Plurality A description of an electoral system that awards a position or seat in the legislature to a candidate who has achieved more votes than any other, even if this does not represent an absolute – 50 per cent plus – majority. The British FPTP system that operates in general elections is an example of plurality at work.

The problem of FPTP

If reform of the electoral system is to be achieved, it is necessary to understand the problem as it is perceived by the proponents of reform. The problems, as stated, are as follows:

● Governments are being elected on a minority of the votes cast in a general election. In the past two elections this problem worsened, to the extent that the Labour victory of 2005 was secured with a mere 35.2 per cent of the total vote (though the problem was solved in 2010 with the formation of a coalition).

● The fact that governments are claiming a mandate on a minority of the votes calls into question the democratic legitimacy of a government. This lack of legitimacy may lead increasingly to sustained and violent dissent. Supporters of reform, indeed, suggest that the coalition government formed in May 2010 was *more* legitimate than single-party governments elected on a minority of votes. This was because it could, at least, claim the support of 59 per cent of the popular vote (36 per cent Conservative plus 23 per cent Liberal Democrat).

- The House of Commons does not represent the range of political opinion in the UK. Support for the Liberal Democrats is seriously under-represented.

- Too many votes are wasted. Those who support small parties such as the Greens or UKIP, together with those who support parties which are inevitably going to lose in a 'safe' seat, know that their votes are wasted.

- Voters are given a very narrow choice. They have only one vote and no say in which candidates shall be put forward from each party.

- Because so many voters feel their vote is wasted they are forced to vote tactically, that is, to vote for their second-choice party in order to have some say in the result in their constituency. Wasted votes may also have become a cause of low turnouts since 2001.

- The discrimination against the Liberal Democrats effectively means that votes are of unequal value. It needed, on average,

33,000–34,000 votes to elect a Labour or Conservative MP in 2010, but 120,000 to elect a Liberal Democrat (see page 102 above).

- It is almost impossible to establish a new party from modest roots. This creates political 'atrophy', that is, a stagnant situation where new political ideas or movements are stifled by the big parties that have such a huge advantage.

- Though there are several reasons for declining voter turnouts, it is believed that disillusionment with an electoral system that is widely perceived to be unfair may be one of the causes of political disengagement.

Student activity

Study the two tables below.

Answer these questions:

1. Identify the main examples of evidence from the two tables suggesting that first-past-the-post is unfair.

2. Identify the evidence suggesting that first-past-the-post has desirable effects.

3. Identify the evidence suggesting that smaller parties are making progress in the British political system.

The effects of FPTP, 1979–2010								
Year	Winning party	% of vote	No. of seats won	% of seats won	Third party	% of vote	No. of seats won	% of seats won
1979	Cons.	43.9	339	53.4	Liberal	13.8	11	1.7
1983	Cons.	42.4	397	61.1	Alliance	25.4	23	3.5

The effects of FPTP, 1979–2010 (continued)								
Year	Winning party	% of vote	No. of seats won	% of seats won	Third party	% of vote	No. of seats won	% of seats won
1987	Cons.	42.3	376	57.8	Alliance	22.6	22	3.4
1992	Cons.	41.9	336	51.6	Lib Dem	17.8	20	3.1
1997	Lab.	43.3	418	63.4	Lib Dem	16.7	46	7.0
2001	Lab.	40.7	412	62.5	Lib Dem	18.3	52	7.9
2005	Lab.	35.2	356	55.1	Lib Dem	22.0	62	9.6
2010	Cons (minority)	36.1	307	47.2	Lib Dem	23.0	57	8.8

Source: Chapter 1.2 of this book

The general election of 6 May 2010				
Party	Seats won	No. votes (millions)	% votes	% seats
Conservative	307	10.73	36.1	47.5
Labour	258	8.61	29.0	39.7
Lib Dem.	57	6.84	23.0	8.8
Green	1	0.29	1.0	0.2
Scots. Nats	6	0.49	1.7	0.9
Plaid Cymru	3	0.17	0.6	0.5
DUP	8	0.17	0.6	1.2
Sinn Fein	5	0.17	0.6	0.8
SDLP	3	0.11	0.4	0.5

The general election of 6 May 2010 (continued)				
Party	Seats won	No. votes (millions)	% votes	% seats
Alliance	1	0.04	0.1	0.2
Others	1	1.93	6.9	0.2
Total	**650**	**25.69**		

The consequences of reform

As we have said, the consequences of changing the UK's electoral system from FPTP to one of the alternatives are uncertain. We can only speculate as to what would happen, using such evidence as we can find from experience elsewhere. The result of reform also depends upon which electoral system might be adopted.

Under AMS

If we begin by considering the additional member system, it may be instructive to look at what has happened in recent times in Germany and Scotland, both of which use a form of additional member system (AMS).

AMS in Germany operates so that half the parliamentary seats are based on a FPTP constituency system, as in the UK, but the other half of the seats available is based on a regional list system where seats are awarded in proportion to the votes cast for each party. For many years after 1969 this system produced a parliament where no single party had an overall majority, but where one of the two main parties – the right-of-centre Christian Democrats or the left-of-centre Social Democrats – was always able to form a government in coalition with a smaller party. These coalitions, either with the Greens

or the liberal Free Democrat Party, were remarkably stable and usually lasted for the four-year term of parliament. But in 2005 all this certainty suddenly collapsed. In that year the election produced a totally inconclusive result, as shown below.

Party	% of the vote	Seats won
Christian Democrats	35.2	226
Social Democrats	34.3	222
Free Democrats	9.8	61
Left Socialists	8.7	54
Greens	8.1	51

We can see that neither of the large parties enjoyed an overall majority and, more importantly, neither could form a majority coalition with only one of the small parties. The result was virtually a dead heat. Furthermore, it was not clear which of the two main parties should provide the chancellor (prime minister). The political deadlock that resulted created major problems for a country that desperately needed strong leadership to deal with its serious economic problems at the time. Ultimately a grand coalition – of the two major parties – was formed, but it proved to be an uneasy alliance. The CDU leader, Angela Merkel, became Germany's first female chancellor, but she led a Social Democrat-dominated government.

By a strange coincidence, the largest party (by a whisker), the Christian Democrats, secured exactly the same proportion of the total vote – 35.2 – as Labour had done in the UK. But Labour came home with a 66-seat majority in Britain. This demonstrates very clearly how different the result can be under FPTP. It also suggests that a move to AMS in the UK might create the same problems experienced by Germany.

Turning to the elections to the Scottish Parliament in 2007 (see the table top right), where a slightly modified form of AMS is used, we see a similar outcome – again virtually a dead heat. In this case all attempts to form a coalition failed and so the Scottish National Party – the largest party by a whisker – formed a minority government. Without an overall majority in the Parliament the SNP must rely on forming a temporary coalition of support for each individual issue.

If we then apply the effects of AMS in Scotland to the UK general election result in 2010, we find the predicted outcome shown in the table opposite.

The estimated result (and it is only an estimate) would see the Conservatives as still the largest party in the UK, but well short of an overall majority. However, the UK would certainly develop a genuine three-party system, with the Liberal Democrats holding the balance of power.

In Scotland in 2007, where the Scottish Nationalists also enjoyed a strong showing, there was clearly a four-party system.

Result of the election to the Scottish Parliament, 2007	
Party	Seats won
Labour	46
Scottish Nationalist	47
Conservative	17
Liberal Democrat	16
Greens	2
Others	1

Party	% of vote	Estimated seats*
Conservative	36.1	299
Labour	29.0	204
Liberal Democrat	23.0	114
Others	11.9	33

* This predicted outcome was calculated by the author by applying the same statistical method of converting votes into seats used in the Scottish election of 2007 to the UK general election of 2010.

The devolved Welsh Assembly uses the same electoral system as Scotland. In the 2007 election to that Assembly, Labour won 32.2 per cent of the vote and 44 per cent of the seats. In the 2005 general election, under FPTP, Labour's 42.7 per cent of the vote in Wales secured the party 29 of the 40 seats available. Meanwhile, the Tories won 11 of the 60 seats in 2007, having won no seats at all in the 2005 General Election. As in Scotland, AMS produces a four-party system in the Welsh Assembly, whereas in a general election the results are totally dominated by one party – Labour.

Under proportional list

The result of a proportional list system is easier to predict. This can be estimated by taking the proportion of the total vote won in 2010 by the three main parties and awarding seats to each in the same proportion as follows:

Party	% of vote won	Seats won (predicted)
Conservative	36.1	233
Labour	29.0	187
Liberal Democrat	23.0	149
Others	11.9	77

Under these circumstances, the UK would undoubtedly be a three-party system. The only feasible structure of government would be a coalition between one of the major parties and the Liberal Democrats.

Under STV

The outcome of the single transferable vote system in the UK cannot be estimated with any certainty. However, we can say that a number of consequences would be discernible:

● The Liberal Democrats would do well from STV and win a substantial proportion of the seats.

● Smaller parties such as the Greens and UKIP would be able to win a significant, though not very large, number of seats.

● The nationalist parties in Scotland and Wales would gain considerable ground.

● Independents and representatives of very small parties would win a handful of seats.

Coalition governments would also be inevitable under STV. But the nature of Parliament might also change as a large number of MPs from very small parties would probably gain seats. This would perhaps persuade more voters to support them in the future (as votes for them would no longer be wasted). As a result, some of the small parties might gain a good deal of ground.

In the Northern Ireland Assembly election of 2007, STV certainly produced a multi-party result. This was as follows:

Northern Ireland Assembly election, 2007	
Party	Seats won
Democratic Unionists	36
Ulster Unionists	18
Sinn Fein	28
Social Democratic Labour Party	16
Alliance	7
Others	3

We can use the Northern Ireland outcome as something of a guide to the possible result of using STV in UK general elections. We do need to be wary, however. Northern Ireland is a fragmented society, so a multi-party result is appropriate. The UK as a whole is certainly more homogeneous, so fewer parties are likely to flourish.

Under the Alternative Vote (AV)

This system gives voters a second choice. It might very well be, therefore, that the Liberal Democrats would gain considerably. Many voters see the Liberal Democrats as their second choice so there could be wins for the party in seats where neither Labour nor Conservative candidates are able to dominate. The smaller parties would probably not win many, if any, seats. The system would possibly be to the Conservatives' disadvantage as the party is not often the second choice of either Labour or Liberal Democrat voters.

So AV would probably create a genuinely three-party system and would offer the chance for the Liberal Democrats to become as significant as the two traditional main parties.

Some overseas clues

If we look at the results of elections among the 15 members of the European Union (before the 2004 enlargement), we can also find some indications of the relationship between electoral systems and party systems in Europe.

Electoral systems and party systems in Europe		
Country	**Electoral system**	**Form of government**
Belgium	PR List	Multi-party coalition (2007)
Austria	PR List	Two-party coalition (2008)
Luxembourg	PR List	Two-party coalition (2009)
Finland	PR List	Two-party coalition (2007)
Netherlands	PR List	Three-party coalition (2006)
Greece	PR List	Single-party minority (2009)
Portugal	PR List	Single-party minority (2009)
Spain	PR List	Single-party minority (2008)
Sweden	PR List	Multi-party coalition (2006)
Denmark	PR List	Single-party minority (2007)
Germany	AMS	Two-party coalition (2009)
Italy	AMS	Multi-party coalition (2006)
Ireland	STV	Two-party coalition (2007)

Electoral systems and party systems in Europe (continued)		
Country	**Electoral system**	**Form of government**
France	Second ballot	Single-party govt. (2007)
UK	FPTP	Single-party majority (2005)

Source: Electoral Reform Society

It can be seen immediately that PR list systems are the most popular and that this system normally produces coalition governments. The main alternatives are minority administrations, though in two countries the list system has produced single-party majorities in Greece and Portugal (though both have since fallen). Whatever system is used, however, coalitions are the most common type of party system. The UK, meanwhile, looks like the odd one out with its unusual electoral system and its clear, single-party majority government.

Key Word

Electoral reform A process whereby the electoral system is changed or where there is campaign for such change.

The forces of reform

The movement for **electoral reform** consists of a number of groups. The Liberal Democrat Party (and its predecessor, the Liberal Party) has supported electoral reform for many decades. Of course, cynics claim that they support reform because it is in their own interests. This is true, but Liberal Democrats argue that their case is based on democratic principles and is held in the interests of good government for the UK.

There is also a substantial group within the Labour Party that supports reform. This movement has declined in influence since Labour's three successive victories in 1997, 2001 and 2005, but it remains significant. Small parties such as the Scottish Nationalists, Plaid Cymru and the Greens also support change, partly because they are discriminated against and partly because they feel Britain is not democratic enough with its current system in operation. There is little support for reform within the Conservative Party, but after 2005 there were signs that support for change might be growing, albeit in a modest way.

Two significant pressure groups campaign for reform. The Electoral Reform Society is the prime example, especially as it is concerned with this one issue alone. The Society publicises the faults in the current system and the benefits of alternatives. It campaigns both among the public and within Parliament itself. Unlock Democracy is concerned with democratic reform in general, but places electoral reform near the centre of its campaign for constitutional reform.

The election campaign in the spring of 2010 changed the whole picture, however. The Liberal Democrats still favoured STV but suggested the introduction of the less radical AV system might be a compromise position. Labour recognised that support for electoral reform might be a vote winner and so adopted either AV or AV+ as an election commitment. Most dramatically, however, the Conservatives offered a referendum on whether to adopt the AV system. This was an election policy that turned into a commitment when the Liberal Democrats nominated it as part of the price for the coalition agreement. Of course, the Conservatives believed they could secure a 'no' vote in the referendum, but had to concede that reform is a possibility. A referendum on the issue is due to be held in May 2011.

The positive arguments for reform

Having considered the main problems of FPTP that have been identified by its opponents, we can look at some positive benefits that reformers believe would come about if the system were changed. On the whole the benefits described below would occur *whichever* alternative system was adopted. These include the following:

● Voters would be given more choices. This may be an increase from one to two, as with the alternative vote, second ballot or additional member systems, but it could also be extremely wide, as with STV.

● The value of votes would be largely equalised. This would be especially true if a proportional list system were adopted.

● If STV or an open list system were adopted, voters would also have the opportunity to choose between candidates *of the same party*.

● Any alternative system would produce a result that was more accurately representative of the political views of the electorate. A proportional list system would be the most accurate, but it is argued that any change from FPTP would be more representative.

● It is argued that the current system places too much power into the hands of a single party that does not enjoy majority support.

This is seen as undemocratic at best and dangerous at worst. Electoral reform would almost certainly result in *no* party winning an overall majority in Parliament on its own. This would force the big parties to compromise and probably enter into coalitions with other parties. Such circumstances would prevent the accumulation of too much power in too few hands. Furthermore, if the winning party were no longer guaranteed a majority in the Commons, MPs themselves would gain influence and so make government more accountable.

● A 'fairer' electoral system may restore some respect for the political system and so reduce disengagement and encourage higher levels of voting and political participation in general.

● The political system would become more dynamic, with smaller and newer parties having more opportunity to establish themselves.

● Every other country in the European Union uses a different electoral system, either proportional, mixed or majority. Britain is therefore out of step with most of the rest of the democratic world. Of course, many argue that this is irrelevant and that special circumstances such as the two party system prevail here, but the reformers suggest that other European countries do have a superior democratic record to Britain's.

● Many argue that the experience of the use of PR in Scotland, Wales and Northern Ireland has been a good one, producing more open, representative forms of political systems.

The arguments against reform

Though electoral reform is a popular issue among the general public, there is probably a minority of support for it within the political community itself. The Conservative Party has staunchly resisted change – not surprisingly as the party is generally suspicious of change where the constitution is concerned. The Labour leadership is largely (though not unanimously) opposed. This is also not surprising, given the fact that, since the mid-1990s, FPTP has favoured Labour heavily. The rest of the Labour party is divided on the issue and even those who favour reform have been mostly silent in recent times.

Labour was elected in 1997 with a mandate to hold a referendum on the issue. After 18 years of uninterrupted rule by the Conservatives it was to be expected that the electoral system would be partly blamed. In the event, the startlingly decisive victory for the party in 1997 changed the situation drastically. The leadership lost interest and stalled on the issue. Eventually apathy in Labour ranks turned into opposition to reform. Now that it was clear that the old system could produce governments from either party, there was less impetus for change. Furthermore, the prospect of either party being forced into coalition with the Liberal Democrats under a proportional system concentrated the minds of the party leaders on opposition to reform.

A number of arguments have been deployed against reform. These have included:

- The FPTP system had successfully delivered decisive, single-party government with comfortable working majorities in the House of Commons for over 60 years. Whatever the arguments in favour of reform, this simple fact could not be denied. The classic conservative argument, therefore, is that we should beware of exchanging what we *know* for the *unknown* consequences of a different electoral system. Of course, this argument was severely weakened when the May 2010 election failed to produce a decisive result.

- The current system also delivered government with a clear mandate to govern, based on its election manifesto. If reform meant that coalition governments became more common or even inevitable, the difficulties in creating a working coalition would be reproduced every four or five years. The predictable outcome of reform, as we have seen above, is likely to be that no party would win an overall majority in the House of Commons. This would result in either minority or coalition governments. Coalitions, it is often claimed, are inherently unstable. Critics point to the experience of Italy and Belgium, for example (where governments come and go frequently), to demonstrate how difficult it can be to establish permanent governments under **proportional representation**. The experience of coalition government in the UK from 2010 onwards may, in the event, prove to be decisive.

- A fourth argument against is more subtle. This suggests that the UK is naturally a two-party system. The conflict between government and opposition, between the two traditional parties, is part of the political culture. The people are used to it and it gives them a sense of security and stability. The FPTP system underpins the two-party system and so maintains the political traditions of the country. This, say many conservative thinkers, is worth preserving. By contrast, reform threatens this firmly established tradition.

- The use of PR in Scotland, Wales and Northern Ireland, though welcomed by many, has also been criticised for producing coalitions or minority governments which lack decisiveness.

Discussion topic

Should the UK now adopt an alternative electoral system in general elections? Which system would be best suited to Britain?

The future of electoral reform

The remarkable outcome of the May 2010 general election has placed electoral reform firmly on the agenda and the arguments will come to a head in 2011, when a referendum is held on whether to adopt the AV system for general elections. A 'yes' vote is likely to settle the matter for some time to come. A 'no' vote may also end the debate, though some are likely to question whether the people might prefer proportional representation.

Key concepts in this chapter

Electoral manifesto A statement produced by a political party at election times, stating what policies it intends to implement if it gains power.

Electoral mandate Refers to the authority to govern granted to the winning party at an election by the voters. The mandate suggests that the government may implement the measures in its election manifesto. It also implies that the government has authority to use its judgement in dealing with unforeseen circumstances (the 'doctor's mandate').

Electoral system A system that converts votes in an election into seats. It may also refer to the process of electing a single leader such as a president or a mayor.

Proportional representation Describes any electoral system that converts votes into seats in a broadly proportional way.

Party system Refers to the typical structure of parties within a political system. It describes the normal number of parties that compete effectively. Thus we may speak of two-, three- or multi-party systems. It also refers to the typical party make-up of governments – for example, single-party government or coalitions and so on.

Plurality A description of an electoral system that awards a position or a seat in the legislature to a candidate who has achieved more votes than any other, even if this does not represent an absolute – 50 per cent plus – majority. The British FPTP system that operates in general elections is an example of plurality at work.

Electoral reform A process whereby the electoral system is changed or where there is a campaign for such change.

Coalitions Governments that are formed using representatives from two or more parties. Coalitions are normally necessary when no single party wins an overall majority in the legislature and can therefore not govern alone. Sometimes coalitions are formed in emergency situations, such as war, because of a need to include a wide variety of political representatives in the government and so unite the country.

Revision topics and examination questions

Revision topics

- The functions of elections
- Meaning of the term 'proportional representation'
- How first-past-the-post works
- How STV, AMS and regional list systems work
- The effects of FPTP
- The effects of the use of other electoral systems in the UK
- The nature of mandate and manifesto

Short answers (approximately 120 words)

- Outline the first-past-the-post electoral system.
- What is meant by 'proportional representation'?
- What is meant by the term 'electoral mandate'?
- Outline the main functions of elections.
- Explain the Alternative Vote (AV) system.
- Explain the Single Transferable Vote (STV) system.
- Explain the additional member system (AMS).
- Outline any TWO electoral systems, other than FPTP, used in the UK.

Medium answers (approximately 250 words)

- What are the main effects of the use of FPTP in UK general elections?
- Describe the operation of any THREE electoral systems used in the UK.
- Describe the operation of STV and AMS in the UK.
- What is the significance of the doctrine of mandate and manifesto?
- Does Britain still have a two-party system?

Long answers (approximately 800 words)

- Describe the effects of the use of proportional electoral systems in the UK.
- Distinguish between the effects of FPTP and other electoral systems used in the UK.
- To what extent do elections in the UK produce representative government?
- How effective are elections in the UK?

Resources and web guide

Books

A detailed analysis of the 2010 general election can be found in:
D. Kavanagh and P. Colles, *The British General Election of 2010,* Palgrave, 2010.

For an analysis of the electoral system in general, look at:
R. Blackburn, *The Electoral System in Britain,* Macmillan, 1995.

For a discussion of electoral reform as an issue there is:
M. Drummet, *Principles of Electoral Reform,* Oxford University Press, 1997.

Reform is also fully discussed in the 1998 Jenkins Commission Report:
Report on the Independent Commission on the Voting System, 1998, HMSO, Cmnd 4090.

For consideration of elections and electoral systems, look at:
N. Smith, *Elections and Electoral Reform*, Phillip Allan, 2006.

Useful websites

Issues concerning elections, parties and results can be found on the website of the electoral commission:
www.electoralcommission.gov.uk.

The Constitution Unit at University College, London discusses the issues on:
www.ucl.ac.uk/constitution-unit.ac.uk

There is a full, though one-sided, discussion on the website of the electoral reform society:
www.electoral-reform.org.uk

Another campaign group is Make Votes Count:
www.makevotescount.org.uk

Pressure groups

The nature and functions of pressure groups

The most informative beginning to this section would be to consult two leading authorities on pressure groups, which offer useful definitions:

'[A **pressure group** is] an organisation which seeks to influence the details of a comparatively small range of public policies and which is not a faction of a recognised political party.' (Robert Baggott)

'[A pressure group is] an organisation which seeks as one of its functions to influence the formulation and implementation of public policy, public policy representing a set of authoritative decisions taken by the executive, the legislature and the judiciary, and by local government and the European Union.' (Wyn Grant)

(Both quoted in R. Baggott, *Pressure Groups: A Question of Interest*, Manchester University Press, 1994)

 Key Word

Pressure group An association that may be formal or informal, whose purpose is to further the interests of a specific section of society or to promote a particular cause by influencing government, the public or both.

We now need to examine these definitions in a little more detail.

1. The most important feature is that pressure groups are trying to *influence* decisions. They do not expect to make the decisions themselves.

2. As Grant points out, they may seek to influence not just the decisions themselves but also the details of those decisions and even their implementation. A good example of this occurred in the period 2003–04. Parliament was debating the issue of hunting with dogs, especially fox hunting. At first the pro-hunt lobby – mainly the Countryside Alliance pressure group – opposed any kind of ban. When this was clearly going to fail, they sought to influence the *details* of the legislation. Perhaps hunting could be allowed, for example, if it was to be strictly regulated to prevent cruelty. When that failed and the full ban was enacted, they turned their attention to ways in which they could thwart the police's attempts to enforce the ban. So the Alliance had operated at every stage of the decision-making process, including implementation.

3. Baggott's quote suggests that pressure groups operate on a relatively *narrow* range of issues. Often this may be a single issue, such as that of Fathers4Justice, which emerged in 2003 and campaigns for better child-custody rights for

Actress Joanna Lumley with some of the Gurkhas she has supported

divorced and separated fathers. A more recent single-issue group was the Justice for Gurkhas campaign, which argued that Gurkhas (natives of Nepal who have traditionally fought in the British army) should have the right to settle in Britain after retirement. These issues have affected only a few thousand people and applied to very specific purposes. It may also be a whole cluster of related issues, for example the environment, where Greenpeace and Friends of the Earth operate.

4. Grant points out that pressure groups operate at different *levels* of government. They must first identify where key decisions are made and then apply their pressure in that location. This may be at the level of central ministers and civil servants, the Westminster Parliament, the Welsh, Scottish or Northern Ireland governments or local government. Issues that are resolved at the European Union level, such as agriculture, fisheries and trade, force pressure groups to work with the relevant institutions in Brussels, Strasbourg and the other centres of power. Grant also mentions the judiciary. Why would pressure groups be interested in legal cases? The answer is that there are some issues that may have to be resolved in the courts because the law is not clear or because there may be disputes about the meaning of law. In such cases pressure groups may promote legal cases themselves, or may seek to give evidence in court in support of their position.

Two examples of pressure group activity in the courts from recent times have been:

● **November 2009 in the Supreme Court.** Seven banks, backed by the British Bankers Association, successfully overturned a ruling that the Office of Fair Trading could investigate their system of charging customers for unauthorised overdrafts. This was an interesting example of pressure groups ranged against each other in the courts. The unsuccessful Office of Fair Trading was representing the interests of bank customers.

● **March 2010 in the High Court.** A coalition of environmental groups, including Greenpeace and the Campaign to Protect Rural England, successfully forced the government to conduct additional reviews into its decision to build a third runway at Heathrow airport, on the grounds that the plans conflicted with official carbon-emissions control targets.

5. The Countryside Alliance can be used as an example again. Having lost the battle against anti-hunting legislation in Parliament in 2004, the Alliance turned to the courts. First they tried to claim that the government had misused parliamentary procedures so the law was invalid. When this failed they returned to the High Court to protest that the anti-hunting ban conflicted with the European Convention on Human Rights. Again they failed, but the process indicates how widely some groups seek to cast their net of influence. Trade unions and consumer groups also use the courts when they feel their members' rights may not have been enforced satisfactorily. After the 2010 election the Alliance promised to go back to Parliament in an attempt to overturn the legislation again.

It must also be pointed out that many government policies take several years to develop. During that time they can be considered by a variety of committees, commissions and agencies. As they begin to take shape, ministers and civil servants become involved. Once the details are published, MPs, peers and the media will seek to add their contributions to the debate. And, of course, public opinion has to be considered. All this happens before any legislation appears at Westminster. Pressure groups need to be aware of these processes and become involved at every stage if they are to be successful.

Our description of what pressure groups seek to do, however, perhaps remains a little narrow. They also have a number of general functions that go well beyond simply influencing government decisions.

We have discussed the nature of representative democracy above. Most of that discussion revolved around political parties, but it is important to remember that pressure groups also have a representative function. Those that have a formal membership, such as the Automobile Association (AA) or any trade union, clearly wish to further their interests. But some pressure groups claim that they represent the best interests of the whole community, for example environmentalists, the anti-smoking lobby and the Campaign for Better Transport, which argues for an improved public transport system.

Like parties, pressure groups have a function of educating the public. They inform us about issues, offering both specific facts and competing points of views, which can help us to form our own opinions. Before the Countryside Alliance emerged in the late 1990s, few sections of the population were aware of the problems of those who live in rural areas. Similarly, Liberty and Unlock Democracy, which promote individual human rights, have alerted us to various examples of shortcomings in the British experience of rights. The passage of the Human Rights Act in 1998 was a crowning achievement for them.

The relationship between pressure groups and parties is explored in some depth below, but it should be pointed out at this stage that there has been some transfer of functions from parties to pressure groups. Members of the public who are not directly involved in politics may wish, nevertheless, to have more influence than merely by voting. Party membership may also demand an excessive degree of involvement. Pressure groups can provide opportunities for a less intensive form of political activity. Furthermore, such groups deal specifically with narrower issues. Parties require support across the whole spectrum of public policy. Most people do not think about politics in that way; they think more of individual issues and how they feel about them. So pressure groups today offer a more relevant and acceptable form of political participation than parties are able to.

The functions of pressure groups

We can now usefully summarise the various functions that pressure groups perform:

- They play a key part in the governing process. Their involvement at all stages of the policy- and decision-making process helps to inform government itself and ensures that the interests and views of sections of the public are taken into account. In this sense, they can improve the quality of policy making.

- They have a representative function. Either they represent specific sections of the public or they claim to represent the best interests of the whole community.

- Pressure groups help to educate and inform the public about politically important issues. (They also try to educate and inform governing institutions.)

- They provide a less intensive but more relevant opportunity for political participation than political parties do.

- Pressure groups often scrutinise legislative and policy proposals, suggesting how they may be improved or amended to make them fairer or more effective.

- One further general function can be added. We may call this 'tension release'. There are times when significant sections of society feel very strongly about a particular issue. If we are to remain a peaceful society it is vital that there is an outlet for such feelings that does not necessarily result in violence. From time to time, people need the opportunity to give full expression to their feelings, sometimes their outrage. Issues such as opposition to the 2003 Iraq war, to hunting with dogs and protests against expanding airports or excessive bonus payments to bankers all create extremely strong feelings. Relevant pressure groups were able to channel the emotions that were generated by these issues into limited forms of political action. (Some violence did occur, but it was limited and controlled.)

The distinctions between pressure groups and parties

Clearly there are a number of areas where the roles of parties and pressure groups overlap. Both types of organisation attempt to influence the policy-making process. In different ways they are also both representative bodies, claiming to be channels of communication between sections of the community and those who govern us. They also try to mould and to mobilise public opinion in order to promote the issues that concern them.

But there are also critical differences. The most important of these is that parties are seeking to achieve power, either as the governing party or as part of a governing coalition. Pressure groups do not seek governmental power. If they do, they must turn themselves into political parties. This begs the question: how does being a party rather than a pressure group affect the way in which members behave? There are two main answers to this question. First, a party must address the full range of political issues. If it were to become part of government it would have to address *all* government responsibilities. Second, parties must accept responsibility for all the policies that they propose. Governments must be accountable for what they do. Pressure groups do not face this problem. They will never be in power and will never have to account for their actions and beliefs. This truth affects their attitudes fundamentally. Two examples can illustrate this.

The environmental action group Greenpeace has waged a long campaign against trials of genetically modified (GM) food crops. They believe that such developments are dangerous and environmentally unsound. But there are also great potential benefits in GM foods, including long-term solutions to poverty in some developing countries. Greenpeace can safely oppose GM crops without having to be accountable for the fact that its opposition might condemn millions of people to starvation. Governments cannot abdicate such responsibility. They have to weigh up the benefits of GM foods against the possible problems. Similarly, Action on Smoking and Health (ASH) successfully campaigned for a smoking ban in public places, it did not have to be responsible for the loss in government revenue from the consequent reduction in smoking.

Some confusion may arise from the fact that some pressure groups offer candidates for election to Parliament, to the Scottish Parliament and other devolved assemblies or to local councils. They do this in order to create publicity for themselves. In the 2010 election, for example, single-issue parties such as Animals Count and the Senior Citizens Party offered the electorate a few alternative candidates. But does this make them into political parties? The answer must be no, because they are not seeking power, they merely want representation and publicity.

However, there is, it has to be noted, a history of pressure groups turning themselves into parties in this way. Most significantly, at the start of the twentieth century the trade union movement began to put up candidates for election. At first they were simply drawing attention to the fact that the working class was under-represented and had a wide range of grievances. But the trade unions had considerable success in having their candidates elected, so much so that they decided in 1906 to become a political party. Thus was created the Labour Party. Similarly, but with less impact, the British Ecology movement fought a number of elections in the 1980s and eventually decided to become a party – the Greens. More recently, the single-issue United Kingdom Independence Party (UKIP) was a pressure group in the 1990s, campaigning to bring the UK out of the European Union, but by 2005 it had become a fully fledged party, with policies on all issues.

We can now summarise the main distinctions between parties and pressure groups, together with the features that serve to blur the differences.

Parties	Pressure groups	Blurring
Seek governmental power.	Do not seek power.	Both may put up candidates for election. In addition, some pressure groups may be converting themselves into parties.
Adopt policies across full range of government responsibility.	Usually have a narrow range of issues.	Some pressure groups such as trade unions or business groups may develop a wide range of policies.
Have to be accountable for their policies.	Do not have to be accountable.	Should be accountable to their members.
Must behave in a responsible way.	Some pressure groups may act illegally or promote civil disobedience.	Some pressure groups work so closely with parties and government it is difficult to distinguish between their roles.

Classification of pressure groups

It is important to establish a classification of pressure groups because it can help us to explain their behaviour. It is normal to divide them into two types: sectional (or interest) groups and cause, issue or promotional groups.

- **Sectional** or **interest groups** are those that represent a specific section of society. They are self-interested and thus concerned only with promoting the best interests of their members. The best examples are trade unions, but there are many groups that represent other economic sections, such as the Institute of Directors (employers in general), the Taxpayers' Alliance, the National Farmers Union or the Engineering Employers' Federation. Medical groups are also prominent. They represent members who are suffering from specific diseases or conditions. The Multiple Sclerosis Society and the Heart Foundation are important examples. There are also sectional groups that represent various sports organisations, pensioners, children, students, industries and the like. Wherever there is an identifiable social section or organisation, it is very likely that it will be represented by a pressure group.

- **Cause, issue or promotional groups** do not have a specific section of the community to represent. They claim to be serving the interests of the whole community. They have one issue or a cluster of issues that they are seeking to promote. They often do not have a specific

 Key Word

Sectional group A pressure group that represents a specific section of society such as a trade union or an employer's association. Also known as an *interest group*.

 Key Word

Promotional group A pressure group that seeks to promote a cause rather than the interests of its own members. Also known as a *cause group* or an *issue group*.

membership, or, at most, only have a small group of activists. They are altruistic in that they consider that they serve us all, not their own members.

The most obvious examples are environmental groups such as *Greenpeace* and *Friends of the Earth*. Many other organisations that flourish in Britain are concerned with both specific environmental issues and the quality of life in general. The Royal Society for the Protection of Birds (RSPB) and the National Trust are typical. Some campaign for changes in the political system itself, such as the Electoral Reform Society and Liberty. These groups may also be temporary in nature, as the issue with which they are concerned may be short-lived. The Anti Poll Tax Federation was an example of this in 1989–90. Campaigning against the unpopular local poll tax, it succeeded in persuading the government to relent and abolish the tax. Naturally the group immediately ceased to exist. It may be that Fathers4Justice (described above) will experience the same fate.

- **Dual-function** groups may be both sectional and cause-based, so we should not be too inflexible in our classification. The Countryside Alliance, for example, represents people who live in rural areas, but also campaigns for a better quality of life in the countryside, which can benefit us all. Similarly, Transport 2000 believes that better public transport is an issue that affects us all, but it also represents existing users of such transport. It is, therefore, both cause and sectional in nature.

There are other types of dual-function pressure groups. These are groups that perform a specific service or set of services for their members as well as campaigning within the political system on their behalf. Trade unions are an obvious example, as is the AA or the RAC. Many charities such as Cancer Research and the National Society for the Prevention of Cruelty to Children (NSPCC) are also pressure groups. They are seeking funds and/or legislation from government to help those whom they serve. But they also offer a wide range of other care services and expend much effort in raising finance from the general public.

- It should not be forgotten that there are many thousands of *local* pressure groups operating within communities. Often they are environmental in nature, being concerned with local areas of natural beauty, parks, and problems arising from industry or agriculture. Local action groups are also often concerned with temporary issues such as the building of bypasses, threatened closure of hospitals and schools, erection of wind turbines, various planning issues and so on. Whenever a major change is proposed for a locality, you can be almost sure that groups will spring up to oppose, amend or support the initiative. Indeed, it is in this domain that the majority of political activity probably takes place. It is much more likely that citizens will become motivated to act locally than to become involved in national politics.

- Finally, there are some examples of organisations where it is not clear whether they are pressure groups at all. For instance, are terrorist groups, such as the IRA, pressure groups? Similarly, what about so-called 'think tanks' – agencies that obtain funds from a variety of sources to carry out research into policy issues and report their findings to governing bodies? The Adam Smith Institute, which researches issues concerning free markets, is an example of such a think tank. Arguably they

are pressure groups, but for our purposes they will not be considered as such.

Insiders and outsiders

Professor Wyn Grant (whose definition of pressure groups opens this chapter) introduced another classification of pressure groups. This divided them into **insider groups** and **outsider groups**.

Insiders

An insider pressure group is one that has succeeded in becoming a part of the decision-making process itself. They are 'inside' the process, not outside, hoping to influence it. Naturally we would expect that insiders have something of an advantage. They take part in the development of policy and so can hope to mould it to their own benefit. They may also be able to prevent unfavourable legislation at an early stage. Their activities can be understood better by identifying the ways in which they are considered to be insiders:

 Key Word

Insider groups Pressure groups that operate inside the political system through contacts with ministers, MPs, peers and official committees. They are regularly consulted by government.

- They may be consulted regularly by government bodies. This is because they can provide useful information and may also be able to express the views of their members. If policies are to secure support, it is important for government to understand the attitudes of those who will be affected. The Confederation of British Industry (CBI) is a typical example of such an insider. The CBI regularly produces reports on how businesses are operating and what are its attitudes towards such issues as business taxation, employment regulations, trade and economic policy in general. It also informs government about how business is performing with regard to such issues as investment, sales expectations, exports and production costs.

- Some pressure groups have permanent seats on government policy committees and agencies. These groups therefore find themselves at the centre of the decision-making process. The National Farmers Union (NFU) is a typical example. It is advantageous to government that all agricultural policy should be considered by representatives of the farming community at an early stage as they will have to conform to these policies.

- There are groups that have actually been set up by government itself and may be funded from taxpayers' money. Naturally these are insiders of a special kind. They are almost *part* of government, not just insiders. The Commission for Equality and Human Rights (CEHR), for example, was set up specifically to advise government on matters of rights, racial discrimination and equality of opportunity. The Office of Fair Trading is an example of an 'ultra insider' group.

- Select committees in both the House of Commons and the Lords investigate the work of government departments and produce reports of policy proposals. They have the power to call witnesses in the course of their proceedings. Insider pressure groups are often called to their meetings and so have a direct input into the process of making government fully accountable.

It should also be noted that some groups need to achieve insider status at local, regional and European levels.

European insider groups, typically trade unions and business employers' organisations, have been able to attach themselves to the various sections of the European Commission, which develops policy for the EU. They also operate extensively with the European Parliament, which is having an increasing impact on policy. Representation is notoriously weak in the European Union as members of its Parliament (MEPs) have huge constituencies and relatively modest influence as individuals or even as political groupings. By 2007 more than 2,000 such groups had been registered with the European Commission, a status that gives them official access to commissioners who develop new policy. Pressure groups – some of them joined up into Europe-wide organisations – therefore have a special role to play in the flow of information and influence.

We can see a similar phenomenon in the governments of Scotland, Northern Ireland and Wales, which have institutions akin to those to be found at central level. In local government there are some insider groups that operate with council committees, but more often they work with the permanent council officials who run local services.

Although insider status may appear to be an enormous advantage for those groups that enjoy it, there is a price to be paid. Insiders must, by implication, act in a responsible way. Government institutions cannot be seen to be closely associated with groups that are prepared to operate outside the parliamentary system and even engage in illegal activities. Insiders, therefore, are constrained in the kinds of methods they use. There is also a danger that they will lose their independence. If they begin to work too closely with government they may find that their position is compromised – in other words, they will begin to adopt the same policies as their political contacts. If this occurs their membership may well feel that they are ceasing to be genuinely representative. Organisations such as environmental groups and trade unions in particular must guard against this danger. For these reasons some groups prefer to remain as outsiders.

Outsiders

There may be two reasons why a pressure group is not an insider. One is that it prefers to remain outside the governing process in order to preserve its independence and its freedom of action. This is certainly true of Greenpeace, for instance. As an organisation it undertakes acts of civil disobedience such as destroying GM crops or disrupting international conferences. If it enjoyed insider status it would not have the option of doing this. The group certainly feels it can make more impact by remaining as outsiders.

The other reason is that the group would like to be insiders but has simply not been invited into the governing process. These have been described as **aspiring insiders**. No doubt the Association of British Drivers would like to find itself in the position of an insider. However, it is relatively young as an organisation and, throughout its existence, has been faced with an unsympathetic Labour government. Certainly the most important factor in outsider status is conflict

between the aims of government and the aims of the group. Trade unions, for example, having enjoyed a special status within the Labour Party since 1900, found themselves total outsiders after Margaret Thatcher came to power in 1979. She was opposed to trade union power in general and therefore had no intention of consulting with them regularly. Even after Labour took power in 1997 unions were unable to regain their insider status fully. Having attracted the support of business, Labour under Tony Blair decided to retain business pressure groups as insiders. This left unions still out in the cold.

New social movements

The 1980s saw the rise of a new kind of political action group that did not fit into any of the existing pressure group classifications. These have been described as **new social movements** or NSMs.

An NSM is a broadly based, fairly informal movement that emerges, sometimes very rapidly, around a particular issue. They are characterised by the organisation of mass demonstrations and media campaigns that are designed to create maximum publicity and to put political pressure upon decision makers. They have become possible largely because of the development of telecommunications such as the Internet and mobile-phone texting. Opinion can spread like a forest fire by means of such communications.

Perhaps the first modern example (mass movements in a very general sense are nothing new) of a new social movement was the Anti-Poll Tax Federation of the late 1980s. This arose out of widespread discontent about the replacement of domestic property rates with a flat-rate tax per head (poll tax) to finance local government services. This movement organised demonstrations, some of which led to considerable violence and damaged property, as well as a 'tax strike'. The tax strike involved hundreds of thousands of people

Key Word

Outsider groups Unlike insider groups, outsiders have no special links with government but seek to influence decision makers by mobilising public opinion.

who simply refused to pay the tax. It was highly successful and the poll tax was abolished in 1991.

In 2000 sharp rises in fuel prices led to the formation of the People's Fuel Lobby, an alliance of farmers, motorists, road hauliers and other interested parties. This group blockaded fuel depots and blocked main roads to publicise the issue. Though the government criticised its tactics, it did lead to a cancellation that year of a tax increase on petrol. In the same period, the Countryside Alliance was developing, campaigning on a variety of rural issues including the proposed ban on hunting with dogs. In the event, the Alliance formed itself into a permanent pressure group and now seeks insider status.

More recent examples have been the Anti Iraq War Coalition of 2002–04 and Make Poverty History (backed by Bob Geldof's Live Aid and Live 8 movements) in the early years of the new century, which campaigned for more aid for poor countries. Make Poverty History has now been absorbed into an even larger, global group, known as Global Call to Action Against Poverty. In a looser sense there is a recognised movement of anarchists, radical environmentalists and anti-globalisation campaigners that regularly appears at international conferences such as the G8 or the World Trade Organisation. This has become known as the Anti-Globalisation Movement. In 2007 a 'Climate Camp' was set up near Heathrow to raise awareness of the detrimental environmental effects of expanding the airport there. A similar movement was set up to inhibit the expansion of Stansted Airport in Essex.

A further new phenomenon arose in 2007 when Downing Street began to accept Internet petitions on a variety of issues. As we have seen above, the Association of British Drivers (a very small organisation at the time) was able to muster 1.8 million signatures, protesting against a road-pricing scheme. Here again it was technology that enabled a modest organisation to mount a rapid and effective campaign. The much larger

motorists' organisations – the AA and the RAC – could certainly not rival the impact of the BDA, despite their immense resources.

Such movements are also often locally based. Campaigns to save hospitals from closure or to prevent new roads being built, green-belt land being developed or footpaths being blocked tend to use similar methods to those employed by national groups.

Global movements, in such areas as environmental protection, human or animal rights, world poverty and fair trade, naturally concentrate their efforts on international conferences such as EU ministerial councils, G8 summits or World Trade Organisation meetings. But once again the methods are the same – publicity stunts, public demonstrations, disruptions and, occasionally, damage to property. The aims are also similar – raising awareness and mobilising mass support to put pressure on decision makers.

The main common characteristics of new social movements are as follows:

- They appear on the political scene very rapidly.

- They are mass movements with many thousands of instant followers.

- They are concerned with a narrow range of issues or one single issue.

- They are often temporary, especially when they achieve some success.

- Their methods are striking and flamboyant, sometimes including acts of civil disobedience.

- They have loose, informal organisations.

- Their followers tend to have an intense attachment to the issue(s) in question.

As we shall see below, insiders and outsiders tend to adopt very different methods. At this stage, however, we can say that an outsider group will always try to mobilise widespread public support as a means of influencing government. Insiders, by contrast, may welcome such support but prefer to work directly with decision makers and opinion formers.

We can now formalise our classification of pressure groups.

Pressure group classification

Type	Examples	Insider or outsider
Cause (promotional or issue)	Action on Smoking and Health (ASH)	Insider
	Greenpeace	Outsider
	Shelter (homelessness)	Insider
	Plane Stupid (anti airport expansion)	Outsider
Sectional	British Medical Association	Insider
	Fuel Forum (against high fuel prices for road users)	Outsider
	Confederation of British Industry (CBI)	Insider
	British Film Council	Insider
Mixed, both cause and sectional	Countryside Alliance	Outsider
	Forest (pro smoking rights)	Outsider

Pressure group classification (continued)

Type	Examples	Insider or outsider
New social movements	Campaign for Better Transport	Insider
	Anti-Poll Tax Federation	Outsider
	People's Fuel Lobby	Outsider
	Anti Globalisation Movement	Outsider

Student activities

Find examples of pressure groups that conform to the following criteria:

- **A group that used to be an insider but is now an outsider.**
- **An outsider group that seeks to be an insider.**
- **A group that is a cause group but is an insider.**
- **A group that is a sectional group but is an outsider.**
- **A group that has been apparently successful despite being small and having few resources.**

Pluralist democracy

Now that we have established the nature and main functions of pressure groups it is important to consider how they fit into modern political society. It is common to refer to the political culture in the UK as being one of **pluralism** in nature. This means that we expect a wide range of groups, interests, beliefs and ideologies to flourish together, all competing for attention and influence. The UK is fundamentally a free society, tolerant of different cultures, ideas and demands. As long as a group does not break the law, threaten the security of the state or incite others to commit crime or adopt racist ideas, it will be tolerated and protected from discrimination. Thus, pressure groups are able to operate in an extremely free and tolerant environment. In short, they are a key element in a pluralist society.

Key Word

Pluralism A description of a political system where a wide range of beliefs, ideologies and ideas is tolerated and allowed to flourish. It also implies a system where power is widely dispersed and not concentrated in a few hands

Britain also enjoys an extremely free and active civil society. The term *civil society* refers to the many types of groups that flourish and to which people owe some kind of allegiance or sense of attachment. Civil society includes individual families, but also larger sections of the community such as religions, political parties, the media, the Arts, sports organisations, associations, schools, universities and so on. A key part of civil society is taken up by pressure groups.

Until the 1970s politics in the UK was largely based upon social class and the two-party system. Most political issues were seen in terms of party conflict. They were also usually based upon class conflict. Political conflict was a reflection of class conflict. On the whole, policies supported by Conservatives were seen as middle-class based (whether or not they were actually aimed at middle-class interests). Conversely, Labour was considered to be the party of the working class. The political attitudes of the electorate tended to revolve around these certainties. But in the 1970s two processes began to take shape.

First, the class divisions in the UK were breaking down. Fewer and fewer people could be identified as members of one particular class. Much of the working class was becoming affluent, thus adopting formerly 'middle-class' lifestyles and attitudes. The middle class was dividing itself up into sub-groups – those who worked in the private sector and those who were part of the public sector, for example. There were increasing differences between those who were 'professionals' – doctors, teachers, lawyers and so on – and those who were employed in managerial positions. There was also a growing distinction between the self-employed and the employed. As such groups no longer identified with one great common class, they began to concern themselves with the narrower interests of their own smaller section of society. Thus so-called 'group politics' was coming into being.

Second, there was a process called 'partisan dealignment' taking place. This was a process whereby people identified less and less closely with the aims of political parties. Group politics, as described above, was taking hold. Parties were unable to represent satisfactorily the smaller sections of society that were now making political demands because they seek to develop policies that attract broad, not specialised support. The gap had to be filled and the growth in the number, membership and influence of pressure groups has gone a long way to filling that gap.

Discussion topic

Has government become too sensitive to pressure from pressure groups, especially from NSMs? Is it preferable for government to take the lead, doing what it believes is in the interests of the whole country, and ignore the demands of powerful groups in society?

Pressure groups and democracy

Here we ask, what is a healthy modern democracy and what part do pressure groups play in such a democracy? As a supplementary issue we can also ask whether there are any ways in which pressure groups may be seen to be *undemocratic.*

A generalised view of democracy suggests that it should enjoy the following features:

● It is a society where knowledge flows freely and people have wide access to sources of information independent of government. In other words, there is a well-informed citizenry.

● People will feel they are effectively represented in government circles. Furthermore, institutions should be politically and socially representative.

● Government itself is fully accountable to the people and to the people's representatives.

● There are free and extensive opportunities for people to participate actively in political processes. Participation can range from deep and intensive to shallow and sporadic, depending on a citizen's preferences.

● The rights and interests of individuals and groups are taken into account in decision-making processes.

● The full range of constitutional, democratic principles are in place, notably free and fair elections and the rule of law, including equal rights, an independent judiciary and defences against arbitrary government.

We can now ask what part pressure groups play in sustaining the features described above.

Democratic features of pressure groups

Education

It is clear that groups offer a considerable amount of information to the people. They are, by definition, independent of government (if they were not, we could not describe them as pressure groups), so we are receiving important messages from which we can make sound judgements. Of course, we cannot always rely upon the information being totally accurate, but if we combine all the various sources of information available to us we are able to form some kind of reasonable judgement. So pressure groups certainly help to inform and educate us.

Representation

Whether we take an active part or not, pressure groups represent our interests to those who govern. In virtually all our activities there is probably a group that is seeking to secure favourable legislation or decisions and to avoid unfavourable ones. As motorists, hospital patients, students, sportspeople, environmentalists, cyclists, walkers, bird-watchers, holidaymakers, workers and so on, we can be sure there is a group that is fighting our corner. In some cases we may be active members and so know exactly what issues are being addressed. In other cases we are not active but are nevertheless being passively represented. Even the smallest minorities are likely to enjoy such benefits. So pressure groups have important representative functions to perform.

Participation

A passive citizenry is often seen as a danger to democracy. When people do not involve themselves in political activity there is a strong probability that government will become dictatorial, safe in the knowledge that its power is unlikely to be challenged. Political activism is therefore important both to prevent excessive accumulations of power and to ensure that government remains accountable to the people. With declining levels of popular involvement in political parties, pressure groups have provided a vital opportunity for political participation.

Minority interests

But perhaps the most important democratic function of pressure groups is to ensure that all of us, in small or large groups, are taken account of, protected and awarded equal status. If this does not occur there is a danger that democracy simply becomes rule by the majority. The nineteenth-century Liberal philosopher John Stuart Mill referred to the dangers of the 'tyranny of the majority' in this context. Majority rule, he argued, is not true democracy. Seeking majority support, political parties will inevitably have to ignore the interests of many minorities. It is therefore necessary for pressure groups to exist in order to ensure that party rule is not converted into tyranny.

The dispersal of power (pluralism)

The conventional view of pressure groups is that they help to spread power more widely. This would be seen by most commentators as an enhancement of democracy. Governments and parties tend to *concentrate* power in the hands of leaderships. Pressure groups, meanwhile, can empower their wider memberships. They represent the full range of the population and allow many voices to be heard. As long as they have any influence, they give the politically active part of the population access to decision makers, either directly or indirectly. We see this particularly effectively when considering mass-membership groups such as Age UK or unions representing public service workers.

The picture is not completely rosy where pressure groups are concerned, however. There are a number of senses in which they may not fulfil democratic principles.

Some undemocratic features of pressure groups

Disproportionate influence

The question of whether some pressure groups do not conform to democratic principles revolves around the nature of influence. If all groups enjoyed the amount of influence that their size and importance warranted, the outcome might be considered democratic. But this perfect state of affairs does not exist. Some groups wield more power than their relative importance might suggest.

Some sectional groups, for example, hold a particularly strategic position in society; that is, we rely on them a great deal and therefore have to take their demands into account. The farming community, for instance, accounts for a tiny proportion of the total population, but farmers are responsible for much of our food supply and create much of the countryside that many of us enjoy. Similarly, transport, emergency and medical workers may have more power than groups that are employed in the private sector. Possibly the most important example in recent times has been the finance lobby. After the credit crunch of 2007–08, the economic recession that followed and the public fury over the size of top bankers' pay, the banking sector came under huge pressure. Yet it was pointed out that the finance sector accounted for a vital part of the British economy, London's in particular. This may have inhibited the Labour government, preventing it from proposing serious controls on the behaviour of the big banks in case they relocated abroad seeking more sympathetic treatment.

Finance

Related to their position in society is the issue of wealth. Clearly some groups have access to considerably more funds than others. All those sectional interests that represent employers and business in general inevitably have far more

Edexcel Government and Politics for AS

finance available to them than charities, which have to rely on handouts from the public or scarce lottery funding. The banking community, referred to above, is a similar example. In particular, wealthy groups, including individual companies, have adopted the practice of giving donations to political parties. Clearly they are hoping for a sympathetic attitude if their chosen party wins power. Perhaps more seriously, in 2006–07 it was alleged that a number of individuals had donated to political parties in return for the granting of peerages. The so-called 'cash for peerages' scandal did much to undermine faith in British democracy and further highlighted the issue of undue influence by those who command great wealth.

Size

Finance undoubtedly can distort the democratic process. So, too, can sheer weight of numbers. When the Countryside Alliance put an estimated 300,000 sympathisers on the streets in 2003 to protest about the ban on hunting with dogs and other rural issues, the government was panicked into action on a number of fronts, including an attempt to water down the hunting bill in Parliament. But the huge numbers involved in the demonstration certainly did not reflect public opinion on the main issue of fox hunting – this was firmly in favour of a full ban. More compelling, perhaps, is the powerful motoring lobby, which campaigns against taxation on fuel, increasing curbs on parking and the possibility of road pricing. No doubt it represents a large proportion of the population, but it does not necessarily reflect the views of most motorists, perhaps only the more vociferous ones.

The concentration of power (elitism)

We saw above that the conventional view of pressure groups is that they disperse power effectively, thus improving the state of democracy. However, when we look at the wealthy, strategically important groups we can see evidence of elitism. Some pressure groups may, in fact, concentrate power

Pressure groups and democracy	
Democratic features	**Undemocratic features**
• Educating and informing the public about important political issues. • A channel of representation between the people and the government, keeping government in touch with public opinion. • Providing opportunities for political participation. • Protecting the interests of groups and opinions. • Acting as a safeguard against the power of the state. • Dispersing power more widely.	• Some groups wield more influence than their place in society warrants. • Some groups have influence simply because they have large financial resources available to them. This may be to the detriment of poorer groups that might have a stronger case. • Insiders have influence at the expense of outsiders. • Some groups' leaderships may not represent accurately the views of their members, i.e. they are undemocratic internally. • Pressure groups cannot be made democratically accountable for what they do and propose. • Wealthy, influential groups may give influence to elites rather than their wider memberships.

in the hands of a few. The banking lobby can be seen as a prominent example, as can the various producer groups representing major industries. Producer groups, in particular, tend to represent their shareholders and management rather than their workers (a view that might be contested on the grounds that what is good for the industry is also good for its employees). When such elites are 'insider' groups, they might form a powerful elite in combination with government. Ministers who are more influenced by group leaderships than by wider memberships could be accused of further elitism.

Internal democracy

Finally, we must accept that some pressure group leaders may not truly represent the views of their members. In other words, groups may not be internally democratic. This used to be a charge levelled at trade union leaders (less so since democratic reforms were introduced to unions in the 1980s) and it remains a danger. Party politicians are made accountable for their actions through the electoral process and through representative institutions. This may not be the case with pressure group leaders. Though such a problem may not be widespread, it is certainly true that democratic controls on pressure groups are weaker than those affecting parties and politicians.

Discussion topic

Is it particularly important that parties are in decline and that pressure groups are replacing them? Which are more 'democratic' – parties or pressure groups?

Methods of pressure groups

Lobbying

The way in which insider pressure groups operate has been described above. Much of what they do is hidden behind closed doors and receives little publicity. Britain, though, is a consultative democracy and so we should expect discussions with pressure groups to be going on all the time. For insiders this is a constant process. Committees and commissions, including group representatives, meet to develop policy; ministers consult with interested groups to ensure consent to their policies; MPs and peers use pressure groups as a source of information or to help in their task of scrutinising legislation and investigating the work of government departments. Outsiders may attempt to lobby policy makers directly, but tend to have less access than insiders.

Parliamentary methods

Although Parliament has been increasingly marginalised in modern times, pressure groups recognise that Westminster remains fertile ground for their causes. Some groups, indeed, pay retaining fees to MPs in return for which they will raise relevant issues as much as possible in the House (it should be pointed out that it is unlawful to attempt to persuade an MP actually to vote in a certain way or to ask a parliamentary question in return for money). All the large pressure groups have a number of MPs who are committed to representing them in Parliament, either for financial return or simply because the MP is a sympathiser. Of course, the party whips usually have the final say, but where MPs have the opportunity to act independently, they often engage in group politics rather than party politics.

The House of Lords has become more significant since it was reformed and there has certainly been a corresponding growth in interest from pressure groups. The Lords is mainly an amending chamber and it is in this field that interested pressure groups seek to gain some leverage. On issues such as university tuition fees, the foxhunting ban, the protection of human rights and the extension of pub licensing hours, the Lords has been successful in securing amendments in recent times. In such examples, campaigning peers have been backed by the relevant pressure groups. Peers are more independent of party control than are MPs in the Commons, so pressure groups are more likely to find a sympathetic ear there than in the Commons.

An ideal example of this occurred in March 2010 over the Equality Bill (later Act). The bill was intended to prevent discrimination against groups such as women, the disabled, members of ethnic minorities and gay people, notably in employment practices. A coalition of Christian churches sought an exemption on the grounds that they were a 'special case' who have a particular reason to exclude gay people. Their amendment to the bill was successful and the government conceded the point.

Outsider pressure groups rarely use such methods and are therefore described as 'extra-parliamentary' in nature.

Direct action

At the other end of the spectrum to such private consultations lies direct action. This occurs when pressure groups seek to obtain the maximum amount of publicity for the cause as possible. The mass demonstration is the most common example. In recent years there have been impressive demonstrations of mass support over such issues as the 2003 Iraq war, the grievances of the Countryside Alliance and opposition to the expansion of Heathrow and Stansted Airports. During international conferences, the anti-globalisation campaign has been able to mobilise huge demonstrations from all over the world.

Direct action can also involve 'stunts' and provocative action to draw attention to an issue. These may be both legal or illegal. Most famously, members of Fathers4Justice have dressed up as 'super-heroes' and placed themselves in positions, such as at Buckingham Palace, where they will attract media attention. Peter Tatchell, the gay rights campaigner, has made something of an art of the 'political stunt' (calling it 'protest as performance'). The anti-fuel tax lobby group has blockaded fuel depots in order to publicise its case for lower petrol taxes. Similarly, Greenpeace destroys GM crops and the Animal Liberation Front lives up to its name by freeing animals from experimentation laboratories or by threatening laboratory workers.

There is no doubt that such direct forms of action have been increasing in recent years. The reason is, quite simply, that it often works. Governments are forced to respond to powerful demonstrations of feeling, especially when the media take up the same cause. Furthermore, technological advances such as the Internet and mobile phones have made such direct action more feasible. Campaigns can be mounted at short notice and large numbers of people can be mobilised simply because communications systems have improved so much.

Mobilising public opinion

As public attachment to political parties has weakened in modern times, so governments have become increasingly sensitive to the shifting sands of public opinion. If a party wishes to retain or regain power it can no longer rely upon a large and permanent bedrock of support. Instead it must try to ensure that it promotes issues that will win it votes at elections. This reality gives pressure groups a great deal of political leverage. If they can demonstrate to political leaders that the issue or issues they support command widespread interest among the people and so deliver many votes, those leaders are forced to listen.

Plane Stupid has successfully compaigned against airport expansion

In the 2005 election campaign, for instance, there is no doubt that the old-age pensioner vote was a critical factor. The elderly vote in much larger numbers than the young. For this reason politicians are forced to woo the so-called 'grey vote'. The main pressure group that represents the elderly – *Age UK* – knew that they were in a position to influence policy in the run-up to the election. Thus they pushed hard on issues such as the size of the pension, rebates on council tax for the elderly, and law and order measures (older people display a greater fear of crime than the rest of the population). By demonstrating that this particular group of voters was interested in these demands, they were able to force concessions from aspiring party leaders. In the 2010 election, such groups as the Taxpayers' Alliance and large business groupings saw the campaign as an opportunity to further their causes and interests.

Similarly, some smaller groups have attempted to publicise their concerns forcefully enough to bring public opinion round to their cause. The anti-air travel group Plane Stupid has been highly successful in publicising the environmental dangers of increasing air transport. The media play a key role in such mobilisation of opinion. Thus many groups employ professional public relations operators whose role it is to ensure good press or TV coverage for a particular campaign. Sometimes, too, the press take it upon themselves to mount their own campaigns in fields such as law and order and opposition to closer European integration.

Why some groups are more successful than others

It is worth asking first: what do we mean by 'success'? Clearly a pressure group can be considered successful if it achieves the passage of particular legislation for which it has been campaigning. This has certainly been the case for ASH, which successfully campaigned for a ban on tobacco advertising and on smoking in public places. But groups sometimes seek to *prevent* unfriendly legislation. Business groups such as the Institute of Directors helped to persuade the British government to negotiate an opt-out from the European Union 'Working Time Directive', which limited the working week to 48 hours. In 2007, anti-gambling groups secured a vote in the House of Lords that forced the Government to rethink its plans to approve the opening of a 'super-casino' in Manchester. As we have seen above, too, religious groups secured concessions on the Equality Act of 2010.

However, pressure group success should not be measured merely in terms of legislation. In some cases such groups simply wish to raise the profile of an issue, to place it on the political agenda where it has, in the past, been ignored. In recent years, such issues as rural problems, child abuse, mental health, infertility treatment, euthanasia and abortion have all risen up the political agenda as a result of pressure group activity.

So, success can come in a number of ways. But why are some groups more successful than others?

Philosophy

Where a group's beliefs and aspirations are close to those of the government of the day, success is very likely. Business groups have certainly done well under the Conservatives and achieved success under New Labour after 1997. Trade unions used to be highly favoured by Labour, but have now lost their strategic position. Meanwhile, the anti-poverty policies pursued by Gordon Brown under Labour put pensioner and lone-parent groups in a good position. After 1997 Labour also placed great emphasis on improving the quality of public services, so that teacher and medical associations have been influential. By contrast, rights campaigners, such as Liberty and Unlock Democracy, have discovered resistance to their demands from recent governments, which have sought to introduce a more authoritarian stance on law and order and asylum seeking. In 2010 some business groups tied themselves to the fortunes of the Conservative Party in the hope of securing a more favourable tax regime. Public-sector trade unions, meanwhile, remained more committed to a Labour victory in the hope that the party would protect public services.

Finance

Being wealthy is no guarantee of a group's success, as the tobacco lobby has discovered over smoking curbs, but it can yield positive results. The Electoral Commission, in its report on the 2005 general election, noted that £20 million had been donated to political parties towards their election expenses. This figure is likely to have been much larger in 2010. Clearly the groups that spent this money felt that it could lead to favourable outcomes. Donations to political parties do not represent the only use of money, however. Those groups that have considerable funds can mount expensive campaigns to press their cause. Many industries, such as farming, oil, tobacco, supermarkets and banks, spend large sums on lobbying behind the scenes and on public campaigning. This is not to say, however, that wealthy groups will automatically be successful. Large trade unions, for example, have considerable funds available for political purposes, but with an unsympathetic government, even this can be futile.

Size

We have seen above how large some groups have become. Age UK, Friends of the Earth (200,000) and the Countryside Alliance (100,000) all claim influence through the weight of public opinion. If we consider the two major motoring organisations – the AA and the RAC – as pressure groups, we can see how much leverage they have, since both have several million members. The private motoring lobby has a considerable advantage as so many of us are motorists.

Size often translates itself into finance and also voting power. The recent success of groups that represent the elderly – Age Concern and Help the Aged (now amalgamated into Age UK) – can be largely put down to the fact that this age-group votes in much larger numbers than the rest of the population. Turnout among pensioners is usually 70–80 per cent compared with less than 40 per cent among the under-30s.

Of course, there is no guarantee that a large pressure group will be successful. As we have seen, trade unions have fallen out of favour with governments from both parties so that even the biggest unions, such as UNISON (1.2 million members working in the public services) and AMACUS (1.1. million general workers), do not 'punch their weight' in political circles as they used to do before the 1980s.

Organisation

The ability of a group to organise successful demonstrations, to raise its public profile and to persuade its members to take visible action can replace both size and finance as factors in success. The Countryside Alliance, Plane Stupid and Greenpeace are all examples of movements that have been successful because they have been well led and have captured the imagination of the public and the media. Images of these and other similar groups appear regularly on our TV screens. Careful planning and organisation are behind their successes.

Opposition groups

It is often the case that groups are faced with adversaries who are arguing the opposite case. When this happens, pressure group activity becomes a battle of wills and the result is uncertain. Where a group is lucky enough to have no serious opposition, such as old-age pensioners, poor families and financial establishments, there is a greater chance of success. The table below shows some examples of how some groups line up against each other.

Group	Opposition
Action on Smoking and Health	The tobacco industry, Forest (pro smoking)
The private motoring lobby	Environmentalists and public transport campaigners
The airline industry	Environmental groups
Farming industry	Animal welfare groups
The Countryside Alliance	Anti-hunting lobby
Animal rights groups	The pharmaceutical industry

These groups that face powerful opposition have to hope they can capture the attention of government and attract the support of public opinion. But they do have special problems that other groups do not face.

Insider status

There is no certainty that insider groups will be more successful than outsiders and it would be a mistake to assume that insiders are always treated favourably. However, there is no doubt that those groups that have ongoing contact with government and Parliament do enjoy some advantage. They are regularly consulted and governments rely upon them for both information and support.

Celebrity involvement

Most groups attempt to gain endorsements from celebrities. One well-placed individual or one useful photo opportunity can replace huge amounts of finance and public support in terms of influence. In 2009 the actress Joanna Lumley triumphed in her campaign on behalf of Gurkhas in the UK. The Gurkhas are Nepalese soldiers who serve in the British army. Ms Lumley led a campaign to win for former Gurkhas the right to settle in the UK after their retirement. There is little doubt that the popular actress was the key factor in this campaign, known as the Gurkha Justice Campaign. Other celebrities such as Elton John (gay rights), Jamie Oliver (healthier food in schools) and Sadie Frost (anti fur trade) have also led influential campaigns.

Jamie Oliver campaigned for healthier food in schools

The changing nature and activities of pressure groups

There is no doubt that pressure groups have a significant place in British society in general and the political system in particular. Furthermore, it is clear that the importance of their role has been increasing and is likely to continue to do so. We can identify a number of reasons for this.

Participation

We have seen that the importance of parties has been declining. Membership of parties has fallen dramatically, as have voting turnouts, and the ordinary members of parties now have relatively little influence over the policy-making process. But membership of pressure groups has been growing. So, too, have their activities. Social and political research indicates strongly that political participation and a general interest in politics is not declining as statistics might suggest. Rather, the nature of interest and participation is changing. The large numbers of non-voters and apparently disillusioned non-participants (concentrated among the young) have shifted their political awareness away from party politics in favour of specific political issues. Clearly, pressure groups provide a more appropriate vehicle for such interest than do parties.

Access points

Pressure groups now have many more 'access points' to the decision-making institutions than has been true in the past. It used to be the case that pressure groups concentrated the vast majority of their efforts on government ministers, civil servants and their advisers, or on Parliament. But decision making in Britain today has tended to become spread over a much wider range of institutions. This process has four facets:

- the importance of the European Union,

- devolution of power to national regions,

- the growth of policy making bodies outside the traditional party system, and

- the increasing importance of the courts as a result of the passage of the Human Rights Act.

The European Union

The clearest example has been the growing jurisdiction of the European Union. Those decisions that are made in the Union have forced pressure groups to adopt two new methods. First, they have switched many of their activities to the European Commission, the Committee of the Regions, the Social and Economic Committee and various other Union institutions whose task it is to develop policy. At the same time, the European Parliament is becoming more influential. Therefore, lobby groups have sent increasing numbers of representatives to the Parliament and its committees. In 2010 there were more than 4,400 accredited (that is permitted to operate freely) lobbyists attached to the European Parliament.

Of course, pressure groups continue to lobby national ministers who make the final decisions, but there is ample opportunity for groups to put pressure on permanent institutions that have consciously opened their doors to representatives of interest groups. It is often argued that the European Union is an undemocratic body, and

in the traditional sense of 'parliamentary democracy' that is probably so. But it is also noteworthy that the European Union accepts that the representation of interests is vital if it is to recommend policy that will enjoy popular consent.

Second, groups have understood that they must unite with their European counterparts if they are to exert effective pressure. So we have seen the development of an increasing number of 'federated' groups in Europe. All major trade unions, producer groups and environmental campaign organisations, for example, have developed their own European-wide institutions. The brief list of examples of European pressure and interest groups shown below gives a flavour of the range of issues being treated in this way:

- The European Automobile Manufacturers' Association

- Friends of the Earth Europe

- Association of Electricity Producers

- European Fair Trade Association

- European Mine, Chemical and Energy Workers' Federation

- European Small Business Alliance

- Association of Commercial Television in Europe

- European Association for the Defence of Human Rights.

Devolution

A considerable amount of power has been devolved to Scottish, Welsh and Northern Ireland government. The main policy areas that have been devolved are health, education, transport, planning, industrial development, agriculture and local government services. Pressure groups that are involved in these policy areas have naturally been forced to move some of their operations to Edinburgh, Cardiff and Belfast. Of course, the main thrust of their activities remains in London or Brussels, but there has been a considerable shift in their operations.

Extra-party institutions

As we have seen, the early consideration of policy has shifted away from party institutions. Instead there is now a wide range of external think tanks, policy units, private advisers and working parties that have the task of feeding policy options into the government machinery. Pressure groups have a vital interest in becoming involved in the *early stages* of policy consideration. The main way in which they can achieve this is by employing *professional* lobbyists who can find their way through the maze of policy-making institutions that now flourishes at the centre of British politics. Professional lobbyists undertake the critical task of identifying the key decision makers, securing contacts with them and ensuring that the information that a pressure group wishes to disseminate finds the appropriate targets.

The Human Rights Act

This Act was passed in 1998 and brought the European Convention on Human Rights into British law in 2000. Its effect was to reinforce and introduce a wide range of rights, many of which were designed to protect minority interests. Since many pressure and interest groups represent such minorities, the Act provided many new opportunities for them to assert their interests. By applying to the courts, a minority group may be able to seek a judgment that protects it from oppressive legislation. The human rights campaign group, Liberty, for example, has been especially active in this judicial field since the passage of the Act, as have environment groups.

Direct action

It used to be the case that *insider* pressure groups were seen to have a distinct advantage in gaining the attention of policy and decision makers over *outsider groups*. This was because they had direct access, were generally felt to be more responsible in their demands and had developed long-term links with government and Parliament. This picture has been changing, however. Many groups now feel that they can exert more pressure on government by mobilising public opinion than by pursuing direct links with decision makers. Certainly, there is a good deal of evidence to suggest that modern governments are responsive to mass political movements – nearly always outsiders – provided they can demonstrate widespread support. The Countryside Alliance has found this, as have old-age pensioner groups, development aid campaigners and environmentalists. Direct action, when properly organised and well supported, is growing in importance.

Summary

Millions of British citizens consider themselves to be detached from the political process. There has been growing disillusionment with traditional party politics, fewer people than ever bother to vote in elections and party membership has been falling steadily. But there is a different perspective that we can adopt. In terms of pressure group activity, especially since the emergence of new social movements, it could indeed be claimed that political activity and participation have never been higher.

Though a decreasing number of people identify closely with any political party or ideology, a growing number are willing to take positive action in pursuit of a cause about which they feel passionate. Furthermore, as representative institutions – especially parties and Parliament – have become increasingly marginalised and impotent, there has been a renewed interest in the influence of direct action. As long as we enjoy an independent civil society, and as long as politicians remain sensitive to public opinion, pressure groups will remain a key feature of British democracy.

Key concepts in this chapter

Pressure group An association that may be formal or informal, whose purpose is to further the interests of a specific section of society or to promote a particular cause.

Sectional group A pressure group that represents a specific section of society, such as a trade union or an employers' association. Also known as an *interest group.*

Promotional group A pressure group that seeks to promote a cause rather than the interests of its own members. Also known as a *cause group* or an *issue group.*

Insider groups Pressure groups that operate inside the political system through contacts with ministers, MPs, peers and official committees. They are regularly consulted by government.

Outsider groups Unlike insider groups, outsiders have no special links with government but seek to influence decision makers by mobilising public opinion.

Pluralism A description of a political system where a wide range of beliefs, ideologies and ideas is tolerated and allowed to flourish. It also implies a society where many different groups are active and are free to operate.

Elitism A tendency for power to be monopolised by small groups of influential people. Elitism exists mainly within business and finance groups, some trade unions, government, the armed forces, etc.

Revision topics and examination questions

Revision topics

- Classification of groups
- Functions of pressure groups
- Methods of groups
- Changing role of pressure groups
- Nature of direct action
- Factors in success or failure of groups
- Distinctions between parties and pressure groups
- Democratic role of pressure groups
- Nature of pluralism
- Nature of elitism
- Undemocratic features of pressure groups

Short answers (approx. 120 words)

- What is a pressure group?
- Describe briefly any TWO types of pressure group.
- Outline THREE functions of pressure groups.
- Distinguish between a pressure group and a party.
- Distinguish between a sectional and a promotional (cause) pressure group.
- Distinguish between an insider and an outsider pressure group.

Medium answers (approx. 250 words)

- Why is it sometimes difficult to distinguish pressure groups from parties?
- Describe the main methods used by modern pressure groups.
- What is meant by the term 'direct action'?
- How do pressure groups encourage political participation?

Long answers (approx. 800 words)

- In what ways do pressure groups enhance democracy?
- In what senses can pressure groups be considered undemocratic?
- Why are some pressure groups more successful than others?
- How has the role of pressure groups changed in recent years?
- How and why have the methods of pressure groups changed in recent years?
- How and why have pressure groups become more important in recent years?

Resources and web guide

Books

Two books stand out as classic works:
    W. Grant, *Pressure Groups and British Politics*, Palgrave, 2000.
    R. Baggott, *Pressure Groups Today*, Manchester University Press, 1995.

A good modern guide is:
    D. Watts, *Pressure Groups*, Edinburgh University Press, 2008.

Useful websites

A sample of prominent groups is:
    www.ash.org.uk (Action on Smoking and Health)
    www.cbi.org.uk (Confederation of British Industry)
    www.rspb.org.uk (Royal Society for the Protection of Birds)
    www.greenpeace.org (obviously, Greenpeace)
    www.ageuk.org.uk (Age UK)
    www.cpag.org.uk (Child Poverty Action Group)

Governing the UK

The UK constitution

The nature and functions of a constitution

Virtually every country in the world operates its political system within the constraints of a constitution. In most cases, too, the **constitution** of the state is a written document that has been agreed on some particular occasion. Such constitutions are usually described as *codified*.

 Key Word

Constitution A set of principles, which may be written or unwritten, that establishes the distribution of power within a political system, relationships between political institutions, the limits of government jurisdiction, the rights of citizens and the method of amending the constitution itself.

There are, however, a few countries, including the UK, that operate without such a specifically written constitution. Even so, these countries have a general 'sense' that a set of constitutional rules exists. So, constitutions, whether codified or not, are a vital aspect of most stable political systems. All constitutions, no matter where they exist, perform the same set of functions. These are as follows:

1. They determine how political power should be distributed within the state. This includes federal settlements where power is divided between the central government and regional institutions, as in the USA, or unitary states where ultimate power lies firmly in one place, as with the UK's parliamentary system. Similarly, constitutions determine the balance of power between government and Parliament, between president and prime minister and between two chambers in systems that are bicameral (two Houses of Parliament).

2. Linked to this first function, constitutions also establish the political processes that make the system work. This includes the relationships between institutions and the rules that govern how they operate.

3. A constitution normally states what the limits of governmental power should be – in other words, what is the competence of government. The British constitution is unusual in this sense as it places no limits at all on the competence of Parliament. Being sovereign, Parliament is able to do what it likes. Of course, we would not expect it to act in a dictatorial way, but it has the legal power to do what it likes. By contrast, US government is circumscribed by that country's constitution.

4. Just as constitutions limit governmental power, so do they assert the rights of the

citizens against the state. Most countries that at least claim to be democratic have some kind of 'bill of rights', a statement that prevents the government from trampling on the civil liberties of its citizens.

5. Constitutions establish the rules by which nationality is established – in other words, who is entitled to be a citizen and how outsiders may become citizens. This also implies that a constitution defines the territory that makes up the state.

6. Finally, we must remember that constitutions have to be amended from time to time. It is therefore essential that a constitution contains within itself the rules for its own amendment. The UK is, once again, unusual in this respect as its constitution changes in two ways. One is through a simple parliamentary statute; the other is the slow evolution of unwritten rules, known as conventions. Normally states have special arrangements for amending their constitution. In France and Ireland, for example, a referendum is needed to approve a change. In the USA it is necessary to secure a two-thirds majority of both houses of Congress and the approval of three-quarters of the 50 states that make up the Union. Britain has no such methods of amendment; its constitution has largely evolved naturally over the course of history.

So we have established six main functions of a constitution. Issues that concern any of these matters are therefore described as 'constitutional' in nature.

Codification

Two aspects of constitutionalism need further explanation. They are **codification** and entrenchment.

Key Word

Codification The process of setting out a constitution in an organised way in a single document.

A codified constitution is one that is written in an organised way in a single document. In other words, it has a *single source*. The advantage of this arrangement is that the constitution is clear and every citizen is able to access it. Similarly, when there is a dispute concerning constitutional arrangements, a codified document is a considerable advantage. Codification of a constitution normally occurs at some critical moment in a country's history. This may be the aftermath of a revolution, civil war or coup d'état; it may come about following the creation of a new state or the re-formation of a troubled country. The following examples demonstrate how constitutions can come about.

The Constitution of the USA, the first example of a codified constitution

Country	Year of current constitution	Circumstances
USA	1787	The creation of a new political union after independence of 13 former British colonies.
Norway	1814	On the country's freedom from Danish rule.
Irish	1937	Renounced the British Crown and became a republic.
China	1949	Upon the victory of communist forces after a civil war.
Malaysia	1957	On independence from Britain.
France	1958	After a coup d'état when a new President – Charles de Gaulle – took over.
Iraq	2005	Following the removal of the regime of Saddam Hussein.

A **codified** constitution has one additional benefit. As a single document it can provide the people of a state with something with which they can identify. The Americans, for example, virtually worship their historic constitution, treating it with great reverence and pledging allegiance to it regularly. When each new President takes office, indeed, it is part of his oath of allegiance that he agrees to 'protect and defend' the constitution.

Two-tier legal systems

When a country has a codified constitution it also has what is known as a *two-tier* or *dual* legal system. This means that there are two levels of law. Higher laws are those that concern constitutional arrangements – who has power, the relationship between institutions, the rights of citizens, etc. – and these are safeguarded and entrenched (see below). In Germany, for example, these higher laws are known as *basic laws*. Such higher laws often have special arrangements for their enactment – referendum approval, two-thirds majority in the legislature, etc. – and so have a different status. Below these are ordinary laws, which concern relations between citizens, administration of the state, criminality, etc. These lower laws can normally be changed without special procedures and are not safeguarded by any special procedures.

Uncodified constitutions

The British constitution is unusual in that it is uncodified. Many even argue, therefore, that it does not actually exist at all. Parts of it are written, but there is certainly no single document and there are important parts of it that are not written at all. Israel, New Zealand and Canada also lack fully codified constitutions, but in all three cases there are 'basic laws' that describe constitutional principles and which are differentiated from other laws. By contrast, the UK makes no distinction between constitutional and other laws. In other words, the UK has a *single-tier* legal system. It is also true that Britain's uncodified nature means that we say it has many sources, not just a single source. The sources of the UK constitution are described below.

We do need to be careful here in relation to Britain. The British constitution is not codified *as a whole*, but there are *parts* of the constitution that *are* codified. In particular, the European Convention on Human Rights is part of British law and it is a codified document. Similarly, the Treaties of the European Union are codified documents that describe the relationship between Britain and the EU. So we can say that, today, the British constitution is *partly codified,* but mostly not.

Entrenchment

This is a rather more important matter than codification. Entrenchment is the device that protects a constitution from short-term amendment. It is important because constitutional change makes a fundamental and important difference to the political system of a country. The constitution is too important to be placed in the hands of a *temporary* government. A country must be sure that any proposed constitutional change meets two tests: one is that there is widespread popular support for it; the other is that it is in the long-term interests of the country.

An example of this principle concerns the guarantees of human rights that exist in most states. It may be in the interests of a particular government to set aside some of these rights by amending that part of the constitution that deals with civil rights. But this would clearly damage the long-term interests of the people. Similarly, a dictatorial government might seek to grant itself additional powers to protect its own position. If this occurred, democracy in general would be under threat.

To ensure that the two tests are met, therefore, special arrangements need to be established. Thus a referendum, for example, ensures popular support for change, while special parliamentary procedures can ensure that constitutional amendment is in the long-term interests of the state.

But the situation in the UK is unusual. It is not possible to entrench constitutional principles. This is because Parliament is sovereign. The sovereignty of Parliament asserts that each individual Parliament cannot be bound by its predecessors, nor can it bind its successors. This

means, in effect, that every new Parliament is able to amend the constitution as it wishes. All Parliament has to do is to pass a new parliamentary statute, using the same procedure as for any other statute. It can be done in as little as two days. Furthermore, of course, government in the UK is normally able to dominate Parliament, using its majority in the House of Commons and the mandate of the people that is granted at elections. So a dominant government can effectively control the constitution.

An example of executive power was demonstrated when the UK Parliament passed the Human Rights Act in 1998. This incorporated the European Convention on Human Rights into British law. It became binding on all political bodies other than Parliament itself. No special procedures were needed. A fundamental change to the British constitution was made through a simple Act of Parliament. It occurred in this way because the British constitution is not entrenched.

Having said that, it is becoming common practice in the UK to hold a referendum when constitutional change is proposed. This was done for devolution of power to Scotland and Wales in 1997, the introduction of elected mayors in London and a number of other locations, and to approve the Good Friday Agreement in Northern Ireland in 1998. Referendums have also been proposed to approve the adoption of the single European currency, the introduction of the AV voting system and the new European Union constitution. The effect of such referendums is to entrench constitutional developments. It is inconceivable that the changes would be reversed without another referendum to approve such a reversal. In the 2010 general campaign, the Labour Party promised referendums on two issues – reform of the House of Lords and a change in the electoral system. Liberal Democrats also support referendums for key constitutional changes.

The table below shows a selection of methods by which various countries have entrenched their constitutions.

Country	Date of constitution	Method of amendment	Number of amendments	Constitutional court
France	1958	Referendum or three-fifths majority of Parliament.	18	Constitutional Council
Germany (constitution known as Basic Law)	1949	Two-thirds majority in Parliament. Some sections cannot be amended at all.	4	Constitutional Court
USA	1787	Two-thirds majority of Congress plus approval of three-quarters (38) of the 50 states.	27	Supreme Court
Irish Republic	1937	Referendum.	23	Supreme Court
UK	Not applicable	Simple Act of Parliament, judicial rulings or gradual development of unwritten conventions.	Innumerable	Supreme Court
Iraq	2005	Constitutional Review Committee recommends change, but this must be ratified by referendum.	0	Supreme Court

The table indicates immediately how different the UK is in this field.

Judicial review

Whether a constitution is codified or not, it is often necessary for the courts of justice to interpret the meaning of some of its terms. Usually this is the result of a challenge made by a citizen or an association against an action or law made by a public body. When the challenge is based on the belief that the action or law has broken the strict rules of the country's constitution, it is necessary for senior judges to review the challenged action in the light of those constitutional rules. Very often the constitution is not clear; its real meaning may need interpreting, it may, indeed, need updating in the light of new developments in society. So the judges are constantly being called upon to re-interpret and re-evaluate the meaning of parts of a constitution. The process is known as **judicial review**.

Judicial review A process undertaken by senior courts where judges are required to interpret, re-interpret or clarify constitutional rules. Judicial reviews take place in response to appeals by citizens or associations. In this way the meaning of a constitution can be clarified, adapted or applied to new circumstances.

When the judges have made their ruling, they have, in effect, rewritten the constitution (though they do not change the actual wording). They have clarified or even altered its accepted meaning. In a democratic system, such rulings are binding on the political system. This means that even strictly codified and entrenched constitutions are constantly evolving as judges make new rulings and interpretations.

When a constitution is codified, as in the USA for example, judicial review takes place with close reference to the actual wording of the constitution. It is also true that judicial reviews by the US Supreme Court have often become key features of US social and political history. Three such celebrated cases are shown here.

Case	Details
Brown v Board of Education 1954	A key case in US history. The court declared that the segregation of education on the grounds of race violated the constitutional principle of equal rights for all. The case was a boost for the growing civil rights movement in the USA.
Roe v Wade 1973	Feminist groups challenged anti-abortion laws on the grounds that such laws violated the basic constitutional rights of

Case	Details
	women. The court ruled that anti-abortion legislation was indeed unconstitutional. A feature film was subsequently made about this case.
Gregg v Georgia 1976	The court was asked to decide whether capital punishment should be abolished on the grounds that the constitution forbids 'cruel and unusual punishment'. The court decided humane execution was not cruel or unusual so states were free to maintain or introduce the death penalty.

In contrast, senior judges in the UK do not have a codified constitution to which they can refer for guidance. Nevertheless, such judicial reviews do happen frequently in Britain. Judges can interpret laws and actions in the light of the European Convention on Human Rights, or of the many constitutional laws and conventions that exist in the UK. Here again they are effectively writing constitutional law. But, as we have seen above, there is one key difference from the US experience. British judges in the Supreme Court (House of Lords) may interpret the constitution how they wish, but it is Parliament that ultimately has the power to overrule them and declare what the constitution means to them. This is explained in the section on entrenchment above. In the US and similar systems, by contrast, the government and legislature have to accept the findings of a judicial review. The only way they can rewrite the constitution is by engaging in complex amendment procedures. The UK Parliament can amend the UK Constitution by simple Act of Parliament.

An important example of this principle occurred in 2007 and serves as an illustration of how judicial review works, but also how Parliament is ultimately sovereign. In 2004, nine suspected terrorists, held without trial in Belmarsh prison, appealed to the House of Lords senior judges on the grounds that their detention without trial violated an ancient British constitutional principle – that the state cannot imprison people without formally charging them and bringing them to trial (a principle known as *habeas corpus)*. Much dissatisfied, the Government persuaded Parliament in 2007 to pass legislation allowing such suspects to be held for up to 28 days without charge. Thus Parliament had effectively set aside the principle of *habeas corpus*. This could not have happened in the USA without a formal constitutional amendment. (The prisoners held at Guantanamo Bay in connection with the Iraq war were not US citizens so the constitution did not apply to them.) A similar case occurred in 2010 when the UK Supreme Court ruled that the government did not have the constitutional power to freeze the bank accounts of *suspected* (i.e. not convicted) terrorists. The Government immediately introduced a parliamentary measure to give itself such power.

Evaluating codification

Should Britain introduce a codified constitution? In the main it is conservatives who oppose such a proposal. However, Labour governments have also avoided the issue. Labour, on the whole, has preferred to make *incremental* changes to the constitution, gradually introducing new legislation such as the Human Rights Act, the Freedom of Information Act, the Devolution Acts and House of Lords reform, to create a clearer set of arrangements. But, like the conservatives, Labour does not believe the time is right for a fully codified constitution.

Ranged against these conservative forces are the Liberal Democrats and pressure groups such as Unlock Democracy. They present a number of powerful arguments in favour of coming into

line with nearly all other modern democracies by writing a new British constitution. In particular they are concerned with the need for robust human rights and controls on the power of government.

The arguments for and against codification are summarised below.

Arguments for retaining an uncodified constitution

Flexibility

The supporters of the current arrangements say that the flexibility of the constitution is a positive quality. The constitution can, they say, adapt to a changing world without major upheavals. It is said that Britain's constitution is 'organic'. This means that it is rooted in society, not separate from society. Thus, when society and its needs and values change, the constitution can do so automatically without undue delay or confusion. Parliament can pass a new Act relatively quickly and new unwritten conventions can simply develop to take account of social and political change. Some examples of such 'organic' and natural development can help to illustrate this quality:

● As the authority of the British monarchy gradually declined from the eighteenth century, to be replaced by elected bodies – government and Parliament – no specific amendments needed to be made. Power and authority simply moved naturally away from the Crown towards government and the Parliament and practices changed. In particular, many of the so-called 'prerogative' powers of the monarch have been taken over by the prime minister – to declare war, to negotiate foreign treaties and to appoint ministers, for example. The power of the monarchy to make law had already largely been lost in a peaceful process known as the Glorious Revolution in 1688–89.

In countries where such powers are codified and entrenched, such changes have tended to cause major upheaval and even violent revolutions. We can think of nineteenth-century France or Germany between the two world wars in this context.

- Since the 1960s the position of the prime minister has become more significant, largely as a result of media concentration on the importance of that office. Here again the growth in prime ministerial power, largely at the expense of the cabinet, has been a gradual and natural process.

- After the 9/11 attack on New York in 2001, the threat of international terrorism became more acute. Had Britain featured an entrenched and codified constitution, it would have been extremely difficult for Parliament to pass a wide range of anti-terrorist measures because of too many constitutional constraints. The lack of a constitution meant that Parliament could do as it wished. The USA and many European countries have had much greater problems dealing with terrorism because of a fixed constitution. (The same applies to the stubborn refusal in the USA to introduce stricter gun laws in case such a measure falls foul of the constitutional right of citizens to bear arms.)

Executive power

Because constitutional safeguards in Britain are weak or absent, government can be more powerful. Clearly this can be viewed positively or negatively. Supporters of the current uncodified constitution argue that, on balance, it is better to have a government that can deal with problems or crises without too much inhibition. They point to the USA where government and Congress are frequently prevented from acting decisively by the fear that the constitution will prevent them doing so. The constant battle against crime in the USA, for instance, has been compromised by such constraints. Conversely, the constitutional weakness of the Congress in controlling the military powers of the president has also created much tension. In the UK, the relationship between government and Parliament is flexible; in countries with codified constitutions it tends to be fixed and can inhibit effective governance.

Conservative pragmatism

The typical conservative attitude to the British constitution suggests that it has served Britain well for centuries. There have been no violent revolutions and no major political unrest. Change has occurred naturally and when it has been necessary rather than when reformers have campaigned for it. Furthermore, say conservatives, codifying the constitution would be an extremely difficult exercise and the meagre benefits would not be worth the problems incurred.

Politicising the courts and judiciability

A codified constitution would undoubtedly involve the courts, the Supreme Court in particular, in disputes over its precise meaning and application. As seen in the USA, many of these issues would be intensely political. For example, there would be conflicts over the exact powers of government, the nature of rights, relations with the EU or relations between England, Scotland, Wales and Northern Ireland. Of course, disputes like these can arise with an uncodified constitution, but they could become more common following codification. In other words, the constitution would become *judiciable*. The problem with such a development is that judges are not elected and therefore not accountable. Critics point out that such political issues should not be resolved by such judges – it is for elected representatives, they say, to make final decisions on constitutional meaning.

Arguments for introducing a codified constitution

Human rights

Perhaps at the top of the reformers' shopping list is the need for stronger safeguards for individual and minority rights. Britain has adopted the European Convention on Human Rights (by passing the Human Rights Act in 1998), but this remains weak in that it can be overridden by Parliament. Parliament remains sovereign and no constitutional legislation can remove that sovereignty. In a codified constitution Parliament could not pass any legislation that offended human rights protection.

Executive power

We have seen above that conservatives and others have wished to retain the powerful position of government in the UK. Liberals and other reformers, however, argue that executive, governmental power is excessive in Britain. They say over-powerful governmental power threatens individual rights, the position of minorities and the influence of public opinion. A clear, codified constitution would, they assert, inhibit the apparently irreversible drift towards greater executive power. In particular, supporters of a codified constitution suggest that there are no real 'checks and balances' – a principle upon which the US constitution is based. It is argued that Parliament needs to have more codified powers to enable it to control government on behalf of the people.

Clarity

Most British citizens do not understand the concept of a constitution. This is hardly surprising as there is no such thing as the 'British Constitution' in any concrete form. There is, therefore, an argument for creating a real constitution so that public awareness and support can grow. If people know their rights and understand better how government works, it is suggested, this might cure the problem of political ignorance and apathy that prevails.

Modernity

As we have seen, Britain is unusual in not having a codified constitution. Many people regard this as an indication that Britain is backward in a political sense and has not entered the modern world. This has become more pressing since Britain joined the European Community. The lack of a constitution makes political relations with the EU difficult and it has been frustrating both for British governments and for their European partners when attempts have been made to create coherent relations with Europe.

Should Britain have a codified constitution?	
For	**Against**
• It would clarify the nature of the political system to citizens, especially after changes such as devolution and House of Lords reform. • Britain would have a two-tier legal system and so constitutional laws would be more clearly identified. • The process of judicial review would be more precise and transparent.	• The uncodified constitution is flexible and can easily adapt to changing circumstances such as referendum use and the changing role of the House of Lords. If codified, constitutional changes would be difficult and time-consuming. It can also respond quickly to a changing political climate. • Conservatives argue that it is simply not necessary – the UK has enjoyed a stable

Should Britain have a codified constitution? (continued)	
For	**Against**
• Liberals argue that it would have the effect of better safeguarding citizens' rights. • It might prevent the further drift towards excessive executive power. • The UK needs to clarify its relationship with the European Union. • It would bring the UK into line with most other modern democracies.	political system without a constitution. • As the UK operates under a large number of unwritten conventions, especially in relation to the monarchy and prerogative powers, it would be very difficult to transfer them into written form. • The lack of constitutional constraints allows executive government to be strong and decisive. • A codified constitution would bring unelected judges into the political arena.

Arguably Britain is in the process, particularly since 1997, of creating a codified constitution bit by bit. True, it may never be contained in a single document for the foreseeable future, but increasingly large parts of the constitution are now both written and effectively entrenched. The aspects of the constitution that conform to this analysis are as follows:

• The European Convention on Human Rights, brought into law by the Human Rights Act (1998), is effectively a Bill of Rights. Though it could be fully or partly repealed in the future, this seems politically unlikely.

• The Devolution Acts (1998) codify the powers enjoyed by the Scottish Parliament and the Welsh, Northern Ireland and Greater London assemblies.

• The UK's relationship with the European Union is codified in the various treaties that Britain has signed, such as Maastricht (1992) and Nice (2001).

• The public's right to see public information is codified in the Freedom of Information Act (2000).

• The status and conduct of political parties is now codified in the Political Parties, Elections and Referendums Act (2000).

• Important constitutional changes are effectively entrenched by the fact that they have been approved by referendum and can therefore be repealed only by referendum.

• The Electoral Commission has created a codified set of rules for the conduct of elections and referendums.

So the old boast, or perhaps criticism, that the British constitution simply evolves and remains in the control of the Parliament of the day is out of date. Labour's stated intention to modernise the constitution was substantially achieved in the sense that Britain's constitutional arrangements bear a much closer resemblance to those of the rest of the democratic world than ever before. There is still no codified constitution, but the vast majority of Britain's constitutional arrangements are now certainly written.

Unitary and federal constitutions

There are two fundamental types of constitution in the world of politics. These are *unitary* and *federal*.

A unitary constitution is one where sovereignty – ultimate political power – resides in one location. This is at the centre. It is possible that some power may be distributed to regions and local government, but this is not the same as sovereignty. In a unitary constitution, the central sovereign power can overrule all other bodies and has the right to restore all political power to itself. Thus, although Britain has devolved much power to Wales, Scotland and Northern Ireland, the Westminster Parliament remains firmly sovereign.

It has sometimes been claimed that Britain is now a *quasi federation*. What this implies is that the powers that have been devolved to Scotland, Wales and Northern Ireland are *effectively entrenched* and therefore cannot be returned to Westminster. They are not legally entrenched, but it seems inconceivable that they will ever be surrendered. Certainly they could not be returned without the approval of a referendum. So, Britain is not a federal system, but it is sometimes described as quasi federal.

In a federal constitution, sovereignty is divided between central bodies and regional institutions. Such constitutions normally arise when a number of sovereign states come together and agree to surrender some, but not all, of their sovereignty to a central authority. The political reason for such an arrangement is usually that a country contains strong regional differences and identities. These can be protected by ensuring that regions retain some of their own sovereignty.

The USA is possibly the best-known federal constitution, negotiated and written in 1787 and ratified by the 13 states in the three years that followed (there are now 50 states). To illustrate the principle, some of the main sovereign powers as they are divided in the USA are shown in the box top right.

US federal powers	US state powers
Economic management	Most criminal law
Currency control	Education
Foreign policy	Property and sales taxes
Defence policy	Most policing
Foreign trade	Industrial development

Both systems, federal and unitary, are popular, as illustrated by the list of major countries below, showing which type of constitution they use.

Unitary constitutions	Federal constitutions
United Kingdom	USA
France	Germany
Italy	Australia
Zimbabwe	Nigeria
Thailand	Malaysia
China	Russia
Pakistan	India
New Zealand	Canada

Student activities

Through the Internet, access the codified constitutions of some or all of these countries:

- France

- USA

- Germany

In each case, establish the following:

- **Three powers enjoyed by the president. Who exercises these powers in the UK?**

- **The make-up of both houses of the legislature. How do these differ from the UK?**

- **Two are federal systems – the USA and Germany. In each of these two cases establish two powers reserved to the individual states (USA) or Länder (Germany) and two powers enjoyed by the federal (central) government.**

Sources of the UK constitution

So the British constitution is neither codified nor entrenched. Some even suggest it does not really exist but is simply 'whatever Parliament says it is at any given time'. It is certainly difficult to define and is constantly evolving. But there is no doubt that there is an 'idea' of the British constitution, so we can attempt to identify the components that make it up.

Parliamentary (Constitutional) statutes

These are Acts of Parliament that have the effect of establishing constitutional principles. The Human Rights Act has been described above as an example, but we can add the Parliament Act of 1949, which established limitations to the power of the House of Lords, and the Scotland and Wales Acts, which devolved power to those countries. Further examples of constitutional statutes are shown in the table on page 181.

Constitutional conventions

A convention is an unwritten rule that is considered binding on all members of the political community. Such conventions cannot be challenged in law but have so much moral force that they are rarely, if ever, disputed. Many of the powers of the prime minister are governed by such conventions. It is, for example, merely a convention that the prime minister exercises the Queen's power to appoint and dismiss ministers, to choose the date of the general election and to grant various answers. It is also a convention (known as the Salisbury Convention) that the House of Lords should not block any legislation that appeared in the governing party's most recent election manifesto.

Historical principles

Similar to conventions, these principles have become effectively binding because they have been established over a long period of time. The most important is the **sovereignty of Parliament**. We could add a similar concept, which is **parliamentary government**, the principle that the authority of the government is drawn from Parliament and not directly from the people. The **rule of law** is a more recent development, originating in the second part of the nineteenth century. The rule of law establishes, among other things, the principles of equal rights for citizens and that government is itself limited by legal limitations. On the whole, historical principles are attributed to important constitutional theorists such as Blackstone (parliamentary sovereignty) and A.V. Dicey (rule of law).

Common law

The term 'common law' is a largely Anglo-Saxon principle. It refers to the development of laws through historical usage and tradition. Judges, who occasionally must declare and enforce common law, treat it as any rule of conduct that is both well established and generally acknowledged by most people.

The most important application of common law has concerned the protection of basic rights and freedoms from encroachment by government and/or Parliament. The right of people to free movement and to gather for public demonstrations, for example, are ancient freedoms, jealously guarded by the courts. So, too, was the principle that the Crown could not detain citizens without trial. For the most part common law principles have been replaced by statutes and by the European Convention on Human Rights, which became UK law in 2000. But from time to time, when there is no relevant statute, the common law is invoked in courts by citizens with a grievance against government. The prerogative powers of the prime minister are considered common law powers. They have never been codified or put into formal legislation. These powers are exercised by the prime minister on behalf of the monarch and include commanding the armed forces, negotiating foreign treaties, calling general elections and making appointments to government. More information on prerogative powers can be seen below.

Tradition

Similar to common law, constitutional traditions govern many of the rituals of parliamentary government. The procedures of both Houses of Parliament are traditional in nature, as are some of their rituals. The practice of allowing the Queen to announce the legislative programme for the coming year (the so-called Queen's Speech) is such a tradition, as are many of the rules of debate.

The table below summarises the main sources of the British constitution.

The main sources of the British Constitution	
Type of source	**Examples**
Statutes	Equal Franchise Act 1928 established full and equal voting rights to women.
	Life Peerages Act 1958 introduced the appointment of life peers to add to the hereditary peerage.
	Human Rights Act 1998 incorporates the codified European Convention of Human Rights into UK law.
	Scotland Act 1998 established a Scottish Parliament with legislative powers.
	House of Lords Act 1999 abolished all but 92 of the hereditary peers in the House of Lords.
	Freedom of Information Act 2000 introduced the right of citizens to see all official documents not excluded on grounds of national security.
Conventions	Salisbury Convention states that the House of Lords should not block any legislation that appeared in the governing party's most recent election manifesto.

Edexcel Government and Politics for AS

The main sources of the British Constitution (continued)	
Type of source	Examples
Historical principles	Collective responsibility means that all members of the government must support official policy in public or resign or face dismissal. Government formation is based on the rule that, following an election, the Queen must invite the leader of the largest party in the Commons to form a government. The sovereignty of Parliament establishes the supremacy of Parliament in legislation. The rule of law states that all, including government itself, are equal under the law. Constitutional monarchy is a principle that the monarch is limited in its role and can play no active role in politics.
Common law	Most common law concerns principles of rights and justice. These have mostly been replaced by the European Convention on Human Rights. However, some of Parliament's powers and procedures are contained in common law. The prerogative powers of the prime minister, exercised on behalf of the monarch, are essentially common law powers, which have never been codified.
Tradition	The practices and traditions of Parliament.

Main characteristics of the UK constitution

Having established how the various parts of the British constitution have come about historically and how it continues to develop, we can examine its main characteristics.

Its uncodified nature

Unusually, the British constitution is not contained in a single document. Instead, as we have seen above, it has a variety of sources. Thus we say it is 'uncodified'. In a sense, therefore, it does have statutes and books of authority or EU treaties, but much of it is unwritten, in the form of conventions and common law or tradition.

It is not entrenched

When a constitution is entrenched it means that it is specially safeguarded against change. In practice this means that an entrenched constitution has arrangements for amendment that are more complex than the normal legislative process. The

Key Word

Royal prerogative This refers to the ancient, traditional powers enjoyed by the monarch. These powers do not require the sanction of Parliament, but are arbitrary. Since the latter part of the nineteenth century these powers have passed from the monarch to the prime minister of the day.

British constitution is not entrenched. It can be changed very easily and quickly by Parliament. There are no restrictions on how Parliament can amend the British constitution.

Constitutional monarchy and royal prerogative

Britain is a monarchy and has been for most of its history. Since 1688, however, it has been a constitutional monarchy. Until then the monarchy enjoyed almost absolute power. Parliament only restrained the king or queen's ability to raise taxes. All other powers, known as the **royal prerogative,** were effectively arbitrary. But when William of Orange was invited to take the throne with his wife, Mary, following the largely peaceful 'Glorious Revolution' in 1688, the price of the invitation was that he should accept the supremacy of Parliament in law making.

Since that time the prerogative powers of the monarchy have been gradually eroded. Though no constitution has ever been enacted, there is a sense that the monarch is constrained by fixed constitutional principles. This erosion has taken place from two directions. First, all law-making power has passed to Parliament. The monarch must give the royal assent to make bills into laws, but it is accepted that they must never refuse the royal assent. Not since 1707, when Queen Anne attempted to block the Act of Union (which abolished the separate Scottish Parliament), has royal assent been withheld. The other direction comes from the office of the prime minister.

Since the development of the idea of a separate head of government in the 1720s, the remaining prerogative powers of the monarch have been gradually taken over by the prime minister. By the 1870s Queen Victoria had to accept that she and her successors would never again have discretion over the appointment of ministers. Nor would they be able to dissolve Parliament and call an election, negotiate foreign treaties, command

forces in combat, create peerages, or interfere in any significant way in policy making. The constitutional monarchy thus means that many actions are taken *in the name* of the monarch, but she is not *actually* making any decisions. So we still speak of 'Her Majesty's Forces', 'Her Majesty's ministers and government' and the 'crown courts', etc., but in fact we know that these are all under the control of the government and/or Parliament.

In practice, the monarch remains head of state, but since the head of government – the prime minister – carries out most of her functions, it is he who *appears* to be the head of state. It is the prime minister who negotiates with other heads of government and heads of state; it is he who represents the nation abroad. In other words, the British prime minister is *effectively* head of state and behaves in that way. The monarchy, now playing a largely ceremonial role, is limited by firm constitutional rules.

Parliamentary government and parliamentary sovereignty

Writing in 1867, in his famous work *The English Constitution*, the great English political journalist Walter Bagehot declared that he understood the 'efficient secret' of the British political system. This was the 'fusion' of executive and legislative power. What he meant was that Britain did not recognise a separation between Parliament and government. In most modern political systems, especially that of the USA, there is a strict separation between the power and membership of the government and the legislature. This is practised in order to ensure that each branch controls the other. No such separation existed in Britain in 1867, and it does not to this day.

The so-called separation of powers is usually praised for keeping governmental power under democratic control. But it can also hinder the effectiveness of strong government. In the UK, government members are drawn from Parliament (all ministers must, by convention, be members of either the Commons or the Lords). Furthermore, we expect the government to control the legislature by manipulating its majority in the House of Commons. Parliament grants authority to government ministers and then expects them to be accountable to it. In return, Parliament allows ministers to dominate it. This system of parliamentary accountability combined with executive supremacy is known as **parliamentary government**.

Key Word

Parliamentary government A political system where Parliament is a central feature. Government is drawn from Parliament and is accountable to Parliament.

Though the government is politically dominant, as Bagehot had pointed out, this does not make it legally sovereign. Legal sovereignty – the ultimate power to make laws that will be enforced – lies only with Parliament. This means that government has to accept the final word of Parliament when proposing legislation. Of course, we expect Parliament to approve most government proposals because government has a mandate from the people. But Parliament retains a reserve power to veto such proposals. In extreme circumstances Parliament can even dismiss a government, normally forcing an election, through a vote of no confidence. This was last done in 1979 when James Callaghan's Labour government was defeated on the floor of the House of Commons and was forced to resign.

This principle of **parliamentary sovereignty** must not, however, deflect our attention away from the fact that *most* political power still normally lies with the government. Some describe this as 'political sovereignty' to distinguish it from 'legal sovereignty'.

Key Word

Parliamentary sovereignty The principle that Parliament is the ultimate source of all authority and power within the political system. It also means that Parliament is the ultimate source of all law and there is no higher legal authority.

Party government

The British constitutional system can operate only in the context of party control. In particular, the arrangements concerning the operation of both the cabinet and the House of Commons depend upon the fact that a single party is in control of the executive branch and is usually able to control its majority in the Commons. The principles of collective responsibility, mandate and manifesto, government and opposition, and patronage all depend upon the reality that one party wins an election outright and forms a government alone.

When no party won overall control after the May 2010 election the whole basis of 'party government' was called into question. Government in the UK was no longer in the hands of a single party, but was controlled by a coalition. Furthermore, the new government had no clear mandate. The agreed policies of the coalition had not been presented to the electorate so the doctrine of the mandate was severely weakened. The coalition can no longer guarantee the support of the majority in the House of Commons. How this situation will play out in practice remains to be seen.

Unitary government

Finally it should be re-stated that the UK is a unitary political system. Legal sovereignty is located at the centre, in one body: Parliament. Though a great deal of power has been decentralised through devolution, and much sovereignty has been delegated to the European Union, ultimately Parliament has the final say in all political and constitutional matters.

An assessment of the British constitution

What are the strengths and weaknesses of the British constitution? There is certainly a balanced assessment to be made. The main features of such a discussion are these.

Strengths

● Because it is neither codified nor entrenched, it is flexible and adaptable. It can be easily changed to react to changing circumstances. This was shown most clearly when the May 2010 election produced an indecisive result. There were no fixed constitutional rules to deal with the circumstances that emerged. The Cabinet Secretary (Britain's most senior civil servant), Gus O'Donnell, had drawn up some draft procedures for the possibility of a hung parliament. His plan worked well and the new coalition government was installed with relatively little disruption or conflict. All this was done without directly involving the Queen, which would have put her into a difficult position as she is required to remain 'above politics'.

● It is highly traditional and has stood the test of time. The fact that Britain has never suffered a violent revolution or major political unrest suggests that the constitution has enduring qualities.

● It ensures that Parliament, and therefore government, can act decisively, unrestricted by excessive constitutional restraints.

● It contains traditional elements such as the House of Lords and the monarchy. These help to maintain public support for the system.

Weaknesses

● The lack of restraints on the powers of government and Parliament may be dangerous, especially to individual and minority rights.

● It contains traditional and outdated institutions such as the FPTP electoral system, the monarchy and the House of Lords. Not only are such institutions often seen as outdated, they are also accused of being undemocratic.

● The lack of separation of powers between government and Parliament means that government tends to dominate Parliament. This is often seen as undemocratic as Parliament represents the interests of the people.

● The fact that the constitution is uncodified means that many people are ignorant of it. This may result in political apathy and lack of support for the political system.

This relatively balanced assessment makes the issue of reform a difficult one. Should the constitution be reformed when there seem to be several important strengths? Yet there are perhaps enough weaknesses to suggest that reform is indeed necessary. The issue of constitutional reform is considered later in this chapter. We *can* say, however, that if the uncertain consequences of the May 2010 election are reproduced regularly, there will be louder calls for the creation of a codified constitution that can manage the new realities of coalition politics.

Sovereignty in the UK

Before considering this issue we need to remind ourselves of what we mean by the term sovereignty:

Legal sovereignty – the ultimate power to make laws that will be enforced within the state.

Political sovereignty – where political power lies in reality. Whoever may possess legal sovereignty, *real* power lies with those bodies that are able to determine what political decisions are made.

Legal sovereignty

In the UK, legal sovereignty lies firmly with Parliament. This means that no other body has the power to make laws or to overrule laws made by Parliament. This second point does, however, need to be qualified in the light of the UK's membership of the European Union. This is explored further below, but at this stage it is sufficient to say that Parliament can restore all its legal sovereignty at any time by withdrawing from the EU.

It is also true that statutory powers can be granted to a subsidiary body or to a minister only by Parliament. In such cases Parliament is *delegating* its legal sovereignty. It can take it back at any time. Thus the Scottish Parliament has *primary* legislative powers under the Scotland Act 1998, but the Act could be repealed.

When we use the term *a Parliament*, it means the group of MPs which has been elected at each general election (together with the House of Lords over the same period). Thus each Parliament normally exists for about four or five years between elections. Each successive Parliament is legally sovereign. It is not bound by the laws made by previous Parliaments. In theory, a new Parliament can undo all the laws in existence (not

that it would have the time to do so, of course). Similarly, each Parliament cannot entrench any laws; it cannot prevent future Parliaments from repealing or amending them. This is a contrast with New Zealand and Canada (neither of which has a codified constitution), where the Parliaments can pass *basic laws* that cannot be repealed in future without a special procedure.

Political sovereignty

This is a more difficult matter. We can certainly say that, at an election, the people become politically sovereign. They determine who shall make up both government and Parliament. They also choose between the competing manifestos of the parties. But between elections the people lose control of the decision-making process.

In general terms we can say that it is the government that is politically sovereign. We expect that ministers will control the decision-making process. The executive branch dominates Parliament and that is generally what we expect to happen. It is the government that has a mandate from the people and it is a tight-knit group of ministers from the same party that can provide firm political direction. Parliament may have the ultimate power to pass or veto proposed laws, but it is not normally expected that it should be a decision-making body.

At this stage the question of the constitutional status of the monarch needs to be addressed. Confusingly, the monarch is sometimes referred to as the 'sovereign' or as 'Her Sovereign Majesty'. But this is misleading. It refers to a historical reality that no longer persists. The monarch is certainly *technically* a part of Parliament and so shares its legal sovereignty, but this is only because the royal assent is required to make bills into laws. As the monarch cannot realistically refuse the royal assent, this aspect of her legal sovereignty is purely ceremonial. The status of the royal prerogative is, however, a different matter.

As we have seen above, the prime minister, by convention, exercises the prerogative powers of the monarchy. These include the following:

● appointing and dismissing all government ministers

● creating peerages

● granting honours such as knighthoods

● appointing ambassadors

● the final appointment of senior judges and bishops of the Church of England

● commanding the armed forces and declaring wars

● agreeing foreign treaties

● conducting relations with foreign powers

● declaring a state of emergency and thus suspending normal government

● granting pardons to convicted persons.

This represents an impressive amount of power. So the prime minister can be said to have a great deal of political sovereignty that is not controlled directly by Parliament. We do, however, need to add a word of caution here. It is conceivable – only *just* conceivable – that the monarch could take back her prerogative powers under exceptional circumstances. If, for example, a prime minister or government acted in a totally unconstitutional manner (e.g. taking powers not granted to it by Parliament), it is possible that the monarch could dismiss them. More likely, if an election failed to produce a decisive result, the monarch might have to take it upon herself to appoint ministers in the absence of a clear candidate for the post of prime minister.

So the monarch could restore to herself political sovereignty in highly unusual circumstances. But for the most part, the monarch is politically passive and powerless – and certainly has been for more than a century.

The EU and the constitution

Britain joined the European Community (now known as the European Union) on 1 January 1973. Parliament had passed the European Communities Act in 1972, allowing this to happen. It has had a profound effect on the UK's constitutional arrangements.

We should note at the outset that there are some areas of government jurisdiction that are virtually unaffected by membership of the EU. Yet some policy areas *are* deeply affected, so much so that they are largely controlled by the EU. In between these two extremes are a number of policy areas that are certainly influenced by membership of the EU, though they do not fall under European control. These are shown in the table on the next page.

The relationship between the UK and the EU is constantly changing and the Union treaties have gradually moved powers from London to Brussels, i.e. from the UK Parliament to the EU Council of Ministers. The Maastricht Treaty of 1992 and the Reform (Lisbon) Treaty of 2007 have been prime examples of this process.

So we can certainly say that the question of where political and legal sovereignty lie has been clouded. However, we can summarise the situation thus:

● EU laws are superior to UK law. This was established in 1990 in the Factortame case (*Regina versus Secretary of State for Transport*) in the appeal court of the House of Lords. It

Areas where jurisdiction has passed largely to the EU	Areas where EU membership influences but does not control government policy	Areas where virtually no jurisdiction has passed to the EU
Trade	Economic policy	Education
Agriculture	Environmental protection	Health provision
Fishing		
	Defence	Social security
Employment law	Foreign policy	Law, order and justice
Consumer law		
Competition control	Overseas development	Moral legislation
Regional economic development	Asylum and immigration	Local government services
		Personal taxation
		Internal political system

- British courts must implement EU laws.

- Where an interpretation of EU law is required it must be referred upwards to the European Court of Justice. Thus the Supreme Court is not the highest court of appeal in all cases. This principle was established in the 1993 case, *Regina versus International Stock Exchange*, by Lord Bingham.

- For proposals that require a unanimous vote in the EU Council of ministers to become EU law, the UK does not sacrifice sovereignty as it has an effective veto. For example, the UK has consistently vetoed any attempts to harmonise taxation throughout Europe.

- However, where proposals can become EU law with only a qualified majority vote (about 71 per cent) in the Council of Ministers, the UK must submit to the shared sovereignty of the EU.

- Parliament should not pass any statute that conflicts with existing EU law (for example, removing workers' rights guaranteed by the EU Social Chapter). If it does so, the courts will not enforce such a law.

Thus the constitutional status of the UK Parliament and the courts has been significantly altered by British membership of the EU.

We can now summarise the answers to the question: *Where has sovereignty in the UK gone?*

- Whatever we say, Parliament remains *legally* sovereign. Even where Parliament has granted, or delegated, power to other bodies or individuals, it can reclaim those powers at any time. This applies, for example, to the devolved governments of Scotland, Wales and Northern Ireland.

- Nevertheless, a good deal of *political* sovereignty – that is *effective power* – has been

was ruled that the Merchant Shipping Act, a UK law, was inferior to the EU fisheries regulations. In this case Spanish fishing vessels were given rights to operate in British waters against the wishes of the UK Parliament.

transferred away from Parliament. This has mainly gone to the prime minister and/or government. It has also gone to the people when a referendum is held. Parliament does not have to accept the result of a referendum, but *effectively* it is unlikely that Parliament would overrule the people.

- Some legal sovereignty has been transferred to the European Union. Such transfers of sovereignty are often referred to as 'pooled sovereignty' to denote sharing, rather than losing sovereignty. This applies to a range of government responsibilities such as trade, environment and employment law. However, many areas of government have not been transferred. Furthermore, where EU decisions require a unanimous vote, such as the proposed admission of new member states, Britain retains a veto and so does not give up sovereignty. Overall, however, it must be remembered that Britain is free to leave the EU at any time and so restore all legal sovereignty to Parliament.

Constitutional reform since 1997

Key Word

Constitutional reform A process whereby the fundamental nature of the system of government (as well as the relationships between governing institutions) is changed, or where change is proposed. In the case of the UK this may also involve the process of codification.

Labour's agenda in 1997

Why Labour came to support radical constitutional reform

Significant **constitutional reform** was a key element in the New Labour 'project' developed by Neil Kinnock, John Smith and Tony Blair in the 1990s. The party, which had been transformed by the three leaders and their allies, was essentially a 'modernising' force. It was committed to reforming economic policy making, industry, foreign and defence policy and the public services. Partly for its own sake, and partly to pave the way for pushing through reforms, it was seen as necessary to make significant constitutional reforms. Three factors made a constitutional reform programme possible and desirable when Labour took power in 1997.

1. The Labour Party has always wished to promote constitutional reform but has rarely had sufficient political control to be able to do so. To some extent it has always been something of an ideological commitment among socialists and social democrats. As a party, Labour has always sought to promote popular democracy, equal rights and the reduction of traditional 'establishment' powers. The ancient constitution was seen by many to be the embodiment of traditional privilege and inequality. The 'undemocratic' status of the House of Lords was a particularly powerful example. By the mid-1990s it was clear that the party was going to win the next general election comfortably and, what is more, had the prospect of at least two consecutive terms in office. Reasonably secure in this knowledge, the party could include constitutional change in its political programme.

2. Despite the prospect of power, the Labour Party had experienced two long periods of Conservative government – 1951–64 and 1979–97 – during which it had felt totally

excluded from influence. The constitutional reforms proposed were, therefore, partly designed to prevent a situation where one party would be able to dominate the political agenda so completely. It is, of course, ironic that Labour's hold on power had become, by 2005, so secure that the constitutional changes it proposed could be directed against itself when it had in fact been developed to break Conservative hegemony.

3. There was clearly considerable public support for reform. Public opinion polls had long since indicated that a majority would be in favour of change, but this support had always been considered 'soft'. In other words, it was not high on anybody's list of concerns. By the mid-1990s, however, it was becoming obvious that demands for reform were hardening. This was demonstrated by growing support for the Liberal Democrats, who strongly advocated reform, for campaign groups such as Charter 88 and for Scottish and Welsh Nationalists.

The principles of Labour's reform

We can divide Labour's reform programme into the following processes.

Democratisation

Too much of the British political system was seen as undemocratic. The prime targets were the unelected House of Lords and the notoriously unrepresentative electoral system.

Decentralisation

As we have seen above, Labour had been scarred by the experience of watching powerlessly as successive Conservative administrations gathered increasing amounts of power into the centre. Part of the programme was, therefore, designed to disperse power away from central government to the regions and localities.

Restoration of rights

During the 1980s there had been fears that the rights of citizens in Britain had been consistently eroded. In fact, the process could be traced back to earlier periods, but Labour concentrated on what had occurred under the Conservatives. In addition, Labour wished to bring Britain more into line with European practice in constitutional matters. The party therefore proposed the incorporation of the European Convention on Human Rights into British law. In addition, a Freedom of Information Act was seen as essential in a drive to create more open and accountable government.

Modernisation

The Conservative Party had done much to modernise the civil service during the 1980s and 1990s. The Labour Party wished to extend this programme, but also turned its attention to Parliament. Changes in the composition of the House of Lords were a key element in this, but there were also hopes that reform of the House of Commons to make it more efficient and effective could be undertaken.

We can now see how extensive the Labour proposals were in 1997. Of course, experience tells us that the new government fell some way short of implementing the whole plan. However, in order to evaluate the process, it is important to be able to compare Labour's original aspirations with its subsequent actions. These can now be considered in more detail.

Before moving on to examine the detailed changes, however, it is worth summarising the totality of constitutional reform that had occurred by the time of the general election of 2010. These reforms are shown in the table below.

Constitutional reforms, 1997–2009	
Reform	**Detail**
House of Lords	Abolition of voting rights of most hereditary peers.
House of Commons	Limited changes to the committee system.
Human Rights Act 1998	Inclusion of the European Convention on Human Rights into British law. Effective from 2000.
Electoral reform	The introduction of new electoral systems for the Scottish Parliament, Welsh and Northern Ireland assemblies, elections to the European Parliament, for the Greater London assembly and for elected mayors.
Freedom of information	Introduction of freedom of information, effective from 2005. Public right to see official documents.
London government	Introduction of an elected mayor and assembly for Greater London.
Local government	Introduction of a cabinet system in local government and the opportunity for local people to introduce elected mayors by initiative and referendum.
Devolution	Transfer of large amounts of power from Westminster and Whitehall to elected bodies and governments in Scotland, Wales and Northern Ireland.
Referendums	Introduction of the principle that any proposal to transfer power within the UK should be approved by a referendum.
Party registration and the electoral commission	A new electoral commission was set up to regulate elections and referendums, including the funding of parties. This reform also required the first ever registration of political parties.
Reform of the judiciary	The 'political' office of Lord Chancellor was abolished. He was no longer head of the judiciary or speaker of the House of Lords. He was replaced by an office known as Justice Minister. The House of Lords Appeal Court was replaced by a separate Supreme Court in 2009. Senior judicial appointments are controlled by an independent committee of senior judges.

Parliamentary reform

> ### Key Word
>
> **Parliamentary reform** A process whereby reforms in the membership, powers or procedures of either or both Houses of Parliament are made or proposed.

A full account of reform of both houses of Parliament can be found below, in Chapter 2.2. However, the main principles can be described at this stage.

It was clear in 1997 that reform of the House of Lords was overdue. It was no longer acceptable in a modern democracy for part of the legislature to be based on the historical principle of hereditary peerages. Furthermore, the new Labour government of 1997 was afraid that, like its predecessors, its programme of reform might be obstructed by a notoriously conservative second chamber. There was political will for change and Labour enjoyed a thumping House of Commons majority with which to force reform through.

The easy part was to remove most of the hereditary peers from the chamber and so, by 1998, after some tricky negotiations with Conservative peers who held a majority in the Lords, the number of hereditary peers was reduced from several hundred to just 92. At a stroke this reform removed the automatic Conservative majority in the Lords and enhanced the democratic legitimacy of the second chamber. But it was intended as a first step only.

The difficult part of the reform was to determine the best composition for the new chamber in the long term. As will be described below, this proved to be difficult and frustrating. By 2008 there was still no agreement on whether to leave the Lords as it largely is – fully appointed, but without any hereditary peers at all, or fully elected, or a combination of each. This issue remains to be resolved following the general election of May 2010, though it seems likely that Lords reform will be implemented.

Reform of the Commons, meanwhile, has been piecemeal and largely superficial. There has been some strengthening of the departmental select committees and some tinkering with working hours and prime minister's question time, but little else. In 2007, Gordon Brown did propose a more radical shift in the balance of power away from the prime minister and government and towards the Commons, but the changes were never implemented.

Inevitably attention has shifted to reform of the pay and expenses system following the MPs' expenses scandals of 2009. Revelations that the system of expenses was flawed and open to abuse led to a new system whereby the issue of expenses and pay of MPs will be placed in the hands of an independent commission. Meanwhile, the knowledge that many MPs had acted either illegally or 'immorally' over their expenses claims seriously damaged the reputation of the Commons. Though the expenses issue was perhaps the most contentious political issue of 2009, its outcome will have relatively little long-term impact and is not, therefore, a significant parliamentary reform. What it may do, however, is to improve public confidence in the House of Commons once the 'offending' MPs have been removed.

> ### Key Word
>
>
>
> **Human rights** Basic rights that all citizens can expect to enjoy. Key examples include freedom of expression, freedom of association, freedom of worship, right to privacy and freedom from imprisonment without trial.

Human rights

Why the Human Rights Act was proposed

A number of factors led the Labour Party to incorporate the European Convention on **Human Rights** into British law:

- A general desire to bring the British constitution into line with the rest of Europe, all of whose states have special arrangements to protect individual rights.

- The increase in the powers of the police and the courts that had occurred in the 1980s and 1990s were now seen as a major threat to our rights.

- The British government had been brought before the European Court of Human Rights (which seeks to enforce the Convention) more than 50 times since 1966 and had lost most of the cases. Although the decisions of the court are not legally binding, these cases had been an embarrassment to the government.

- New Labour stressed the idea of active citizenship. This concept included the principle that citizens have responsibilities to their communities and to the country as a whole. In return for these responsibilities it was believed that rights should be better understood and safeguarded.

- It was part of the devolution settlements that the Welsh and Northern Ireland assemblies and the Scottish Parliament should be bound by the Convention. This was designed to reassure the citizens of these nations that devolution would not threaten their rights.

So it was that the Human Rights Act (passed in 1998) made the European Convention part of British law in 2000.

How the Human Rights Act works

The Human Rights Act states that the European Convention on Human Rights is binding on virtually all public bodies in virtually all circumstances. Furthermore, it can be enforced by any British court of law. In essence, therefore, the following individuals and bodies are bound by the Act:

- the Welsh, Scottish and Northern Irish political systems in their entirety

- local authorities

- government ministers, civil servants and their departments

- all government executive agencies

- all quangos (non-government public bodies)

- any other organisation engaged in 'public business' – this includes the media, all schools and colleges, charities, etc.

Any regulation or action by any of these bodies can be scrutinised in a court of law and may be declared unlawful. This will result in the action being cancelled and may result in compensation.

The main exception to this law concerns parliamentary legislation. In order to preserve the constitutional principle of parliamentary sovereignty, the convention cannot be considered superior to Parliament. A minister who introduces proposed legislation in Parliament must make a declaration. This declaration will state whether the government believes the proposal to be either compatible or incompatible with the convention. If it is thought to be *incompatible,* the fact will be taken into consideration when Parliament debates the bill. However, if a bill receives parliamentary approval it will be enforced by the courts.

The European Court of Human Rights may still hear appeals against UK national legislation and may declare an Act to be in breach of the convention, but its judgments are still not binding in Britain.

The Human Rights Act in context

In some senses the Act can be considered to be an extremely radical example of constitutional reform. Indeed, some commentators have suggested that it is the most important development since the Great Reform Act of 1832, when Parliament began the road to democratisation.

Certainly it is the first example of the codification of rights in British history. What is familiar to most Europeans and all Americans – a clear statement of enforceable individual rights – has not been seen here since Magna Carta in 1215. It also represents a huge advance in the protection of individuals against the power of the state.

Critics, however, suggest that the Human Rights Act does not go far enough. By preserving parliamentary sovereignty and making parliamentary legislation an exception to its jurisdiction, the Act fails to deal with a fundamental problem in the British constitution: the enormous power of central government and its almost complete control over Parliament. Had the Human Rights Act been binding on parliamentary legislation it would have represented a major check on governmental power. But it stopped short of this.

Nevertheless, an incident late in 2004 seemed to contradict the criticisms that the Act was too weak. Under the anti-terrorism legislation of 2001, the security services were granted power to detain, without trial, British citizens who were suspected of planning or carrying out terrorist acts. Eight such detainees were being held in Belmarsh prison, but decided to appeal on the grounds that their detention contravened the European Convention on Human Rights. Their appeal was upheld in the House of Lords. Parliamentary sovereignty dictated that the government did not need to obey this judgment. The European Convention is not binding on Parliament and the legislation had been lawfully enacted. But the political repercussions of the judgment were so great that the government felt it had to act. Thus the legislation was amended so that a number of safeguards for suspects were added to the Anti-Terrorism Act.

The Belmarsh case suggested that the passage of the Human Rights Act is a more dramatic constitutional change than had been envisaged. Furthermore, in 2005, the rules on the deportation of foreign terrorist suspects also had to be amended. The European Convention forbids the use of torture. This also implies that the UK should not deport any individual to a country where they are likely to be tortured. This appeared to tie the government's hands in the fight against terrorist infiltration. In this case the government had to gain assurances from other countries that deportees would not suffer torture. Here, again, the force of the Human Rights Act has been demonstrated.

It is now the case that all policy and decision makers in Britain must have a thorough knowledge of what is contained in the European Convention on Human Rights. They know that any possible transgression of these rights can lead to a legal challenge in the courts.

Electoral reform

The relationship of electoral systems to the party system is analysed in the first chapter of this section. The operation of electoral systems in the UK is also described in section 1 of this book. Here we examine the political background to reform.

Key Word

Electoral reform A process whereby the electoral system is changed or where there is a campaign for such a change.

New Labour and electoral reform

In truth, the Labour Party that prepared itself for power in the 1990s was completely split on the issue of **electoral reform**. From a pragmatic, self-interested point of view, a change looked attractive. The dominance of the Conservative Party since 1951 showed no signs of disappearing, especially after the party's 'against-all-odds' victory at the 1992 general election. If this hegemony could not be broken by political means, argued many in Labour, perhaps electoral reform would do the trick. But this was not the only factor.

As we have seen, New Labour was committed to modernising elements of the British constitution. The old electoral system was beginning to look out of date, whatever the consequences of reform. There were powerful voices in the party who suggested that Britain had become fundamentally undemocratic. The doubts within Labour were demonstrated by the party's indecisive approach to possible reform. In opposition they had commissioned Lord Plant to recommend a course of action. The Plant Committee

did opt for reform, albeit unenthusiastically, suggesting something like the German additional member system as an alternative. Still unconvinced, Tony Blair offered the electorate a referendum on the issue if Labour won power in 1997. Labour duly won, but no referendum was forthcoming. Instead, another commission was appointed, this time under Liberal Democrat Lord Jenkins.

Jenkins reported in 1998. He strongly advocated a more radical system than Plant had done. This was known as AV Plus. Its basic operation is described in the table on p.197. The party leadership demonstrated little enthusiasm for the Jenkins proposals and they have effectively been shelved. Labour continued to delay and, having won again in 2001, was far from ready to consult the electorate. However, this did not mean that electoral reform was a dead issue. On the contrary, various forms of proportional representation were steadily creeping into the political system.

Electoral reform after 1997

While little progress has been made by the electoral reform movement in terms of *general elections,* there has been great progress in other forms of election. Indeed, Britain since 1997 has resembled a great experiment in how different electoral systems can work. The descriptions below demonstrate how electoral reform has progressed, with the dates of the introduction of the system shown in each case.

Northern Ireland, Scottish local elections	
System:	Single transferable vote (STV)
Operation:	Multi-member constituencies in elections for the Northern Ireland Assembly and in local government. There are several seats in each constituency (normally four). Parties may put up any number of candidates up to the number of seats available. Voters may vote for all candidates, from any party, in any order of preference. First preferences count more, but all preferences may be relevant. An electoral 'quota' is calculated, which is the minimum

Northern Ireland, Scottish local elections (continued)	
System:	**Single transferable vote (STV)**
	votes a candidate needs to be elected. The quota is roughly the number of votes cast divided by seats available, but not exactly. The first four (if that is the number of seats) to achieve the quota are elected. First-preference votes are counted first and a candidate achieving the quota is elected automatically. Very few can do this, so second- and subsequent preference votes are progressively added until enough candidates have achieved the quota.
Effect:	This is a highly proportional system. Party representation is very close to the proportion of votes cast for each. Small parties do well and a number of independents have won seats. It also maximises voter choice, allowing them to show all their preferences and to discriminate between candidates of the *same* party.
Why used:	It was vital in such a divided society as Northern Ireland to reflect the many different groups in the Assembly. So a highly proportional system was needed. Fourteen different parties or independents were elected in a small assembly.

Scottish Parliament, Welsh Assembly, Greater London Assembly	
System:	**Additional member system (AMS)**
Operation:	A mixed or hybrid system. About two-thirds of the seats are elected by the FPTP system. However, each voter has a second vote; this is for a party. About one-third of the seats (known as 'top-up seats') are elected from a list of candidates put up by the parties. These seats are awarded according to the proportion of these second votes won by each party. However, this proportion is adjusted. Parties that do well on the constituency votes will have their list proportion adjusted downwards. Conversely, those that do poorly in constituencies will win more than the normal proportion of seats on their list. In this way small parties receive a boost from the top-up list system.
Effect:	The system has meant that Labour still dominates. However, in all three places where it has been used, no party has won an overall majority. In Scotland and Wales, Labour has had to go into coalition with the Liberal Democrats. After 2007 Scotland was governed by a minority administration run by the Scottish National Party. In the Greater London Assembly, no party dominates and there are signs of political inertia as a result. The Conservatives, who lost all their parliamentary seats in Scotland and Wales, won a fair proportion of seats in the elections to the devolved Parliament and Assembly. The Welsh and Scottish Nationalists did well from the system.
Why used:	Had FPTP alone been used in these elections, Labour would probably have won decisive majorities at the first elections. This would have defeated part of the object of the exercise – to disperse power *away* from Westminster. By introducing an element of proportional representation, the Nationalists have received fair representation and the systems do appear truly democratic.

Elections to the European Parliament	
System:	**Regional list system (closed list)**
Operation:	A common system in Europe. The country is divided into large regions. In each region voters are presented with a list of candidates from each party. They vote for a list, not an individual candidate. Seats are awarded off each list in accordance with the proportion of votes cast for each party. Therefore it is strictly proportional. The system first used (there are proposals for change in the future) was a 'closed list'. This means that the party leaderships decide which individuals are elected off their lists. An open system would mean that the voters would not only choose a party list but would also be able to determine which individuals are elected off their chosen list.
Effect:	There are no constituencies, though members do represent a region in an indirect way. The result is fully proportional. Small parties do well and the Green (two seats) and UK Independence (three seats) parties won representation. It was roundly criticised because the closed list system means that voters have no say in which individuals are elected – this is in the hands of party leaderships.
Why used:	Something of an experiment in an election that was not considered of great importance at the time. It brought Britain more into line with most other European states. It also satisfied, in some small way, demands for greater proportional representation. Constituencies were abandoned as this is not seen as particularly important in the context of the European Parliament.

The Jenkins Proposal (1998)	
System:	**AV Plus. In full, Alternative Vote plus list top-up.**
Operation:	This is the same as the additional member system described above. However, the constituency MPs would be elected differently. This would be by the alternative vote system, which is used in Australia. Voters make a first and second choice on the ballot paper. If a candidate wins at least 50 per cent of the first-choice votes, they are elected. If no candidate achieves this, the second-choice votes (i.e. the alternative votes) are added to those who have come first or second. In this way, one of the two must have an overall majority of first- plus second-choice votes.
Effect:	Though never used, it was estimated that this system would most favour the third party, i.e. the Liberal Democrats. Very small parties would probably gain few or no seats. It would be difficult but not impossible for a major party to win an overall majority. Voter choice would be greatly enhanced without electing too many small-party candidates.

The future of electoral reform

Following the election of a Conservative–Liberal Democratic coalition in 2010, it appeared that electoral reform was assured. The new government proposed an early referendum on whether to adopt the Alternative Vote (AV) system in general elections. The question of reform was, thereby, placed into the hands of the electorate.

Freedom of information

The lack of any citizen's right to obtain publicly held information was one of the features of the British constitution that lagged behind the European and US experience in the 1990s. The Labour Party, supported by the Liberal Democrats, made a firm commitment to introduce such a measure. However, the legislation, when it appeared in 1997, proved to be a disappointment to civil rights campaigners.

There are two strands to freedom of information. The first gives the right to citizens to see information that is held about them by public bodies. These include government, schools, medical bodies and other institutions of the welfare state. This has been relatively uncontroversial. Indeed, the right to view records held on computer files had long been established already under the Data Protection Act (1998). The main disappointment here was that the right would not come into existence until 2005.

The second strand has caused more problems. This concerns the right to see documents and reports that are held by government and its agencies. In other words, there was to be a public right to see inside the very workings of government. The ability to suppress information would be limited, while the media and Parliament would have much greater access to information. In theory this represents a major move towards more open government. If implemented in full, freedom of information would have virtually ended the British culture of secrecy in government.

As with electoral reform, the new Labour government proved to be less enthusiastic about reform once it was in office than when it had been in opposition. The legislation that appeared in 2000 was very much a watered-down version of similar measures in operation elsewhere in Europe. The security services were exempt while the rest of government was given a key concession. The 'normal' situation is that governments have to justify any reason for suppressing information. The British version, however, gives government the right to conceal information if it feels it might prejudice the activities of government. In other words, the onus is on the 'outsider' to prove that a document or other information should be released. Nevertheless, an Information Tribunal was also set up. The tribunal can rule on what information can and should be released. In the event this tribunal has proved to be more sympathetic to freedom of information than was envisaged.

When the Freedom of Information Act was passed, human rights campaigners thought it was too weak. Experience tells us otherwise, however. One major development illustrates its power. In 2008 a request was made to the Information Tribunal to release details of expenses claims made by MPs. Parliament attempted to block the request through the High Court, but failed. The information was released and immediately leaked to the *Daily Telegraph*. When the revelations were made in the newspaper it became clear that there had been widespread abuse of the generous expenses system. As a result a kind of 'witch-hunt' was undertaken in which hundreds of MPs were accused of 'milking' the system for their own benefit (though most claimed successfully that they had operated within the rules). The results of the revelations were far reaching. Many MPs were forced to give up their seats, Parliament was subjected to widespread ridicule and public condemnation, and the expenses system had to be radically reformed.

The Freedom of Information Act also proved to be significant in such areas as health care provision, defence procurement and local authority procedures. It is, therefore, one of the most important constitutional reforms of recent times.

London government

In 1985 the Greater London Council (GLC), a powerful local government body with wide powers and responsibilities, was abolished by the Conservative government. Prime minister Thatcher was determined to remove from power what she saw as a socialist enclave in the centre of Conservative Britain. Led by left-winger Ken Livingstone, the GLC was seen by her as a wasteful, over-bureaucratic and excessive burden on London taxpayers. Above all, however, the policies of the controlling Labour group on the GLC were viewed as dangerously socialist in nature. Abolition left London without any central government. Instead it was divided into 33 boroughs, each with their own powers. Central functions, such as the planning, ambulance, fire and police services, were left under the oversight of unelected 'quangos'.

Labour was determined to restore government to London, a measure that has been seen as an extension of local government, rather than devolution, when it returned to power in 1997. In addition a new innovation was to be introduced. This was the election of a mayor with a fair degree of executive powers. Elected mayors were unheard of in British history. In the past, mayors had been ceremonial offices, appointed by councils and with no executive power at all.

In 2000, following a decisive referendum in which the people of London approved the introduction of an elected mayor and assembly, elections were held for the two new institutions. However, the legislation seemed to ensure that neither would enjoy a significant amount of political power.

The mayor controls the allocation of funds to different uses in London, funds that are distributed and administered by the elected assembly of 25 members. But at the same time, the assembly has the power to veto the mayor's budgetary and other proposals, provided there is a two-thirds majority for such a veto. Similarly, while the mayor has powers of patronage, controlling a variety of appointments, the assembly again had rights of veto. This was a classic example of the introduction of a system of 'checks and balances', on the American model. Furthermore, the electoral system used for the assembly – AMS as in Scotland and Wales – meant that there was no possibility of a single party enjoying an overall majority. This ensured that the mayor would always face obstruction for controversial measures. The table below shows the result of the Greater London assembly election of 2008.

Greater London Assembly election, 2008	
Party	Seats
Conservative	11
Labour	8
Liberal Democrat	3
Green	2
British National Party (BNP)	1

Has the mayor made a difference?

The office of London mayor was granted relatively limited power under the legislation. He cannot be said to enjoy a similar position to powerful mayors in New York and Paris, for instance. However, within the limitations, it could be said that Ken Livingstone and his successor Boris Johnson have been involved in several significant

Boris Johnson, London's second elected mayor

developments in London. Accepting that the mayor possesses *influence* rather than power, Livingstone and Johnson have been wholly or partially instrumental in the following initiatives:

- The introduction of the congestion charge, together with its extension after 2007, was Ken Livingstone's most decisive action. Motorists must pay to drive in London's centre on weekdays. The revenue from this has been diverted into public transport. The scheme has not been a major revenue-earner but has cut traffic in central London by about a quarter.

- Livingstone lost his battle with central government to prevent the privatisation of the London Underground system, but did gain approval for a huge investment programme from 2004–09.

- He was influential in gaining central government approval for a Crossrail system in London, in effect the construction of a new east–west rail link. Boris Johnson also supports Crossrail.

- While the mayor does not control expenditure on the police, both Livingstone and Johnson secured Home Office funding for an increase in the number of police officers in the capital to its highest ever level. They also introduced about 3,000 community support officers to support the police.

- But it was Livingstone's part in the securing of the 2012 Olympic Games for the capital that may prove to be most important in the long run. Livingstone was only one element of a large team that bid for the games, but his support was certainly critical – without it the Games could not have come to London. Boris Johnson has added his support for the Games and is one of the team overseeing the development of the Olympic sites.

- A keen cyclist, Johnson has led developments to make London more cyclist-friendly. He also promises to improve the bus system in the city.

So, the range of powers available to the mayor and the assembly that oversees his work is limited, but the impact of this innovation has been considerable and high profile.

Local government

The government's enthusiasm for reform of local government in general withered very quickly after Labour was elected to office in 1997. Cities, towns and districts have been given the opportunity to elect mayors following a local referendum. However, very few held referendums and fewer still voted in favour of an elected mayor (only 11 by 2005). Furthermore, if the new mayors suffer the same fate as Livingstone in London (i.e. becoming marginalised), it will prove to be an ineffective reform.

Similarly, local authorities have been given the option of changing to a 'cabinet' system of government. This involves the creation of a central cabinet of leading councillors from the dominant party or from a coalition who may take over central control of the council's work, making key decisions and setting general policy. This replaces the former system where the work of the council was divided between a number of functional committees. But, as with elected mayors, the take-up for the new cabinet system has been patchy. Moreover, it is generally acknowledged that this kind of internal change does not tackle the real problems of local government. These are seen as threefold:

1. Lack of autonomy from central government

2. Lack of accountability to local electorates

3. Largely as a result of the first two problems, very low public interest in local government and politics.

In 2010 David Cameron's 'Big Society' ideal could mean a shift away from local authority responsibility towards local voluntary groups, but radical reform remains unlikely.

Devolution

Background

Movements that were dedicated to the introduction of greater self-government for Britain's national regions can be traced back as far as the nineteenth century. There has been a Scottish Nationalist movement for more than a century, although the Scottish National Party (SNP) did not come into existence until 1928. The Welsh Nationalist Party dates back to 1925. Both these movements were certainly influenced by the fact that Ireland had been granted virtually full independence in 1921.

The situation in Northern Ireland has been, quite clearly, very different. **Devolution** had existed there after the partition of Ireland in 1921. The province was largely self-governing under the British Crown. When inter-community violence began in the late 1960s it soon became clear that direct rule from London was necessary. In 1972, therefore, devolution was abolished. In the 1990s there was progress towards a peace settlement between the nationalist and unionist communities. Part of such a peace settlement was a new devolution arrangement and in 1998, when the Belfast Agreement (more commonly known as the Good Friday Agreement) was signed, it contained a new system of devolved government for Northern Ireland.

The demand for devolution in the 1990s

As the 1990s progressed, demands for devolution in Scotland and Wales grew steadily. There was widespread dissatisfaction with London government, especially after the recession of the early 1990s. Furthermore, nationalists in both countries were inspired by the experience of small countries that were gaining full independence after the end of the Cold War and the collapse of the Soviet Union.

Key Word

Devolution A process of constitutional reform whereby power, but not legal sovereignty, is distributed to national or regional institutions. In the UK this has meant transfer of power to institutions in Scotland, Wales and Northern Ireland, but not to the regions of England.

The Labour Party proposed devolution in its 1997 general election manifesto. This was part of its larger constitutional reform package, but was also a defensive measure. The rise of Scottish and Welsh nationalism threatened the party's domination of the two countries. By granting a degree of autonomy, though short of full independence, Labour hoped to retain their strong voting support. Meanwhile, Conservative opposition to devolution certainly undermined the party's position and it lost virtually all its seats in Wales and Scotland in 1997.

How devolution came about

In some ways the introduction of devolution can be seen as a model of how constitutional change can be effected in a parliamentary democracy such as Britain's. The stages were as follows:

- Of course, Labour had to win the general election with devolution as a clear part of its manifesto. This would provide a mandate for change. It was important for Labour to win decisively to prevent any questioning of its authority to carry through radical changes. This was achieved comfortably.

- It was not just important for Labour to win – it also needed to win well in Scotland and Wales. A resurgence of Conservative voting there would call the devolution idea into question. If, however, the nationalists were to make significant gains, it would suggest that the proposals were not radical enough. In the event the Conservatives failed to win a single seat in Scotland and Wales in the 1997 general election. The nationalist parties, meanwhile, made little progress. Labour support held up well, suggesting that it had got its devolution plans about right.

- Before the legislation was to be considered, referendums were held. These took place in 1997, soon after the general election. Two factors were important in these referendums. First, there needed to be a good turnout. In the event a little over 60 per cent of Scots voted – just enough to give the result authority. In Wales, however, the turnout was only just over 50 per cent and this has certainly had the effect of reducing the effectiveness of Welsh self-government. Second, of course, a 'Yes' vote was needed. There were no problems in Scotland – 74.3 per cent voted in favour of devolution and 63.5 per cent voted separately for the tax-varying powers that had been hotly contested in the general election campaign. In Wales, however, the 'Yes' majority was only 50.3 per cent. Nevertheless, the government decided to approve Welsh as well as Scottish devolution.

- The legislation had to be passed. With a huge parliamentary majority, this was unlikely to be a problem and so it proved. The only major stumbling block was the proposal to allow the Scottish Parliament to vary UK income tax in its own country by 3 per cent up or down. The Conservatives had dubbed this a 'tartan tax' – a means of raising taxes by stealth (so-called 'stealth taxes' had formed a major element in the Conservatives' 1997 election campaign). The new government, however, was not to be diverted and the legislation – the Scotland and Wales Acts – survived largely intact. The Acts were passed in 1998.

- The final hurdles were the actual elections to the Scottish Parliament and Welsh Assembly. Would enough people turn out to vote? Would the results be such that it was possible to form viable governments? As with the referendums, support in Wales was lukewarm, with a turnout of 46 per cent. In Scotland, there was a better turnout – 58 per cent – but there was still some concern that too few people were interested in the devolution project. The results by party, however, were more encouraging. Though Labour dominated both elections, the party failed narrowly to win overall majorities in both countries.

So it was that, in 1999, the Scottish Parliament and the Welsh Assembly came into existence. The Scottish executive was formed from a coalition between Labour and the Liberal Democrats. Donald Dewar, the Labour leader in Scotland (who then died in 2001), became the country's first minister. In Wales, Labour formed a minority executive under Alun Michael. Michael was replaced by Rhodri Morgan in 2001 following a kind of coup d'état by Labour assembly members.

In the same year Labour gave up trying to govern with a minority and formed a coalition with the Liberal Democrats. Since then Wales and Scotland have experienced both coalition and minority governments.

The table below summarises the main arguments that have been deployed in favour of, and against, the process of devolution.

The arguments for and against devolution	
For	**Against**
<ul><li>There has been growing popular demand for more self-government in the national regions.</li><li>The national regions have different needs to England, which should be reflected in stronger regional government.</li><li>By conceding devolution the demands for fuller independence will be headed off, thus preventing the break-up of the United Kingdom.</li><li>It is more democratic because government will be brought closer to the people.</li><li>It will reduce the workload of the British Parliament and government.</li><li>It recognises the new idea of a 'Europe of the regions' rather than separate states, that is, national boundaries will become less important than regional differences.</li></ul>	<ul><li>Conservatives in particular believe it may lead to the break-up of the United Kingdom because demands for independence will be fuelled by devolution.</li><li>It was argued that demand for devolution was over-exaggerated, especially in Wales, so it was unnecessary.</li><li>It creates an extra layer of government, which will increase costs to the taxpayer.</li><li>In Scotland it was feared that taxes there would inevitably rise because Scotland is less prosperous than the United Kingdom as a whole.</li><li>It will lead to confusion because there is an additional layer of bureaucracy.</li><li>Nationalists have argued that devolution does not go far enough. British government has retained all the important powers for itself.</li><li>Nationalists also argue they should have a separate voice in Europe, but devolution does not give them this.</li><li>The West Lothian Question – see p. 207.</li></ul>

Three types of devolution

The process of devolution can be divided into three levels. These are as follows:

- **Administrative devolution** is the transfer of limited powers to devolved administrations. This effectively means control over the allocation of public funds, the nature of administration, the way in which laws, enacted elsewhere, should be implemented and the passage of secondary legislation. Secondary legislation refers to the various rules and regulations that can be imposed within the country under powers granted by Parliament in Westminster.

- **Financial devolution** is the ability of the devolved administration to raise its own taxes.

Most funds available to devolved administrations are in the form of central government grants. This allows relatively little financial independence. Granting taxation powers, by contrast, conveys a great deal of autonomy. The Scottish Parliament was given very limited financial power, restricted to increasing or reducing the level of income tax by 3 per cent either way.

- **Legislative devolution** is the transfer of power to make primary legislation. It is this distinction that makes the Scottish representative body a parliament rather than an assembly.

The table below summarises the way in which these three types of devolution were granted to the nations of Britain.

The distribution of devolution			
Country	**Administrative devolution granted?**	**Legislative devolution granted?**	**Financial devolution granted?**
Scotland	Yes	Yes	Yes
Northern Ireland	Yes	Yes	No
Wales	Yes	No	No

Devolution in Scotland

The Scottish Parliament

This came into existence, after a gap of 292 years, in 1999. There are 129 seats, 73 of which are elected by normal, FPTP constituency elections. The other 56 seats are the result of voting for party lists, where each party is awarded seats from its list according to a combination of what proportion of the votes was won by them in both the constituency and the party list elections. In other

words, each Scottish voter has two votes – one for a constituency MSP (Member of the Scottish Parliament), the other for a party. The electoral system is known as the **additional member system**. The Parliament sits in Edinburgh. It has fixed electoral terms. Elections take place every four years.

In the first election in 1999 Labour won most seats, but not enough for an overall majority. Labour therefore entered a coalition with the Liberal Democrats. Following the third election to the Scottish Parliament in 2007, the strength of the parties was as shown in the table below.

Allocation of seats in the Scottish Parliament after 2007	
Party	Seats won
Labour	46
Scottish Nationalist	47
Conservative	17
Liberal Democrat	16
Greens	2
Other	1

The Labour–Lib Dem coalition collapsed. The Scottish Nationalists therefore formed a minority government. Potentially this development will lead to further demands for full independence for Scotland. However, opinion polls suggest that the Scottish people are not ready for independence, so it remains a distant prospect.

The powers and functions of the Scottish Parliament

It is important to note that the Scottish Parliament was granted the power to make primary legislation in selected areas. The term 'primary legislation' essentially means two things. First, it refers to the laws as we understand them – what is prohibited, how organisations must behave, what responsibilities citizens are expected to carry out. Second, it

The Scottish Parliament in session

grants powers to other bodies to make regulations and rules that are as binding as other laws. We call this *enabling legislation*. Thus, for example, local authorities, members of the executive and other public bodies will be given powers to make *secondary legislation*. Secondary legislation involves orders that do not need to be passed through the same process as primary legislation. They are simply announced and become law if there is no successful objection to them in Parliament.

The decision to grant powers of primary legislation was crucial to Scottish devolution. It meant that the Scots were given the opportunity to make themselves and their society distinctive. It should also be remembered that Scotland has always had its own laws, especially criminal and civil law, but that after 1707 these laws were made by the British Parliament in Westminster. In other words, the final say on Scottish law rested with the British government. With its own primary legislating powers after devolution, however, Scotland was granted a significant amount of autonomy. As we shall see below, the Welsh Assembly was not granted the power to make primary legislation and so has to consider itself very much an inferior body.

The functions of the Scottish Parliament are as follows:

1. To pass primary legislation in those areas of policy making that have been devolved to Scotland:

   ● criminal law
   ● civil law
   ● education
   ● social services
   ● local government
   ● building and planning regulations
   ● agriculture
   ● fisheries
   ● health

   ● transport
   ● emergency services.

2. To determine the level of income tax to within 3 per cent higher or lower than the general British rate set in London.

3. To approve the overall Scottish budget.

4. To call the executive to account for its actions and policies.

5. To elect a first minister to form the executive (i.e. government).

6. To form committees to scrutinise legislation and the work of Scottish executive departments.

7. To oversee and scrutinise secondary legislation produced by Scottish ministers, local authorities and other public bodies.

The constraints on the Scottish Parliament are as follows:

1. It can pass legislation only in areas allowed under devolution legislation.

2. It cannot pass legislation that conflicts with British law.

3. It cannot pass legislation that conflicts with European Union law.

4. Its legislation must conform to the European Convention on Human Rights.

5. It cannot raise its own national taxes, other than a 3 per cent variation in income tax levels.

6. It cannot amend the devolution legislation, i.e. it cannot change the system of government in Scotland.

The Scottish executive

The term 'executive' is used in the devolved systems to replace 'government'. This is to avoid confusion with British government in London.

The Scottish executive is headed by a first minister, who is effectively the prime minister of Scotland, without being given that title. The first minister is chosen, in practice, by being leader of the largest party in the Parliament. However, they must be elected to office by the whole Parliament. That is to say that the Parliament must confirm the first minister's appointment (in contrast to Westminster where the appointment of the prime minister is a very 'private' process).

The rest of the executive is formed by the heads of the various departments that make up Scottish government. The role of the executive is as follows:

1. To formulate policy for Scotland and draft appropriate legislation to be presented in Parliament.

2. To negotiate with the British government for funds.

3. To implement policies that have been developed within the executive and approved by the Scottish Parliament.

4. To make decisions under powers delegated to it by either the British or the Scottish Parliament.

5. Liaison with the British government where there are overlapping functions such as law enforcement, environmental and industrial policies.

6. To negotiate with institutions of the European Union (though Scotland has no seat at the Council of Ministers) for regional funds and favourable policies.

7. To organise and oversee the provision of services by executive departments (i.e. the Scottish civil service), local authorities and other public bodies.

A note on the West Lothian Question

This thorny issue is named after the parliamentary constituency of long-term Labour opponent of devolution Tam Dalyell. Dalyell it was who first gave voice to a particular problem arising from Scottish legislative devolution. In the Westminster Parliament all MPs have a vote on all issues. This means that Westminster MPs representing Scottish parliamentary constituencies can vote on issues that affect England and Wales *only*. To make matters worse, however, English and Welsh MPs have no such voting rights over affairs affecting Scotland as they are voted on in the new Scottish Parliament.

It can be argued that MPs representing constituencies in Scotland could be denied a vote on any issues that affect only England and Wales. But this presents another problem. What if the government cannot rely on a majority from MPs representing only Welsh and English constituencies? In such circumstances it would have to recruit Scottish MPs to support the government. Of course, this applies only to a Labour government as only Labour holds a significant number of seats in Scotland. In other words, we could be faced with a situation where a government had a working majority for the UK as a whole but not for England and Wales.

As it happens this has not yet been a problem. Labour has enjoyed a large majority of seats in England and Wales since 1997. It has not had to rely on the support of MPs from Scotland. But there could come a time in the future when this West Lothian Question could become a constitutional crisis. For now, though, it remains unresolved.

The future of devolution in Scotland

It has been said that devolution is a process, not an event. This is certainly the case in Scotland. Thus there are now moves to give additional financial independence to Scottish government. Certainly the SNP wants full financial independence in the future. However, there must be some doubt whether the new coalition government in London will allow this to happen.

More dramatically, the SNP hopes to move towards full independence. It therefore proposes a referendum on the issue. However, this will require the approval of the Scottish Parliament and this is by no means assured. In addition, opinion polls suggest that a referendum would produce a 'No' vote. That said, the arrival of a coalition Government in London may change the political landscape in Scotland as far as independence is concerned. Most Scots remain staunchly anti-Conservative, which may change the attitude of the senior coalition partner.

Devolution in Wales

The Welsh Assembly

In Wales, the representative body is known as an assembly rather than a parliament. This reflects the fact that it has considerably fewer powers than its Scottish counterpart. In particular, it has no powers to make any primary legislation. This is a key difference. It means that the British Parliament and government still rule Wales.

The assembly was elected at the same time as the Scottish Parliament, using the same AMS electoral system. There are 60 seats in all. The Assembly meets in Cardiff and, like Scotland, has a fixed term of four years. The result of the first election is shown in the table below.

Seats in the Welsh Assembly after 1999	
Party	Seats won
Labour	28
Plaid Cymru (Welsh Nationalist)	17
Conservative	9
Liberal Democrat	6

As in Scotland, Labour failed to win an overall majority but was the largest party. However, unlike in Scotland the party decided to try to govern alone, without a coalition party. Within two years this proved to be impractical and so it formed a coalition, again with the Liberal Democrats.

In 2007 the election result was somewhat different, as shown in the following table.

Seats in the Welsh Assembly after 2007	
Party	Seats won
Labour	26
Plaid Cymru (Welsh Nationalist)	15
Conservative	12
Liberal Democrat	6
Independent	1

The coalition between Labour and the Liberal Democrats collapsed after the 2007 election. Instead, Labour went into coalition with Plaid Cymru.

The powers and functions of the Assembly

The following list indicates the main policy areas devolved to Wales:

- education
- social services
- local government
- building and planning regulations
- agriculture
- fisheries
- health
- transport
- housing
- Welsh language regulations
- sport and recreation
- emergency services.

The most important element of Welsh devolution is that the assembly (note again that it is not called a *parliament*) does not have the power to make primary legislation. This means it has to rely on Westminster for all its legislation. This is a considerable limitation. The assembly can make secondary legislation. This involves more minor laws and regulations under the general limitations of the primary legislation passed in Westminster. What is left to the Welsh Assembly, therefore, is as follows.

Functions:

1. It calls the Welsh executive (see below) to account by questioning department heads both in committee and through the full assembly.

2. It elects the head of the Welsh executive. It can also dismiss that person.

3. It discusses Welsh affairs and makes resolutions that it hopes will be influential on London and on Cardiff.

4. It discusses the implementation of policy on Welsh affairs.

5. It attempts to direct the Welsh executive in its implementation of policy and allocation of funds to various uses.

6. It debates and requests changes to the Welsh budget.

Restraints on its powers:

1. It can pass only limited primary legislation.

2. It cannot grant powers to members of the Welsh executive.

3. It cannot call London government to account directly.

4. It cannot raise any special taxes in Wales.

The Welsh executive

This is, to a large extent, the government of Wales. However, because relatively few powers were devolved it must share this function with London – with the Welsh Office, in particular. The head of the executive is elected by the assembly and that person appoints the heads of the Welsh departments. These department heads are accountable to the assembly, which can effectively remove them. As we have seen above, the first Welsh executive was a Labour minority government but it has since become a Labour–Plaid Cymru coalition.

The functions of the executive are as follows:

- To allocate funds, which are provided by the British government, among competing needs such as health, education, transport and industrial development.

- To negotiate with the Welsh Office in London for those funds.

- To negotiate appropriate legislation for Wales with the Welsh Office.

- To organise the implementation of devolved policy areas in Wales.

- To represent the interests of Wales at various institutions of the European Union, even though Wales is not separately represented in the Council of Ministers.

The future of devolution in Wales

The powers of the Welsh Assembly were increased modestly in 2007, but it now seems likely that the assembly will take power to pass primary legislation. This would give Wales nearly as much autonomy as Scotland. In February 2010 the assembly voted in favour of holding a referendum on this issue. If the vote is 'Yes' it will give Wales similar powers to those enjoyed by Scotland. Of course, even if that hurdle is cleared it remains to be seen whether the Coalition Government in London will allow such powers to be transferred. Ultimately the sovereign Westminster Parliament will decide.

An evaluation of devolution in Wales and Scotland

Before attempting to assess how well devolution is working it is useful to consider what pieces of evidence we should look for. If we are to judge devolution a 'success', what are the signs to look for? Here are some suggestions:

1. Public opinion surveys indicating high levels of satisfaction with devolved government

2. A rise in the sense of 'national identity' in the two countries. This may be assessed by surveys, but is generally difficult to judge and the evidence is likely to be uncertain

3. Have Scotland and Wales developed significantly different policies to those that apply in England when we remind ourselves of why devolution was introduced – because it was felt that Scotland and Wales may have different needs and demands to England? If this assumption is true, it must follow that there will be differing policies. In this respect, it is clear that Scotland, with powers of legislation, is bound to have become more independent.

4. Arguably we could consider whether demands for federalism or full independence have subsided. If they have, devolution could be said to have achieved one of its objectives – to satisfy demands for more self-government. If not, it could be argued that devolution has failed in its primary objective.

At the time of writing, devolution is only 12 years old – too soon to make a valid assessment. However, the early signs are interesting.

Wales

Welsh devolution undoubtedly enjoys less support than in Scotland. It is also true that, at first, it appeared to be unpopular. In recent years, however, there has been a distinct revival of interest in devolution in Wales. The Nationalists, Plaid Cymru, made considerable progress in the 2007 assembly election and now share government with Labour.

The assembly certainly increased its popularity when it abolished prescription charges and reduced the tuition fees paid by Welsh students in higher education. There are now proposals to give the Welsh Assembly legislative powers similar to those enjoyed by the Scottish Parliament. It is likely that this will be implemented by 2011.

Scotland

The picture here looks even brighter for devolution. The first indication is that Scottish government has made a difference in some areas. Five examples are interesting:

1. The bovine foot-and-mouth crisis, when many thousands of cattle had to be slaughtered and beef and dairy farming was severely affected, was handled more successfully in Scotland and it therefore escaped the worst effects.

2. The Scottish Parliament forced through a measure to make all care of the elderly in special homes free on demand (only *medical* care is free in England and Wales).

3. The extra tuition fees for Scottish students in higher education were abolished. They were retained in England and Wales.

4. While the House of Commons was locked in an exercise of mutual frustration with the Lords over fox hunting, the unicameral (single chamber) Scottish Parliament had little difficulty in responding to public demands for its abolition (though it remains subject to a possible legal appeal).

5. The Scottish Parliament has introduced proportional representation (STV) for local government elections under its jurisdiction.

While these legislative innovations were taking place, the feared rises in Scottish taxation have not emerged. Surveys indicate reasonable levels of satisfaction with the operation of the Scottish Parliament and executive. As in Wales,

there are few signs that demands for full independence are rising. The Scottish National Party made no progress in the general election of 2001 – a sure sign that nationalism remains quite weak.

Yet there is little evidence of a stronger sense of Scottish identity emerging. There has always been a strong feeling of Scottish cultural identity, but there is little evidence that this is turning into patriotism, which involves pride in one's political institutions.

Devolution in Northern Ireland

Devolution in Northern Ireland has to be seen in the context of the Good Friday Agreement of 1998. However, we can identify a number of reasons why devolution in Northern Ireland had to be very different in character from the constitutional developments in Wales and Scotland.

●   There is a deep sectarian divide in Northern Ireland. This is more fundamental in character than the division between those English people who favour a close union within the United Kingdom (largely conservatives) and those who wish for more independence in Scotland and Wales, mostly nationalists and liberals. The Northern Ireland devolution arrangements had to take into account the fact that, in many policy areas, it would be difficult to find any consensus.

●   The normal 'British' model of parliamentary government tends to ensure that a clear *majority* government emerges. Both the electoral system of first-past-the-post and the practice of forming executives from one single party, or at least *dominated* by one party, have ensured one-party government. In Wales and Scotland, Labour is the dominant party in the new executives and is likely to remain so for some time, even though it has a junior coalition party. In Northern Ireland, the domination of all political life by the Protestant Unionists as a result of the **St Andrews Agreement**. Since then further problems between Nationalists and Loyalists have created uncertain progress towards a final settlement. However, a further breakthrough in February 2010 saw all parties agreeing to the transfer of law and order and security issues to the Northern Ireland executive. This event was highly significant as it seemed to remove the final obstacle to permanent power sharing.

English regional devolution

In 2001 the establishment of regional assemblies in parts of England was a Labour policy. It was supported by the Liberal Democrats, but vehemently opposed by the Conservatives. However, there was also a commitment to hold referendums in the regions (as had occurred in Scotland, Wales and Northern Ireland) to determine whether there was public consent for such a development.

In 2004 a referendum was held in the North-East to ask whether devolution, very much along Welsh lines, was supported. The proposal was firmly rejected by a majority of 77.9 per cent against as opposed to 22.1 per cent in favour. This shocked the government and it promptly cancelled all the other proposed referendums. Regional devolution seemed to be a dead duck and is likely to remain so for the foreseeable future.

Nevertheless, some English devolution has certainly occurred. England is now divided into eight regions (not including London). Since 2001 some of the activities of government departments in London have been transferred to these regions. Thus, civil service planning in such areas as industrial development, transport and the environment is now undertaken at regional rather than national level. This does not add up to regional devolution, as such, but can be described as devolved administration.

Referendums

There has not been a piece of legislation establishing the practice of holding **referendums** to provide popular consent for constitutional changes. Nevertheless, it has become firmly established that a referendum will be held if any power is to be transferred away from central government in the UK. This transfer could be upwards to the European Union or downwards to regional or local bodies.

In other parts of the democratic world referendums are often used as a special arrangement for constitutional reform. In the past, Britain has not had special arrangements for constitutional amendments – they have been created either by Act of Parliament or by the emergence of new unwritten conventions. But the referendum is now a regular feature in the UK, so much so that we can describe its use as an important constitutional reform.

Key Word

Referendum A popular vote in which the people rather than their elected representatives resolve a political issue. It is used as a way of gaining consent for constitutional reforms.

The registration of political parties

The Political Parties, Elections and Referendums Act of 2000 was a landmark in the codification of the party system in the UK. Before then the existence and conduct of parties was largely conventional and voluntary in nature. Now all parties must be registered if they are to take part in elections. By registering, they subject themselves to a variety of strict rules on finance and conduct.

But behind the legislation there lies a more fundamental change. This is the admission, in a constitutional statute, that elections are about parties rather than about individuals. Individuals can still stand for election, but if they are to use a party label, they become subject to a new, stricter set of regulations.

Reform of the judiciary

A fuller account of this area of reform can be found below, in Chapter 2.4. However, we can specify the main principles of reform here.

First, and most importantly, it was seen as crucial that there be a clearer separation between the senior members of the judiciary and the government. In the past, the position of the Lord Chancellor had been ambiguous. He was a cabinet minister and senior member of the governing party. At the same time he was head of the judiciary and presided over the proceedings of the House of Lords. This placed him in all three branches of government. Although the occupant of the post might protest that he understood the difference between his neutral *judicial* role and his *political* role as a cabinet minister, suspicions persisted that one role would interfere with another. This perception of lack of independence had to be addressed in a modern system. The judicial role of the Lord Chancellor was therefore largely removed.

Second, the highest court of appeal was the House of Lords, meeting as a court rather than as part of Parliament. The senior 'law lords' – usually in groups of five – would hear important appeal cases, often with great political consequences. There was disquiet over recent years that it was not appropriate that members of the legislature (i.e. the law lords) should also be the highest level of the judiciary. In other words, it was seen as vital that law and politics should be completely separated to safeguard the rule of law. It was therefore decided to take the senior judges out of the Lords and to create a separate Supreme Court. The Supreme Court was opened in the autumn of 2009 and began work immediately to establish its new independence. In reality the change to a Supreme Court is a cosmetic exercise. The new court has the same powers as the old House of Lords. However, it is symbolically important and the early signs have indicated that it will indeed prove to be a genuinely independent body.

Third, there was opposition to the continued practice of senior appointments to the judiciary being in the hands of politicians – mainly the Lord Chancellor and the prime minister. There was a constant danger that such appointments might be made on the basis of the political views of prospective judges rather than on their legal qualifications. A Judicial Appointments Commission (JAC) was therefore set up in 2005 to ensure that all candidates should be suitable, using purely legal considerations. The government has the final say on who shall become a senior judge, but this must be after approval by the JAC. The most senior appointments – to the Supreme Court – have been placed in the hands of a non-political committee of senior judicial figures.

The principles of judicial reform have been fourfold:

1. To increase the separation of powers between government, legislature and judiciary.

2. To improve the independence of the judiciary.

3. To eliminate the ambiguity of the role of the Lord Chancellor.

4. To bring Britain into line with modern constitutional practice.

An assessment of constitutional reform after 1997

The position with regard to constitutional reform in Britain at the start of the twenty-first century is certainly paradoxical. On the one hand, the years after 1997 have seen the greatest constitutional changes in Britain probably since 1832 – and, some have suggested, even since Parliament became effectively sovereign in 1688. The list of reforms shown in the table at the start of this chapter is certainly impressive. Yet New Labour's reforms disappointed many, both inside and outside the party.

The Liberal Democrats and constitutional pressure groups such as Unlock Democracy and Liberty see reform as only half completed. They point to the following gaps in the programme needed to make Britain a truly modern democracy:

● The new, largely appointed House of Lords falls well short of being properly accountable, authoritative and representative. Only a fully elected second chamber, they argue, is acceptable.

● The House of Commons remains ineffective and inefficient. Lack of government accountability is seen as a fundamental problem and only a reformed, revitalised House of Commons can provide this.

● The Human Rights Act, though a vital development, has not been given the political status it needs. The fact that the European Convention cannot overrule Acts of Parliament means that rights can still be trampled on by powerful governments. The anti-terrorism measures were enacted that after the September 11th terrorist attacks on the USA were seen as a case in point.

● The Freedom of Information Act is too weak and allows government to remain over-secretive.

● Perhaps most importantly, Labour had failed, up to 2010, to deliver electoral reform for parliamentary or local elections. It is this measure that is most often seen as the way in which the political system can be fundamentally changed for the better.

Prospects for constitutional reform after 2010

The coalition government that took office in May 2010 promised a good deal of constitutional reform. The proposals for reform were as follows:

● the introduction of the Alternative Vote for general elections (if approved by referendum)

● the introduction of a fully elected second chamber to replace the House of Lords

● the introduction of fixed-term parliaments, taking away the prime minister's power to dissolve parliament and call a general election. The term is likely to be five years and governments will not be removable unless a 67 per cent majority in the Commons votes for its own dissolution

● local constituents will have the power to 'recall' an MP who proves to be corrupt or unsatisfactory. Recall would require a petition to call a fresh by-election

● reduction of the size of the Commons by 10 per cent and the equalisation of the size of parliamentary constituencies.

● the possible introduction of elected mayors in ten more major cities

● greater powers granted to the Scottish Parliament and Welsh Assembly

● the compulsory registration of lobby groups (i.e. pressure groups) in order to regulate their operation in Parliament.

If most of these reforms are implemented it will represent a similarly radical programme to that of the first three years of the previous Labour government. Specifically, it will change the following features of the political system:

- the party system (potentially to a three-party system)

- the way governments are formed

- the powers of the prime minister

- the role and status of Parliament

- the relationship between Parliament and the executive

- the relationship between voters and MPs.

Key concepts in this chapter

Constitution A set of principles, which may be written or unwritten, that establishes the distribution of power within a political system, relationships between political institutions, the limits of government jurisdiction, the rights of citizens and the method of amending the constitution itself.

Codification The process of setting out a constitution in an organised way in a single document.

Parliamentary sovereignty The British principle that Parliament is the source of all political power (with the exception of the prerogative powers of the prime minister) and that all enforceable laws must be approved by Parliament.

Constitutional reform A process whereby the fundamental nature of the system of government (as well as the relationships between governing institutions) are changed, or where change is proposed. In the case of the UK, this may also involve the process of codification.

Parliamentary reform A process whereby reforms in the membership, powers or procedures of either or both Houses of Parliament are made or proposed.

Human rights Basic rights that all citizens can expect to enjoy. Key examples include freedom of expression, freedom of association, freedom of worship, right to privacy and freedom from imprisonment without trial.

Devolution A process whereby power, but not sovereignty, is transferred to regions and countries. It means the establishment of assemblies and governments in those regions.

Referendum A popular vote in which the people rather than their elected representatives resolve a political issue. It is used as a way of gaining consent for constitutional reforms.

Constitutional government Government that is limited by a constitution and by constitutional principles.

Legal sovereignty The location of ultimate power to make laws, together with the location of the source of all legal power within the political system. In the UK legal sovereignty lies in Parliament.

Revision topics and examination questions

Revision topics

- Nature and functions of constitutions
- Nature of codification and entrenchment
- Sources of the British Constitution
- Main features and characteristics of the British Constitution
- The nature and location of sovereignty in the UK
- The changing location of sovereignty
- Federal and unitary constitutions
- Sovereignty and Parliamentary sovereignty
- Impact of the EU on the British constitution
- The arguments for and against codification of the constitution
- Constitutional reform – past and future
- The impact of EU membership on UK sovereignty
- The impact of devolution

Essay questions

40 minutes

1. Assess the arguments for and against introducing a codified constitution in the UK.
2. Discuss the view that Parliament is no longer truly sovereign.
3. Assess the strengths and weaknesses of the British constitution.
4. How and to what extent has the British constitution been criticised?
5. Why did Labour governments introduce a series of constitutional reforms after 1997?
6. 'The reform of the British constitution remains unfinished business.' Explain and discuss.

Stimulus questions

Question 1

40 minutes

Read the following passage and answer the questions that follow:

'What constitutes citizens' rights – beyond voting – and citizens' responsibilities – like jury service – should itself be a matter for public deliberation. And as we focus on the challenges we face and what unites us and integrates our country, our starting point should be to discuss together and then – as other countries do – agree and set down the values, founded in liberty, which define our citizenship and help define our country.

And there is a case that we should go further still than this statement of values to codify either in concordats or in a single document both the duties and rights of citizens and the balance of power between government, Parliament and the people.

In Britain we have a largely unwritten constitution. To change that would represent a fundamental and historic shift in our constitutional arrangements. So it is right to involve the public in a sustained debate whether there is a case for the United Kingdom developing a full British Bill of Rights and Duties, or for moving towards a written constitution.

And because such fundamental changes should happen only where there is a settled consensus on whether to proceed, I have asked my Right Honourable Friend the Secretary for Justice to lead a dialogue within Parliament and with people across the United Kingdom by holding a series of hearings, starting in the autumn, in all regions and nations of this country – and he will consult with the other parties on this process.'

Gordon Brown, statement to the House of Commons, Hansard, 3 July 2007

(a) From the source, explain what is meant by the expression 'we have a largely unwritten constitution'. **(5 marks)**
(b) From the source and your own knowledge, assess the current 'balance of power between government, Parliament and the people' in relation to the British constitution. **(10 marks)**
(c) Assess the arguments in favour of and against the introduction of a codified constitution for Britain. **(25 marks)**

Question 2

40 minutes

Read the following passage and answer the questions that follow:

The coalition government which took office in May 2010 promised a major programme of constitutional reform. Led by Nick Clegg, who claimed they were embarking on the most radical set of reforms since 1832, plans were unveiled for a possible new electoral system, an elected House of Lords and fixed-term parliaments. A number of other reforms to parliament were also proposed. An eye-catching measure was the idea to allow local constituencies to recall an MP who was unsatisfactory in some way.

The purposes of these reforms included an attempt to restore public faith in politics and to usher in an era of 'new politics' which would break the old two party control over governmental power. They were also designed to move power away from central government towards the people. The Liberal Democrats had a special interest in reform as they were hoping to cement their position at the centre of British politics. For the Conservatives it was a matter of necessity. If they did not agree to reforms, they could not rely on the support of their coalition partner.

(a) From the source, briefly explain three constitutional reforms proposed by the coalition government in May 2010 **(5 marks)**
(b) From the source and your own knowledge, why was a programme of constitutional reform proposed in 2010? **(10 marks)**
(c) Analyse the arguments against further reform of the constitution **(25 marks)**

Resources and web guide

Books

The classic work on the British Constitution was written in 1867 by journalist Walter Bagehot. Though clearly dated, it is an interesting insight. This was:
   Walter Bagehot, *The English Constitution*, various editions.

A detailed account is given by:
   Peter Hennessy, *The Hidden Wiring,* Gollancz, 1995.

However, this may be too detailed for all but the most committed students.

Perhaps the single chapter on the constitution from Gillian Peele's work is best for modest further reading:
   Gillian Peele, *Governing the UK,* Blackwell, 2004.

An excellent discussion is:
   K. Harrison and T. Boyd, *The Changing Constitution*, Edinburgh University Press, 2006

or:
   D. Oliver, *Constitutional Reform in the UK*, Oxford University Press, 2003

A major new work is:
   V. Bogdanor, *The New British Constitution*, Oxford University Press, 2009

Useful websites

The best site for comprehensive information is:
   www.ucl.ac.uk/constitution-unit.ac.uk

The government service on the constitution is published by the Department for Constitutional Affairs.
   www.dca.gov.uk

The main campaign group for reform is Unlock Democracy.
www.unlockdemocracy.org.uk

Parliament

2.2

Introduction

Parliament is normally known as the 'legislature'. This suggests that it has something to do with making law (from the Latin *legis – of the law)*. This is undoubtedly appropriate, but it would be a mistake to assume therefore that law making is Parliament's primary function. It is not. As we shall see below, most law certainly does have to pass through parliamentary procedure, but this is not to say that *making* law is what Parliament does. It is more accurate to say that it makes laws *legitimate*.

So, if Parliament is not *primarily* a law-making body we will have to ask what its main purposes are. This chapter will explore the functions of Parliament, will explain how it carries them out and will evaluate how well it performs those functions. It will then consider the ways in which Parliament has been reformed in recent times and how such reforms might continue into the future.

It is perhaps worth examining briefly the historic role of Parliament as such a perspective can help us to understand many of its current activities and procedures.

From the Middle Ages onwards it became the practice of English monarchs to call representatives of the aristocracy (a council that became the House of Lords) and of the boroughs (towns) and the counties (a gathering that became the House of Commons) to advise them. It is immediately interesting to note that early parliaments were called by the monarch themselves, not by the people. Thus Parliament existed to assist the monarch rather than as an expression of democracy.

Parliaments up to the latter part of the seventeenth century had two main functions: one was to give legitimacy to laws that the monarch wished to see enacted; the other was to give consent to taxation (taxation also implied expenditure on a war or a public building development, etc.). There have been lengthy periods when monarchs attempted to govern without Parliament, but these became briefer and briefer as time went by. Indeed, it was Charles I who paid the ultimate price (he was executed by Parliament in 1649) for attempting to govern without Parliament. King Charles' successors certainly learned the lesson!

In other words, the role of Parliament was to *support* the monarch, *not to control* the monarch's power. Though Parliament insisted on being consulted, its role was subordinate to the monarchy through most of its history. To some extent this legacy remains, except that we have replaced the monarchy with the elected government of the day.

Parliament did demand something in return for its support. This was the 'redress of grievances'. The Commons in particular expected that

The House of Commons in session

the monarch would listen to the complaints of the representatives on behalf of the inhabitants of their boroughs or counties. Many such disputes were about tax, of course, but there would also be problems of, for example, land tenure, inheritance and military service.

It was only after the Glorious Revolution of 1688, when the Stuart monarchy was replaced by William and Mary, that we can say that Parliament began to assume its current role. At that time, responsibility for legislation began to pass decisively from the monarch to Parliament. But even then it was not expected that Parliament would actually *initiate* any legislation. This function was gradually transferred from the monarch to the leaders of Parliament, that is, the most prominent members of both Houses. It was this leadership group that eventually was to become the more formal *cabinet,* and the cabinet's most senior figure became known as prime minister in the 1720s. By the end of the nineteenth century cabinet also came to be exclusively made up of leading members of the dominant party in Parliament.

If we look back at this brief parliamentary history, we can see that the basic functions of Parliament remain the same as they always were. Parliament exists to make government legitimate, to give consent to legislation without actually making that legislation, to approve the government's financial arrangements and, in return, to expect to raise grievances against the government and thus make it accountable. On the whole, therefore, Parliament's key role – or at least the role of the governing majority – is to support government, not to threaten it. But one major function has been added: this is Parliament's ability to dismiss a government through a vote of no confidence. This reserve power, a constant reality that governments are aware of, means that every government must make itself responsible to Parliament.

Parliamentary and presidential government

Before proceeding it is important to make clear the constitutional basis of parliamentary government. At the same time it can usefully be contrasted with presidential government, as it operates in the USA, to bring into focus its important elements.

Parliamentary government

Parliamentary government implies the following features:

- Parliament is the highest (in the UK the *only*) source of political authority. That is, political power may be exercised only if it has been authorised by Parliament.

- The government must be drawn from Parliament – either the Commons or the Lords. In other words, all members of the government must also be members of one of the two houses.

- There is, therefore, no strict separation of powers between that of the legislature and that of the executive. Instead, we say that the powers of the government and legislature are *fused*.

- Government must be accountable to Parliament.

As we can see, these principles place Parliament at the very centre of the British political system.

Presidential government (the US model mainly) is quite different. These are its main features:

- The legislature and the executive, in the form of the presidency, have separate sources of authority. They are separately elected.

- The president is not part of the legislature.

- The president (and therefore executive government as a whole) is accountable directly to the people, not to the legislature.

- There is a clear **separation of powers** between the executive and the legislature.

- This implies that there must be a codified constitutional arrangement that separates those powers.

 Key Word

Presidential government In contrast to parliamentary government, a president normally has a separate source of authority from that of the legislature. This means that the executive (president) is accountable to the people directly, not to the legislature.

 Key Word

Separation of powers A constitutional principle that the three branches of government – legislature, executive and judiciary – should have separate membership and separate powers and should be able to control each other's powers. It is largely absent in the UK.

 Key Word

Parliamentary government A system of politics where government is drawn from Parliament and is accountable to Parliament. In other words, the government has no separate authority from that of Parliament.

Parliamentary sovereignty

This is perhaps the most important reality in the whole of the British political system. The general meaning of the term 'sovereignty' is explained in the first section of this book. But it is important to place this concept in the context of Parliament itself.

Parliament in the UK is said to be *legally sovereign.* This means the following:

- Parliament is the source of all political power. No individual or body may exercise power unless it has been granted by Parliament. In effect, of course, Parliament does delegate most of its powers – to ministers, to devolved governments in Scotland, Wales and sometimes Northern Ireland, to local authorities and to the courts of law.

- Parliament may restore to itself any powers that have been delegated to others.

- Parliament may make any laws it wishes and they shall be enforced by the courts and other authorities. There are no restrictions on what laws Parliament may make. In this sense Parliament is said to be *omnicompetent* (literally, capable of any act).

- Parliament is not bound by its predecessors. In other words, laws passed by parliaments in the past are not binding on the current Parliament. Existing laws may be amended or repealed at will.

- Parliament cannot bind its successors. This means that the current Parliament cannot pass any laws that will prevent future parliaments from amending or repealing them. In effect, therefore, we can say that laws cannot be *entrenched* against future change. For this reason, Britain cannot have a fixed, entrenched constitution as long as the current principle of parliamentary sovereignty endures.

If, however, we consider another type of sovereignty – **political sovereignty** – we can certainly say that Parliament has lost much of its sovereignty. Political sovereignty refers not to strictly *legal* power but to where political power lies *in reality.* It is the practical location of power rather than its theoretical location.

In reality, most political power lies with government. Normally, though obviously not always, the government of the day enjoys a majority in the House of Commons and can therefore virtually guarantee that its proposals will be passed by Parliament. It is sometimes said, therefore, that 'the sovereignty of Parliament is, in reality, the sovereignty of the majority party'. It is generally understood that the government has an electoral mandate to carry out its manifesto commitments and Parliament should not thwart that authority. We expect Parliament to block government plans only if it is seen to be abusing its mandate or operating beyond it. In addition, of course, at a general election, political sovereignty returns to the people, who are both electing a new Parliament and giving a new government a fresh mandate.

But before we dismiss Parliament as the sovereign body in theory only, we must remember that Parliament retains enormous *reserve* powers. In some circumstances it can block legislation (in modern times the House of Lords does this quite frequently) and in really exceptional circumstances Parliament can dismiss a government by passing a vote of no confidence. This was last done in 1979 when James Callaghan's Labour government was removed prematurely from office.

In summary, therefore, we can say that Parliament in the UK is legally sovereign, but that political sovereignty is less clearly located. It lies with the people at elections, with the government between elections, but with the proviso that Parliament can ultimately overrule the government.

The erosion of parliamentary sovereignty

There are five main senses in which it can be said that parliamentary sovereignty has been eroded. These are as follows:

1. Clearly a great deal of legislative power has moved to the European Union. European law is superior to British law so if there is any conflict, EU law must prevail. At the same time, Parliament may not pass any law that conflicts with EU law. There remain large areas of policy that have not passed to Brussels, including criminal law, tax law, social security, health and education, but there are also significant shifts of legislative authority – over trade, environment, employment rights and consumer protection, for example.

2. As we have seen above, executive power has grown considerably in recent decades. This involves a transfer of political but not legal sovereignty.

3. It is increasingly the practice to hold referendums when important constitutional changes are being proposed, such as devolution or the election of city mayors. Although the results of such referendums are not technically binding on Parliament, it is almost inconceivable that Parliament would ignore the popular will of the people. So, in effect, sovereignty in such cases returns to the people.

4. There is also some room for controversy over the status of the Human Rights Act and the European Convention on Human Rights, which it establishes in law. The ECHR is not legally binding on Parliament, so Parliament retains its sovereignty. However, it is also clear that Parliament treats the ECHR largely as if it *were* supreme. In other words, it would only be in extraordinary circumstances that Parliament would assert its sovereignty over the ECHR.

5. Finally, there is devolution, especially to Scotland. As with referendums, Parliament can restore to itself all the powers that it has delegated, but it is difficult to imagine circumstances in which the powers granted to the Scottish Parliament and the Welsh Assembly would be removed. Here again sovereignty has been transferred in reality, though not in constitutional law.

So we could say that parliamentary sovereignty is now something of a myth. But before we jump to such a conclusion we must remind ourselves again of Parliament's reserve powers. Britain can leave the EU at any time and so restore all her sovereignty. Parliament can thwart the will of the government, devolution could be cancelled – bear in mind that the Northern Ireland Assembly has been suspended and direct rule from London restored on several occasions, Parliament could, under exceptional circumstances, decide not to accept the verdict of a referendum. Furthermore, if there comes a time when the government does not enjoy a secure parliamentary majority, it could be that the balance of power – both legal and political – could return to Parliament, much as it did in the middle part of the nineteenth century.

The structure of Parliament

Parliament is divided into three parts. These are the House of Commons – known as the *Lower House*, the House of Lords – known as the *Upper House* – and the Queen-in-Parliament. The House of Lords is known as the Upper House not because it is senior or more important but as a reflection of its more illustrious history. In practice, and paradoxically, the House of Commons is considered the senior chamber, even though it remains the Lower House in name.

One aspect of this triple personality – the monarchy – is immediately puzzling, especially as the Queen is not welcome at the Palace of

Westminster except when she is performing the ceremonial opening of the new session of Parliament, normally in the autumn. Indeed, the monarch is never allowed in the House of Commons. This is a relic of the past occasions when the monarch's presence in the chamber was seen as a direct threat to the independence of its members. So the Queen must deliver her annual speech in the Lords. The only reason today why the Queen is considered part of the legislature is that proposed legislation requires her signature

(the Royal Assent) to become legitimate. But the monarch plays no *active* role in parliamentary politics and the Royal Assent has not been refused since 1708. On that occasion Queen Anne resisted the passage of the Scottish Militia Bill, which abolished the Scottish Parliament. She was brought quickly into line, the Act was passed and no monarch since has tried to defy Parliament.

We can now examine Parliament in more detail.

The House of Commons, May 2010			
Party	Male MPs	Female MPs	Total
Conservative	257	49	306
Labour	178	80	258
Liberal Democrat	49	8	57
Democratic Unionist	8	0	8
Scottish National	6	0	6
Sinn Fein	4	1	5
Plaid Cymru	3	0	3
SDLP (N. Ireland)	2	1	3
Alliance (N. Ireland)	0	1	1
Green Party	0	1	1
Independent	0	1	1
The Speaker (independent)	1	0	1
Total	**508**	**142**	**650**

Plenary sessions

Neither the House of Lords nor the Commons meets very often in full, or plenary, session. Indeed, there are not nearly enough seats for all the members! The occasions when the Houses are most full are normally for prime minister's Question Time in the Commons every Wednesday, or when a great issue of the day is to be debated. In recent years the debates on the banning of hunting with dogs, on the 2003 war in Iraq, on the 2001 Anti-Terrorism Act and on student tuition fees have all attracted full houses. But for the most part the two chambers are only part filled. It is true that all loyal party members are expected to *vote* on government legislation, but this does not mean that members of either House have to be present during debates.

General committees of either House

Much of the legislative business of both houses of Parliment is carried on through general committes. They typically contain between 20–40 members. There are various types dealing with secondary (minor) legislation and regional issues. Occasionally a general commitee will conduct a debate on the general principles of a bill when it is not contentious. However, the main kind of general committee is a **public bill committee.**

Public bill committees are specially formed to consider proposed amendments to government legislation (the vast majority of legislation is produced by government). Each important amendments is debated in commitee and a vote is held to decide whether to include it. As most key general committees are concerned with legislation we will call them 'legislative committees' below.

Before we assume that this role grants much power to MPs and peers we must be aware that these committees are not free from party discipline. The governing party is always granted a majority on the committees (that is, positions are allocated in rough proportion to party membership in the two Houses as a whole). Party loyalty is expected to apply in committee. Members of the governing party are required only to vote for amendments that are approved by the government (indeed, many amendments are proposed by ministers as a result of consultations with pressure groups or other interested parties). Similarly, governing party members normally vote against any amendment that is not approved by government. It is rare for an amendment to succeed against government wishes.

The government does, indeed, have a further precaution against unwanted amendments. Any changes proposed in the House of Lords' committees must also be approved by the House of Commons. It is normal that Lords' amendments that are hostile to government intentions will be overturned in the Commons. However, as we shall see below, the Lords can make such a nuisance of itself, holding up important legislation in legislative committees, that the government will sometimes be forced to concede. Unwanted amendments from House of Commons legislative committees can also be overturned when the *'Report Stage'* is reached. The whole House in plenary session is invited to vote on proposed amendments and the party whips can get to work at this stage, reversing unwanted changes.

Membership of legislative committees can be a frustrating experience and it is not a particularly popular role for members. Of course, MPs and peers who have a special interest in and/or experience of a particular issue will be keen to be on a particular committee and will request specially to be allocated to them. It should also be pointed out that pressure groups tend to be very active at this committee stage of a bill's progress through Parliament. They seek to persuade both committee members and relevant ministers to include amendments that are supportive of their cause. It is in committee that any changes can be made.

Committees of the whole House

In the House of Lords it is often, though not always, the case that the committee (amendment) stage of a bill is considered by plenary session of the whole House. In the Commons, however, such 'committees of the whole House' are rare. When a bill is of special significance and if it is of constitutional significance (i.e. it is about the structure and powers of government), a committee of the whole House of Commons will be called. But, here again, party discipline applies.

Departmental select committees

There are 19 such committees, each one of which is concerned with a specific area of government responsibility (i.e. they mostly 'shadow' a government department). The following 19 departmental select committees existed in April 2010:

● Business Innovation and Skills

● Children, Schools and Families

● Communities and Local Government

● Culture, Media and Sport

● Defence

● Energy and Climate Change

● Environment, Food and Rural Affairs

● Foreign Affairs

● Health

● Home Affairs

● International Development

● Justice

● Northern Ireland Affairs

● Science and Technology

● Scottish Affairs

● Transport

● Treasury

● Welsh Affairs

● Work and Pensions.

Select committees are normally made up of between 11 and 14 members. They are elected by all members of the House of Commons. The chairperson of these committees is a significant parliamentary personality with a good deal of influence. Such positions are, therefore, much sought after, not least because they carry an additional salary above normal MPs' pay. Although the governing party has a majority of its members on select committees, all members are expected to behave in a non-partisan, neutral fashion. Indeed, when the select committees produce their reports the chair will normally attempt to achieve unanimous support for their conclusions. If the members simply split along party lines, reports have little interest for Parliament as a whole. A unanimous report, however, carries significant weight.

The select committees have considerable powers. They can call for ministers, civil servants, external witnesses and official papers in their investigations. Their role is multi-faceted and includes the following tasks:

● To investigate the work of government departments to determine whether they have acted efficiently and effectively.

● To consider major departmental policies, determining whether they are well considered and have taken into account relevant opinion.

● To consider proposed legislation, not with a view to blocking it but to consider whether it is likely to be effective.

- To consider matters of major public concern that fall within the remit of the committee and the government department that it shadows.

- To investigate any serious errors or omissions made by the department, making recommendations to correct the problem.

- Occasionally to propose future legislation where there is an overwhelming need.

The committees have a wide range of responsibilities and their work is taken seriously. In addition, they tend to adopt an adversarial style of questioning, which can, on occasions, be aggressive. Indeed, many ministers and civil servants have admitted to approaching select committee hearings with some trepidation.

The committees have a small research staff to assist them and, after years of service, the MPs can develop a high degree of knowledge and experience. Most select committee members end up serving for more years than the ministers they are investigating.

There is no equivalent of departmental committees in the House of Lords.

The following lists show a selection of reports of the Defence Select Committee and the Environment and Rural Affairs Committee in their sessions 2008–09 and 2009–10.

Defence Committee

- February 2009   Defence equipment

- March 2009   Department of Defence annual accounts

- May 2009   Defence contribution to national security

- July 2009   Defence Department annual budget proposals

- July 2009   Helicopter capability

- November 2009   Russia – a new confrontation?

- February 2010   Readiness of the armed forces

- March 2010   Defence equipment 2010

- March 2010   Control of arms exports.

Environment and Rural Affairs Committee

- January 2009   The English pig industry

- June 2009   Energy efficiency and fuel poverty

- July 2009   Securing food supplies up to 2050

- March 2010   The national forest

- March 2010   Dairy farmers of Britain

- March 2010   Waste strategy for England.

Other select committees of either House

There are a number of committees in Parliament as a whole that deal with domestic issues with which we need not concern ourselves here. However, there are a number of committees that *are* of political significance.

The most important select committee is the **Public Accounts Committee (PAC)**, the oldest in Parliament. It is a highly independent body, so much so that its chairperson is, by tradition, a member of the opposition party. The PAC is charged with the task of investigating the financial arrangements of the government. In particular it checks that public spending has been used for the purpose intended by Parliament. In this respect it is also searching for any possible examples of corruption (mercifully very rare in British politics). But its main work has proved to be investigations of how efficiently public money has been used. Its reports often highlight examples of government wastefulness and inefficiency. Membership of the PAC is much sought after by MPs.

The **Standards and Privileges Committee** is concerned mainly with standards of public life. It deals with disciplinary matters against MPs and comments on the way in which ministers and other public officials have conducted their relationship with Parliament. The **Statutory Instruments Committee** exists to check the government's use of 'secondary legislation' (Acts of Parliament are known as 'primary legislation'). Parliament grants wide powers to ministers to make detailed legislation without recourse to parliamentary debate. The device used by ministers for this purpose is known as a 'statutory instrument'. Though Parliament does not debate these,

it is important that a check is kept on the use of such powers. This committee looks at statutory instruments and alerts Parliament to any that might be contentious.

Both Houses of Parliament have **European Scrutiny Committees** whose role is to examine proposed legislation or regulations coming from the European Commission. They may alert Parliament as a whole to any concerns they have. In particular, they attempt to guide ministers in their negotiations with the Commission and their European partners. Finally, the **Liaison Committee** comprises the chairs of all the select committees. Its best-known task is to question the prime minister twice a year.

It would be a mistake to over-emphasise the power and influence of these committees. They are a vital part of the process of making government accountable, but they suffer from the problem of lacking any powers of enforcement. They can criticise, publicise and recommend action, but there is no guarantee that their conclusions will result in action. That said, a sample of some recent reports made by such committees shown in the table below demonstrates that they do sometimes find themselves at the centre of major controversy.

Important action by select committees		
Committee	**Report**	**Detail**
Home Affairs	Detention of terrorist suspects 2006	The committee rejected the government case for up to 90-day detention without trial for terrorist suspects, recommending instead 28 days maximum. The recommendation was accepted by the whole House of Commons.
Culture, Media and Sport	Call-in TV quiz shows 2007	The committee criticised TV companies running call-in quiz shows where it was not clear what

Important action by select committees (continued)		
Committee	Report	Detail
		the chances of winning were and how much callers were paying. As a result investigations led to cancellation of many such shows.
Home Affairs	Domestic violence and forced marriage 2008	Called for better policing and law enforcement in relation to domestic violence and forced marriages. Resulted in new police guidelines.
Culture, Media and Sport	Press standards and libel laws 2010	Opposed proposals for new laws guaranteeing greater privacy against press intrusion. Suggested the Human Rights Act and common law were sufficient safeguards for privacy.
Science and Technology	Climate change 2010	Called for greater transparency from the science community over the evidence concerning climate change.

The Speakers

Both Houses have a Speaker, whose role it is to oversee the debates, select speakers from the floor and arrange the business of their House with party leaders. They are expected to be entirely neutral and even-handed. The Speaker of the Commons is a senior MP who is elected by the House. It is someone who has no political ambitions and so is prepared to retire from party politics.

Normally the role of the Speaker is not controversial. All that changed, however, in 2009. In that year the then Speaker, Michael Martin, became involved in a major political controversy, which led to his downfall. When revelations emerged about the way in which many MPs had been taking advantage of an over-generous expenses system (some illegally), Speaker Martin was put at the centre of the conflict that followed. It was widely accepted that his response was inadequate, that he was blocking calls for reform and that he was too defensive of the conduct of MPs. The wave of demands for reform of the expenses system and the clearing out of those MPs who had been accused of abusing the system to their own benefit also carried him out of office. He was forced to resign. In his place, John Bercow promised to lead the reforms of the system and to become more actively involved in the general reform of the House of Commons. Thus the office of Speaker has ceased to be a passive, administrative role and has become a key element in restoring the reputation of MPs and Parliament in general.

The Speaker of the Lords is the Lord Speaker, chosen by the members. In 2006, this figure

John Bercow, Speaker of the House of Commons who leads attempts to 'clean up politics'

replaced the former office holder, who was the Lord Chancellor, a controversial figure. The Lord Chancellor was a member of the cabinet, an appointee of the prime minister. This placed his neutrality into some doubt. His replacement by a neutral figure, chosen by members, marks a small step towards greater independence of the House of Lords. The first Lord Speaker was Baroness Hayman. Her role is to chair debates, decide on who shall speak and organise the business of the House with the leaderships of the main parties.

The functions of Parliament

As we have seen above, it would be wrong to see Parliament as primarily a legislature in the strict sense of the word. Parliament does *pass* law, but it does not usually *make* law. Professor Philip

Norton, a leading constitutional expert, has classified parliaments in various countries into three main types:

1. Policy-making legislatures

2. Policy-influencing legislatures

3. Weak legislatures.

Norton suggested that the British Parliament falls into the second category, though many might argue it belongs in the third. In order to make such a judgement we need to examine the role of Parliament in more detail.

Legitimation

Our brief history of Parliament demonstrated that a traditional role was to provide consent for the monarch's legislation. This remains a key function. Although any government enjoys a mandate from the electorate, it is still important that its authority to legislate is underpinned by Parliament. For any law or executive action to be implemented and respected it requires parliamentary sanction. This is effectively granting popular consent *indirectly*. Parliament is, in short, making legislation legitimate. In this sense Parliament is supporting government, not challenging it.

As Parliament is acting on behalf of the people it is clear that the House of Commons plays the leading role in this regard because it is elected. The unelected House of Lords cannot claim the same authority.

We can also employ the term *'promulgation'* to this function. The formal procedures by which laws are passed (see details below) serve the purpose of proclaiming the law and announcing its legitimacy.

Scrutiny

Though Parliament does not normally make law it has the important function of scrutinising proposed legislation. Scrutiny involves close inspection and, where it is seen as necessary, amendments may be proposed. Detailed scrutiny is carried out by standing committees of both Houses (see above) and more generalised consideration by plenary sessions of each House.

In this respect Parliament is representing various interests in society, ensuring that unnecessary discrimination does not take place, that minorities are not unfairly discriminated against and that laws will be clear in their application. Scrutiny does not normally involve blocking legislation, but important changes can be proposed and accepted.

It is not only major, or primary, legislation that is scrutinised. Parliament also looks at secondary legislation – decisions made by ministers under statutory powers granted by Parliament – and at proposed European laws or regulations. It is not expected that Parliament will make substantial changes to such legislation, but it does warn and inform government as far as it can.

Opposition

This function applies only to the parties that do not make up government – in other words, the opposition parties. Governments virtually always enjoy a majority in the House of Commons, though obviously not always. So opposition does not imply that any proposals will be defeated on the floor of the House. The government does not command a loyal majority in the Lords, but it is understood that occasions when the Lords can defy the government and the Commons will be rare and exceptional. Opposition is more of a ritualised process, but one that nevertheless plays an important role.

It is expected that parliamentary politics in Britain will be *adversarial* in nature. That is, whenever government makes a proposal, it normally expects it to be robustly challenged in Parliament. This process ensures that the government is forced to explain and justify its policies. The opposition parties do not expect to overturn the government majority, but they do hope to expose any weaknesses in the government's position. It is often said that 'the role of the opposition is to oppose'. This apparently bland expression suggests that all proposals have to be challenged as a matter of course. It is a process that ensures that government prepares its case effectively.

Accountability

In a modern democracy the accountability of government is essential. At election times, of course, government becomes directly accountable to the people. Thus, in 2005, when the Labour government saw its popular support fall from 41 per cent of the voters in 2001 to just over 36 per cent, the people were delivering something of a negative verdict on Labour's performance (even though the government survived). But continuous accountability is not yet feasible, so Parliament must act on behalf of the people between elections.

Accountability implies a number of activities:

● It means forcing the government, its ministers in particular, to justify their policies, explaining why they were developed and what their effects are likely to be.

● It may mean criticism of those policies. Obviously it is mainly the role of opposition parties to criticise, but MPs representing the government party itself may also have their say.

● For opposition parties accountability can also imply the presentation of alternatives to the government's proposals. This represents a more positive form of criticism.

● Where it is believed that there have been serious errors, it is largely the role of Parliament to expose such mistakes. The doctrine of **individual ministerial responsibility** is particularly relevant here.

Individual ministerial responsibility

This doctrine suggests that every minister is individually responsible for *all* the activities of their department. Ministers are also, quite naturally, responsible for their personal conduct. Responsibility means that they must be prepared to face criticism from Parliament, including its select committees, and, in extreme circumstances, it is expected that they should resign.

The issue of when ministers are expected to resign is a contentious one. It used to be the case – perhaps up to the 1970s – that *any* serious mistake made within a department, whether or not the minister knew anything about it, should result in ministerial resignation. In other words, ministers were considered to be responsible for the actions of their senior civil servants. It was, in fact, considered a matter of honour that the minister was responsible. The principle has been considerably eroded in recent decades, however.

Perhaps the most celebrated example of the doctrine at work occurred in 1982 when Foreign Secretary Lord Carrington resigned. He accepted responsibility (it has never been clarified whether his department was *actually* responsible) for the fact that British forces were unprepared for the Argentine invasion of the British Falkland Islands in that year. More recently, Education Secretary Estelle Morris resigned in 2002 over the generally poor performance of her department and in the same year Stephen Byers was forced to resign as Trade and Industry Secretary after his personal advisers were accused of behaving unprofessionally.

But ministers today are more likely to hang on to their jobs when serious errors are revealed. Michael Howard, for example, suffered a number of embarrassing criticisms over his running of the prison service when he was Home Secretary in the 1990s, but he survived. Similarly, Defence Secretary Geoff Hoon refused to resign despite a number of problems relating to the inadequate equipping of British forces in the 2003 Iraq war. In practice, it is up to the prime minister whether a minister 'takes the rap'. Once a minister has lost the confidence of the prime minister, they are then likely to be undermined by excessive errors.

Where personal conduct is concerned, however, ministerial resignations are more common. In 2004, for example, Home Secretary David Blunkett was forced to resign following a major parliamentary and media campaign against him. His resignation followed the finding of an independent inquiry that his office was linked to the speeding up of a visa application made by his then partner's nanny. He agreed to accept overall responsibility, although there was no finding that he had personally intervened in the application.

But it was during the 1990s that resignations over personal conduct had reached their height. In the so-called era of 'Tory sleaze' a succession of ministers was forced out of office as a result of sexual or financial scandals. Perhaps the best known of these was Neil Hamilton, a junior minister who became involved in the 'cash-for-questions' scandal. Outside interests were found to be paying MPs and junior ministers to ask parliamentary questions to bring their interests to public attention. This is against parliamentary rules and Hamilton, who had to admit his role in the practice, resigned in a blaze of publicity.

It is more difficult for ministers to resist calls for their resignation over personal conduct than over political errors. In essence, Parliament has more influence over the former than the latter. It has, therefore, become difficult to assert that individual ministerial responsibility is effective.

What we can say is that it is often the case that an individual minister is required to accept responsibility for problems in order to save the embarrassment of the government as a whole.

It should be pointed out that Parliament does not have the power to remove an individual minister from office – only the prime minister can do that. Parliament can only apply pressure for a resignation and often MPs do not succeed. Conversely, however, Parliament can remove the government as a whole. But, as we shall see below, the removal of the whole government, through a vote of no confidence, will normally result in a general election. MPs, especially from the governing party, are naturally reluctant to precipitate a general election in which many of them may lose their seats. Turkeys, as they say, do not vote for Christmas.

So accountability normally stops short of forcing resignations and involves investigation and criticism. There are a number of ways in which Parliament can call government to account, as follows.

Questions to ministers

This is the best-known device. Every minister is expected to appear regularly in the House. (Ministers who are peers will also face questions in the Lords.) They will face many questions from MPs, some of which are expected (notice must be given), some of which are unexpected (notice is not needed for supplementary questions). Questions may be relatively gentle, being designed merely to obtain factual information. Others, however, may be hostile and can create a good deal of discomfort. Ministers must face criticism and be prepared to answer it. Many questions are also written, in which case the minister (in fact, his senior civil servants) has time to frame an answer. Written questions are far less hostile than oral questions.

MPs relish the opportunity to question ministers, especially in areas of special interest to them. It is one of the rare occasions when they feel they may be able to make an impact freed from the discipline of the party whips. It is also vital that ministers, whatever their department does, know that they may be subject to parliamentary scrutiny at some stage. But it also has to be said that the ministers have a great advantage in such exchanges. They have an army of civil servants to prepare answers for them. MPs do not have access to this kind of help. Clever ministers are also able to deflect attention away from their shortcomings and are notoriously difficult to pin down with sensitive material.

Prime Minister's Question Time used to be an occasion for making the head of government accountable. For many years, however, it has been reduced to a ritualised contest between party leaders. It is designed more as a 'media show' than an attempt to shed light on the activities of the government. It is entertaining to the public and to MPs, but does little to support accountability.

The following is an extract from the proceedings of the House of Commons on 23 February 2010. The Minister of State for Health, Mike O'Brien, had to answer questions on the provision of free health care to participants in the 2012 Olympic Games in London.

NHS London (2012 Olympics)

James Duddridge (Rochford and Southend, East) (Con): What discussions he has had with the Minister for the Olympics on the preparedness of NHS London for the London 2012 Olympics; and if he will make a statement.

The Minister of State, Department of Health (Mr. Mike O'Brien): The Department of Health has been working jointly with NHS London, the London Organising Committee of the Olympic Games and Paralympic Games – LOCOG, as I understand it is known – and the Government Olympic Executive to ensure that the NHS will be fully prepared for the 2012 games.

James Duddridge: How does the Minister reconcile those comments with those of Azara Mukhtar, the deputy director of NHS London, who said at a recent meeting that

'additional funding was not going to be forthcoming to support the commitment to offer free healthcare for those participating in the 2012 Olympics,'

and that there were therefore serious

'concerns about how to resolve the cost and resource implications without diverting funding from services for Londoners'?

Mr. O'Brien: Fairly easily. The Department of Health has provided NHS London with an extra £1.5 million for this financial year, which it has confirmed meets its current requirements. The Department is also in discussions with NHS London authorities on the provision of further funding, and we are going through some figures that they have provided us with. At the moment they look to be figures for a worst-case scenario, but we want to go through the detail and examine what is needed. However, we are certainly clear that the health needs of Londoners will not be compromised and that the health needs of visitors will be met.

Mike Penning (Hemel Hempstead) (Con): But the figure of £1.5 million that the Minister just cited is well short of the £30 million that is the estimated cost to London of putting on the games. Will the Minister publish the information that NHS London has given him, as well as the understanding reached when the games were bid for, about how much they would cost Londoners through the NHS?

Mr. O'Brien: First, the figure that the hon. gentleman gave is contrary to some of the figures that have been circulated recently, which have actually been larger. NHS London has put forward a figure of £41 million, as a cost spread over four years. That is based on planning assumptions

that appear to be based on a worst-case scenario, and were made last summer. We know that there is a good deal more planning work to do, to ensure that we estimate the cost much more carefully and get the figures right, and that we must work with NHS London so that our health care needs are delivered.

Source: Hansard

We can see that the Minister concerned is subject to close scrutiny of his answers and an implied criticism that insufficient money has been set aside for health-care for participants in the games. He is also forced to explain more clearly how the funding will work.

Select committees

Select committees, especially departmental select committees of the House of Commons, are a different matter altogether. Committees of 11–14 MPs have the power to question, and indeed cross-examine, ministers, their civil servants and any witnesses they may call from external organisations. Unlike questions to ministers, there is no ritual and questioning may go on for some time. Furthermore, MPs usually spend several years on the committees and so develop a good deal of knowledge and expertise. The examples of important select committee reports shown above demonstrate how important they have become since they were introduced in 1979.

We can usefully look at an extract from an important report from the Defence Select Committee from March 2010 as an illustration of the kind of work undertaken by departmental select committees of the House of Commons. The composition of the Defence Select Committee at the time was as follows:

Labour members	8
Conservative members	4
Liberal Democrat members	2.

The chairman was James Arbuthnot, a Conservative, and thus not a member of the governing party at the time, demonstrating the capacity of the committee to be independent of government.

The Comprehensive Approach: the point of war is not just to win but to make a better peace.
March 2010
Extract from the conclusions

'It is evident that the need for a clear strategy and vision has been recognised for Afghanistan. It is important that all parties share an understanding of the context and the nature of the challenges faced. In future situations where the Comprehensive Approach is adopted, all relevant government departments and the armed forces should agree a clear set of objectives with appropriate measures of achievement and with a clearly defined end state set in the context of the nature of the challenges faced. The need for post-conflict reconstruction and stabilisation should be recognised and incorporated into planning at the earliest stages...

We understand why, for major situations such as those in Iraq and Afghanistan, it is inevitable that the Prime Minister should take overall responsibility for the Comprehensive Approach. We note there has been a debate about whether this is necessary, whether it provides effective leadership and clarity for all missions and whether it might be appropriate for the Prime Minister to appoint a Lead Minister... Certainly as missions evolve these matters should be kept under review.'

Source: Hansard

In general, the report was urging future governments to learn the lessons of Iraq and Afghanistan, to plan for the post-war peace as well as the war itself, and to ensure that different government departments and agencies should work together to create a comprehensive plan for peace. In this way the committee was making an important contribution to future policy.

Debates on legislation

These are further occasions when accountability can be achieved. Every proposed piece of legislation must be fully debated at least twice. Here again ministers must justify the proposals. It is extremely rare for the government to lose a vote on a major bill, but the procedure ensures that every aspect of legislation is carefully examined in a public forum.

We would expect members of opposition parties to question proposed legislation, but MPs from the governing party may also subject bills to scrutiny, especially if they have a particular impact on their constituency. Some MPs also represent the interest of outside pressure groups and may well question parts of a bill on their behalf. However, as we shall see, it is more likely that close and effective scrutiny of legislation will take place in the more independent House of Lords.

Financial control

Although the approval of the government's financial arrangements is one of Parliament's oldest functions, dating back to the Middle Ages, it is also an area where it is seen at its weakest. Governments depend on their ability to collect taxes and to spend money on key functions. These financial powers have to be renewed every year, while any changes to the tax system or to spending allocations must also be approved in Parliament. If Parliament were to withhold consent, government would cease to function very rapidly and would almost certainly be forced to seek a fresh popular mandate by calling a general election. As the position is so critical it is customary for Parliament to renew financial powers with relatively little obstruction.

The House of Lords has long since lost any powers over financial affairs. The 1911 Parliament Act took away the Lords' ability to vote on financial matters. Having attempted to block the

Liberal government's annual budget in 1909, it was clear that the unelected House of Lords could no longer be allowed to jeopardise the position of the elected government. Meanwhile, in the Commons the MPs representing the governing party tend to be at their most loyal when the annual budget is being voted.

When we consider the operation of the **Public Accounts Committee**, however, the picture changes. This committee considers the *effectiveness* of government expenditure. Its members feel that they represent the interests of the taxpayers, trying to ensure that they get value for money. Some of their reports can be highly critical and can result in remedial action by government. It should be stressed that the PAC does not consider the way in which public funds are allocated among different functions – that is the role of Parliament as a whole. Its task is to root out waste and inefficiency, to raise awareness of examples of poor administration within government departments and agencies.

Student activity

Each student should choose one of the departmental select committees. The reports of that committee for the current session of Parliament should be accessed using the Parliament website. The main conclusions of the committee for any one of its reports should be briefly summarised and presented to the rest of the class to illustrate the range of work of the committees.

Representation

The role that Parliament undoubtedly has, of representing the people, is a difficult one to grasp. The problem for MPs is that they are required to represent so many different sections of society and so many ideas. We can identify the following responsibilities:

- They are elected to represent their party and its manifesto. Therefore we normally expect an MP to 'toe the party line'. An exception to this occurs when an MP, during the general election campaign, declares openly that he does not support a particular aspect of his party's official policy. In 2005, for example, a large number of Labour candidates openly stated that they did not support British military involvement in Iraq. Conversely, a smaller number of Conservatives asserted that they supported British withdrawal from the European Union.

- MPs must represent the interests of their own constituency whenever they are involved in government policy or with a ministerial decision. When, for example, it was proposed to set up a number of centres for asylum seekers in rural areas in 2004–05, the MPs involved set up an ultimately successful campaign to reverse the policy. It is typical for local MPs to become active in decisions to build, for example, road by-passes (or not to build them), nuclear power stations, airport terminals and the like. During debates in 2006–07 on the possible introduction of a number of casinos in Britain, some MPs were concerned with attracting casinos to their constituencies to provide employment, while others were anxious to prevent such developments in their regions on the grounds that it might attract crime or cause excessive gambling. When there emerged a proposal to build a third runway at Heathrow airport in 2009–10, the relevant MPs from constituencies in the Thames Valley actively opposed the plans or sought to change the details of those plans.

There are times when the national interest can be at stake and MPs or peers will take this into account when parliamentary debates are held. Here our representatives in both Houses must weigh up their party's attitude to the issue against *what they perceive* to be in the nation's best interests. The 2003 war in Iraq, Britain's relations with the European Union, how we should deal with suspected terrorists (in particular whether we could suspend civil liberties in the fight against terrorism) and whether identity cards should become compulsory are all examples of where our representative may step out of traditional party allegiance and consider the country as a whole on non-partisan lines.

It is currently estimated that about 75 per cent of MPs are either paid a retainer to represent an outside group or regularly support the interests of a group without payment. Many peers fulfil a similar role in the House of Lords. This is considered normal and part of the democratic process. As a safeguard, any representative who is paid to represent groups must declare their interest and so avoid any possibility of corrupt practices. It is well known, therefore, that many trade unions, professional associations, industrial organisations, large companies and campaign groups have friendly representatives in both Houses. They will alert the groups to any hostile policies, promote their interests and attempt to gain publicity for their aims.

The main occasions when this process occurs are during debates, committee hearings, questions to ministers and three special types of parliamentary opportunities for MPs to raise such issues. These are *adjournment debates, early day motions* and *ten minute rules.* They are gaps in normal procedure that have been protected to give MPs the chance to raise a matter of constituency interest or one that concerns any external group which they represent. In all these cases no direct response from government is expected, but at least the issue becomes a matter of public record and may be used for later campaigns.

In the House of Lords, external groups are particularly active when legislative amendments are being considered. Most peers are not strongly tied down by party discipline and many see their role in terms of protecting minority interests. The Lords amendment process – when the government is at its most vulnerable in Parliament – is where representation on interests can be seen at its most intense.

Redress of grievances

Along with consent to finance, the redress of citizens' grievances is an ancient parliamentary function. It is necessarily carried out by individual MPs on behalf of their constituents. Where a constituent feels they have been unfairly or unjustly treated by the government or by one of its agencies such as the NHS, the police, immigration authorities, the social security system or the taxation authorities, that constituent may well complain to their local MP. This privilege remains part of an unwritten contract between MPs and the government – it is that Parliament will normally support the government in its key functions, in return for which MPs will be given special access to ministers.

The degree to which MPs undertake such work varies a good deal. Some are known as dutiful constituency workers, others are less enthusiastic. Ministers find the constituency role particularly difficult (remember that most ministers are also constituency MPs, including the prime minister), but their role is usually performed by friendly neighbouring MPs or by their own paid constituency agent. MPs will either raise issues on the floor of the House or will see ministers and civil servants directly.

Private members' legislation

Most legislation is presented by the government. Opposition parties are not permitted to do this. However, a few lucky MPs and peers, who win an annual ballot, are allowed to present their own private legislation. Though such proposals are nearly always blocked by the government, occasionally a so-called 'private members' bill' does find its way through to law. This requires an enormous effort by the MP or peer concerned, who must both persuade a large number of his colleagues to support it and persuade the government to keep their hands off it. Sometimes, of course, the government actively supports a private members' bill, in which case it is almost certain to pass.

In effect, therefore, private members' legislation can succeed only if the government either supports it or has its own reasons for not opposing it. Thus, successes are rare. Yet one of the most significant pieces of legislation in modern history was a private members' bill. This was David Steele's Abortion Act of 1967, which legalised abortion for the first time. In the same era private acts between homosexuals were also legalised under such legislation. More recently, private members' legislation has tended to be less momentous and often affects small numbers of people. It has concerned such issues as dog breeding, energy conservation in private homes, guide dogs in taxis and employee share-owning schemes. However, in 2007, a significant Act was passed following the initiative of Lord Lester in the House of Lords. This was the Forced Marriages Act, protecting individuals against being forced to marry against their will.

An indication of how few private members' bills pass is demonstrated by the following figures showing how many such bills were passed in recent sessions of Parliament (whether they were initiated in the Commons or the Lords):

2003–4	5
2004–5	0
2005–6	3
2006–7	4
2007–8	3
2008–9	5

Deliberation

Occasionally – and it is only occasionally – Parliament is given the opportunity to hold a great debate on a vital issue. Such debates can form part of a national process of deliberation. These are moments in history when a nation must take a moment to draw breath and make a critical decision that will affect its future. The debates on the war with Iraq in 2003 were such an example. So, too, were the debates in the House of Lords on the issue of detention without trial for terrorist suspects.

Delving further back into history we can find many examples of where Parliament has made a significant contribution to national debate. Independence for India, Britain's imperial future, the 1956 invasion of the Suez Canal zone, the Falklands crisis of 1982 and Britain's reaction to the 9/11 atrocity in New York in 2001, the Iraq war of 2003 and the current Afghan war were all occasions when Parliament played a full role.

Reserve powers

Parliament enjoys two powers that it rarely uses (hence the term 'reserve powers') but which nevertheless give it great authority. These are the ability to veto government legislation and to dismiss a government.

The House of Lords has voted down legislation on a number of occasions, but such decisions will normally be reversed by the House of Commons in the next session. If the Commons rejects a bill, however, that is normally the end of the matter, at least until after the next general election. As we have seen above, it is not the role of Parliament to defy the will of the elected government, but the threat that any government which attempts to act in an arbitrary way may be blocked remains an important discipline.

The 1986 Second Reading defeat of the Sunday Trading Bill, intended to allow more stores to remain open on a Sunday, occurred because a determined coalition of MPs from all parties was opposed on the grounds of either religion or the need to protect workers' rights. The government whips miscalculated the level of opposition and were too late to withdraw the bill before the embarrassing defeat. The rarity of such defeats disguises the reality that government does face such a threat from time to time and usually responds by making concessions to head off opposition. Just because government defeats on the Second Reading come once in a blue moon does not mean that Parliament is toothless. Indeed, John Major's second administration, from 1992–97, was beset by such threats from a House of Commons in which he enjoyed only a narrow majority. Since then, the most significant veto occurred in 2006 when the Commons rejected government plans to extend the period during which terrorist suspects could be imprisoned without trial to 90 days. A more recent embarrassment for the government occurred in 2009 when many Labour MPs defied the whips and voted to allow Gurkhas (Nepalese soldiers in the British army) to settle in the UK after retirement. This followed a sustained media campaign by the actress Joanna Lumley. In 2009, MPs in general obstructed attempts by all parties to reform their expenses system, again in defiance of the whips.

The threat to remove a government by a vote of no confidence in the Commons is also constant. Of course, when a government enjoys a large majority it remains a distant threat, but the people can be comforted by the fact that there is an ever-present safeguard against arbitrary government. James Callaghan's Labour government was removed in March 1979, the last time this happened. He had lost his Commons majority, but tried to continue too long. The impatient Conservatives, led by Margaret Thatcher, could not wait for the impending election and organised a no-confidence vote, which they won by a majority of one.

Specific Lords powers

Although it is the junior House, the Lords does have two specific powers not necessarily enjoyed by the Commons. One is the power of delay. The Parliament Act of 1949 states that if a bill is rejected in the Lords, it will automatically become law if the Commons passes the same piece of legislation in the next session (year) of Parliament. This effectively means that the House of Lords has the special power to delay a proposal for a year. The Commons does not do this because MPs are whipped to support the party and so government defeats are, as we have seen above, very rare. The Lords, however, has more freedom to defy the government in the knowledge that, if it is determined enough, the government will have its way in the long run. The purpose of delay is twofold. First, it forces the government to think again and so ensure that there is sufficient support for a proposal. Second, the threat of delay is often enough to obtain important concessions by way of amendments.

The 1991 defeat of the War Crimes Bill – passed under the Parliament Act rule in the following year – was an important example of the use of the power of delay. So, too, was the Hunting with Dogs Act, which was passed twice, in 2004 and 2005. On that occasion attempts to compromise failed, but the Lords succeeded in ensuring a full debate on the issue. Similarly, the Lords' rejection of the bill to outlaw incitement to religious hatred in 2004 provoked a full debate on the issue. This kind of obstruction, negotiation and compromise is a luxury that the strictly controlled House of Commons does not enjoy.

The Lords also has slightly more opportunity for amending legislation than the Commons. Here again the greater political independence of peers plays its part. But perhaps more importantly, Lords' amendments have the effect of delaying legislation. Every Lords amendment must be confirmed by the Commons. If there is a disagreement between the two Houses, a bill will simply pass backwards and forwards between the two Houses (a process known, not surprisingly, as ping-pong), much to the frustration of the government. The result is often important compromises.

In 2004–05 a most important example of ping-pong created critical changes to a key piece of legislation. The 2001 Anti-Terrorism Act had been declared unlawful under the European

The House of Lords in ceremonial session

Convention on Human Rights. This forced the government to return the legislation to Parliament in a modified form. But the Lords decided to add some critical amendments, preventing the Home Office from detaining suspected terrorists without trial or process of law. The Lords' amendment was passed back and forth along the long straight corridor that leads from the Commons to the Lords. Eventually the government, running out of time and patience, was forced to concede the point to the determined peers.

We can now summarise the principal functions of Parliament, noting the main limitations of each. These are shown in the table below.

The functions of Parliament	
Functions	**Limitations**
Private members' legislation	• The House of Lords is not elected. • The Commons is seen to be dominated by the executive and therefore not independent. • The electoral system means the Commons is not politically representative of the electorate. • Little time is devoted to private members' legislation. • Government is easily able to 'kill' any bills it opposes. • It is difficult for MPs and peers to gather enough support to force bills through.
Deliberation	• Both Houses lack enough time to consider bills thoroughly. • Standing committees are whipped so fall under government control.

The functions of Parliament (continued)	
Functions	**Limitations**
Calling government to account	• Collective government responsibility makes it difficult to examine government decisions. • The opposition lacks the administrative back-up of the government. • Skilful ministers and civil servants can evade questioning by MPs and peers. • MPs and peers may lack expertise and knowledge. • The power of patronage prevents governing MPs and peers being hostile or too inquisitive. • There remains a good deal of government secrecy, especially in the fields of defence, security and foreign policy.
Financial control	• Parliament is traditionally not expected to challenge government seriously in this area. • House of Lords has no jurisdiction at all.
Representation	• The electoral system makes the Commons highly unrepresentative. • The House of Lords is not elected. • Both Houses are socially unrepresentative, especially in terms of women or social and ethnic background.
Redress of grievances	• MPs lack time to deal with many constituents' grievances.
Reserve powers	• MPs of the governing party are especially reluctant to use reserve powers for fear of precipitating a general election in which they might lose their seats and/or their party might lose power.
Scrutiny of proposed legislation	• Legislative committees are whipped and rarely defy government.
Delaying (House of Lords)	• The Parliament Act limits this power to one year.
Amending (House of Lords)	• Proposed Lords' amendments must be approved by the House of Commons, where the government dominates.

Agencies supporting Parliament

Parliament is assisted in its work by a number of specialist agencies that have the task of investigating various aspects of government work and reporting back to Parliament on their findings. The departmental select committees have a particular interest in their work. Some of the key organisations are described below.

The parliamentary ombudsman

Despite the name – of Scandinavian origin – it is not necessarily a man. Nor is it a single person but is, in fact, an extensive office staffed by experienced officials.

The parliamentary ombudsman investigates complaints that are routed through MPs from

The Legislative Process

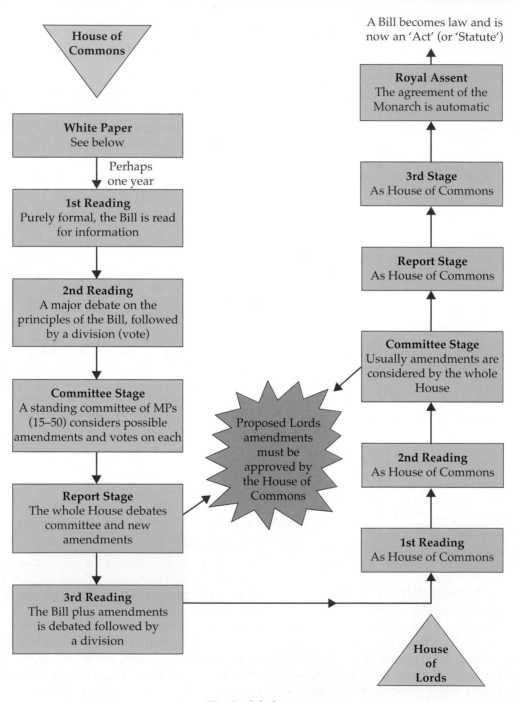

The legislative process

constituents or groups of constituents. Their role is to investigate claims of what is known as 'maladministration'. These are cases where a government department is accused of not dealing fairly or thoroughly enough with a member of the public. It may be that standard procedures have not been followed, or that a civil servant has been negligent, if there has been undue delay or citizens have not been granted equal treatment. The ombudsman cannot deal with all complaints, but normally concentrates on matters that are likely to affect large numbers of people. In the past it was a role carried out by constituency MPs, but they no longer have enough time to deal with them thoroughly enough.

The parliamentary ombudsman receives about 2,000 complaints per year (the number varies considerably) and decides to investigate about half of them. Where a complaint is upheld the ombudsman makes a report to a special select committee that deals with their work. The committee for the parliamentary ombudsman or Parliament as a whole may order that compensatory action be taken by the department concerned. Over the years the role of the ombudsman has expanded and has now become a key element in Parliament's role in the redress of grievances.

Several other industries in the private sector have also set up ombudsman systems and these should not be confused with the parliamentary ombudsman, who deals only with central government. The banking and insurance industries are examples of private ombudsman systems. There is also an ombudsman for local government.

The comptroller and auditor general

This extensive office works directly for the Public Accounts Committee. It has two main functions. One is to ensure that government revenues are spent on the purposes for which Parliament has given approval. In other words, the government is not permitted to shift expenditure from one use to another without seeking parliamentary sanction. Second, it checks the government accounts to ensure that money has been spent carefully and effectively. It therefore forms part of the wider role of Parliament in trying to ensure that government is run efficiently. Major criticisms are reported to the Public Accounts Committee, which may then summon ministers and/or civil servants to account for the problem.

National Audit Office

Closely connected to the role of the comptroller, the much expanded National Audit Office provides a service both to government itself and to parliamentary select committees. It looks at various aspects of the work of government departments to check for efficiency, guard against wastefulness and ensure that services serve the public effectively. It looks especially at what are known as 'front-line services' – those where the service deals directly with the public, such as the NHS, social security system and tax authorities. Its reports, often highly critical, are used by government to improve its performance and by select committees as a basis for their own investigations.

Audit Commission

Like the National Audit Office the Audit Commission serves both government and Parliament. It investigates the operations of local government specifically. All local authorities are expected to provide services on the basis of *best value.* This means that they should combine value for money with the best possible standard of service within the financial constraints. Audit Commission reports are used by central government to control the activities of local government, but may also be used by Parliament to monitor the quality of services at local level.

Membership of the House of Lords

The House of Lords in May 2010	
Categories of membership	Number
Life peers	590
Hereditary peers	91
Bishops	24
Archbishops	2
Party strengths in the House of Lords (May 2010)	
Party	Number
Conservative	186
Labour	211
Crossbenchers (no party)	186
Liberal Democrat	72
Bishops/Archbishops (no party)	26
Total	681

Looking at the nature of the membership of the House of Lords is essential in understanding how it behaves. The immediate thing to notice in the table above is that no single party enjoys an overall majority. Even the two-party coalition formed in May 2010 could not command a Lords majority.

The **life peers** are appointed mostly on political grounds, with each of the main parties having the privilege of regularly nominating a number of new life peers each year to replace those who have died. The parties are able to nominate new peers in proportion to their representation in the Commons. This means that the Conservatives were able to nominate more peers in 1979–97, but since then Labour has had an advantage. The Liberal Democrats naturally have a limited number of nominations. Most – but not all – party nominations are either retired politicians such as Lord Coe (former MP and athlete) and Lord Lawson (former Chancellor of the Exchequer), or current professional politicians who do not wish to be a constituency MP such as Lord Adonis (former Junior Education minister and prime ministerial adviser) and Baroness Warsi (cabinet minister).

In order to prevent total domination by the parties a number of life peers with no party allegiance are nominated each year. They become crossbenchers and represent a large presence in the Lords who are extremely independent. They also guarantee that the government can never enjoy an overall majority. The neutral life peers can be nominated by anyone, though they are normally nominated by existing peers, and are ultimately appointed by the independent Appointments Commission. Most of them are prominent citizens who are 'life achievers' such as Lord Hastings (former TV executive) and Lord Ramsbotham (prison reformer).

The 91 **hereditary peers** are a legacy of the time before 1999 when the Lords was dominated in terms of numbers, by hereditary peers who owed their position to being the eldest son of a hereditary peer who had died. Though many of them rarely attended the debates, if ever, the minority who were active created a permanent in-built Conservative majority. The Labour government that came to power in 1997 was determined to abolish the right of hereditary peers to sit and vote in the Lords. In the event the House of Lords was extremely obstructive and so a compromise was reached, allowing 92 (currently reduced to 91) hereditary peers to retain their seats. It is intended (and now widely accepted) that even these hereditary peers will lose their right to vote in the near future. So their political significance will be short-lived.

The **bishops and archbishops** are all members of the Church of England. They represent the fact that the Church of England remains the 'established' religion of the UK. Their position is controversial for two reasons. One is that the majority of citizens in the UK do not regularly observe *any* religion. The second is that they no longer represent the religious traditions of the UK. Why, many ask, are the Catholic, Muslim, Jewish and Hindu religions not represented formally in the same way? This, among other membership issues, is discussed in the final section of this book. Though a small group, the bishops can be influential when moral and religious issues are at issue. They are politically neutral and therefore form a kind of pressure group within the Lords.

Until 2009 it was true that the House of Lords contained all the most senior members of the judiciary, the so-called 'law lords'. However, from 2009 their function, as the highest appeal court in the UK, was replaced by the Supreme Court, a separate body. Nevertheless, as a legacy of the House of Lords's connection with the top levels of the legal system, there remain many senior judges in the House, both active and retired. Though these peers have no formal function, their presence remains important. The wealth of legal experience in the House of Lords gives it a special ability to make a great contribution to the legislative process. Apart from law and order issues, the lawyers in the Lords can also examine proposals from a legal point of view. Thus, they are in a good position to examine and improve the legal aspects of proposals, checking that they are both clear and enforceable. Nevertheless, members of the Supreme Court who are also peers are not expected to take part in contentious proceedings. This is to preserve their independent status (see Chapter 2.4).

We can now summarise the significance of the membership structure of the Lords:

● The government is prevented from enjoying an absolute majority.

● Even peers who have a party allegiance tend to be more independent that MPs because politics is not their principal occupation, so the whips have little leverage over them.

● Because most peers have had a previous occupation they have a wider variety of experience than MPs and so represent a wide range of interests in society.

● The Church of England is strongly represented, as is the legal profession and the judiciary.

● Despite its greater independence, the House of Lords is subject to the political patronage of party leaders.

● It is likely that the membership structure of the House of Lords will be significantly reformed in the years after 2010.

Why the House of Lords is becoming more significant

Until the 1980s the House of Lords was considered to be of relatively little significance in the British political process. It contained a large majority of hereditary peers, many of whom did not attend at all or had only a passing interest in it proceedings. More importantly there was a permanent in-built Conservative majority, largely because the vast majority of the hereditary peers were, as one might expect, Conservatives. These two realities meant that the Lords simply could not be allowed to wield any great influence as it was so clearly undemocratic in nature. Furthermore, before 1983, it was the norm for the government to enjoy relatively modest majorities in the House of Commons. The lack of a comfortable majority meant that there was a reasonable amount of effective opposition to the government among MPs. So much was the Lords held in modest esteem, indeed, that its complete abolition remained a well-supported proposal, mainly among Labour members of the Commons.

But there has been a remarkable change in both the prestige and the influence of the Lords since that time. There have been a number of factors at work in this process, among them:

● Large government majorities in the Commons became normal. Governments enjoyed majorities of over 100 following the elections of 1983, 1987, 1997 and 2001. This meant that opposition in the Commons was weak. Members of the House of Lords therefore felt it their duty to bolster parliamentary opposition to make up for Commons' weakness.

● At the same time the House of Lords began to develop a new 'professionalism'. An increasing proportion of its membership began to take their role more seriously, attending regularly and making themselves specialists in certain fields of policy. To some extent this is the result of party leaderships selecting professional politicians for the Lords to a greater degree.

● The reform of the Lords in 2000, removing all but 92 of the hereditary peers, gave the Lords greater authority. It was still not a democratic body, but at least it was seen as more politically and socially representative of the country.

● There is now a stronger 'rights culture' in the UK, especially since the incorporation of the European Convention on Human Rights into British law in 2000. The Lords, which contains many lawyers and human rights experts, has taken upon itself the role of guardian of

individual rights against governments that have been accused (whether justifiably or not) of being too dictatorial.

We can demonstrate the potential and actual power of the House of Lords by looking at the number of defeats on bills or amendments to bills suffered by governments since 1997:

Session	Number of defeats
2008–09	25
2007–08	29
2006–07	45
2005–06	62
2004–05	37
2003–04	64
2002–03	88
2001–02	56
2000–01	2
1999–2000	36
1998–99	31
1997–98	39

Source: House of Commons Library, www.parliament.uk

A more illuminating statistic is this: the average number of government defeats per annum in the Lords under Labour 1997–2009 was 43. This compares with a figure of only 13 under Conservative governments from 1979–97. There are two probable explanations for this. One is that, up to 2000, there was a built-in Conservative majority in the Lords because there were still hundreds of hereditary peers allowed to vote and most were Conservatives. The other is that, after reform in 2000, the Lords gained more democratic credibility and legitimacy and so acted in a more independent, confident manner.

The following table sets out prominent examples of the House of Lords' defiance of the will of government and the House of Commons.

Issue	Detail	Outcome
House of Lords Reform, late 1998–9	The Lords objected to the complete abolition of the voting rights of hereditary peers.	The government was forced to compromise, allowing 92 hereditary peers to retain their rights.
The legal age of consent for homosexual males, 1998–9	The Lords voted twice, in 1998 and 1999, against lowering the age of consent to sex for homosexual males from 18 to 16.	In November 2000 the government forced the measure through by using the 1949 Parliament Act. The legislation had been passed in two consecutive sessions of the Commons.
Anti-Terrorism legislation 2001	The Lords defeated the government on ten occasions, proposing key amendments.	The government compromised, removing incitement to religious hatred as an offence from the legislation.
Hunting with dogs 2001	The Lords blocked the proposal to ban hunting with dogs (mainly fox hunting). Time ran out for the bill because of the 2001 general election.	The ban was postponed, but did pass both houses by 2004.
Anti-Terrorism Legislation, 2004–05	The Lords insisted that the Anti-Terrorism Act, 2001, following a successful appeal by several Belmarsh prisoners in the law lords, was unacceptable on the grounds that it allowed suspects to be detained without trial.	The government was forced to accept amendments, ensuring that terror suspects could have movements restricted with permission of a judge, but could not be detained in prison.
Gambling Order 2007	The Lords rejected a plan to allow the construction of a 'super-casino' in Manchester, a measure that had been narrowly passed in the Commons.	The government was forced to completely review its plans to allow more casinos to be opened in Britain.

Issue	Detail	Outcome
Political Parties and Elections Bill 2009	The Lords rejected a clause that stated that all donors to UK political parties should be resident in the UK for tax purposes.	The clause was dropped.
Equality Bill 2010	The Lords carried an amendment excluding the Church of England from the terms of the new Act designed to end discrimination against the old, gay people, the disabled, etc. This was against government opposition but it was accepted.	The Lord's amendment was accepted.

The Commons and Lords compared and contrasted

On the face of it the Commons and the Lords appear to be remarkably similar. The procedures of each house are similar and both spend a high proportion of their time passing legislation. Even the shape of both chambers is similar – rectangles with the Speaker at the end and government and opposition benches ranged opposite each other on either side. But when we scratch the surface, crucial differences appear.

If we stay for a moment with the shape of the chambers, there is an immediately noticeable contrast. In the Lords there are benches – known as 'crossbenches' that sit in the middle facing towards the Speaker. These are absent in the Commons. The crossbenches seat a large number of peers who are politically independent. They are said 'not to take a party whip'. The crossbenchers are in a minority, but there are enough of them to ensure that the governing party can never enjoy an overall majority. So, when the House of Lords divides on strict party lines, the fate of a bill or an amendment lies with the independent crossbenchers.

Even those peers who do 'take the party whip' and declare themselves members of one party or another are far more independent minded than their counterparts in the Commons. A relatively small number of party supporters in the Lords have political ambitions. Many are retired from their professions (a large number are former professional politicians, often ex-ministers) or have other major roles in society (for example, as lawyers, journalists, pressure group leaders, university professors or business men and women), which means they are effectively very much part-time politicians. Such individuals may well have strong party allegiances, but they are no longer subject to prime-ministerial patronage and do not have to submit themselves to the discipline meted out by the whips. Nor do they have a constituency to worry about if they decide to defy their party leadership.

But perhaps the most important distinction lies hidden behind the apparent likenesses – which is that the House of Lords simply lacks the legitimacy of the Commons. While it remains unelected (as we shall see later there are proposals for a partly elected Lords in the future) it is an undemocratic body. Its members are fully aware of this and therefore do not even *claim* to enjoy the same degree of authority as the Commons. The following restrictions on the Lords therefore apply:

- It can delay the passages of bills for only one year under the terms of the Parliament Act 1949.

- It has no power over the financial arrangements of the government. This is under the Parliament Act of 1911.

- Its members agree voluntarily that they will not block any legislation that clearly appeared in the government's previous election manifesto. This is under the unwritten 'Salisbury Convention'.

- Any amendments proposed by the Lords must be approved by the Commons (although the Lords can delay legislation simply by repeatedly passing the same amendments over and over again until a compromise with the government is reached).

As a result of these restrictions we can identify a much more traditionally limited role as played by the Lords. It looks like this:

- To delay any legislation where peers felt it was desirable for the government to think again and perhaps consult more widely. This was certainly the case with the legislation to ban hunting with dogs in 2004–05.

- To make helpful and friendly suggestions for amendments to bills, often to protect minority interests or to improve the quality of the legislation. This was done with the proposals to introduce top-up tuition fees for university students in 2003–04.

- Sometimes to make hostile suggestions for amendments in the hope that constant obstruction will force the government to compromise. This tactic worked with the amendment of the Anti-Terrorism Act of 2004–05. Similarly, in 2010 a hostile amendment was passed when the Lords agreed to make an exemption for Christian churches to the Equality Act, allowing them to discriminate on the basis of sexuality when employing priests, etc.

- To debate some of the great issues of the day in order to ensure that the government and the House of Commons hear representations from a wide variety of groups in society and from experts in the Lords who have great experience of the issue concerned. Such issues as mercy killing, abortion, *in-vitro* fertilisation and embryo research have been debated in this way in recent times.

The relationship between government and Parliament

The domination of the legislature by executive government in the UK is one of the key features of the political system. Indeed, it could be considered to be its most important feature. The nineteenth-century political journalist Walter Bagehot called the 'fusion' of executive and legislative power the *efficient secret* of the British system. Certainly the power of government creates two important realities:

1. It means that governments are rarely removed from office prematurely. Most governments last the full legal maximum of five years in office or decide to call an election before that on a voluntary basis. The stability of government in the UK is certainly envied by countries whose governments are much less secure and are often shorter lived.

2. It also means that governments are generally able to carry out virtually all of their manifesto commitments with relatively little obstruction. The electorate are therefore able to vote for a party, confident in the knowledge that they are granting them a solid mandate.

Of course, these are the advantages of executive domination. There are also two very striking problems that arise:

1. Governments can become dictatorial in nature. Legislation may not be properly scrutinised and may survive with undesirable features.

2. There may be times when the government has lost the confidence of the public. The public cannot remove a government, but Parliament can. However, as long as the government whips can maintain control, the government will survive, even with a small majority in the House of Commons.

So, the question of whether executive dominance is desirable is a balanced one. When governments appear to be popular and successful, the weakness of Parliament is of little concern. But when the opposite is true, the public bemoan the fact that MPs do not seem willing to exercise their considerable reserve powers.

Why government dominates Parliament

We should now examine the reasons why the government is able to control Parliament so effectively. The following factors are important:

- The electoral system used to guarantee that one party would win an absolute majority in the Commons. Furthermore, the government's parliamentary majority tends to be very large. Here again the electoral system is the cause. It tends to exaggerate even a modest lead in the popular vote. For example, Labour's 3 per cent lead over the Conservatives in the 2005 election was translated into a majority of more than 60 seats. Thus we can say that single-party majorities help the executive to dominate, but when there is no party majority, as after 2010, this control is inevitably weakened.

- Party loyalty in the UK is traditionally strong. Political parties are normally ideologically unified so the number of dissidents is usually low. Governments can therefore rely on their

parliamentary majority with some confidence. However, when there is coalition government, party loyalties can become problematic.

- Prime ministerial patronage is extremely important. There is virtually only one career path for a professional politician and that is to achieve ministerial office. Since all posts in the government are controlled by the prime minister he can demand loyalty from a high proportion of his party's MPs. There are more than 100 members of both Houses who are already ministers and therefore bound by collective majority. They will always support the government. Of the others, the majority retain hopes that they will one day be promoted to ministerial office. One of the important qualities that an aspiring minister must display is loyalty. Here again, however, coalitions weaken the prime minister's power as some ministerial posts are inevitably controlled by their coalition partner.

- The ultimate sanction a whip can use against a dissident MP is to suspend or remove them permanently from the party. This will have no short-term effect, but if an MP loses the nomination of his party at the next general election, they will almost certainly lose their seat. Even if the whips do not remove an MP's party membership, the constituency party of the MP in question may well 'de-select' them if they feel that there has been excessive disloyalty. De-selection means that they will not be the official party candidate any more, with the effect described above.

- Prime ministers used to be able to threaten dissident MPs with the dissolution of Parliament, pitching them into an unwanted election. However, the introduction of fixed-term parliaments effectively will remove this threat.

- The House of Lords can be a thorn in the government's side. But its lack of authority and powers means that the government can often sidestep its attempts to be obstructive. As we have seen above, there is no doubt that the Lords is stronger and more obstinate than it used to be, but ultimately it will nearly always have to bow to the authority of the government and its majority in the House of Commons.

Having said all this, it must be emphasised that the relationship between government and Parliament (the House of Commons in particular) is constantly changing. A number of observations can be made in this respect:

- When the government has a modest majority in the Commons – for example 1992–97 and 2005 onwards – it is more vulnerable. A coalition of opposition parties and a relatively small number of dissidents in the governing party can defeat the government. This occurred in 2006, for example, when proposals for 90-day detention orders for suspected terrorists was roundly defeated.

- Similarly, when there is no overall majority for the government, its control is reduced. This may also be true of coalition government. Relatively small groups of dissident MPs from either of the coalition partner parties can thwart the will of the government.

- It has been the case that, when the government has a large majority in the Commons, the House of Lords becomes more active in an attempt to replace the weaker opposition. In the period 1997–2005, when Labour enjoyed huge majorities, the House of Lords certainly became more obstructive than normal.

- Under Labour after 2001 there was a persistent group of MPs in the governing party who proved to be consistently obstructive, particularly in matters concerning human rights, foreign policy and welfare issues. This so called 'Labour Left' was small in number but relatively important in terms of influence.

But, despite this, the dice are very much loaded against parliamentary power. It is usually the case that government will have its way. Victories for Parliament are relatively rare, but they do occur.

We can now summarise the relative strengths and weaknesses of the Commons and the Lords.

Commons strengths	Commons weaknesses
<ul><li>The Commons has the ultimate power to remove a government from office.</li><li>Under exceptional circumstances the MPs can veto legislation, or threaten to do so and thus force compromises.</li><li>Also under exceptional circumstances, MPs can force legislative amendments from the government.</li><li>MPs can call ministers to account. This is particularly effective when conducted by select committees.</li><li>Every constituency can be effectively represented by its own MP who can raise grievances in the Commons.</li></ul>	<ul><li>Governments normally have a comfortable majority and so can dominate MPs through patronage and discipline in general.</li><li>The legislative standing committees are largely controlled by the party whips, so the amending function of the Commons is weak.</li><li>MPs have insufficient time and support to be able to call government effectively to account. Ministers are also adept at avoiding intrusive questioning.</li><li>MPs have a limited role in developing legislation.</li><li>The Commons is not socially representative, especially lacking women and members of minority-ethnic groups.</li></ul>

Commons strengths	Commons weaknesses
• Various interest and cause groups are represented by MPs. • With a coalition government, small groups of MPs can have influence as they can thwart the will of the government.	• Governments are increasingly ignoring Parliament and consulting groups and the public directly. • The belief that the government may fall at any time can promote obedience as, generally, MPs do not relish elections.

Lords strengths	Lords weaknesses
• Many members of the Lords are more independent from party control than MPs. They can therefore be more effective in controlling government. • Peers represent a wide variety of interests and expertise, being largely prominent citizens with considerable specialised experience. • The Lords can delay legislation and so force compromises by government. • The Lords has more effective time to conduct debates and to scrutinise legislation.	• In its unreformed state, the Lords lacks democratic legitimacy. • The powers of the Lords are limited by law. It has no power over financial matters and cannot veto legislation in the long term. • Its proposed amendments can be overturned by the Commons. • Like the Commons, the Lords has a very limited role in developing legislation. • Peers face the same problems as MPs in calling government to account.

Discussion topic

Does the second chamber have a useful role to play? If so, what should that role be?

Parliamentary Reform

The House of Lords

We start with the Lords rather than the Commons in this section mainly because it is this area that the most significant reforms have occurred and are likely to develop in the future.

Modern reform has occurred in two stages.

Stage 1

Immediately after taking office in 1997 the Labour government took steps to remove the voting rights of hereditary peers. These eight hundred or so members of the nobility were either permanent absentees or were invariably committed to the Conservative cause. The number of Labour or Liberal Democrat hereditary peers was extremely limited. The party had also been severely affected by an incident in 1988 (discussed below) which was to spell the ultimate demise of the political role of the hereditary peerage. This incident entered the collective memory of the Labour party so that, when they returned to power, it was hardly surprising that it should occupy their immediate attention.

In 1988 Margaret Thatcher's government was trying to force through legislation to introduce the Poll Tax into local government. The Poll Tax was extremely controversial, being seen in many quarters as unfair as it was not based on ability to pay. The whips forced the bill through the House of Commons with relatively little difficulty. The Lords, on the other hand, were threatening to thwart the government's will. It was at this stage that the government, with its back to the wall, decided to persuade large numbers of hereditary peers to come to London to vote through the new tax. Many of these peers – sometimes known as 'backwoodsmen' – never normally voted. Some did not even know where to go to vote. However, the plan worked and the legislation was passed through. Labour, as we have said, never forgot these events. The days of the hereditary peerage were numbered, though no one knew it at the time.

At first the legislation to remove the voting rights of hereditary peers was held up. Not surprisingly the large Conservative majority there were unhappy with the proposals. Many meetings were held behind closed doors to find a compromise. Conservative leader, William Hague, feared that the obstruction would lead Labour to even more radical reform. He therefore persuaded his colleagues in the Lords to accept a limited reform: 92 hereditary peers – less than an eighth of the total – were to remain on a temporary basis. These peers were to be elected by the rest of the hereditaries. They were still a Conservative majority, but the government now had the opportunity to redress the political balance by creating many new Labour-supporting life peers.

It was always asserted that this was only the first stage of reform. The next stage was initiated with the appointment of a Commission to consider a long-term solution. By appointing a Conservative peer – Lord Wakeham – Tony Blair signalled the fact that he did not expect any radical change. Wakeham obliged with a moderate report. Its main principles were as follows:

- The powers of the Lords were to remain substantially unchanged. It was to be clearly subordinate to the House of Commons.

- A minority – possibly as few as 20 per cent – was to be elected by proportional representation on a regional basis.

- There were to be no more hereditary peers in the House.

- The rest of the House was to be appointed.

- An independent Appointments Commission would ensure that appropriate people were appointed and to prevent the excessive use of political patronage by party leaders.

- The political balance of the House would prevent domination by any one party. Independent 'crossbenchers' would hold the balance of power.

The Wakeham report was not implemented, but it formed the basis for the debate on reform that was to follow.

Stage 2

After a second decisive election victory in 2001, the Labour government was encouraged to complete its reforms. However, attempt after attempt failed. Between 2001–05, the political forces lined up as follows:

- **Tony Blair and senior colleagues** wanted an all-appointed House of Lords. The fact that it was not elected would prevent it gaining too much authority and therefore influence. Thus executive power would not be seriously threatened by reform. Gordon Brown was relatively non-committal, but expressed willingness to be guided by the will of the House of Commons.

- **Most Labour MPs** support either a fully elected House of Lords or one with a large elected element.

- **Liberal Democrats** insist that the second chamber should be fully elected by proportional representation. It could then act as a counterweight to the power of government and the House of Commons.

- **Conservatives** hoped after 2001 that the issue of reform would either simply fade into obscurity or would be blocked once again by the peers themselves. They watched with satisfaction as successive proposals to introduce a fully or partly elected second chamber failed through lack of consensus. By 2005, however, the party had made a complete u-turn and decided to support the idea of a chamber that was to be half elected and half appointed. On becoming Conservative leader, David Cameron re-affirmed his support for a mixed elected–appointed solution.

By the time of the 2005 general election no progress had been made. However, the Labour leadership reluctantly agreed to allow the House of Commons a free vote (i.e. the whips would not try to influence voting) on the issue. It was hoped that a final solution was imminent if compromises could be made on all sides. One thing seemed certain – that the final 92 hereditary peers would ultimately lose their voting rights.

When David Cameron came to lead the Conservative Party he declared himself 'interested' in Lords reform. By the election of 2010 this interest had turned into a relatively firm commitment.

The future of Lords reform

Gordon Brown, who governed from 2007 to 2010, was unable to complete reform of the House of Lords. Beset as he was by a major economic crisis,

he simply did not have the time or the will to make the changes he wanted. When the Conservative–Liberal Democrat coalition came to office in 2010, however, the whole picture changed. Both coalition partners were committed to reform and the Liberal Democrats made the issue part of their price for forming a coalition. It was agreed that there should be an all-elected second chamber, elected by proportional representation (probably a regional list system). Reform was promised within the life of the Parliament that started life in 2010, i.e. by 2015.

Assessments of Lords reform

We can now consider and evaluate the main alternatives for future reform. The three likely structures of the House of Lords are:

1. A fully elected chamber

2. A fully appointed chamber

3. A partly elected, partly appointed chamber.

The two tables below summarise the cases for or against each of the first two alternatives.

| A fully elected second chamber ||
Arguments for	Arguments against
<ul><li>It is more democratic than current arrangements.</li><li>It will eliminate any corrupt practices in relation to appointments to the Lords.</li><li>It might act as a democratic balance against the power</li></ul>	<ul><li>If an elected second chamber simply mirrored the Commons it would create a deadlock between the two houses or no balancing effect at all.</li><li>Too many elections might lead to</li></ul>

A fully elected second chamber (continued)	
Arguments for	**Arguments against**
of the government, especially if elected by proportional representation so that no party will win an overall majority. • If elected proportionally, it will allow smaller parties to be better represented.	voter fatigue and therefore apathy. • A more powerful second chamber might lead to less decisive government. • It might simply be another part of the legislature dominated by the parties, with too many 'party hacks'.

A fully appointed second chamber	
Arguments for	**Arguments against**
• It is an opportunity to bring people into the political process who would not wish to stand for election. • The membership can be controlled to ensure that all major groups and associations in society could be represented. • It can bring more independents into the political process.	• It could put too much power into the hands of those responsible for appointing members and could lead to corruption. • It is undemocratic and holds back progress towards a modern system. • It might lack legitimacy and public support because the people have no part in its composition.

The argument is relatively balanced. There are strong impulses for both solutions. It is therefore not surprising than many propose a compromise between the two. A part-elected, part-appointed

chamber would have greater democratic legitimacy than current arrangements and the fact that many members would be appointed would prevent too much party domination. After the 2010 election, however, the balance of opinion had firmly shifted towards the fully elected option and this seems to be the most likely outcome.

The House of Commons

New Labour also pledged to make reforms to the House of Commons in order to modernise it after 1997. In the event, however, this proved to be one area of reform that appeared to be stillborn, despite widespread and growing concern that the Commons was becoming at best ineffective and at worst impotent and irrelevant. It was in need of streamlining, certainly – though whether it needed more power was problematic.

A modernisation committee was set up early in Labour's administration, but it had little effect. A few cosmetic changes were made, including the reduction of Prime Minister's Question Time from two short sessions to one longer one. The facilities for MPs were improved with a new office block and there were increased allowances for secretarial and research backing. But nothing *substantial* altered. Indeed, after 1997, most commentators saw the Commons as declining in importance, especially as Labour won two thumping majorities in succession.

Robin Cook, who took over as Leader of the House in 2001, showed some willingness to promote change, but he could make little headway. The one major change that Cook made was, in fact, forced on him by his own backbenchers. They insisted that membership of the departmental select committees should be placed in the hands of MPs rather than the party whips. In the long term this may prove to be a significant reform, but if the government has a large majority, the balance of power is likely to remain firmly with the executive. When Robin Cook left office in

2003 (over his opposition to the war in Iraq), the impetus for reform seemed to be lost.

Prime minister Tony Blair also promoted one other change that, again, may become significant in the future. Blair decided to submit himself to a twice-yearly questioning session at the hands of a liaison committee comprised of the chairs of all the departmental select committees. It was a small step in the direction of more government accountability, but nobody can claim it is of great significance.

Ironically, it has been the Conservatives who have made most of the running on Commons reform. It was Margaret Thatcher herself who had backed the creation of departmental select committees in 1979, perhaps the most important parliamentary development of the twentieth century. These committees certainly improved the Commons' ability to call ministers to account and are still the main way in which our representatives are able to scrutinise the work of government. In fields such as foreign policy, defence spending, health administration and police matters they have been especially effective in throwing extra light on official or unofficial policies.

More recently, the Norton Committee, led by a Conservative peer, has headed calls for further changes. His report, published in 2000, contained many recommendations, the most important of which included:

- the restoration of two Prime Minister's Question Times

- longer ministerial question-time sessions with more in-depth questions

- more opportunities for back-bench MPs to raise issues

- debates should have shorter speeches so that more can participate

- more research resources available for the opposition parties

- more research facilities for select committees

- MPs should control their own select committees rather than the party whips

- standing committees that consider legislation should have more time to use outside witnesses, along the model of the US Congress

- more resources for the Commons to consider EU legislation

- select committee chairmen to be paid a minister's salary so that there is an alternative career option for MPs to being a minister. This would break much of the influence of the prime minister and the whips.

These recommendations represent something of a consensus on how the Commons' work could be made more effective. However, Blair's government showed no enthusiasm for them, especially as it had been too busy struggling with a rebellious House of Lords to worry about the Commons. We may also reflect on the comments of former cabinet secretary Lord Butler in a 2001 lecture to the Politics Association. He suggested that only the reform of the electoral system could bring about any truly meaningful change in the role and influence of the Commons.

The future of Commons reform

The importance of electoral reform was recognised by the Liberal Democrat Party and it has remained their main proposal. When, therefore, they achieved a share of power after 2010 it became a key policy. They easily persuaded the Conservatives to agree to a referendum on the issue. Electoral reform in favour of the Alternative Vote will have marked effects on the Commons, including the following:

- It seems likely that it will prevent any party from winning an overall majority. If this is the case, the governing party or coalition will be unable to dominate MPs in the way they have done historically.

- Many issues will have to be resolved on the basis of consensus, rather than being bulldozed through the Commons by a dominant majority government. This implies that there will be more meaningful debates in the chamber.

- The power of the party whips will be reduced when there is no decisive government majority.

- MPs will have increased authority and public esteem as the AV system guarantees that they will achieve a majority of votes in their constituencies.

The 2010 coalition government made further proposals for reform. These were:

- Power is to be given to constituents to 'recall' unsatisfactory or corrupt MPs. This would entail a petition followed by a by-election.

- The constituency boundaries are to be redrawn to make their size more equal, effectively removing the built-in Labour advantage.

- The size of the Commons is to be reduced by 10 per cent to make it more streamlined and effective.

Discussion topic

How else could the House of Commons be reformed and strengthened to enable it to better control the power of government?

Key concepts in this chapter

Legislature The name given to the political institution whose main role is to pass laws. In the UK this is Parliament, in the USA it is the Congress. This does not necessarily mean that the legislature develops the laws, but certainly that laws are considered legitimate only if passed by the legislature. Legislatures often have the additional role of scrutinising the work of government and acting as a check on its power.

Parliamentary government A system of politics where government is drawn from Parliament and is accountable to Parliament. In other words, the government has no separate authority from that of Parliament.

Presidential government In contrast to parliamentary government, a president normally has a separate source of authority from that of the legislature. This means that the executive (president) is accountable to the people directly, not to the legislature.

Separation of powers A constitutional principle that the three branches of government – legislature, executive and judiciary – should have separate membership and separate powers and should be able to control each other's powers. It is largely absent in the UK.

Representative government A form of government where political power is largely exercised by elected representatives, through individual MPs, Parliament as a whole and parties.

Second chamber A second House of Parliament, normally seen as subordinate to the first house. Currently in the UK this is the House of Lords. In France it is known as the Senate.

Revision topics and examination questions

Revision topics

- The main functions of Parliament
- Differences in functions between the House of Commons and the House of Lords
- Meaning of parliamentary government
- How Parliament calls government to account
- How Parliament scrutinises legislation
- Strengths and weaknesses of Parliament
- Factors that prevent Parliament controlling executive power
- Extent to which Parliament is representative
- Nature of parliamentary sovereignty
- The erosion of parliamentary sovereignty
- The reform of the House of Lords
- The reform of the House of Commons

Essay questions

40 minutes

1. Is Parliament now an irrelevant institution?
2. Analyse the main distinctions between the role and importance of the House of Commons and the House of Lords.
3. To what extent is Parliament an effective check on the power of government?
4. Evaluate the various arguments concerning reform of the House of Lords.

Stimulus response questions

Question 1

Read the following passage and answer the questions which follow.

Department select committees have existed since 1979 and have the responsibility of examining the work of government departments on behalf of parliament. They are independent of party and attempt to produce unanimous conclusions. Typically they examine such matters as whether the department has been efficient, fair and effective and whether its policies and legislation are justified. They can call witnesses from inside and outside government as well as official reports and papers. Here is an extract from a report of the Public Accounts Committee that looks at the financial performance of government as a whole:

Public Accounts Committee. First three conclusions of its report on child obesity, December 2006

1. The 2004 Health Survey for England showed an overall rise in obesity amongst children aged 2–10 from 9.9 per cent in 1995 to 13.4 per cent in 2004. Despite the introduction of a specific PSA target in July 2004 aimed at tackling the growing problem of child obesity, the Departments have been slow to react and have still not published key sections of the Delivery Plan. The

Departments need to increase the pace of their response and improve their leadership by, for example, appointing a senior, high profile champion, to lead and galvanise activity.

2. The three Departments have set up a complex delivery chain for tackling child obesity involving 26 different bodies or groups of bodies. Our predecessors' report on obesity identified confusion over roles and responsibilities both between different departments and others charged with tackling the problem. This confusion still exists. The Departments need to clarify responsibilities throughout the delivery chain and introduce measures to judge the performance and contribution of the respective parties, perhaps similar to those under development for Local Area Agreements.

3. Parents have not been engaged; the only initiative planned by the Departments that will directly target parents and children is a social marketing campaign which will not be launched until 2007. The campaign should be started as soon as possible. It should present some simple but high profile messages and advice to parents, children and teachers, outlining the risks of obesity and show simple ways in which children can make a difference to their lifestyles: for example, the message that consuming one less chocolate biscuit per day can help lead a child out of obesity (the Departments' own example).

(a) From the source, what is a select committee of Parliament? **(5 marks)**

(b) From the source and your own knowledge, what is the role of such select committees? **(10 marks)**

(c) How effective is the House of Commons in scrutinising the work of government? **(25 marks)**

Question 2

Read the following passage and answer the questions that follow is.

Extract from a Consultation Paper by the Department for Constitutional Affairs, September 2003

The government believes that the UK must remain a bicameral democracy. The second chamber has an important part to play in our system of government. It has a distinctive role: to be a complement to the House of Commons; to bring a less partisan viewpoint to the consideration of legislation; and to have the time to undertake longer-term enquiries into the work of government. There are a number of areas where the present House could be better equipped to carry out its role and functions. The proposals which follow in this consultation document are directed to that end.

There is widespread agreement about the proper role and functions of the House and about the principles which should inform its composition.

These areas of agreement include the following:

● The Lords should not challenge the pre-eminence of the House of Commons. It should be a complement to it, not a copy or a rival. The present constitutional conventions which govern how the Lords conducts its business and behaves towards the Commons should remain basically unchanged.

● The most important role of the Lords is to be a revising chamber for legislation. In undertaking this role, it should bring a distinctive perspective, not simply duplicate the work of the House of Commons.

● The Lords also has important functions in relation to the scrutiny of government action and holding ministers to account.

Any proposals for the composition of the House, and indeed for the way in which it does its business, should spring from a clear understanding of its role and functions.

(a) What does the statement mean by the term 'revising chamber'? **(5 marks)**

(b) The statement refers to the pre-eminence of the House of Commons. In what senses is the House of Commons more important than the House of Lords? **(10 marks)**

(c) How might the House of Lords be reformed to make it more effective? **(25 marks)**

Resources and web guide

Books

The classic modern work and still very relevant is:
   P. Norton, *Does Parliament Matter?*, Harvester Wheatsheaf, 1993.

A full description is given in:
   R. Rogers and R. Walters, *How Parliament Works*, Pearson, 2006.

A more journalistic account, but very readable, is:
   P. Riddell, *Parliament Under Blair,* Politicos, 2000.

A very authoritative discussion of the current state of Parliament as well as possible reform is:
   Hansard Society, *The Challenge for Parliament: Making government Accountable,* Hansard, 2001.

A modern account is:
   M. Grant, *The UK Parliament*, Edinburgh University Press, 2009

Useful websites

The official website is
   www.parliament.uk

The other useful site is the Hansard Society:
   www.hansardsociety.org.uk

Acts of Parliament can be viewed on
   www.hmso.gov.uk

For information and chat about the activities of MPs:
   www.revolts.co.uk

The prime minister and cabinet

How governments are formed

Before looking at how governments come into existence in the UK, we need to be clear about what is meant by the term 'government'. Essentially, there is a broad and a narrow definition. The broader meaning of 'government' includes elected ministers together with the army of civil servants, advisers, committees and other bodies that are involved in the formulation of policy and the implementation of decisions and services. The narrow definition includes only the 100-plus ministers and senior party officials who are appointed by the prime minister and thus form the 'inner circle' that governs the country. It is this narrow definition with which we are concerned here.

There are no codified rules operating in the UK to state how a government is formed. Instead it is the natural consequence of the outcome of general elections. In theory we do not need rules because the choice of government – both which party will govern and which members of that party will be make up that government – is in the hands of the reigning monarch. Up until the nineteenth century, indeed, this was largely a reality. The King would choose his preferred ministers and as long as it was felt they could command the support of Parliament, they would form a government that ran the country on behalf of the monarch. But, of course, the monarch no longer plays any active role in this process.

Fortunately, the way elections *usually* turn out in Britain makes the intervention of the monarch unnecessary.

As long as one party has won an absolute majority of the seats in the House of Commons after a general election, its leader will be invited by the monarch to form a government. However, when no party wins an overall majority, as occurred in February 1974 and May 2010, the situation becomes more confused. The aftermath of the 2010 election demonstrates the problem and the likely outcome of such a situation. This was the order of events:

1. It became clear on the day after the election that no party would have an overall majority.

2. The Conservatives were the largest party in the new House of Commons but were 20 seats short of an overall majority.

3. Prime minister Gordon Brown did not resign, though Labour had come well behind the Conservatives. The Labour leadership entered negotiations to form a coalition with the Liberal Democrats.

4. Over several days, the Liberal Democrats conducted simultaneous negotiations with both the main parties with a view to forming a coalition.

5. It became apparent that a Labour–Liberal Democrat coalition was more logical in terms of policy, but there was a major problem: the Liberal Democrat and Labour MPs together did not make up a majority. They would have to rely on a 'rainbow coalition' of 'progressive' MPs including members of the nationalist parties, the Northern Ireland SDLP and a single Green Party MP. Such a coalition would have enjoyed a majority of only three and would have been extremely fragile.

6. Gordon Brown, who remained prime minister while negotiations continued, bowed to the inevitable. He resigned both as prime minister and as Labour leader. He went to Buckingham Palace and advised the Queen that she should ask David Cameron to form a government, either as a minority or in coalition with the Liberal Democrats.

7. Cameron accepted and shortly afterwards announced that negotiations for coalition with the Liberal Democrats had been successfully concluded.

Thus was a new government formed. The whole process took a mere five days. It is likely to be a 'blueprint' for procedures in the event of more hung parliaments. Nevertheless, though the formation of a coalition had run relatively smoothly, the nature of government was radically changed.

'The government'

Bearing in mind that we are still using the narrow definition of government (i.e. only elected ministers), we can look at a typical structure of a modern British government. The exact structure of every government may change, but the figures shown opposite are normal.

Type of member	Typical number	Role
Cabinet members	23	These include the prime minister, the heads of large government departments, plus a small number of other senior party (single party or coalition) members. They are the ultimate source of official government policy.
Senior non-cabinet posts	15	The holders of important offices, such as Attorney General, who are not quite senior enough to be in the cabinet.
Junior ministers not in the cabinet	60	These are subordinates of those cabinet ministers who run departments. Most are known as 'ministers of State'.
Whips	17	The Chief Whip sits in cabinet. All other whips do not. They have the task of ensuring party discipline among MPs and peers, running the administration of debates and votes in Parliament, and keeping MPs and peers informed.
Total	115	The complete 'government'

Because government must have a substantial presence in both Houses of Parliament it always contains a number of peers. Again, the proportion will vary from one administration to another, but it is typical for 25 members of the government to be members of the House of Lords. The other 90 are all MPs.

We can now establish a number of characteristics of the body we know as 'the government':

- All members of the government must sit in Parliament as well as being ministers, etc. As we have seen above, most, but not all, are MPs in the Commons. It can therefore be noted that members of the government who are MPs – 90 or so – also have a constituency to look after, even the prime minister.

- MPs from the party that is in government are *not* members of the government. It is a common misconception that they are. They are known as *back-benchers*, while government members are known as *front-benchers*. Back-benchers from the party in government are not bound by the same rules as front-benchers.

- All members of the government are appointed by the prime minister. Though he may seek advice from trusted colleagues, the decision is his alone. This also means that only the prime minister may dismiss a member of government.

- All members of government are bound by the principle of **collective responsibility**. This means that they must all take public responsibility for all policies of the government, even if they disagree privately or had nothing to do with the formulation of policy. If a minister, however junior, publicly disagrees with government policy they are expected to resign or face rapid dismissal. In fact, it is the prime minister and cabinet who make virtually all policy, so the 90 or so government members who are not cabinet members are required to support policies in whose formulation they may have played no direct part.

- The full government – 100-plus members – would never normally meet together in one body. The cabinet, usually of 22–23 members, does, however, meet regularly.

Ministerial selection

The next question to be posed is, how does a prime minister decide whom to put in his government? This is a complex issue, mainly because there are two considerations that may well conflict with each other. One concerns the competence of the individual in question. This may be simple enough. But there are also political considerations. Furthermore, the principles of selection also change when there is a coalition government. Here we will first consider the issues when there is single-party government.

The best person for the job may have unorthodox views, may be considered to be something of a 'rebel' and may well have clashed with the prime minister in the past. The prime minister must, therefore, weigh up the qualities of individuals against the political consequences of appointing them. Nevertheless we can identify a number of qualities that ideal ministers should possess:

- They must be politically reliable. This does not necessarily mean that they should agree with the prime minister on every issue, but it does mean that they will be willing to accept collective responsibility and support the government, at least in public. Well-known dissidents are occasionally appointed. Tony Blair, for example, appointed such characters as Mo Mowlem (Northern Ireland Secretary), Robin Cook (Foreign Secretary) and Clare Short (Overseas Development Secretary), knowing that they were potentially difficult to control. He chose them for their personal qualities and because they had a substantial following in the party. In the event all three left the government, Short and Cook over policy in Iraq and Mowlem because she became disillusioned with politics in general. Tony Benn, however, Labour's best-known left winger, was not considered for government office as it was highly unlikely that he would ever accept collective responsibility.

● Junior ministers, on the first rungs of the promotion ladder that leads to cabinet office, must have potential. Prime ministers are always looking for younger MPs who will be able to fill senior posts in the future. 'Potential' generally means an ability to cope under pressure, to be a good debater in Parliament and to be a good 'politician'. This means displaying such skills as negotiation, persuasion and a general 'feel' for how opinion is moving.

● Political leaders like Tony Blair and Margaret Thatcher, who have a strong political philosophy and wish to put that philosophy into practice, will normally try to recruit a team of ministers that shares their political views. This creates a united and dynamic government. Dissension within government can hold back progress towards specific political goals. Sometimes, of course, as was the case with John Major from 1992–97, this is not always possible. Major had to accept a number of colleagues who were not his political allies. This was because, in his position as prime minister, he was constantly undermined by having a small parliamentary majority and by serious political rifts within the Conservative Party.

● Potential ministers must have managerial skills. Those who will head a government department or a section of a department will have a large number of civil servants, advisers and other bodies to manage. If they cannot do this they will inevitably fail.

The variations in these considerations under a coalition government are considered below. Overall, however, it is clear that the selection of ministers in a coalition must partly be the result of negotiation between the coalition partners.

Other forms of government

So far we have looked at the conventional form of government seen in the UK. That is a government made up of members of the same party and which is able to command an absolute majority in the House of Commons – where it really matters. However, we should also look at two other forms of government. This is for two reasons. First, the British model of dominant, single-party government is unusual in most other so-called liberal democracies. The proportional representation and majority electoral systems that are used almost everywhere in the democratic world rarely throw up a single party with an absolute parliamentary majority. Therefore they have to form other types of government. Second, it could well be that we will have to adapt to new forms of government formation in the future, either if we change our electoral system, or if the Liberal Democrats continue to make progress and create a three-party system.

The two types we will consider are minority and coalition governments.

Minority government

Minority governments are unusual, unstable and normally short-lived. But they are not unheard of and have been known in the UK. It is a situation where a party forms a government without a parliamentary majority. This was the case in Britain from February to October 1974 (see above) and it also occurred in the 1920s. Usually a minority is a caretaker government, waiting for a fresh general election in the hope that it will produce a decisive result.

A minority government can never rely on getting its legislation or its financial budgets passed. It must, therefore, take each issue separately and try to build a coalition of support from other parties, or sections of other parties. It cannot hope to pass legislation without such a consensus of support. In effect, minority governments cannot attempt to do anything radical. They can keep government 'ticking over', but little more.

Coalition government

A coalition government is one in which two or more parties take part. There are two conditions that must be met:

1. Ministerial posts are shared between two or more parties. In the British system this also means shared cabinet posts. Which posts are given to which parties would be the subject of considerable negotiation. Thus in the Conservative–Liberal Democrat coalition formed in May 2010, there were five Liberal Democrat ministers in cabinet and eighteen Conservatives. Lower ministerial posts were allocated on a similar basis.

2. There needs to be agreement among all the coalition partners on which policies can be accepted. All the parties need to be willing to give up some policies and perhaps agree to some of their rivals' proposals. Such an agreement was achieved in 2010 and its main elements can be seen in the section on the General Election of May 2010 on page 111.

Coalitions can be remarkably stable, as has been the case in countries such as Germany, Japan and Sweden. There coalitions are the norm and have tended to last for many years. But they can also be very unstable and typically short-lived. Italy and Israel are notorious for such instability. We consider the relative merits and drawbacks of coalition government in the chapter on electoral reform.

There had been no coalition government in Britain from 1945 until 2010 and it is certainly a kind of administration that is considered to be unnatural, to be avoided at virtually all costs. But we have now seen coalition government at work in Scottish government, where Labour and the Liberal Democrats have worked together since devolution was introduced in 1998. There was also a brief agreement between the same two parties in the Welsh Assembly. In local government coalitions are very common, with all combinations of parties being possible. So the British are coming round to the idea that coalitions are not a disaster. The advent of a coalition government in 2010 was certainly feared by many but also welcomed as a new kind of politics based on more consensus and less conflict.

There are a number of different types of coalition, any one of which might be seen in the future:

- **Majority coalitions**: Normally formed by just two parties, such coalitions are formed simply to create a parliamentary majority. This was the type of arrangement that was forged in 2010.

- **Grand coalitions**: These are coalitions between two major parties, formed to create an overwhelming majority. They would normally be considered in times of national emergency or crisis.

- **Rainbow coalitions**: These are agreements between a larger number of parties, often of greatly varying philosophies. It would normally be one large party and several other smaller parties.

- **National coalitions**: These are coalitions where all parties (or sections of parties) are invited to participate. They occur at times of national crisis and are designed to create unity. Britain used such a coalition in the 1930s, when there was a major economic depression, and in the Second World War.

Before leaving coalitions we can consider the alternatives that were presented in May 2010:

1. Conservative minority government. This would have been 20 seats short of a majority and would have relied on support from the Democratic Unionists in Northern Ireland plus any elements of the other parties that would support it on specific issues. It seems unlikely that such a government could have lasted more than a few months.

2. A progressive rainbow coalition. Made up of Labour, the Scottish Nationalists, Plaid Cymru, the Northern Ireland SDLP and a Green MP, this would have made a total 329 MPs, giving a majority of eight.

3. A Conservative–Liberal Democrat coalition. This was the successful option. It commanded the theoretical support of 363 MPs, a majority of 76.

Three other options – a minority Labour government, a grand coalition of Labour and Conservatives or a national coalition of all main parties – were not seriously considered.

The decision tree below represents the range of outcomes following a general election.

Cabinet government

Until the 1960s most, if not all, textbooks would describe the British system of government as '**cabinet government**'. Since then, however, the concept of cabinet government has been gradually eroded and replaced by the notion of 'prime ministerial government'. We will consider the conflict between these two ideas below, but before doing that it is necessary to consider the traditional idea of cabinet government.

The following realities used to be taken for granted:

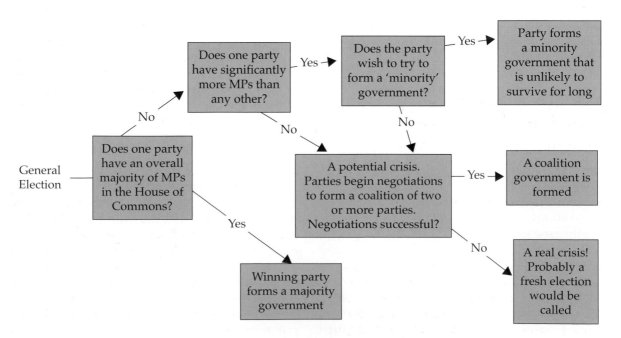

Government formation in the UK

- The cabinet represented the collective identity of the government.

- All important domestic and many foreign policy decisions were made within the cabinet.

- In order for a policy to be official, it would need full cabinet approval.

- Any disputes within the government would be resolved within the cabinet.

- The prime minister was considered *primus inter pares* (first among equals), meaning that he had a higher status than his colleagues, but also implying that he could, and often was, outvoted within the cabinet.

In summary, the cabinet was considered to be the centrepiece of the government and its supreme policy-making institution.

It was during the premiership of Harold Macmillan (Conservative, 1957–63), and more particularly the first administration of Harold Wilson (Labour, 1964–70), that commentators began to realise that the days of cabinet government, as described above, were numbered.

Key Word

Cabinet government A system of government where the cabinet is the central policy-making body.

The changing UK cabinet

What began to happen in the 1960s was that the prime minister became increasingly dominant within the government. Two of Wilson's cabinet colleagues, Richard Crossman and Barbara Castle, began to speak and write openly of 'prime ministerial government'. This was not because they were Wilson's political opponents within the Labour Party, but because their experience of cabinet government was not what they had expected it to be. It certainly did not correspond to the textbook descriptions that they had read. So, it was Wilson who started a process of degradation of cabinet government that continues to this day. What were the changes that constituted this process?

Prime ministerial domination

Harold Wilson soon learned how he could dominate the whole governing process, the cabinet especially. With the help of a small, close-knit team of allies, the cabinet Secretary (the most senior civil servant who came to serve the prime minister almost exclusively), a few trusted private advisers (known in Wilson's day as the *kitchen cabinet* from where it often met to discuss strategy in Downing Street) and his own force of personality he could control the political agenda from Number 10.

Wilson manipulated the agenda of cabinet meetings, reached private agreements with ministers before the meetings so as to control the probable outcome and even, it was reported, had the accounts of the meetings (the secret cabinet 'minutes') written to suit his own conclusions. So even senior cabinet colleagues began to feel that matters were outside their control, even though they sat at the apparent centre of power.

In the same period – the 1960s and early 1970s – the role of the media was becoming increasingly important. TV, radio and the press were taking over from Parliament as the main forums within which political issues were being presented. Wilson was perhaps the first prime minister who understood the power of TV in particular. Meanwhile the media were choosing to centre on the prime minister alone as the spokesman for the whole government. It was therefore almost inevitable that the prime minister would increasingly be both the presenter and the maker of government policy.

Margaret Thatcher (1979–90) took prime ministerial domination to a new level. By 1983, when she had removed most of her political opponents from the government and had won decisive victories over Argentina in the Falklands War (1982) and in the general election that followed it, Thatcher appeared to dominate the whole government machinery. Even more than Wilson, she possessed great strength of purpose and came to be either feared or respected by her colleagues. The cabinet seemed to operate as it had always done, but it was packed with her supporters and she controlled its meetings just as Wilson had done. She was respected abroad, almost as much as Churchill had been, and the media concentrated their attention on her almost exclusively. Even the most senior of her colleagues in cabinet felt marginalised by her and most of them left government in angry circumstances at one stage or another. Nevertheless it was ultimately her own cabinet that removed her in 1990. Tired of her unshakable support for the highly unpopular local poll tax, they replaced her with the mild-mannered and apparently reasonable John Major.

Excited political commentators heralded Thatcher's removal with talk of the 'return of cabinet government'. Indeed, John Major himself promised to restore 'collective' decision making, and for most of his period in office he had to put up with a quarrelsome cabinet that contained some of his deadliest enemies. Surviving close votes of confidence in the House of Commons and a leadership challenge in 1995, he held on in power for seven years. But Major's period in office was not the return of cabinet government, as many thought it was. The cabinet certainly did not operate as it had done in pre-Wilson days. Rather it proved to be an obstacle in the way of Major's attempts to solve the country's economic difficulties and to adopt a coherent policy towards the European Union. It was less a collective decision-making body, more a battleground in which warring factions within the Conservative Party played out a damaging war of self-destruction. It has taken more than a decade for the Conservatives to begin the process of repairing the damage.

To prove that prime-ministerial government had not disappeared, Tony Blair (1997–2007) set about restoring personal control. Combining Wilson's manipulation of the government machinery with Thatcher's media supremacy and adding his own brand of domination by controlling the flow of information to the governing community, he took prime-ministerial control to new heights. This reality was barely disputed by commentators and politicians alike. Blair's style of leadership was often described as 'sofa politics', a reference to his practice of settling issues with individual ministers and officials privately and informally. Sofa politics was seen as a direct challenge to cabinet government. Blair also dominated Labour policy, with the exception of economic management, which he left to his close colleague, Gordon Brown, the Chancellor.

Blair's style was also described as presidential. He was a charismatic, persuasive speaker and often spoke on behalf of the nation, rather than merely as head of the government. He was heavily involved in international affairs, notably concerning the Balkan conflicts, Afghanistan, Iraq, the international terrorism threat, climate change and world poverty. He committed troops to three conflicts – in Kosovo, Sierra Leone and Iraq – and so adopted the role of commander-in chief, which is very much associated with the role of a president. His total domination of foreign affairs and his exceptional use of the 'Downing Street machine' marked Tony Blair out as one of the most dominant prime ministers of the modern era.

Gordon Brown (2007–10) could never dominate as Blair had done. From the beginning of his premiership he was hampered by a lack of media and public support as well as a gap in his legitimacy since he had never faced the electorate in a general election as party leader. He was therefore commonly described as an 'unelected' prime minister. He did exercise a high level of control over international affairs and became a leading statesman in the fields of world poverty action and climate change. He was also able to deal effectively with two leadership challenges, neither of which gained any significant support. But Brown suffered from world events, mostly beyond his control. The credit crunch of 2007–08 and the recession of 2008–09 consumed his premiership to a crippling extent and he was unable to stamp his authority on the country. He did exercise similar control over Whitehall and his party as Blair had done, but he never achieved his predecessor's presidential status.

David Cameron (2010–) faces a new problem: how to dominate the political system in coalition. Clearly this presents a range of new challenges. Cameron shows every inclination to dominate his *party*, but understands that he must also share power with his Liberal Democrat colleagues. Unless he can command a House of Commons majority in the future, David Cameron will remain a limited prime minister.

Cabinet committees

Although cabinet committees have existed since the 1920s, their full use did not emerge until the 1960s. Since then they have increasingly taken over from the full cabinet in terms of policy and decision making. A cabinet committee is a small group (around five) of cabinet ministers who meet regularly to discuss a specific area of government policy. Of course, a decision that is not considered of great strategic importance and that doesn't affect more than one government department will be made within the department itself, but most important decisions need wider approval.

Some committees are permanent, dealing with such matters as the Economy, Defence or Foreign Affairs, but some are temporary in nature, dealing with policy areas that may not be long-lasting, such as the Olympic Games or the terrorist threat. The larger areas of policy making also require

highly specialised sub-committees that report back to the full committee. Below are listed some key cabinet committees operating in January 2010.

- Border and Migration
- Communities and Equality
- Constitution
- Economy
- Environment and Energy
- Europe
- Families, Children and Young People
- Food
- Intelligence
- Health and Wellbeing
- Justice and Crime
- Olympic and Paralympic Games
- Overseas and Defence
- Science and Innovation
- Social Exclusion
- Tackling Extremism
- Talent and Enterprise
- Trade

Over many decades, as the business of government has broadened and become more technical and complex, cabinet committees have increasingly taken over the work of the full cabinet. Decisions are often taken in committee only and, even if a recommendation is passed up from committee to full cabinet, approval tends to be automatic. The cabinet in full session simply has neither the time nor the information to be able to deal with most matters. It is therefore an unusual occurrence when the full cabinet makes its own decision following discussion or decides to over-rule the recommendation of a committee.

The growth in the number and importance of the committees has had the effect of increasing prime-ministerial control. The prime minister controls the creation of the committees and who sits on them. He also has a great deal of influence over their agendas. It is much easier for a prime minister to control a small group of ministers than the whole cabinet. Of course, under Blair, the management of the economy remained the personal empire of Chancellor Gordon Brown, but in all other areas the committee system allowed the prime minister to exercise some control.

Marginalisation

During the 1960s, 1970s and 1980s, cabinet government *appeared* to operate in the traditional way. However, behind the scenes, important rivals to cabinet power were emerging. Some of these were as follows:

- As we have seen above, the personal authority and power of the prime minister alone have grown in contrast to the collective power of cabinet.

- There is a growing tendency for the great departments of state – the Treasury, Home Office, Foreign Office, Department for Constitutional affairs, Department of Education and Skills, etc. – to see themselves as separate 'kingdoms' or 'baronies', as they have sometimes been described. At their head, ministers jealously guard their own empire and resent any attempt at interference by the cabinet. Of course, they must retain allegiance to the prime minister and he may influence what they do, but there is less and less inclination to bring matters of importance to full cabinet.

- As we have seen above, a great deal of policy making now takes place within cabinet

committees. It is, therefore, perhaps best to think of cabinet as a 'system' or 'network' rather than as a single body. In other words, meetings of the full cabinet are almost ceremonial. The real work goes on elsewhere.

- Not only have cabinet functions moved to the prime minister, to departmental ministers and to committees, there has also been a shift in policy-making functions to 10 Downing Street itself. Again since the 1960s, but particularly under Tony Blair, there has been a growing army of private political advisers, 'think tanks' and policy units doing the work previously undertaken by the cabinet and its committees. This has both extended prime ministerial control and tended to reduce cabinet importance.

- Finally, we should remember that the prime minister still conducts much government business on a 'bilateral' basis, that is, by discussing policy with an individual minister, reaching agreement with that minister, and then presenting the decision as a *fait accompli* to the rest of the cabinet.

The cabinet today

We can now see that the nature of the British cabinet is much changed since the 1960s. So we need to ask, what functions does it perform today? The short answer is to say 'far fewer than 50 years ago', but this does not explain its position in the executive branch of government today. It still meets normally every week and it is still a requirement for the prime minister and his colleagues to attend unless they have pressing, unavoidable business elsewhere. But the meetings now tend to be short and can be as little as 45 minutes long, and they attract relatively little publicity. Nevertheless, the endurance of the cabinet has some significance. We can identify the following current functions:

1. On rare occasions when a dispute between ministers cannot be resolved elsewhere, by

the prime minister, the cabinet Secretary or other advisers, the matter may be brought to the full cabinet. In this way the ministers who are in conflict are forced to accept the decision under the doctrine of collective responsibility. The most common kind of dispute concerns public spending, usually when one minister finds his proposed budget is being cut and he or she feels that the cut should fall elsewhere.

2. There may also be circumstances when the prime minister decides that an issue should be resolved by a full cabinet session. This may be because he has no personal interest, or because he would prefer not to commit himself to a decision that may later cause him personal embarrassment. Perhaps the best-known example of such a decision was the commitment to build the notorious Millennium Dome in Greenwich in 1997. Though Tony Blair wanted it built, despite claims it would fail and be a waste of public money, he chose to seek a full cabinet decision to head off the opposition. But there may also be less sinister reasons for seeking cabinet approval – for example, when it was decided in 2005 to press ahead with plans for the introduction of identity cards. As fierce opposition was expected in Parliament and among the public, it was felt that the commitment needed collective government approval.

3. Similarly, in times of national emergency it is often seen as desirable that the whole cabinet should back government policies. This was the case with plans to deal with the terrorist threat after the attack on New York's Trade Center in 9/11, and following terrorist atrocities in London in July 2005.

4. It has become increasingly important for government to present a united front to the media and Parliament and to ensure that policy is seen in the most favourable light possible. Cabinet therefore has the task of making decisions about the *presentation* of policy. This may be little more than a set of instructions by the prime minister on how he would like policy presented.

5. Just as Parliament must legitimise all proposed legislation, so too must cabinet legitimise policy proposals and key decisions. If the political community, especially members of the governing party, are to accept policy as 'official', it needs the cabinet stamp of approval. This is largely a formal process – some call it 'little more than rubber stamping' – but it remains necessary for the effective working of government.

6. We can certainly say that a coalition cabinet gains a further function. This is the settling of conflicts between coalition partners. Of course, the prime minister will seek to avoid such disputes and try to settle them outside cabinet, but it is inevitable that the cabinet will have to give final approval to any coalition agreements.

We can now summarise the current state of cabinet government.

Remaining functions of cabinet	Main weaknesses of cabinet
Settling ministerial disputes	Prime minister is now dominant
Making decisions that cannot be made elsewhere	Most decisions are made in committee
Dealing with domestic emergencies	Meetings are shorter and are stage-managed
Determining presentation of policy	Large departments have become more independent

Remaining functions of cabinet	Main weaknesses of cabinet
Legitimising decisions made elsewhere	More decisions are made in bilateral meetings
Settling coalition disputes	Much decision making has moved to the 10 Downing Street organisation

Cabinet formation – single party

It is one of the key roles of every prime minister to select a cabinet. This is an important role because it can both shape the political direction of the government and, to some extent at least, determine how successful it will be. It is also a vital instrument of power for the prime minister. The power to make senior government appointments and indeed to dismiss office holders is known as *patronage*. The power of patronage is a key element in the prime minister's ability to control the top levels of his party. Every minister, in and out of the cabinet, owes their position to him and may, in theory at least, lose it at any time on his say-so. Added to these office holders there are hundreds of MPs and a smaller number of peers who are hoping to be promoted by him. But it is appointments to the cabinet itself that a prime minister considers to be the most important component in his powers of patronage.

On first coming to power a prime minister has to start afresh in forming a new cabinet. He has two initial decisions to make:

1. Will he choose a 'balanced' cabinet, containing all shades of political opinion in the ruling party, or will he choose a team that is ideologically united? The former option may appear easier because it will please all sections of the party. John Major was forced to do this when he found himself with a reduced majority in 1992 and a divided party. However, to do so runs the risk of internal dissension, as Major was to find to his cost. The second option – the united team – may alienate some sections of the party but is likely to give the prime minister an easier ride. This was Margaret Thatcher's choice in 1983 and Tony Blair's in 1997. Of course, even the united cabinet option may contain one or two dissidents if they have great personal qualities and might cause too much trouble if left outside on the back benches.

2. Which individuals should fill the 22 or so posts that are available in a modern cabinet.

We can offer the following list of criteria that a prime minister might take into consideration when choosing individuals. Beside each consideration is an example of a choice made by Gordon Brown or David Cameron between 2007 and 2010:

● He may have close political allies from the past who have been guaranteed a post if the party gains power (Brown chose Jack Straw, Cameron promoted George Osborne).

● There may be an individual who can represent an important section of the party (Alan Johnson and the trade unionists for Labour; the Conservatives' first Home Secretary, Theresa May, represented the right wing of her party).

● He may decide that a potential rebel who has great ability and is widely respected is better in the cabinet where they will be silenced by the discipline of collective responsibility (John Denham in Brown's cabinet).

● He may identify some individuals who are thought to have great potential to be successful ministers, that is, who will manage a department well (Cameron appointed Oliver Letwin).

● He may even have old personal friends whom he wishes to have close by him (Brown promoted Ed Balls and Cameron favoured Philip Hammond).

- Some individuals may be popular figures with the public and the media (a factor in appointing Liberal Democrat Vince Cable in 2010).

- A number of choices will be based on a desire to retain the political identity of the new government, individuals who symbolise the ideology of the ruling group (Iain Duncan Smith represents Cameron's new Conservatism, which was concerned with social deprivation).

- Some may achieve their position simply because they are thought of as extremely able people who will 'do a good job' (the Conservatives appointed Kenneth Clark as Justice Minister in 2010 – a well-known 'safe pair of hands' and a very experienced politician).

Cabinet formation – coalition

Many of the principles described above apply to the formation of a coalition cabinet. Nevertheless, there are crucial differences. Among them are the following:

- The prime minister must consult with his coalition partner about which members of the 'junior partner' should be included.

- The balance of the membership between the two parties will approximately mirror the balance of the strengths of the two parties in the House of Commons.

- The prime minister must give a prominent role to the leader of the coalition partner. Nick Clegg, the Liberal Democrat leader, was appointed deputy prime minister in 2010.

Of course, as time goes by, some of these ministers will fall by the wayside. Some may find

David Cameron and Nick Clegg formed Britain's first coalition for 65 years

the pressures of high office too much for them, as Labour's Education Secretary, Estelle Morris, found. Others may find themselves isolated from government, out of step with its policies and therefore unable to continue to support the 'party line'. Foreign Secretary Robin Cook found this to be the case and resigned in 2003 over the Iraq war. Some are not considered to be doing a good enough job by the prime minister and are removed during one of his regular 'cabinet re-shuffles'. Occasionally there may be a scandal that forces a minister to resign. Liberal Democrat cabinet minister David Laws resigned after less than three weeks in office because of adverse publicity over his MP's expenses claim. This was an early blow to the coalition government as he was considered a key figure in the new administration. Finally, there is the doctrine of individual ministerial responsibility, which requires that a minister should consider resignation if a serious mistake is made within his or her department. Trade and Industry Secretary, Stephen Byers lost his job in 2002 in such circumstances when one of his private political advisers made a serious error of judgement.

David Laws, the coalition's first casualty after problems over his MP's expenses claims

Collective cabinet responsibility

When a minister joins the government they are immediately bound by the principle of **collective responsibility**. Members of the cabinet are bound especially tightly by it. The doctrine declares that all ministers, in and out of cabinet, must publicly support all decisions made within cabinet. It also implies that cabinet decisions are considered to be *collective* (i.e. joint) decisions for which they are jointly responsible. Ministers may disagree with policy in private and in cabinet meetings, but once a decision has been reached, it must be supported by all.

Under coalition government the doctrine has to be modified. On issues where there is no agreement between the coalition partners, there is an agreement to differ whereby ministers can express their own party's views. For example, in 2010 the new coalition agreed to differ on the issue of whether Britain should renew its Trident nuclear weapon system and over the desirability of promoting nuclear energy. Liberal Democrats oppose the development of new nuclear plants, while Conservatives see it as a key element in the battle against climate change.

Key Word

Individual ministerial responsibility The convention that a minister should resign if their department makes a serious political or personal error. In practice, this usually means that a minister is responsible to Parliament and must face questioning and criticism.

This can be illustrated by what happens at the end of most items of cabinet business. The prime minister is unlikely to ask whether all members of the cabinet agree with a decision. What he will ask is 'Are they all prepared to defend that decision in public?' If an individual is not, then they are expected to resign, as former Foreign Secretary Robin Cook did over the decision to commit troops to the invasion of Iraq in 2003. (Interestingly, Clare Short, who was also known to disagree, did not resign and survived for a few months. However, she did eventually go under great pressure and over the government's handling of the post-war situation in Iraq.)

Collective responsibility can be seen as something of a sham. Political journalists, for example, who are 'in the know', understand perfectly well that many cabinet decisions have been bitterly contested, but, once announced, all members of the government will line up to support it in public without a murmur. On the other hand if collective responsibility did not apply, it is argued, governments would regularly fall apart. Parliament and the public would soon lose respect for a group of ministers who regularly failed to agree on policy and said so in public.

Everyone in the political community, including the opposition parties, understands the working of collective responsibility and most accept it as a necessary reality. It gives government its unity and creates stability. The great disadvantage of collective responsibility, however, is that it stifles public debate and it is difficult for Parliament and the media to understand how government reaches its decisions. If ministers are not prepared to debate government policy in public it becomes difficult to make them accountable for those decisions.

The following table shows the make-up of the British cabinet in May 2010.

The British Cabinet, May 2010		
Minister	**Position**	**Party**
David Cameron	Prime Minister	Conservative
Nick Clegg	Deputy Prime Minister	Liberal Democrat
George Osborne	Chancellor of the Exchequer	Conservative
Theresa May	Home Secretary	Conservative
William Hague	Foreign Secretary	Conservative
Liam Fox	Defence Secretary	Conservative
Kenneth Clark	Justice Secretary	Conservative
Michael Gove	Education Secretary	Conservative
Vince Cable	Business Secretary	Liberal Democrat
Iain Duncan Smith	Work and Pensions Secretary	Conservative

The British Cabinet, May 2010 (continued)		
Minister	**Position**	**Party**
Andrew Lansley	Health Secretary	Conservative
Philip Hammond	Transport Secretary	Conservative
Caroline Spelman	Environment, Food and Rural Affairs Secretary	Conservative
Danny Alexander	Scottish Secretary	Liberal Democrat
Cheryl Gillan	Welsh Secretary	Conservative
Owen Paterson	Northern Ireland Secretary	Conservative
David Laws*	Chief Secretary to the Treasury	Liberal Democrat
Eric Pickles	Communities and Local Government Secretary	Conservative
Chris Huhne	Energy and Climate Change Secretary	Liberal Democrat
Jeremy Hunt	Culture, Media, Olympics and Sport Secretary	Conservative

The British Cabinet, May 2010 (continued)		
Minister	**Position**	**Party**
Lord Strathclyde	Leader of the House of Lords	Conservative
Baroness Warsi	Minister without Portfolio**	Conservative
Andrew Mitchell	International Development Secretary	Conservative

* Resigned after three weeks after problems with his MPs expenses claims

** This means a minister who has no fixed role.

The role of the prime minister

It is worth pausing at this point to consider how the office of prime minister came about. All monarchs, of course, have had their close advisers, and generally there has been one who has been closest of all. However, during the seventeenth century, the political authority and power of the monarchy began to wane. It was also true that the early Hanoverian kings – George I and George II – had relatively little interest in British politics. As a result the cabinet began to assume independent powers of its own, effectively running the country on behalf of the King.

Naturally, one member of the cabinet would come to be thought of as the most senior member and the most trusted ally of the King. In the 1720s, when Robert Walpole filled such a role, the position came to be known as 'prime minister'. But there was still no formality about the position and it was never acknowledged in British law. Walpole happened to be First Lord of the Treasury and it has come to be that the prime

Britain's first Coalition Cabinet since 1945

minister has held this honorary position ever since. This is despite the fact that the Treasury is in fact run by the Chancellor of the Exchequer. But this is the nearest to the formalisation of the post that has ever occurred. In effect, prime ministers were declared to be so by the monarch. Since the late nineteenth century, however, the prime minister has automatically been the leader of the largest party in the House of Commons. As we saw above in the section of government formation, the prime minister is the individual who is called upon to form a government by the monarch. This is where we are today.

The functions of the prime minister

The post of prime minister has been constantly evolving, but we can identify a clear list of functions carried out by today's office-holder.

1. **Chief policy maker**. Although this role is clearly shared to some extent with other ministers, with cabinet and with his party, there is no doubt that the prime minister is completely pre-eminent in making the government's policy. The fact that he must seek wider spread approval for much of what he decides does not alter this political reality.

2. **Head of government.** This is a function that covers a number of roles. The prime minister is in charge of the machinery of government. He can create new posts and new departments as well as abolish them, establish committees and policy units and amalgamate existing ones. It also means he is head of the civil service and can seek advice from its vast machinery. As we have seen above, too, he chairs cabinet meetings, determining their agenda and controlling the system of cabinet committees that underpins it. But above all it includes the task of determining which individuals should hold posts as ministers, senior judges and senior bishops and archbishops of the Church of England.

3. **Chief government spokesperson.** It is now expected that the prime minister must be the ultimate source of the official version of government policy to the media. Though other ministers may be called upon to represent the

government on TV, radio and in the press, the definitive expression of policy must come from the prime minister. To some extent this can create an illusion that the prime minister makes *all* policy. This would be wrong. But it certainly does mean that he can place his own interpretation on policy, whoever has made it. Often this is described by the media and opposition politicians as 'spin'.

4. **Commander-in-chief of the armed forces.** This is a role that is exercised on behalf of the monarch who is no longer permitted to become involved with such matters except on a purely ceremonial level. It is the decision of the prime minister and his alone whether or not to commit British troops to battle or to any other role. He may, of course, seek much advice, but the he has the final say.

   In recent times it is a function that has often had to be carried out. Margaret Thatcher ordered a military task force to the Falkland Islands in 1982 to oust the Argentine invaders. John Major decided to support the USA and other forces in the liberation of Kuwait from Iraqi invaders in 1990–1. Tony Blair has committed British forces to action in Kosovo in 1998 to protect the Muslim population from ethnic cleansing, in Afghanistan in 2001 to oust the Taliban regime, in Sierra Leone in 2002 to protect the democratic government from a rebellion and, most famously, in Iraq in 2003 to topple Saddam Hussein.

   We can add to this impressive list of responsibilities the task of maintaining national security. This means directly controlling the intelligence and counter-terrorism services as well as assuming emergency powers in a time of emergency such as war.

5. **Chief foreign-policy maker.** This again is a function carried out for the monarch. This can mean anything from negotiating with foreign powers, to negotiating and signing treaties, to chairing international meetings. Tony Blair, in particular, concentrated on this role. As well as chairing meetings of the G8 group of leading nations, he chaired the British presidency of the European Union in 2005 and took a leading role on such issues a global warming and the relief of poverty in less developed countries. The prime minister today, must also conduct British relations with the European Union.

6. **Parliamentary leader.** Although government ministers play a substantial role in debates and parliamentary questioning, it is the role of the prime minister to lead his party in Parliament. As we have seen above, he must decide who shall be a minister, but he is also in overall control of the government's strategy within both Houses.

The sources of prime ministerial power and authority

As we have shown, the British prime minister today completely dominates the political system. This accords him tremendous power and huge responsibilities. It is therefore an important question as to how one single office can have accumulated so much authority, which allows him to exercise so much power. The answer lies in the fact that the office stands at the junction of a number of different sources of authority. Authority is turned into power and so we have an extremely potent combination. The prime minister draws his authority from these main sources:

1. **The ruling party.** Although it is possible for the prime minister not be the leader of the governing party, it would be highly unusual and, arguably, unworkable if he were not. So it is safe to assume that the prime minister has the support of his party both in Parliament and in the country in the form of the ordinary members. Since that party has won the right to govern at the last general election, the prime minister carries all the party's elective authority with him. (Note: where there is no overall majority after an election, it is assumed

that the prime minister's authority stems from leading the *largest* party or the party able to form a governing coalition.)

2. **The royal prerogative.** The reigning monarch retains, in theory and in law, the power to carry out functions as head of state. This means commanding the armed forces, conducting relations with foreign powers or international organisations and generally maintaining the security of the state. It also bestows the right to appoint and dismiss ministers, decide the date of the general election by dissolving Parliament, making key appointments of peers, judges and Church of England bishops and controlling the civil service machinery. Of course, in a democracy, we cannot allow the unelected monarch to exercise out any of these powers in reality. The traditional authority of the monarch to exercise these so-called 'prerogative powers' is therefore delegated to the prime minister of the day.

3. **Popular mandate.** Although technically the electorate are choosing MPs and a party when they vote at a general election, it is undeniably true that they are also conscious of the fact they are electing a prime minister. Indeed, research suggests that the leader of each party has become a more significant factor in voting choices than ever before. In this sense, therefore, the victorious prime minister can claim, in some degree at least, to enjoy the authority of the electorate, the popular mandate. Of course this does not apply to a prime minister who has taken office *between* elections, such as Gordon Brown in 2007 and John Major in 1990. In these cases the authority of the prime minister is slightly weakened by the lack of such a popular mandate.

4. **Parliament.** Finally we should remind ourselves that the prime minister is a parliamentary leader. As long as he enjoys the support of the majority in the House of Commons he can claim to have parliamentary authority.

What we see here is at least four sources of authority, providing us with an explanation of why the prime minister can exercise so much power. We could perhaps also add the effects of the office holder's own personal qualities. These, too, can be converted into yet more power. Margaret Thatcher certainly enhanced her inherited authority by becoming such a dominating personality who was admired and respected, at least in conservative circles. Tony Blair, at least in his first term from 1997–2001, was also seen as a charismatic figure and was therefore able to enjoy greatly increased authority and power.

Prime ministerial power

We are now in a position to summarise the prime minister's powers. At the same time we can establish the ways in which these powers may vary, depending on circumstances. This can be done by dividing powers into 'formal' and 'informal' powers, or, put another way, by identifying the powers which *all* prime ministers enjoy, whatever the circumstances, from those which vary according to circumstances.

The powers enjoyed by *all* prime ministers (formal powers) are as follows:

- Appointment and dismissal of ministers.

- Granting peerages and other honours.

- Head of the civil service.

- Appointing senior judges and senior bishops.

- Commanding the armed forces.

- Conducting foreign relations.

- Maintaining national security.

- Chairing cabinet meetings.

The powers of the prime minister that vary according to circumstances (informal powers) are as follows.

Powers	Circumstances
Making government policy	How united is the ruling party? How secure is he as party leader? How forceful is his personality? How much does he wish to dominate the political agenda? How ideologically united is his party? Does he lead a coalition or majority government?
Parliamentary leadership	How large is his parliamentary majority? Does he have a parliamentary majority at all? How united are his party's MPs?
Controlling cabinet	Does he have powerful adversaries in the cabinet? If a coalition, how stable is that coalition? How politically united is the cabinet? How much is he inclined to prevent collective decision making? How secure is he as party leader?
National leadership	How much personal popularity does he enjoy? How high is his media profile? How high is his standing abroad?

Limitations on prime-ministerial power

Having reviewed the circumstances within which a prime minister operates we are able to establish and summarise what the main limitations to his power must be. They are as follows:

● The size of the parliamentary majority is critical. Margaret Thatcher enjoyed huge majorities of over 100 following the 1983 and 1987 elections. So, too, did Tony Blair after 1997 and 2001. But when the majority is low or non-existent the prime minister can never rely on parliamentary approval. They must, therefore take into account forces within both Parliament in general and their own party in particular before taking any initiatives.

● This was the case with John Major from 1992–97. Starting with a majority of 21, he soon found this whittled away by by-election defeats and defections of his MPs to other parties. He therefore found himself governing with his hands almost tied behind his back. There were even times when he had to rely on the support of a handful of Ulster Unionist MPs to survive – a fact that disabled his ability to conduct the policies he wanted in Northern Ireland. James Callaghan faced similar circumstances in 1976–79. In his case it was economic and industrial policy that suffered. Left-wing, union-sponsored MPs in his own party proved to be major obstacles. As a result the economy and industrial relations gradually deteriorated.

● The unity or otherwise of the ruling party or coalition is also critical. A prime minister who leads an ideologically united leadership group can achieve a great deal more than one who is constantly forced to try to maintain some kind of cohesion. Margaret Thatcher's premiership illustrates this well. From 1979–83 she was confronted by a divided party. Many were supportive of her proposals for a new free market economy and reduced state intervention in industry. There was also, however, a substantial group (known by her as 'the wets') who were traditional conservatives and opposed her radical ideas. This meant that too much of her attention was taken by the need to keep the party together and so preserve her leadership. By 1983, however, she had removed most of the dissident wets from the cabinet. This left her with a more tight-knit group that shared her convictions. Her power increased dramatically and there followed seven years of the most dynamic leadership Britain had known in the twentieth century.

- Tony Blair had no such problems in 1997 when he took power. 'New Labour', as his allies were known, was an exceptionally united group. This meant that Blair enjoyed several years of almost total domination. This contrasted with his predecessor, John Major. Between 1992 and 1997 Major led a Conservative party completely split over the issues of Britain's relationship with Europe and over the state's relationship to the economy. This gave him the reputation of one of Britain's weakest prime ministers of modern times.

- Similarly, the public and media profile of the prime minister is important. When a leader loses the confidence of the public and of the media they become an electoral liability. In such circumstances the ruling party will become unwilling to accept their leadership. This is what eventually happened to Margaret Thatcher in 1990 when she was removed. It also weakened Tony Blair, especially after 2003. When Blair announced he would not seek a fourth term in office, he became something of a 'lame duck' and his power and authority ebbed away until his retirement in 2007. His successor, Gordon Brown, enjoyed the traditional 'honeymoon

period' when he took over. The public perceived his virtues to be reliability, calmness and good judgement.

- Prime ministers can survive only if they enjoy the confidence of the cabinet and Parliament. This is the ultimate limitation on their power. If the cabinet overrules the prime minister, there is nothing he can do as cabinet is the ultimate source of government policy. Similarly, the policies of the prime minister are meaningless if he cannot secure parliamentary approval for his proposals. Under coalition government this becomes problematic. The prime minister does not enjoy a parliamentary majority and the cabinet is naturally divided. Thus, support for him is bound to be fragile and potentially transitory.

- Finally, there is the party of which the prime minister is the leader. Today, parties are undoubtedly less important than they used to be. Little policy is made within parties and the members have little influence over the leadership. But, as we have seen above, the prime minister draws much of his authority from the governing party. It is not the norm for parties to remove a sitting prime minister (with Thatcher a notable exception), but prime ministers must always be careful not to lose the confidence of their own party.

It would be wrong to assume that prime ministers always lose office against their will. But as can be seen below they usually do. The following list describes how prime ministers in recent times have ended their period in office.

Prime minister	Period in office	Reason for loss of office
Harold Macmillan	1957–63	Resigned through ill health
Alec Douglas-Hume	1963–64	Lost election
Harold Wilson	1964–70, 1974–76	Retired voluntarily

Prime minister	Period in office	Reason for loss of office
Edward Heath	1970–74	Lost election
James Callaghan	1976–79	Lost vote of no confidence in the Commons
Margaret Thatcher	1979–90	Lost leadership of the Conservative Party
John Major	1990–97	Lost election
Tony Blair	1997–2007	Retired voluntarily
Gordon Brown	2007 – 2010	Lost election

Thus, of the nine prime ministers shown, two resigned for personal reasons, four were removed by the electorate, one by her party and one by Parliament. This gives a good idea of what the main limitations on prime ministerial power are.

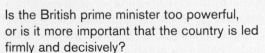

Discussion topic

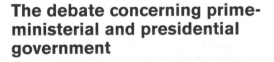

Is the British prime minister too powerful, or is it more important that the country is led firmly and decisively?

The debate concerning prime-ministerial and presidential government

The arguments that used to take place among political academics about 'prime ministerial government' have now largely disappeared. Few, if any, now doubt that the office of prime minister dominates the British political system. As long as the holder of that office is not faced by too many limiting factors, such as a small parliamentary majority or a divided party, the British system has moved away from the traditional 'cabinet government' model to a 'prime ministerial' model.

But a somewhat different question has emerged concerning the role and importance of the prime minister. This asks whether the system has now become 'presidential'. This term implies a number of things:

● That the prime minister has come to be, effectively though not legally, the head of State, the leader of the nation, irrespective of party allegiance. It should be stressed that this is not the same as national 'popularity'. Rather, it means that, in times of difficulty, emergency or crisis such as war or terrorist threats, the country can unite behind its head of government. Nothing new in that, you may say, and certainly it has always been true to a great extent. But it can be argued that there has been a long-term drift towards seeing the prime minister of the day rather than the monarch as national leader.

● That the prime minister now has an extensive network of personal advisers, think tanks, policy units and working groups that serve him alone and are not available to the rest of the government unless he wants them to be so. So, just as the US President has his own White House staff and large executive office, the prime minister has his own 'government department', mostly in Downing Street. It used to be the case that the prime minister was at a disadvantage when negotiating with ministers because they had huge departments of civil servants to assist them, while he, the prime minister had very little.

- The growing importance of the media in politics has contributed to the greater concentration on the individual holder of the office of prime minister rather than the government as a whole. Prime ministers now have large groups of advisers whose sole task is to enhance the media image of their master and to control the flow of information coming out of Downing Street. Perhaps as a result of this, or perhaps coincidentally, the general public have also come to see government in terms of its leading member rather than as a collection of ministers and MPs. This is a double-edged sword for the prime minister. He can often claim credit for the successes of the government in general, but he also takes personal blame for their failures, whatever his own role may have been.

- The undoubted growth in the importance of foreign and military affairs has contributed to a presidential 'feel' for the office of prime minister. When the head of government has to negotiate with foreign powers, attend international conferences, negotiate treaties, conduct wars and meet visiting dignitaries, he is bound to appear presidential. Indeed, at large conferences he will be seen rubbing shoulders with the presidents of France and the USA, who represent their countries on these occasions. Margaret Thatcher (with Reagan), John Major (with Clinton) and Tony Blair (with Clinton and Bush junior) all forged close links with US presidents. Standing on the White House lawn after one of their many bilateral meetings, who could say that both did not appear equally presidential? Furthermore, all these three prime ministers led the country into important foreign wars.

- Finally, we turn to the concept of 'spatial leadership'. This is a relatively new theory of prime ministerial power (and, indeed, of power in general). It suggests that political systems are increasingly led by leaders who consider themselves to be distinctly *separate* from the rest of the government. This separateness gives rise to the term *spatial*. Presidents are naturally spatial leaders, largely because they are elected separately from the rest of the government and therefore have a different source of authority and are accountable directly to the people. This has not been the case with the British prime minister. Nevertheless, as the role has become more dominant there has been a tendency for the office holder to see himself as separate from government and, to some extent, to have his own mandate directly from the people.

We will now examine three of these phenomena in more detail.

The growth of 10 Downing Street

There has long been a body known as the 'cabinet office' situated in Downing Street. A relatively small organisation, the cabinet Office was largely administrative, existed to serve the whole cabinet and did not become directly involved with policy making. This was the situation up to the 1960s. Since then there has been a steady growth in the Downing Street machine. Furthermore it has shifted from serving the government as a whole, to serving mainly the prime minister alone. In addition it has become far more concerned with the development of policy than ever before. This means that, wherever policy needs to be coordinated between different departments the Downing Street organisation is in a position to develop strategy. Measures to combat youth crime, terrorism, drug abuse, child poverty and homelessness in recent times are all examples of such co-ordinated action. This enables the prime minister to play a pivotal role and so appear to be dominating government.

The list below shows the main individuals and bodies that make up the sources of advice available to the prime minister specifically:

- Chief of Staff

- Deputy Chief of Staff

- Principal Private Secretary

- Director of Communications

- Director of Events, Visits and Scheduling

- Director of Political Operations

- Head of the Policy Directorate

- The Policy Directorate

- Chief Adviser on Strategy

- Director of Government Relations.

All these individuals also have sizeable offices to support them. The two most important units are the **Policy Directorate** and the **Strategy Unit**.

Spatial leadership

This concept was developed by Michael Foley in his important work, *The Rise of the British Presidency* (MUP, 1993). In it he looks at leaders such as US President Ronald Reagan and Margaret Thatcher. Above all, he suggests these leaders deliberately make themselves into *outsiders* within government. They separate themselves from its other members and so are able to act independently, but also to remain part of government itself.

Thatcher and Reagan took this a step further. They even criticised governments of which they were the head, suggesting that they tended to be inefficient, wasteful and simply tried to do too much. On taking office in 1981, Reagan expressed the issue thus: 'government is not the solution to our problems. Government is the problem.'

Meanwhile, Margaret Thatcher was promising to 'roll back the frontiers of the state', was roundly criticising the civil service for its conservatism and wastefulness and was not averse to openly opposing her own ministers. Both Thatcher and Reagan were popular leaders who commanded great public support. This enabled them often to appeal to the people above the heads of their own party leadership. Most famously Thatcher eventually decided to use her own advisers on economic policy and to by-pass her own Chancellor of the Exchequer, Nigel Lawson, a tactic which ultimately led to his resignation in 1989 and contributed to her own demise a year later.

John Major was also a spatial leader, though this was not necessarily through choice. He had to separate himself from large parts of his government simply because they were his political enemies. He was not powerful enough to remove them and so had to try to govern without them. He was also something of an outsider in that he was generally more popular in the country than the government as a whole. He was trusted, they were not.

Foley's analysis predates Tony Blair, but Blair fits very much the same mould. He chose to adopt certain areas of policy as his own – foreign affairs, Northern Ireland, education and health – and attempted to dominate the political agenda by introducing his own policy initiatives above the heads of the relevant ministers. In areas where he did not choose to become involved – the economy, poverty relief and the environment, for example – he left matters very much to his ministers. In this way, he too became an outsider. When we add this to his total domination of foreign policy, we see a prime minister who was indeed very separate from the rest of government.

Foley argues that all recent American presidents have been spatial leaders. As British prime ministers have followed their lead, they too appear to be presidential in style.

Labour MP Graham Allen has taken this analysis a stage further. He accepts the general thesis of a 'separate leadership' and suggests that we should embrace the reality of it and make changes to the Constitution to accommodate the 'British Presidency'. He suggests that the prime minister (who is a quasi President anyway) should be elected separately from Parliament, just as occurs in the USA and in Israel. In this way we would acknowledge the inevitable truth and would give the prime minister his own source of authority. The electorate would then be in a position to distinguish the performance of the prime minister from that of the government as a whole.

'President Blair'?

Although, arguably, Margaret Thatcher was a more dominant prime minister than Blair, there is little doubt that Tony Blair brought presidential 'style' to new heights. As we have seen, he dominated some parts of the domestic political agenda, but his real preference lay in foreign and international affairs.

Here he took a world lead in supporting American Middle East policy, took a close interest in world environmental issues (though not domestic ones), in world poverty (along with Gordon Brown, his closest political rival) and in the reform of EU finances and its political structure. He also made periodic attempts to solve the Northern Ireland problem and eventually achieved a final settlement. He appeared more comfortable in these roles, was certainly more popular and gained a good deal of respect abroad. In short, on the world stage Blair looked like a President. To some extent this rebounded on him at home where he became less popular in his second and third terms. Furthermore, the British resented his presidential style, especially after the failure to find the much promised 'weapons

of mass destruction' in Iraq. Thus respect abroad was countered by lack of trust at home.

There is, of course, a counter argument to the thesis that Blair became effectively a president. This is that the political opposition to him and his governments was weak. He saw off four different Conservative leaders, and the Liberal Democrats failed to make the major impact they had hoped for after 1997. It could therefore be said that Blair dominated not through his own efforts, but through the failings of others. But this counter-analysis does not alter the fact that Blair became a major international statesman. It will be of great interest to see whether Blair's successors, either Labour or Conservative, will attempt to emulate his personal style. Certainly Gordon Brown made it clear when he took over in June 2007 that he hoped we would see a change of style, with less spin and fewer 'sound bites' and probably a greater emphasis on a domestic rather than an international agenda.

In the event, as we shall see below, Brown's premiership was seen as a failure, partly because of circumstances he could not control. Yet even the fatally unpopular Brown managed to show statesmanship on the world stage, taking a leading role in the international rescue of the banking system and in international measures to reduce the effects of recession. Brown ended his premiership a more respected statesman abroad than at home.

The counter-arguments to the presidential thesis

So far we have looked at the evidence that suggests that the British prime minister is indeed effectively a president. But there are some important arguments against this thesis:

● Perhaps the most compelling argument has been provided by Professor Peter Hennessy. He suggests that the office of prime minister is an extremely flexible one. In other words, it is what the holder wishes to make of it. Some prime ministers will therefore seek to dominate, while others will be either unable or unwilling to do so. The actual powers and limitations of the office have not, he argues, changed a great deal in modern times. What has happened is that Britain has seen two very dominant individuals – Thatcher and Blair – who have been able to squeeze as much power from the office as possible. The weaker premierships of Edward Heath, John Major and James Callaghan prove that presidential style is not inevitable.

- A second critique is that there has indeed been a change in recent decades but that it has been a change of 'style rather than substance'. In other words, prime ministers now *seem* to be more presidential – largely the result of media attention and the importance of foreign policy – but in fact they are subject to the same constraints that have always existed. This was most clearly seen with Margaret Thatcher, who ultimately was reined in by her own party leadership when she attempted to implement a policy (the introduction of a local poll tax) against their wishes.

- A third analysis has been offered in the past by Professor George Jones. This is the 'elastic' theory. It suggests that, as a prime minister tries to stretch the powers of the office further and further (a tendency among prime ministers who have been in office for a long time), the forces of constraint become increasingly strong. Again this analysis fits well with the experience of Margaret Thatcher, who gained increasing numbers of enemies as she sought to exercise more and more control. Eventually the enemies turned on her when they felt they had enough strength to remove her. Many suggest that Tony Blair went this way in his second and third terms.

- The experience of Gordon Brown gives us much evidence that a prime minister has no right to presidential status. Brown suffered

Is the prime minister now effectively a president?	
Arguments for the proposition	**Arguments against the proposition**
• Prime ministers perform most of the functions of a head of state.	• There has been no permanent change. The dominant role of the prime minister constantly ebbs and flows.
• Prime ministers now have extensive sources of advice of their own. 10 Downing Street increasingly resembles the inner circle in the presidential White House.	• There has been a change to a more presidential *style* but in substance the role of the prime minister has not changed.
• The media tend to concentrate on the prime minister as personal spokesman for the government rather than a president.	• There are important forces that will rein in prime ministerial power. Most of these forces are absent for a true president.
• Foreign and military affairs have become more important. The prime minister dominates these.	• It should not be forgotten that, although the prime minister may appear so, he is not actually head of state.
• The importance of spatial leadership in the UK increasingly looks like the president's style of leadership.	

from lack of personal popularity, from the charge that he had never faced the electorate as prime minister (he became leader of Labour without a general election taking place) and, perhaps above all, he was unfortunate enough to preside over the devastating credit crunch and the economic recession that followed it. We can say that Brown is the classic modern example of a prime minister whose power was destroyed by world events, some of which were beyond his control.

Now that we have considered the positions at the apex of power in Britain, we can study the rest of the machinery of government.

Ministers and departments

The machinery of British government is divided into departments. The precise nature and responsibilities of these departments lies in the hands of the prime minister and is constantly evolving. The following list shows the main departments of state in 2010 as arranged by David Cameron and Nick Clegg:

- Treasury

- Foreign Office

- Department of Justice

- Department for Women and Equality

- Department of Defence

- Department for Business, Innovation and Skills

- Department of Work and Pensions

- Department of Energy and Climate Change

- Department for Health

- Department for Education

- Department for Communities and Local Government

- Department of Transport

- Department for Environment, Food and Rural Affairs

- Department for International Development

- Northern Ireland Office

- Scottish Office

- Welsh Office

- Department for Culture, Olympics, Media and Sport

- Office of the Attorney General

- Department of the Cabinet Office

Each department effectively has two heads. One is a minister, the other is a civil servant. The normal title for the minister is 'Secretary of State', and for the civil servant it is 'Permanent Secretary' The precise nature of the relationship between ministers and civil servants is examined further below. However, at this stage we can establish that the department has a *political structure* standing alongside an *administrative structure.*

The political structure is comprised of the Secretary of State, who is normally also a cabinet minister, with below him junior ministers who are normally known as Ministers of State. Ministers of State do not sit in the cabinet but are bound by the same political rules. To assist these ministers there will also be a number of private political advisers. Their role is to give political advice, conduct research and help ministers deal with Parliament, the media and the public in general. It is expected that political advisers will give advice that is sympathetic to the political aims of the government in general. Indeed, many such advisers go on to become elected politicians themselves. All secretaries and ministers of state are appointed by the prime minister. Political advisers are appointed by the ministers themselves.

The Permanent Secretary is the administrative head of a large number of civil servants. He or she will normally have worked their way up through the ranks of the civil service, will possibly have worked for two or more different government departments and will be considered a highly skilled and experienced manager and administrator. As we shall see below, they must be politically neutral and should not attempt to change official government policy. All their work is expected to take place within the constraints of existing policy as declared by the prime minister, cabinet and the minister him or herself.

The top two levels of the civil service in each department are appointed from a short list by the prime minister in consultation with the minister concerned. A short list is drawn up by the Senior Appointments Selection Committee, which is made up of a number of senior civil servants. They normally chose individuals who are well established in the civil service, but increasingly they are allowed to consider applicants from outside the civil service – for example, from universities or the world of business and commerce.

There were, in 2010, 20 government departments, staffed by 113 ministers. If we count only those civil servants who are close advisers to the minister (i.e. are in regular contact and involved in key decisions), there are about 4,000 very senior civil servants. In addition, departments may form task forces or policy units from outside the structure of the civil service and staffed largely by outside experts to assist in policy making.

As an illustration, the structure of the senior levels of the Home Office is shown immediately below.

Home Office, May 2010 Ministers in post		
Theresa May MP Home Secretary in Cabinet		
Damian Green MP Minister of State for Immigration	**Nick Herbert MP** Minister of State for Police	**Baroness Neville-Jones** Minister of State for Security
Lynne Featherstone MP Parliamentary Under-Secretary for Equalities	**James Brokenshire MP** Parliamentary Under-Secretary (unspecific)	

We can see that the department is divided into three sections, each headed by a junior Minister of State who reports to the Secretary of State, Theresa May. The lowest level of minister is Under-Secretary of State. They have responsibility for smaller areas of the Home Office's jurisdiction.

Ministers and civil servants

The differences between ministers and civil servants are critical to an understanding of how government works in the UK. Unfortunately there is a certain amount of blurring of the distinction between the roles of minister and civil servants, and this confusion has been compounded by the growth in the number and use of private political advisers. However, we can identify the key distinctions.

Essentially ministers are appointed for political reasons – because they are leading members of the ruling party – while civil servants are appointed because they have specialist or administrative skills and, at the same time, are expected to be politically neutral. Ministers are essentially temporary. They hold office as long as the prime minister wishes them to do so. Civil servants are permanent in that they can expect to retain their position, and hopefully climb up the ladder of promotion if they are good enough, whoever is in government. In short, ministers are politicians who come and go, civil servants are administrators and managers who are expected to stay.

This is relatively straightforward. The confusion arises when we seek to identify their separate roles. Ministers are expected to hold political views and they may have a very specific political agenda. They are, after all, representatives of a government that was elected on a popular mandate to carry out certain stated policies. Civil servants, on the other hand, must have no political agenda, whatever their private views might be. The information and advice given to ministers by civil servants should be free of any political bias.

The following scheme will help to distinguish the roles in policy.

Tasks of ministers	Tasks of civil servants
Set the political agenda.	Gather information for policy making.
Determine priorities for action.	Provide alternative courses of action.
Decide between political alternatives.	Advise on consequences of decisions.

Tasks of ministers	Tasks of civil servants
Obtain cabinet and prime-ministerial approval for policies.	Draft legislation.
Steer proposals through Parliament.	Provide briefings for other ministers.
Be accountable to Parliament for policies and their implementation.	Advise on implementation methods.
Account to Parliament for the general performance of their department.	Organise implementation of policy.
	Draft answers to parliamentary questions.

We can see from these tasks that it is only ministers who make political decisions. Civil servants have the task of facilitating decision making and ensuring the successful implementation of those decisions.

Of course, it would be naïve to believe that civil servants never influence ministers. When they prepare alternative courses of action and when they advise on the consequences of each possible decision, there may be a possibility that the advice could be manipulated to steer the minister in a particular direction. If the civil servant is acting strictly in the 'national interest', there may be little harm in this. It only becomes a dangerous – and therefore forbidden – practice if the motives of the civil servant are political in nature.

The following extracts from the Civil Service Code of 1999, gives a strong sense of how civil servants are expected to behave:

'The constitutional and practical role of the civil service is, with integrity, honesty, impartiality and objectivity, to assist the duly constituted government of the United Kingdom, the Scottish Executive or the National Assembly of Wales. ...whatever their political complexion, in formulating their policies, carrying out decisions and in administering public services for which they are responsible.

Civil servants must recognise their accountability to ministers, and their duty to discharge public functions reasonably and according to law.

Civil servants should conduct themselves with integrity, impartiality and honesty. They should give honest and impartial advice to the minister ... without fear or favour, and make all information relevant to a decision available to them. They should not deceive or knowingly mislead ministers, Parliament, the National Assembly or the public.'

Source: Cabinet Office, 1999

There is one other aspect of the relationship between ministers and civil servants that is important. This is the anonymity rule. Civil servants are expected to be anonymous. This means that they should keep a low public profile, never make public statements about policy unless required to do so by Parliament or a parliamentary committee and should avoid revealing their *precise* role in policy making. They are allowed to reveal what department they work for and what is their rank. What they should *not* do in public is to reveal exactly what kind of advice they are giving.

Key Word

Accountability A political principle which suggests that an individual or an institution has to account for what it does and for its policies. Thus, in the UK, MPs are accountable to their constituents and the government is accountable to Parliament.

This rule presents a problem in a democracy. How are civil servants, who are contributing very often to key decisions, to be made accountable for what they do if they are anonymous? The answer lies in the doctrine of ministerial responsibility which has been described above. Briefly it is expected that the minister will answer for his or her civil servants to Parliament or to the public. In other words, the minister is **accountable** *on their behalf*. It used to be the case that ministers were expected to resign or face demotion if their civil servants made serious errors. But this principle has now all but disappeared. Nevertheless, where there is criticism circulating, the minister is the one who must 'take the flak'. Disciplining of civil servants takes place strictly in private.

We are now in a position to summarise the respective status of ministers and civil servants.

Ministers	Civil servants
• Are politically committed to one party.	• Must display no political allegiance.
• Are temporary, they only hold office as long as the P.M. wishes them to.	• Are permanent, or at least will spend a long time in the civil service.
• Are expected to make political decisions.	• May only suggest alternatives in a neutral way.
• Have to use judgements about the outcomes of decisions.	• Identify possible outcomes in a neutral way.
• Have a high public profile.	• Are expected to be largely anonymous.
• Are publicly accountable for the performance of their department.	• Cannot be held publicly accountable for what they do.
• Will lose office if their party loses power.	• Will remain in position even if there is a change of government.

Civil service neutrality has been an important principle of government in the UK since the latter part of the nineteenth century. It is considered essential that ministers have access to advice that is free from political bias. Since the 1870s the principle of neutrality has included the following 'rules':

● Civil servants must not be politically active. The lower ranks of the service may join a political party, but not be active. Senior civil servants should not be party members.

● They should not express politically biased views either in public or in the course of their professional duties.

● Although they are expected to understand government policy and to facilitate such policy, they must separate their service to the government from any political service to the ruling *party*. In other words, they serve a government minister but not his or her party.

● The advice they give should be free of political bias. Instead, it should conform to what the civil servants considers to be in the national interest within the constraints of official government policy.

● They must avoid any situations that might lay them open to external political pressure.

● In giving evidence to a parliamentary committee they must only express views that conform to official government policy; they may not express personal opinions outside their department.

Political advisers to ministers are not expected to be neutral. They serve the interests of both the

 Key Word

Civil service neutrality The constitutional principle in the UK that civil servants must retain political neutrality, must give neutral advice to ministers and should not become involved in party politics.

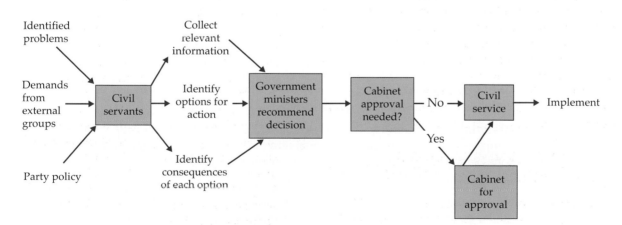

Ministers and civil servants and decision making

government and the ruling party. It is expected that they be politically sympathetic to the aims of the ruling party. This causes tension within government circles. While civil servants are attempting to give neutral advice they may feel that their position is being undermined by the political advisers. It is almost inevitable that rivalry has grown between civil servants and advisers as to who can gain the ear of the minister. There may also be considerable blurring between the roles of the two. Ultimately it is up to the relevant minister to distinguish between neutral and political advice.

Open government

The term **open government** refers to a policy of attempting to allow more access by the media and the public to decision-making processes in government. In particular, the relationship between ministers, civil servants and private advisers remains shrouded in some mystery. The Freedom of Information Act, which came into force in January 2005, has gone some way to opening up the processes of government, but progress has remained limited. Successive governments since the 1970s have promised to open up government, but relatively little has been done.

The requirement for civil servants to be neutral and anonymous has led to a great deal of secrecy in government. Indeed, it is said to be an established part of civil-service culture to be secretive. This culture has made it difficult for members of Parliament to obtain relevant information from government. So, the concept of 'open government' remains more an aspiration than a reality.

 Key Word

Open government A principle and an aspiration that the processes of government should be made as open to the public and parliamentary scrutiny as is possible and reasonable.

Key concepts in this chapter

Collective responsibility In the UK all cabinet decisions must be collectively supported by all members of the government, at least in public. It also implies that the whole government stands or falls as a whole on the decisions made by cabinet

Cabinet government A system of government where the cabinet is the central policy-making body.

Prime-ministerial government Political circumstances in which the prime minister dominates policy making and the whole machinery of government.

Individual ministerial responsibility The convention that a minister should resign if they or their department make a serious political or personal error. In practice this usually means that a minister is responsible to Parliament and must face questioning and criticism.

Accountability A political principle which suggests that an individual or an institution has to account for what it does and for its policies. Thus, in the UK, MPs are accountable to their constituents and the government is accountable to Parliament.

Civil service neutrality The constitutional principle in the UK that civil servants must retain political neutrality, must give neutral advice to ministers and should not become involved in party politics.

Open government A principle and an aspiration that the processes of government should be made as open to the public and parliamentary scrutiny and is possible and reasonable.

Revision topics and examination questions

Revision topics

- The main powers of the prime minister
- Limitations to prime-ministerial power
- The functions of the prime minister
- The sources of prime-ministerial power
- Role of the cabinet
- Nature of cabinet government
- Factors in appointment of ministers and the cabinet
- Reasons why ministers resign or lose office
- Collective and individual ministerial responsibility
- Nature and growth of prime ministerial government
- Extent to which the prime minister has become presidential
- Differences between ministers and civil servants
- Relationship between ministers and civil servants

Essay questions

1. Is the British prime minister now effectively a president?
2. For what reasons and to what extent has cabinet government declined In Britain?
3. Analyse the limitations on the power of the prime minister.
4. Are the doctrines of individual and collective responsibility now effectively dead in British government?

Stimulus response questions

1. Read the following passage and answer the questions that follow:

Britain's first coalition cabinet for 65 years

The formation of a coalition administration in May 2010 marked Britain's first experiment with this form of government since the end of World War Two. The new cabinet contains 23 members, 5 of whom are Liberal Democrats. Other, non-cabinet posts were allocated between the two coalition partners on roughly the same basis. But though all seems well at first, there are dangers ahead.

Only a few weeks previously members of the two coalition parties were criticising many of each other's key policies. Now, however, they were being asked to agree to a common programme containing some controversial policies. For example, the Liberal Democrats opposed the further use of nuclear energy, but it was agreed between the leaderships of the two coalition partners that more nuclear power plants can be built. On the other hand, many Conservatives in cabinet oppose the introduction of the alternative vote in general elections, but the coalition has agreed to hold a referendum on the issue. Thus it seems inevitable that, in the future, there will be stresses and strains on the arrangement as difficult issues arise. It may be that the Conservatives will grow tired of having always to consider Liberal Democrat opinion and wish to end the coalition. Similarly, if any precious Liberal Democrat ideals are abandoned, they too may wish to leave and put the government in jeopardy.

Source: (Original material)

(a) From the source, what is meant by the term 'coalition government' as referred to in the article? **(5 marks)**

(b) From the source and your own knowledge, what problems might arise if a cabinet contained members of both the Conservative and Liberal Democrat parties? **(10 marks)**

(c) What factors might a prime minister take into account in forming a new cabinet? **(25 marks)**

2. Read the following passage and answer the questions.

'The story of Tony Blair's ten years in office is remarkable for the change that took place in the degree of authority he was able to enjoy in the course of his decade in power. When he won the 1997 election Blair seemed to have collected more advantages than any other prime minister in living memory. He was leader of a largely united party and was unrivalled in his leadership of that party. He enjoyed a massive majority in the House of Commons and the opposition parties were in disarray. Blair was also personally popular in the country, even among those who had not voted Labour. The economy was strengthening and the tricky question of the single European currency had not yet emerged as a serious issue. When the new prime minister assembled his new cabinet he could rely on a team of colleagues who were ideologically united and loyal to the 'New Labour project'. But when he left office in 2007 Blair was a very different leader. He had lost the support of much of the party who felt either that he had made a huge mistake in going to war in Iraq or that he had stayed on too long and should have already handed over to Gordon Brown. His party's majority in the Commons had been reduced to 65 and he began to lose key votes, not least over the plan to allow security services to hold suspected terrorists for up to 90 days without trial. His personal popularity was at a low ebb and the Conservatives had found new energy under its young leader, David Cameron.'

Source: Author

(a) From the source, what factors can determine the amount of authority a prime minister may enjoy? **(5 marks)**

(b) From the passage and your own knowledge, analyse the limitations on the power of a prime minister. **(10 marks)**

(c) Should British government now be best described as 'prime-ministerial government'? **(25 marks)**

Resources and web guide

Books

A concise account of PM and cabinet is:
  N. McNaughton, *Prime Minister and Cabinet Government,* Hodder and Stoughton, 1999.

Presidential government issues are covered excellently in:
  M. Foley, *The British Presidency; Tony Blair and the Politics of Public Leadership,* Manchester University Press, 2000.

A modern history of the office of PM, full of useful examples, is:
  P. Hennessy, *The Prime Minister: The Office and its Holders Since 1945,* Penguin, 2001.

A huge book on the civil service, probably too big, is:
  P. Hennessy, *Whitehall,* Fontana, 2001.

A short, manageable guide is:
  P. Fairclough, *The Prime Minister and the Cabinet*, Hodder, 2007

or:

  S. Buckley, *The Prime Minister and Cabinet*, Edinburgh University Press, 2006

Useful websites

There are a number of official government sites:
  www.cabinet-office.gov.uk
  www.number-10.gov.uk
  www.civil-service.gov.uk

Information about recent prime ministers can be found on:
  www.margaret-thatcher.com
  www.johnmajor.co.uk
  www.controversy.net/blair

The judiciary and civil liberties

2.4

The nature of the judiciary

It is important at the outset to distinguish between two definitions of the judiciary. The first is a wide description that includes all those officials who are concerned with the dispensation of justice within the legal system. The other, narrower definition deals only with those judges who are directly involved with the process of law making and politics. When we refer to the 'three branches of government' – the executive, the legislature and the judiciary – it is this second, specific definition to which we are referring.

Therefore we can start by describing the complete judiciary of England and Wales first, including those who have no direct political significance.

Post	Type of post-holder	Main roles
Lay magistrates	Part-time, non-legally qualified members of the public	Hearing minor criminal cases, giving verdicts and setting punishments. Deciding whether to grant bail to arrested persons. Conducting committal hearings to decide whether more serious suspects should be sent for trial at a higher court. Granting licences to pubs, entertainment places, etc. Deciding whether children should be taken into local-authority care.
Stipendiary magistrates	Full-time lawyers	As above, but usually in larger cities.
Circuit and crown court judges	Full-time judges and recorders ('junior judges') who are mostly former barristers. They sit in crown courts or county courts	Hearing more serious criminal cases. Giving verdicts and determining punishments. Hearing disputes such as cases of negligence, commercial issues, divorce.

Post	Type of post-holder	Main roles
Tribunal officials	Lawyers or experts in a particular field, sometimes part-time, who staff special administrative tribunals, which are not courts of law but have a judicial function	Deciding on disputes over issues such as unfair dismissal, taxation, social security payments, compulsory purchase of property by local government.
High Court judges	Senior judges	Hear appeals from county courts. Hear cases involving matters and disputes over large sums of money. **Hearing cases where citizens or organisations have a dispute with some part or agency of government, known as 'judicial review'.**
Appeal courts	Very senior judges	Hearing appeals from criminal courts and the High Court. **Dealing with disputes from lower courts over the accurate meaning of the law.** **Dealing with appeals involving human rights.**
The Supreme Court	The most senior judges – 12 in number	Hearing appeals from the appeal courts in England and Wales. Hearing appeals from Scottish and Northern Ireland Courts. **Settling major disputes over human rights and judicial reviews.** **Dealing with major problems over determining the accurate meaning of law.** **Settling disputes over conflicts between British and EU law.**

Notes:

- The roles shown in bold have greater political significance.

- The court systems in Scotland and Northern Ireland differ slightly, but major appeals and political cases end up in the House of Lords in London.

- The table above does not show the **Judicial Committee of the Privy Council**. This is a highly specialised committee of the otherwise largely ceremonial Privy Council. This committee is the highest appeal court for a few British Commonwealth countries and also deals with any disputes over whether matters are under the jurisdiction of the British government and Parliament or whether they should fall under the jurisdiction of the Scottish Parliament, Welsh Executive or Northern Ireland government (when the latter is not suspended).

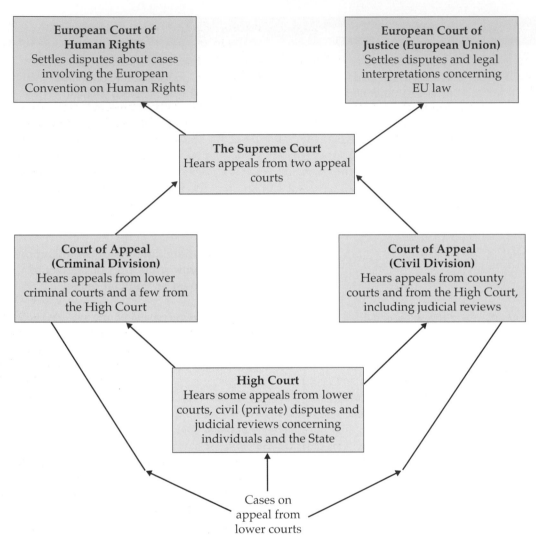

The upper levels of the judiciary

The political role of the judiciary

We can now see that role of the vast majority of the judiciary has no great political significance at all. Its overall task of administering justice is just that: 'administration'. But a minority of the total judiciary is certainly involved with cases of 'political' significance. What do we mean by this? The kinds of issues that we can consider to be political in nature are explored below.

Dispensing justice

Though not of directly political importance, the lower courts – magistrate's, crown and county courts – do have a vital role in ensuring that legal justice is delivered. This implies that all citizens should be treated equally under the law and that the law is applied to them in a fair way. Trials and hearings should all be conducted in such a way as to ensure that all parties gain a fair hearing and that the law is applied in the spirit intended.

Interpretation

The precise meaning of a statute is not always clear. However well the drafters of legislation have done their job, and however much parliamentary standing committees may have tried to make the law easy to understand, there will always be circumstances where those in court – disputants in a civil case, defenders and prosecutors in a criminal case – come into conflict over what the law is supposed to mean. In such cases it is for judges to interpret the meaning of law. In cases involving the powers of government or its agencies, or the rights of citizens, such interpretations may be of great public significance.

Creating case law

Similarly, it is not always clear how the existing laws are to be applied in a particular case. For example, there are laws relating to racial prejudice, discrimination against women and against actions that are likely to incite people to commit crime or to indulge in race hatred. This is all very well, but how should the law operate in *specific circumstances?* It is for judges to decide this. Furthermore, when such a decision is made, it is expected that any similar cases that arise in the future should be dealt with in the same way (the concept of 'judicial precedent' – see below). Once the application of law in specific kinds of case is established, the precedents are known as **case law**. We also refer to such law, including the interpretation of law described above, as **judge-made law** because it is judges, rather than Parliament, who, in effect, are making new law.

Declaring common law

Not all law is made by Parliament. Some law is known as 'common law'. These are rules of behaviour that have developed solely by tradition. In other words, they are common ways of dealing with disputes of various kinds. This law typically relates to such matters as inheritance, commercial practices and, very occasionally, the rights of citizens. Much common law is well enough established for judges to be able to apply it relatively easily. However, from time to time there may be problems in settling disputes for which there is no relevant statute law (made by Parliament) and no clear common law. When this happens a judge must take evidence and decide what the common law is. This is the third example of 'judge-made law'. Once again the rule of judicial precedent applies.

Judicial review

The quantity of cases involving **judicial review** has grown dramatically since the 1960s. The landmark case of *Ridge v Baldwin* in 1964 established the principle that citizens could appeal against decisions by government that appeared to be against 'natural justice'. Natural justice simply suggests that citizens have not been treated fairly as we generally mean that term. Typically, these are cases where a citizen, a group of citizens or an organisation believes it has been mistreated by the government or an agency of government. In such cases they will ask for a judicial review of their case, normally in the High Court. Typical examples of judicial review are cases where a minister or civil servant has not dealt equally

Key Word

Judicial review A process whereby the courts review decisions by the state or any public body in relation to its citizens. Where a review finds that a citizen has not been treated fairly, or that their rights have been abused, or that a public body has exceeded its legal powers, the court may set aside the decision.

with different citizens, or where there has been a clear injustice or where government or a public body has exceeded its statutory powers. Judicial reviews increased still further after 1977 when the procedures for citizens who wished to call for a judicial review of a decision by the courts were considerably simplified.

Judicial review is clearly a critical role because it helps to achieve two democratic objectives. One is to ensure that government does not over-step its powers. The second is to assert the rights of citizens. The courts were given an enormous boost in this area when the Human Rights Act came into force in 2000. This meant that courts could review actions by government and public bodies that might contravene the European Convention on Human Rights. At the same time, the Freedom of Information Act, which came into force in January 2005, gives citizens and the courts a right to see a much wider range of official documents than before. In this way there is considerably more scope for discovering whether injustice has been done and whether rights have been abused.

A number of examples of judicial review and the general political work of the courts are shown on p. 304 in a table that outlines cases of political importance.

Public inquiries

Though it is not necessarily always the case, judges are often called upon to conduct public inquiries into matters of widespread public concern. The reason for using judges is twofold. First, as experienced judges they are used to handling such issues. Second, they are independent of government so that an inquiry led by a judge can be seen to be politically neutral. The table opposite shows a number of such inquiries held in recent times. In each case the chair was a current or former judge. The fact that there were

Public inquiry	Detail
Scott Inquiry, 1996	The British government apparently changed the rules on the sale of **arms to Iraq** without making the matter public. This caused a number of embarrassing legal cases and ministerial errors.
Phillips Inquiry, 1998	Into the government's handling of the crisis over the outbreak of **BSE** (mad cow disease) in the UK.
Macpherson Inquiry, 1999	Into the killing some years earlier of black teenager **Stephen Lawrence** by a group of young white men. Conducted in order to examine the handling of the case by the police and the implications for race relations in the UK.
Hutton Inquiry, 2003	Into the circumstances surrounding the apparent suicide of **David Kelly**, a civil servant and weapons expert, who had been criticised for his role in the issue of Iraq and the search for weapons of mass destruction there.
Gibson Inquiry, 2010	Into allegations that British intelligence services were involved with US forces in the torture of terrorist suspects.

no highly significant inquiries between 2003 and 2010 indicates how reluctant governments have been to order them. The reason may well be that the independence of the judiciary acts as a deterrent.

External jurisdiction

The activities of government are now further constrained by relations with political and legal systems outside England and Wales. First, there is devolution. The courts have to settle any disputes concerning the jurisdiction of the Scottish Parliament and the Welsh or Northern Ireland Assemblies. The Devolution Acts that established devolution could not possibly deal with every single eventuality. It is therefore the role of the courts (especially the Judicial Committee of the Privy Council) to decide who has power in particular cases: London or one of the devolved administrations.

Second, there is the European Union. When there is a dispute over whether a matter falls under the power of British government and courts or whether it is a matter for the European Court of Justice, the case will first be referred to one of Britain's appeal courts – the Court of Appeal or the House of Lords. If there is a further appeal, or more consideration needs to be given to the case, it will pass to the European Court of Justice for a final decision.

Sentencing issues

Finally, we need to turn to the contentious issue of sentencing in criminal cases. In the past this has not been a political issue. Judges were given a free hand in deciding what sentences to give out. The only major restrictions on this power were homicide cases of various kinds where a life sentence was mandatory, or the general use of maximum sentences determined by Parliament.

Since the mid-1990s, however, when growing crime rates became a major political issue, politicians, mostly Home Secretaries, have sought to take control out of the hands of judges and to try to force their hand in various ways. The judges have resisted on the grounds that they should be independent from government and

that they are the best judges of each individual case and should decide them on their own merits. Politicians counter this by saying that judges are not accountable to the public. The public have shown a clear preference for more severe sentencing in general, so judges should be forced to respond to public opinion. The dispute goes on, but politicians appear to be winning by introducing *minimum sentences* for certain offences and for repeat offending. This takes away most of the flexibility that judges formerly enjoyed.

Now that we have established the nature of the judiciary's role, we can review some important legal cases that illustrate that role. See the table on p. 304.

Discussion topic

Who should make ultimate judgements about how the law is to be implemented – unelected and unaccountable judges who are neutral, or politicians who are elected and accountable but are not legally qualified and are not neutral?

The legal and constitutional environment of the judiciary

The judiciary does not operate in a vacuum. There are a number of limitations, principles and safeguards within which it operates. These are as follows.

The sovereignty of Parliament

Since Parliament is the source of all political authority, it cannot be overruled by the judiciary. In particular this means that judges cannot legally defy the legislative will of Parliament. Even if judges believe that a law is an offence to

Cases of political importance	Detail
Factortame 1991	The High Court ruled that the UK Merchant Fishing Act was in conflict with European Union Fisheries directives. The UK law was set aside, establishing the principle that EU law is superior to UK law.
Michael Douglas v Hello *Magazine* 2001	The European Court of Human Rights ruled that Michael Douglas and Catherine Zeta Jones had a right not to allow unauthorised photos of their celebrity wedding to be published. This established a right to privacy, under the Human Rights Act, for such celebrities.
Mental Health Act Case 2002	The UK Mental Health Act required that a person detained with a mental illness had to prove their own fitness to be released. The Court ruled this contradicted the Human Rights Act's individual right to freedom. Instead such detainees have a right to freedom unless it can be proved to be against the public interest.
Belmarsh case 2004	The House of Lords ruled that detainees held against their will under the anti-terrorism legislation contradicted the Human Rights Act on the grounds that citizens have a right not to be detained without trial. This forced the government to amend the anti-terrorism legislation to ensure safeguards for suspected terrorists.
Office of Fair Trading v Abbey National [now Santander] *and others* 2009	The Supreme Court ruled that the Office of Fair Trading had no power to investigate the banks' system of charging customers for overdrafts. This limited the regulatory power of government over the banks.
Suspected terrorist bank assets 2010	The Supreme Court ruled that the government did not have the legal power to freeze the assets of suspected terrorists. This forced the government to pass special legislation to give it such power.

human rights or discriminates unfairly against a particular group within society, they do not have the power to set that law aside – they are obliged to enforce it. They may, of course, give a critical opinion and suggest a change in the law, but that is as far as it goes (see the Belmarsh case above). The advent of the Human Rights Act in 2000 has given the courts a great deal of ammunition in their defence of individual rights, but even so, they cannot overturn a statute that has been properly passed by Parliament.

The rule of law

It is a firm principle of the British constitution that all citizens are considered to be equal under the law. This also applies to the government itself. The judiciary must always apply this principle. All citizens are also entitled to a fair trial. If the courts do not provide this they leave themselves open to appeal to a higher court.

Judicial precedent

As we have seen above, when a judge makes an interpretation of law, creates new case law or declares common law, all courts in the future must abide by that interpretation. Only a higher court is able to overturn an interpretation made by a lower court. Ultimately most disputed interpretations will end up in the House of Lords for a final decision. Of course, if a judge's interpretation of the law causes a problem for the government, ministers are at liberty to ask Parliament to clarify the law by passing a new one or amending existing legislation.

The primacy of EU law

In areas of policy where jurisdiction has been transferred to the European Union, British courts must accept the fact that EU law takes precedence over domestic law (see the Factortame case above). In other words, it is the duty of the British courts to enforce EU law. Only when there are problems of interpretation of EU law will British courts pass a case up to the European Court of Justice.

The independence of the judiciary

An essential feature of any healthy democracy is that the judicial branch should be independent of the government. There are a number of reasons why this is so:

● If judges are not independent there is a danger that the government will exceed its powers without legal justification. Without any effective check on government power, tyranny may result.

● Citizens need to feel certain that any legal cases with which they may become involved will be dealt with on the basis of justice and the rule of law. It may suit government to discriminate against individuals or groups in society for its own benefit. An independent judiciary can prevent such discrimination. The citizens of a democratic state must feel that their rights will be effectively protected.

● In some political systems the judiciary may appear to be independent, but in practice the judges are specially selected by the government to ensure decisions that are friendly to that government. Independence, therefore, also implies that judges are selected on a neutral basis to prevent collusion between the judiciary and the government.

How is independence of the judiciary maintained?

There are four main ways in which **judicial independence** is guaranteed in the UK. These are first, security of tenure, second, rules of *sub judice*, third, the system of appointments and, finally, the background of senior judges.

Key Word

Judicial independence The principle that members of the judiciary should retain independence from any influence by government or parties or other political movements.

The first and key principle that attempts to ensure the political independence of the judiciary is **security of tenure**. This principle says that judges cannot be removed from office on the grounds of the kinds of decisions that they make. The only reason a judge can be removed is if he can be shown to be corrupt as a result of personal conduct incompatible with being a judge. It follows, therefore, that judges are free to make decisions without fear of dismissal, even if such decisions offend the government. For the same reason judges are appointed on the understanding that their salaries cannot be reduced if they make contentious decisions.

Second, it is a **contempt of court** for any servant of the government to attempt to interfere with the result of a court case or even to comment on such a case in public or in Parliament. This rule is designed to prevent any political pressure being placed upon judges. Any such interference would be strongly criticised in Parliament and could result in legal action against the government member concerned.

The **appointments** system was reformed in 2005. Most judges are now appointed by a Judicial Appointments Commission. This is politically independent. Judges in the Supreme Court and Appeal Court (civil division) are appointed by a special committee comprising senior members of those courts and representatives from the Judicial Appointments Commissions in England, Scotland and Northern Ireland. This sounds complex, but the significance is simple – that there can now be little or no political influence over sensitive judicial appointments.

Finally, it should be pointed out that all senior judges must have enjoyed a lengthy career as courtroom lawyers. This means that they are accustomed to the principle that cases must be judged on the strict basis of law and not according to their personal opinions. Indeed, junior judges who gain a reputation for lack of impartiality are most unlikely to be put up for promotion.

In case one is tempted to be sceptical about these safeguards there is a great deal of evidence to suggest that the UK judiciary is indeed politically independent. Under both Conservative and Labour administrations senior members of the judiciary have made a large number of judgments that have been clearly contrary to government interests. This has been especially true since the implementation of the Human Rights Act in 2000. Indeed, it is significant that politicians of *both* the main parties have criticised the judiciary on the grounds that it is politically biased. This certainly implies that there is little or no political bias among judges.

How independence may be threatened

Although the British judiciary has a reputation for political independence it remains true that threats to this independence still exist. These include the following:

- The fact that the government retains control of the legal system through the Justice Ministry. This does not constitute direct control, but suggests a good deal of interference.

- In recent years there has been an increasing tendency for politicians to enter into open political dialogue with judges over such issues as sentencing policy and the protection of rights. Though this does not constitute *direct* interference, it may result in indirect pressure being placed on the judiciary.

- Though the appointment of senior judges is now handled by an independent Judicial Appointments Commission, the prime minister (on the advice of the Lord Chancellor) has a final veto over such appointments. Again this remains a *theoretical* problem, which may or may not be grounded in reality.

The neutrality of the judiciary

This may seem to be the same as independence, but there are crucial differences. Independence implies that judges are kept free from political pressure. **Judicial neutrality,** meanwhile, suggests that judges themselves are free from political or any other bias. The principle of the rule of law insists that every citizen should be treated equally under the law. This makes it essential that judges who preside over cases should conduct them without any personal favour to one side or the other.

Until the 1990s there was a widespread view that the British judiciary was not neutral, however much it claimed to be. Since then, however, there has been a great deal of evidence to suggest that the senior judges in the UK do indeed dispense justice in a politically neutral fashion. Each of these arguments can be examined in turn.

Key Word

Judicial neutrality The principle that members of the judiciary should avoid allowing their political ideas to affect their decisions in cases. It also implies that judges should not show any systematic bias towards or against any groups in society.

The case for lack of neutrality

The main argument here is that judges come from a narrow social and professional background. The majority are from middle- and upper-middle-class backgrounds. They are almost exclusively male and the majority have been educated at independent schools and often graduated from Oxford or Cambridge.

Professor John Griffith, originally writing in 1977, produced an important argument claiming that judges could not be consistently neutral. Their social background, he suggested, inevitably would affect the kind of judgments they make. In cases concerning the rights of women, or gay people, or trade unionists, for example, the gender and social background of the judges might be decisive. But, more importantly, he argued that judges are all lawyers, by definition, and this affects the way they think and act. He believed that judges were naturally inclined to favour the interests of the state and public order against the interests of individuals and minorities. In other words, they were likely to be conservative rather than liberal. In cases where the rights of individuals were in conflict with a public order issue, therefore, it was likely that a judge would favour public order. This might not apply to *every* judge, of course, but he argued that there was a general tendency in this direction.

Up to the time of Griffith's writing there was a good deal of evidence to suggest he was right. During the 1980s in particular there had been a succession of cases concerning trade union rights and activities, conflicts between central and local government, and issues about the powers of the police where judgments seemed to run consistently in favour of the centralised state.

Many of the senior judges also have seats in the House of Lords. Up to the late 1990s this was seen as a particularly conservative institution and the judges, it could be argued, were heavily influenced by their colleagues.

The first Supreme Court, which began work in 2009, certainly did not *appear* to be reasonably balanced in a social sense. Of its 12 members, all but one were educated at Oxford or Cambridge universities. Eleven were male and the average age was 68. We might therefore expect that the new court looks very conservative and from a narrow social base. The question was, however, how did it behave? This is examined below.

The Judges of the Supreme Court in 2010

The case for neutrality

The main argument in favour of the view that the British judiciary is effectively neutral arises from hard evidence. An increasingly large number of judgments in recent years have fallen in favour of individuals and minorities against the government. Indeed, in the mid-1990s, Conservative Home Secretary Michael Howard lost a string of judicial review cases brought against him by prisoners in custody who claimed his prison regime abused their human rights. The Mental Health Act and Belmarsh cases, described above, also provide evidence of the changing attitude of the judiciary.

The implementation of the Human Rights Act in 2000 has given further ammunition for judges to use against the power of the state in favour of individual rights. Indeed, so active have the judges been in this area that Conservative politicians have begun to talk of repealing the Human Rights Act and the Labour government has spoken of amending parts of it. The old charge that the judiciary normally favours the powers of the state against individuals seems no longer to be true. Indeed, the situation seems to have been largely reversed.

The social composition of the judiciary has changed little. As we saw above, the Supreme Court in particular comes from a narrow social base. Nevertheless, there has been a succession of independent-minded, 'liberal' judges appointed to senior positions. Lords Woolf, Hoffman and Bingham are good recent examples. All of these individuals have been quick to criticise government for threatening **civil liberties**. As we have seen above, when the senior judges are being criticised by politicians from both main parties, it suggests they may indeed be largely neutral. The early evidence from the Supreme Court is that it is likely to show itself to be fully independent and therefore neutral. It is as ready as ever to challenge governmental power when it feels citizens' rights are under threat or when the behaviour of government is likely to discriminate against any group in society.

Key Word

Civil liberties The rights and freedoms that citizens enjoy in relation to the state and its laws. These include, for example, the right of all to vote or to stand for office, freedom of expression, freedom of association and the right to a fair trial.

Civil liberties in the UK

We need first to define the term 'civil liberties' precisely. These are those freedoms and rights that the citizen of a state may enjoy at any particular time. They are freedoms seen in relation to the state itself and to its laws. In other words, they are the freedoms that are guaranteed by the state and its constitution (assuming the state has a constitution).

Until the passage of the Human Rights Act in 1998 (implemented in 2000), the UK had no codified set of civil liberties. Freedom was, up to 2000, 'negative' in nature. That meant that the citizens of Britain were considered to be free to do anything up to the point where the law limited their actions. In other words, citizens knew the extent of their freedom only in terms of the *limits* to those freedoms. For example, there was freedom of expression up to the point where that freedom was limited by the laws of libel, slander, pornography, incitement to crime, blasphemy, etc. Similarly, there was freedom of movement up to the point where the laws of private property, trespass, public order, etc. limited citizens' right to go wherever they pleased. There was no specific *statement* of what civil liberties were.

This was for two reasons. The first was that Britain enjoyed a particularly strong common-law tradition of liberty. Magna Carta, drawn up in 1215, was an expression of those traditional rights and freedoms, even though it was largely ignored by monarchs for centuries afterwards. The traditional enjoyment of liberties made the creation of a statement of rights apparently unnecessary. The second reason is the principle of the sovereignty of Parliament. Because Parliament is *omnicompetent* – can pass any legislation it wishes – it is not possible to establish a set of civil liberties (usually referred to as a bill of rights) that will be protected from future erosion. When we put these two realities together – the common-law tradition and the sovereignty of Parliament – we have the state of affairs that means that citizens are completely free up to the point where Parliament places limits on that freedom.

The people of the UK considered themselves to be largely 'free' – arguably freer than most peoples in the world – because Parliament has been traditionally unwilling to erode those liberties. Whenever governments proposed any measure that might threaten British liberties, Parliament had normally been reluctant to allow them to do so. Put another way, we can say that the instinct for civil liberty has always been very strong in the British political culture, strong enough not to need the creation of a binding bill of rights. But in the 1990s the situation changed.

The threat to civil liberties

In the 1990s there was growing concern in the UK that civil liberties were under serious threat. This was the result of a long-term accumulation of developments that seemed to add up to a dangerous growth in the powers of the state. The principal elements of this threat seemed to include the following:

- Increases in police power, notably as a result of the Police and Criminal Evidence Act of 1984 and the Criminal Justice and Public Order Act of 1994. In general terms, the growth in crime rates gave rise to growing calls for even more powers to be granted to law enforcement agencies.

- Legislation, passed in the 1980s, limiting trade union activities.

- Increasing quantities of information about individual citizens being held by the state and its agencies, such as the police, social security system and National Health Service.

- Increasing tension between governments and the media concerning the right of the government to limit what they printed and broadcast.

- A general fear that executive power was growing and the ability of Parliament to limit that power was weakening. This presented a generalised fear that civil liberties might be threatened by over-powerful government.

Citizens did have some ability to challenge the apparent erosion of civil liberties. They could appeal to the European Court of Human Rights, a body set up by the Council of Europe in 1950 (*not* by the European Union – a common misconception) on the grounds that the actions of the state contravened the European Convention on Human Rights. However, this was far from being a satisfactory safeguard. It was slow and extremely expensive – facts that put off most potential appeals. But, more importantly, the European Convention was not binding on British government. For these reasons appeals to the ECHR have remained relatively rare.

The perceived threat to liberties and the unsatisfactory status of the ECHR in the UK led the Labour Party leadership to include proposals to safeguard civil liberties more effectively in its 1997 manifesto. Two measures were included. One was the introduction of a **Freedom of Information Act,** while the other was to incorporate the **European Convention on Human Rights** into British law. These two measures have transformed the status of civil liberties in the UK.

Discussion topic

Can it be justified to set aside civil liberties and basic rights for the sake of protecting society from terrorism and general crime?

Freedom of information and open government

The Freedom of Information Act was passed in 2000, but did not come into force until January 2005. It was intended to be the main stage in a longer-term process of creating more open government.

During the 1970s there was increasing concern that government in the UK was too secretive. Citizens were denied access to information about the institutions and processes of government. This was felt to be detrimental to democracy. Furthermore, other political systems, notably that of the USA, were in the process of opening up government to public scrutiny. Britain was looking out of step with the rest of the democratic world.

The first major development was the introduction of departmental select committees in the House of Commons. These committees, which are described in more detail earlier in this book, had powers to question ministers and civil servants, as well as calling for official papers. The committees have had their limitations, but they were an important step on the road to more open government.

Next came the **Data Protection Act** in 1984. This gives citizens the right to see the contents of any computer file that contains information about them. There are exceptions, of course, notably police records, but in general it has helped to ensure that citizens can check that important personal details are accurately kept.

The Data Protection Act recognised the growing importance of computers in society. The development of the Internet accelerated this process. It is therefore increasingly true that government – central, regional and local – has used the Internet to provide increasing amounts of information about itself for public scrutiny. It has become possible to discover what agencies are serving government, what is their role, how government itself is organised and who is being employed to advise government. Indeed, civil servants and other public officials are now encouraged to publicise their work rather than hide it, which used to be their natural instinct.

The original **Freedom of Information Act (FOA)** was designed to give considerable powers to citizens to see government papers. However, under pressure from the civil service itself and from Conservative politicians, especially in the House of Lords, the final version was watered down. In essence the Act gives all citizens the right to see all public documents. However, the exemptions to this general principle have become extensive. Understandably, matters referring to national security and to private communications within government (such as the minutes of cabinet meetings) cannot be open to the public. But there is also a general rule attached to the legislation. This says that government can withhold information if it is felt publication will cause damage to the public interest. This is considered by critics to be too wide an exemption. It effectively means that government retains the opportunity to maintain a good deal of secrecy about its processes.

Nevertheless, the Act is an important extension to civil rights in the UK. The media in particular are beginning to find that they can obtain more background information on government than ever before. Individual citizens also now have access to papers relating to their own dealings with the state. This was perfectly illustrated when the MPs' expenses affair broke in 2009. As described above, the FOA was used as a means to reveal what expenses MPs had been claiming. It emerged that many had been abusing the generosity of the system. The scandal was so severe that many MPs resigned or did not seek re-election in 2010.

The Human Rights Act

As we have seen, the European Convention on Human Rights has been in existence since 1950. But it had relatively little impact in the UK as governments did not consider it to be binding on them. All this changed when the Labour government of 1997 decided to incorporate the Convention into British law. This was done in 1998 with the passage of the Human Rights Act.

The Act stated that all legislation, actions and decisions made by government, its ministers, regional parliaments, assemblies and governments, local government or by any agency engaged in public business (which includes schools and the media) had to conform to the European Convention on Human Rights. If it did not, the courts could strike the action or legislation down if it were successfully challenged. So at first sight the Act seems to be extremely powerful. But it contained one crucial exemption.

The government (and Parliament itself) were unwilling to set aside the principle of the sovereignty of Parliament. It was therefore decided that the Westminster Parliament would not be subject to the Convention. If the government does introduce legislation that will conflict with the Convention, it must alert Parliament to the fact by making a 'declaration of incompatibility'. In doing this Parliament becomes aware that there is an important rights issue at stake and may wish to refuse to pass the legislation. If, however, the government can persuade Parliament that the legislation is important enough to set aside the Convention, the new law will stand.

There is one other safeguard. If a citizen or group of citizens challenges a law on the basis that it conflicts with the European Convention, the court may agree and declare the law to be incompatible. This does not mean that the law is invalid, but it does mean that the government and Parliament will be made aware of the opinion of the court. This is what occurred in the Belmarsh detainees case in December 2004.

Eight citizens suspected of being Islamic terrorists were being detained without trial in Belmarsh prison. Their detention was legal under the Anti-Terrorism Act of 2001. In a ground-breaking decision, eight of the nine members of the House of Lords who heard the appeal declared that the detention of the suspects without trial contradicted the European Convention. As we have seen above, the verdict did not invalidate the Anti-Terrorism Act (it had been properly passed by Parliament), but the political fallout from the ruling was immense. The government came under pressure to amend the Anti-Terrorism Act to make it compatible with the Convention. After much political wrangling this was achieved and a considerable number of additional legal safeguards were built into the amended Act. This demonstrated the fact that, although Parliament remains legally sovereign, it will find it difficult to resist the pressure of an adverse court decision.

In other areas the European Convention is all-powerful and all bodies other than the Westminster Parliament must conform. The development therefore represents an enormous extension in the protection of rights in the UK. It is likely to have far-reaching effects in years to come.

The list below shows the main areas covered by the European Convention on Human Rights and therefore the Human Rights Act:

1. The protection of property.

2. The right to life.

3. Prohibition of torture.

4. Prohibition of slavery and forced labour.

5. Right to liberty and security.

6. Right to a fair trial.

7. No punishment without law.

8. Right to respect for private and family life.

9. Freedom of thought, conscience and religion.

10. Freedom of expression.

11. Freedom of assembly and association.

12. Right to marry.

13. Prohibition of discrimination.

14. Restrictions on political activity of aliens.

15. Prohibition of abuse of rights.

16. Limitations of restriction of rights.

For the first time in its history the UK has a positive set of rights that is fully codified. These rights are not entrenched, as Parliament can repeal all or part of the Human Rights Act, but it is hard to imagine that Parliament would allow such a development in the foreseeable future.

Human rights in the UK

Having examined the issue of civil liberties, the question of human rights in general can be considered. When we refer to human rights *in general* we are including civil liberties, but also adding two other categories of rights. One is the prevention of discrimination against certain groups in society, notably women, members of ethnic and religious minorities, gay people and the disabled.

The other is usually described as economic and social rights (as opposed to civil rights).

Economic and social rights concern our status as citizens in relation to employment and to welfare benefits, including health and education. Thus, for example, citizens in the UK are entitled to some protection from unfair dismissal from work, have a legal right to join a trade union and to take industrial action as long as it is legally approved and have an equal right to benefits under the welfare state provided they have contributed.

The most important development in the field of economic and employment rights in the UK was the British signing of the EU Social Chapter in 1997. We can now put together all the various kinds of rights that are protected in some way in the UK and the ways in which they are safeguarded – see the table opposite.

We can see, therefore, that human rights are protected in a number of ways in the UK. In each case it is the courts, or perhaps a tribunal, that are involved in the enforcement of laws, conventions and EU directives. In each case appeal procedures can be undertaken and, ultimately, cases may appear in the Supreme Court or one of the European Courts – the Court of Justice (EU) or the Court of Human Rights – if they are considered to be of great importance and to have wider implications.

The government and the judiciary

In theory the executive and judiciary in the UK should be kept entirely separate. This also implies that the government should not interfere with judicial independence, while at the same time judges would remain totally aloof from political issues. In recent years, however, this reciprocal arrangement has begun to break down. A number of issues have emerged that have brought

Protection of rights		
Type of right	Examples of main methods of protection	Enforced by
Civil liberties	European Convention on Human Rights	Judicial review
	Common law rights	European Court of Human Rights
	Parliamentary statutes such as the Habeas Corpus Act	Appeal to common law in the High Court
		Judicial review
Anti-discrimination	Race Relations Acts	Courts and tribunals
	Equal Opportunities Acts	Courts and tribunals
	Equal Pay Acts (for women)	Courts and tribunals
Employment and Union right	Employment Protection Act	Industrial tribunal
	Trade Union Acts	Civil cases
	EU Social Chapter	EU European Court of Justice
Rights to welfare	Welfare state legislation	Judicial review

government ministers and senior judges into serious conflict. There have been three main areas in dispute:

1. As ministers, especially Home Secretaries, have sought to gain more control over sentencing in serious crime cases, they have encountered opposition from judges who believe that the issue of sentencing in criminal cases should remain in their hands. Specifically, judges have resisted the introduction of legally binding *minimum* sentences for some categories of crime. More generally, judges have also expressed a strong view that they would prefer to reserve longer prison sentences for the most serious of crimes. Lord Woolf, the Lord Chief Justice (Britain's most senior judge) until 2005, declared that judges reserved the right to use alternatives to prison when sentencing in less serious cases. In other words, judges resent political interference and believe they should be free to conduct cases as they wish in their own courts. In 2010 a new body came into existence – the **Sentencing Council**. Its role is to set sentencing guidelines that judges should follow. There is some doubt over how tight the new guidelines will be. Many judges fear it will take away their discretion, but many politicians believe the rules are still too loose. Its effects remain to be seen.

2. Many senior members of the judiciary, including Lords Woolf and Phillips, have publicly criticised the erosion of civil liberties that would occur if the government introduced ever tougher anti-terrorism measures. As we have seen above, indeed, eight of the law lords declared the 2001 Anti-Terrorism Act unlawful on these grounds. Judges also criticised the Criminal Justice Bill of 2003. This bill proposed that accused persons could be tried twice for the same crime in some circumstances (so-called double jeopardy), that many types of cases would be heard without a jury and that accused persons' past convictions could be used as evidence against them. Many judges believed these changes would endanger the rights of accused persons and lead to miscarriages of justice. Judges sitting in the Supreme Court appear to be extremely willing to challenge government powers when individual rights may be threatened.

3. The general tendency of judges to become publicly involved in political controversies of the kind described above has angered government ministers, who insist that the judiciary should be seen to be politically neutral. Home Secretaries Blunkett and Clarke, in particular, criticised judges for being too politically active. Their argument was that ministers are elected and accountable, whereas judges are neither. They therefore have no right, the politicians assert, to obstruct the political process. Judges counter that they are guardians of individual rights against the power of over-mighty government.

Finally, we can summarise the position of the judiciary in relation to government by identifying its main strengths and weaknesses. This is shown below.

The judiciary and protection of rights – an evaluation	
Main strengths	**Main weaknesses**
• The Human Rights Act has given the judiciary a codified set of rights upon which to judge whether executive and legislative action threatens civil liberties. As it is binding on all but Parliament, the Act is a key weapon available to judges.	• The sovereignty of Parliament means that judges are forced to accept legislation made at Westminster. • The Human Rights Act is not binding on Parliament.

| The judiciary and protection of rights – an evaluation (continued) ||
Main strengths	Main weaknesses
<ul><li>The judiciary can justifiably claim to be independent.</li><li>It has become considerably easier for citizens to seek judicial review so that judges now hear many more cases of political importance.</li><li>The new Supreme Court is showing signs of being more independent than the House of Lords used to be.</li></ul>	<ul><li>Judges do not have the power to undertake 'pre-legislative review', that is, they cannot take positive action to influence legislation before it is presented to Parliament.</li><li>Judges are neither elected nor accountable and so lack democratic legitimacy.</li><li>Where judges are believed to be obstructing government, the law can be amended to force them to comply with government wishes.</li></ul>

The reform of the judiciary

In 2003, momentum grew for reform of the British senior judiciary. This had always been an aspiration for the Labour government that took office in 1997, but the political will had been lacking until then. The reasons for reform were these:

● The ancient office of Lord Chancellor was an historical oddity. The holder was a cabinet minister, speaker (chairman) of the House of Lords and also head of the judiciary. In this third capacity he advised the government on legal and constitutional matters, appointed senior judges in consultation with the prime minister and was a leading figure in the making of government policy on legal matters. He was, therefore, a member of all three branches of government. His position was the most dramatic example of the lack of separation of powers in the UK. If Britain were to claim to be a modern democracy it had to rid itself of this strange anomaly.

● As senior judges were appointed by the prime minister and the Lord Chancellor, obviously both party politicians, there could be no guarantee that the judiciary would be free from political influence. This would place under threat the principles of the rule of law and the independence of the judiciary.

● It has been confusing and potentially unjust that the highest appeal court – the House of Lords – should be made up of judges who were also members of the legislature and who therefore had a place in the making as well as the implementation of the law.

● In nearly all modern democracies it is firmly established that the judiciary (which upholds the rights of citizens, controls the arbitrary power of government and maintains the principles of justice and the rule of law) should be totally independent of government and protected from influence from government. Such a situation certainly did not exist in Britain.

For these reasons the decision was taken in 2003 to undertake reform. The **Constitutional Reform Act** of 2005 put the proposals into effect. The three main reforms were these:

1. The position of Lord Chancellor was retained, but its holder no longer presides over the House of Lords and is no longer the head of the courts system. Instead the Lord Chief Justice – a non-political post – became head of the judicial system. The post of Secretary of State for Constitutional Affairs was created in the cabinet and its holder is to advise the government on constitutional issues. (As it happens, the first two holders, Lord Falconer and Jack Straw, were also made Lord Chancellor, but this will not necessarily always be the case.)

2. A new Judicial Appointments Commission was set up to propose candidates for promotion to senior judicial positions. The Commission ensures that there is no political influence over the decision. Though senior politicians do have some say in the final appointment, it is expected that there be no more political interference.

3. The 12 law lords who sat in the House of Lords and formed the highest court of appeal in the UK were removed to a new Supreme Court in 2009. Though the powers of the new court remained the same as those enjoyed by the former law lords, it was an important step in establishing its independence. The separation of the Supreme Court from the House of Lords was largely symbolic, but the new name and location may well go some way to persuading the public and the media that the UK's highest court is truly independent.

The British courts and the European Union

Since two key cases (described below) – Factortame (1991) and *ex parte* EOC (1994) – it has been established that European Union law is superior to UK law. This means that where there is a clash between UK and EU law, the British courts must uphold EU law.

In Factortame it was ruled that the UK 1988 Merchant Shipping Act, limiting the rights of foreign shipping vessels to fish in British waters, contravened EU law. The EU allowed foreign vessels to register to fish in other countries' waters. Thus UK law was set aside and replaced by the EU regulation. In *ex parte* EOC it was ruled that British law failed to give part-time workers the same employment rights as full-time workers. EU law stated that part-timers and full-timers must have the same rights throughout the European Union. Here, again, UK law was set aside in favour of EU law.

The effect of the two rulings was to establish clearly that EU law is superior to UK law. In practice this means two things: first, that British courts must enforce EU law and second, that if there is a dispute over UK and EU law, the European Court of Justice shall have the final say.

The European Court of Human Rights (ECHR)

First, a possible confusion must be cleared up. The European Court of Human Rights has nothing to do with the European Union. The ECHR was set up by a body called the Council of Europe, a separate organisation altogether.

The European Convention on Human Rights was incorporated into British law in 1998 and came into force in 2000. This means that any group or citizen can claim that their human rights have been abused if any action by government or any public body contravenes the Convention. British courts have the power to enforce the Convention. However, if a group or individual believes that the British court has not interpreted the Convention correctly, they can take the case to a higher level, the European Court of Human Rights.

If the ECHR rules that the Convention has been broken, it can order a reversal of the decision in question. This is the highest appeal, so a case can go no further. The only exception to this is that the ECHR cannot set aside any law made by the Westminster Parliament as this is not subject to the European Convention.

Up to 2008 the Court had upheld all the decisions made in British courts since the Human Rights Act was implemented. In other words, whenever British citizens had claimed their rights had been abused, appeal to the ECHR had not worked for them. This suggests that British courts have become successful in understanding how to interpret the European Convention.

Key concepts in this chapter

Judicial review A process whereby the courts review decisions by the state or any public body in relation to its citizens. Where a review finds that a citizen has not been treated fairly, or that their rights have been abused, or that a public body has exceeded its legal powers, the court may set the decision aside.

Judicial independence The principle that members of the judiciary should retain independence from any influence by government or parties or other political movements.

Rule of Law The principle that all citizens are equal under the law, that all are entitled to a fair trial if accused of a crime and that the government itself is subject to law. In other words, the rule of law insists that government should not be arbitrary but must always act within the constraints of the law.

Judicial neutrality The principle that members of the judiciary should avoid allowing their political ideas to affect their decisions in cases. It also implies that judges should not show any systematic bias towards or against any groups in society.

Civil liberties The rights and freedoms that citizens enjoy in relation to the state and its laws. These include, for example, the right of all to vote or stand for office, freedom of expression, freedom of association and the right to a fair trial.

Separation of powers The principle that the three branches of government should be kept separate from each other and should have their own, independent powers. In the context of this chapter, this implies the separation of the judiciary from government and Parliament.

Judicial activism The practice of some higher courts and judges in actively seeking to assert the rights of citizens and to limit the power of government. By doing this they are taking an active role in interpreting and revising the constitution.

Revision topics and examination questions

Revision topics

- Nature of civil liberties
- Nature of human rights
- Various roles and functions of the judiciary
- Independence of the judiciary
- Neutrality of the judiciary
- Ways in which the judiciary can protect rights
- Importance of the Human Rights Act
- Nature of the rule of law

- Limitations to the power of the judiciary
- Ways and extent to which the judiciary can control the power of the executive
- Reasons for disputes between the judiciary and governments
- Recent reform of the judiciary.

Essay questions

1. How is the judiciary able to protect civil liberties in the UK?
2. To what extent is the British judiciary able to control the power of government?
3. Why is the independence of the judiciary so important and how is it maintained in the UK.
4. Analyse the relationship between British and European courts.
5. Analyse the ways in which the judiciary can influence constitutional development in the UK.

Stimulus response questions

1. Read the following passage and answer the questions that follow.

'Tony Blair is planning a radical overhaul of Britain's controversial human rights legislation after claims that the present laws put the rights of criminals above those of victims.

In a move which brought immediate criticism from human rights' experts, the prime minister wants the government to have the power to override court rulings. The move comes only days after Blair criticised a senior judge for preventing the deportation of nine Afghan refugees who hijacked a plane to Britain. Downing Street said he was determined to find a way around such 'barmy' court rulings.

Blair unveiled his plans in a letter to the new Home Secretary, John Reid, in which he set out his 'most urgent policy tasks'. Legal experts and civil liberties groups accused Blair of playing politics with fundamental rights. The *Observer* has obtained a copy of the letter, which says it is essential to 'ensure the law-abiding majority can live without fear'.

It adds: 'We will need to look again at whether primary legislation is needed to address the issue of court rulings which overrule the government in a way that is inconsistent with other EU countries' interpretation of the European Convention on Human Rights.'

A Downing Street source said a range of existing laws could be reviewed and new legislation was also possible. One option under consideration was to amend the 1998 Human Rights Act, which wrote the European Convention into British law, to require a 'balance between the rights of the individual and the rights of the community to basic security'. He said that 'although British judges should already take that balance into consideration, it's clear that sometimes they don't'.

Source: *Observer,* 14 May 2006, Ned Temko and Jamie Howard. © Guardian News & Media Ltd 2006

(a) From the source, what was Tony Blair's attitude to the judiciary at that time? (**5 marks**)
(b) From the source and your own knowledge, what is the importance of parliamentary sovereignty in the field of human rights? (**10 marks**)
(c) How much are British judges able to remain independent of government influence? (**25 marks**)

2. Read the following passage and answer the questions which follow.

'The government announced plans for significant constitutional reform on 12 June 2003, designed to enhance the independence of the judiciary and to ensure clarity in the relationship between the Executive and the judiciary. I plan shortly to introduce the required statutory instruments to bring into force those parts of the Constitutional Reform Act 2005 that will deliver the central aspects of those reforms. As of 3 April 2006, I intend to bring the new Judicial Appointments Commission into being and commence those aspects of the Act that give statutory effect to the provisions of the Concordat I agreed with the Lord Chief Justice.

Roles of the Lord Chancellor and Lord Chief Justice

As of 3 April, the Lord Chancellor's role as a judge will cease. The Lord Chief Justice will hold the additional title of President of the Courts of England and Wales and be legally recognised as the head of the judiciary in England and Wales. As set out in the Concordat, the role of the Lord Chief Justice will be significantly reformed and strengthened. To support the Lord Chief Justice, the Judicial Office for England & Wales has been established and the new head of that Office has recently been appointed and taken up post.

In addition, to give effect to the new arrangements for the handling of judicial disciplinary matters, a new Office for Judicial Complaints will be established. The arrangements relating to judicial complaints and discipline will be published shortly.

Judicial Independence and Rule of Law

As of 3 April, for the first time there will be a guarantee of continued judicial independence enshrined in statute, underpinned by particular duties binding on the Lord Chancellor and ministers of the Crown to uphold judicial independence. The Act also formally recognises the constitutional principle of the Rule of Law and the Lord Chancellor's role in relation to that principle.'

Source: Written statement by Lord Falconer to Parliament, 23 January 2006

(a) What reforms of the judiciary are referred to in the statement? **(5 marks)**
(b) From the statement and your own knowledge, how and why is the independence of the judiciary to be guaranteed? **(10 marks)**
(c) Why was it felt necessary to reform the judiciary in 2005? **(25 marks)**

Resources and web guide

Books

The best-known work on the political role of the judiciary was:
  J. Griffiths, *The Politics of the Judiciary,* Fontana, 1991.

Another important work, if now a little dated, is:
  R. Stevens, *The Independence of the Judiciary,* Oxford University Press, 1993.

On rights:
  F. Klug, *Values for a Godless Age: The Story of the UK's New Bill of Rights,* Penguin, 2002.

Though it pre-dates the Human Rights Act, the whole issue is covered very well in:
  M. Zander, *A Bill of Rights?,* Sweet and Maxwell, 1997.

A good short introduction is:
  S. Foster, *The Judiciary, Civil Liberties and Human Rights*, Edinburgh University Press, 2006

A review of the House of Lords and law is:
  L. Blom-Cooper et al, *The Judicial House of Lords*, Oxford University Press, 2009

Useful websites

For information and a full account of the European Convention on Human Rights:
  www.echr.coe.int
The pressure group Liberty has a useful website on human rights:
  www.liberty-human-rights.org.uk

Examination guide

This section is written to help students who are taking Edexcel examinations for AS Government and Politics. A complete specimen examination is shown below, together with guidance about how to answer the questions. The questions are taken from the examination questions shown at the end of each unit. Note that these questions are not 'officially approved' Edexcel questions or answer guidance, but they are certainly typical.

Overall guide to Units 1 and 2

General points

- The principle of 'a mark a minute' applies to Unit 1, as it does to Unit 2. This means that candidates are advised to spend about one minute of their time per mark available. Thus a five-mark question should take up about 5 minutes, and so on. Clearly, a little general time must be reserved for reading and thinking, so allocate slightly less than this to each question.

- Questions may be attempted in any order.

- It is advisable to choose questions on the basis of the most promising (c) parts as these carry five-eighths of the total marks for the question. In other words, it is bad practice to choose questions on the basis of part (a) or part (b) sections if the candidate will be weak on part (c).

- Occasionally similar factual material may be used for different sections of the same. When this occurs the candidate must *repeat* the information and not simply refer to a previous passage that they have written in another section.

- Candidates who run out of time should try to complete the answer using bullet points or a plan of the remaining material.

- Crossing out should be a single clear line through the relevant words.

- Where a candidate has missed out information and wishes to refer to it later, the asterisk should be used, clearly showing where the additional material belongs.

- Examination booklets are divided strictly into sections for each answer. Candidates should not spread an answer into a different section. Where an answer is too long for the relevant section, additional sheets must be used, clearly marking which answer is being included.

- The quality of handwriting is not relevant as long as it can be clearly read. Candidates whose writing is too poor to be read run a strong risk of losing marks.

- Spelling is not marked specifically. However, the quality of general communication is marked in some sections. Spelling may count here. General advice is to make sure that specifically *political* words and phrases are spelled correctly.

● Marking is *positive*, which means that examiners will not deduct marks for errors or for irrelevant material. They will award marks only for accurate and relevant material. That said, too much irrelevance may cause problems with structure and evaluation.

Assessment objectives

Candidates should familiarise themselves with the assessment objectives and how they apply to the different parts of the examination. Examiners award *separate* marks under each assessment objective, so marks will not be transferred from one objective to another. For example, an answer that contains a spectacular quantity of factual knowledge and examples will not compensate for a lack of analysis and evaluation. The same is true of very good analytical answers that lack factual evidence and illustrations.

Here is a brief guide to what the assessment objectives are and what they require:

Assessment Objective 1 (AO1) – Knowledge and Understanding

This means *relevant knowledge*, that is, information that helps to answer the question and provides good evidence. It includes examples and illustrations. *Knowledge* includes the ability to deploy relevant arguments on both sides of a discussion. *Understanding* means that candidates are demonstrating that they comprehend the nature of the question, understand ideas, arguments, concepts and processes, and know what is relevant as opposed to irrelevant.

Assessment Objective 2 (AO2) – Analysis and Evaluation

Analysis refers to the ability to be able to describe links between processes, an understanding of why one set of facts leads to one conclusion, while other facts suggest a different conclusion. For example, demonstrating the relationship between the prime minister's power of patronage (appointment and dismissal of ministers) and his ability to dominate the government is an example of analysis. Similarly, explaining the reasons why pressure groups have become more important but parties are less significant is analysis. *Evaluation* involves demonstrating what is more important and what is less, for example, placing factors in order of importance. It means balancing arguments on one side of an issue against the other side, describing the relevant strengths and weaknesses of each. It also means responding evaluatively to questions that begin with such phrases as *To what extent?*, or *How much?*, or *What are the most important...?*

Assessment Objective 3 (AO3) – Communication

In simple terms this refers to how clearly candidates express themselves. However, it also refers to how well the answer is constructed. Are facts assembled in a logical way? Is there a useful introduction and conclusion? In addition, there is an assessment of how well specifically *political* vocabulary is used. For example, terms such as *legitimacy, authority, accountability, prerogative powers, rule of law, patronage, sovereignty, arbitrary power* and the like will attract marks under AO3 if they are used in the appropriate context.

As we have said, the marks for each assessment objective are not distributed equally among all the questions, so candidates should know the weighting of each for each section. Where there are *no* marks for a particular assessment objective, the candidate should not waste time in trying to meet that objective. For example, *all* section (a) questions in both units offer marks *only* under AO1, Knowledge and Understanding. Candidates should not, therefore, attempt any analysis or evaluation. Marks will not be deducted, but it is simply a waste of valuable time.

When candidates are fully aware of the assessment objectives on offer for a section, they should make a special effort to ensure that they address them. Thus, if analysis and evaluation are to be awarded marks, a conscious attempt should be made to include analysis and evaluation.

A typical examination

(This is NOT an approved specimen examination)

Unit 1 (80 minutes)

Question 1

(a) What is meant by 'direct democracy'? (5 marks)

(b) Under what circumstances have referendums been used in the UK? (10 marks)

(c) Compare the relative merits of direct and representative democracy. (25 marks)

Question 2

(a) Outline three functions of a political party. (5 marks)

(b) In what senses is the UK a two-party system? (10 marks)

(c) How liberal are the beliefs of UK political parties? (25 marks)

Question 3

(a) Explain the additional member system electoral system. (5 marks)

(b) What is the significance of the doctrine of manifesto and mandate? (10 marks)

(c) To what extent do elections in the UK produce representative government? (25 marks)

Question 4

(a) What is a pressure group? (5 marks)

(b) Distinguish between insider and outsider pressure groups. (10 marks)

(c) How and why have the methods of pressure groups changed in recent years? (25 marks)

The distribution of assessment objectives for Unit 1:

(a) sections

All 5 marks are for AO1.

(b) sections

7 marks for AO1, 3 marks for AO2.

(c) sections

8 marks for AO1, 9 marks for AO2, 8 marks for AO3.

A guide to answering Unit 1 specimens above

Question 1

(a) What is meant by 'direct democracy'? (5 marks)

AO1 marks can be gained by simply describing the meaning of the term and referring to referendums. Give an example of a referendum. Do not discuss or analyse direct democracy.

(b) Under what circumstances have referendums been used in the UK? (10 marks)

AO1 marks are for describing some of the referendums held, with understanding shown of the issue and the circumstances surrounding the poll.

AO2 marks can be achieved by showing why a referendum was used rather than a simple parliamentary vote.

(c) Compare the relative merits of direct and representative democracy. (25 marks)

AO1 marks are for demonstrating knowledge and understanding of the various reasons why direct democracy is desirable and why representative democracy can be preferred.

AO2 marks can be gained by successfully evaluating the strengths of the various merits and by reaching conclusions about the circumstance where one is more desirable than the other – e.g. direct democracy may be desirable when constitutional changes are compromised, while representative democracy is more appropriate where complex, technical issues are at stake.

AO3 will largely be gained by creating a logical structure. For example, this might be an introduction describing democratic principle, content including the merits of each type

with evaluation of each, and a conclusion that demonstrates the circumstance when each might be more appropriate.

Question 2

(a) Outline three functions of a political party. (5 marks)

AO1 marks are for accurately identifying three functions (probably 3 marks) and for a brief description of each (an additional 2 marks).

(b) In what senses is the UK a two-party system? (10 marks)

AO1 marks are for knowledge and understanding of the meaning of 'two-party system' and for knowledge of the evidence suggesting Britain is a two-party system.

AO2 marks would be awarded for some analysis of why the relevant evidence points to the argument that it is a two-party system.

(c) How liberal are the beliefs of UK political parties? (25 marks)

AO1 marks for knowledge and understanding of the principles of liberalism in its various forms and the aspects of the philosophies and policies of the three parties that conform to liberal principles.

AO2 marks for evaluating the extent to which the three parties are, indeed, liberal. This means creating a balance with aspects of party policies that are illiberal. A conclusion for each of the parties should be included.

AO3 marks can be gained through appropriate vocabulary such as 'social justice' or 'civil rights' or 'constitutionalism', all of which apply to liberalism. A logical structure might be – an introduction to explain the main principles of liberalism, content looking at the three parties' main policies and ideas, and a conclusion for each, assessing how liberal they actually are by balancing liberal against illiberal ideas in each.

Question 3

(a) Explain the additional member system electoral system. (5 marks)

AO1 marks for a brief but accurate description, with an example of where it is used and its main impacts.

(b) What is the significance of the doctrine of manifesto and mandate? (10 marks)

AO1 marks for a full understanding and accurate description of what the term means and an example of how it operates.

AO2 marks mainly for demonstrating the links between the terms manifesto and mandate and for an analysis of why they are important. Possibly some analysis of their changed significance with a hung parliament and coalition government.

(c) To what extent do elections in the UK produce representative government? (25 marks)

AO1 marks can be gained by explaining clearly what representative government means and for evidence demonstrating both representative and unrepresentative features of the outcome of elections. Knowledge should be shown of different elections – local, regional and national. A response that concentrates on general elections is acceptable, but there should be some material about other elections.

AO2 marks for a full evaluation of the balance between representative and unrepresentative features. There should also be some analysis of why elections produce unrepresentative results, especially for general elections as opposed to, for example, elections to devolved assemblies.

AO3 marks will largely be awarded for structure – probably an introduction describing what the term 'representative' means, content describing

the outcomes of different kinds of election in the UK and a conclusion containing the evaluation.

Question 4

(a) What is a pressure group? (5 marks)

AO1 marks for a clear description of what a pressure group is, of the two main types of pressure group – promotional and sectional – plus an example of each.

(b) Distinguish between insider and outsider pressure groups. (10 marks)

AO1 marks for a clear description of what each term means, how each type operates plus one or two examples of each.

AO2 marks can be gained by drawing out the clear distinctions. These will mainly concern the different types of impact of each, why some are insiders and others are outsiders, and how their methods vary.

(c) How and why have the methods of pressure groups changed in recent years? (25 marks)

AO1 marks for knowledge and understanding of the methods used and the changes in those methods over time. Examples should be included. This is the 'how' part of the question.

AO2 marks are for the 'why' part of the question. Analysis is needed of what changing circumstances have existed and how these link into the changes in pressure-group methods. For example, what the connections are between the growth of social networking and the increased use of direct action by, for instance, motoring groups or anti-airport expansion campaigns.

AO3 marks for structure that should clearly reflect the 'how' and 'why' distinction in the question, and for appropriate use of political language such as 'mobilisation of public support' or 'new social movements'.

A guide to stimulus questions (Unit 2, questions 1 and 2) – below

General points to consider

- The (a) section always requires information *only* from the stimulus. Do not add any additional information not in the supplied material.

- There are only marks for AO1 so no analysis is needed even if it is contained in the stimulus material.

- You are expected, wherever possible, to identify material from the stimulus using your own words, rather than simply quoting directly from a passage. This may not always be possible, in which case quoting is acceptable. Where data is involved this can obviously be directly lifted out.

- The (b) section always requires candidates to use some information from the stimulus material and some from their own knowledge. Ideally, there should be an equal balance between material from the stimulus and from 'own knowledge', but a one third–two thirds split either way is acceptable.

- Material from the stimulus may be purely factual and its explanation and analysis may be from 'own knowledge'. However, it is likely that additional factual material is expected.

- The (c) section is 'free standing'. It is not required that any material from the stimulus is used. Of course, if relevant, such material can be included.

Specific guide to the specimen questions

Unit 2. 80 Minutes

Question 1 (40 marks)
Read the following passage and answer the questions.

'What constitutes citizens' rights – beyond voting – and citizens' responsibilities – like jury service – should itself be a matter for public deliberation. And as we focus on the challenges we face and what unites us and integrates our country, our starting point should be to discuss together and then – as other countries do – agree and set down the values, founded in liberty, which define our citizenship and help define our country.

And there is a case that we should go further still than this statement of values to codify either in concordats or in a single document both the duties and rights of citizens and the balance of power between government, Parliament and the people. For example, issues surrounding the domination of Parliament by the executive.

In Britain we have a largely unwritten constitution. It is made up of conventions, common law, traditions and judgments from the courts. To change that would represent a fundamental and historic shift in our constitutional arrangements. So it is right to involve the public in a sustained debate, whether there is a case for the United Kingdom developing a full British Bill of Rights and Duties, or for moving towards a written constitution.

And because such fundamental changes should happen only where there is a settled consensus on whether to proceed, I have asked my Right Honourable Friend the Secretary for Justice to lead a dialogue within Parliament and with people across the United Kingdom by holding a series of hearings, starting in the autumn, in all regions and nations of this country – and he will consult with the other parties on this process.'

Adapted from a Gordon Brown statement to the House of Commons, Hansard, 3 July 2007

(a) From the source, explain what is meant by the expression 'we have a largely unwritten constitution'. (5 marks)

AO1 marks only can be gained by explaining that the passage refers to why the constitution is largely unwritten, mentioning conventions, and common-law court judgments. Briefly outline why these sources of the constitution are unwritten.

(b) From the source and your own knowledge, assess the current 'balance of power between government, Parliament and the people' in relation to the British constitution. (10 marks)

AO1 marks for identifying issues such as the rights of the people, and the domination of Parliament by the executive. Explain why there are problems in these relationships. From 'own knowledge', explain such issues as prime-ministerial domination, lack of public accountability or similar.

AO2 marks for analysis of why there are problems in these relationships – for example, why Parliament is so weak and why the rights of the people may be in danger.

(c) Assess the arguments in favour of and against the introduction of a codified constitution for Britain. (25 marks)

AO1 marks for knowledge and understanding of the various arguments regarding codification.

AO2 marks for the assessment of these arguments. This would include analysis of the strengths and weaknesses of each argument. In addition, candidates should offer a general conclusion as to whether the case for codification is strong enough

to prompt reform or whether the balance lies with anti-codification.

AO3 marks for the structure of the answer, with an introduction explaining codification, content describing both sides of the argument and a conclusion that gives an overall evaluation of the arguments on either side.

Question 2 (40 marks)

Read the following passage and answer the questions.

Britain's first coalition cabinet for 65 years

The formation of a coalition administration in May 2010 marked Britain's first experiment with this form of government since the end of World War Two. The new cabinet contains 23 members, five of whom are Liberal Democrats. Other, non-cabinet posts were allocated between the two coalition partners on roughly the same basis. But, though all seems well at first, there are dangers ahead.

Only a few weeks ago members of the two coalition parties were criticising many of each other's key policies. Now, however, they were being asked to agree to a common programme containing some controversial policies. For example, the Liberal Democrats opposed the further use of nuclear energy, but it was agreed between the leaderships of the two coalition partners that more nuclear power plants can be built. Also, many Conservatives in cabinet oppose the introduction of the alternative vote in general elections, but the coalition has agreed to hold a referendum on the issue. Thus it seems inevitable that, in the future, there will be stresses and strains on the arrangement as difficult issues arise. It may be that the Conservatives will grow tired of having always to consider Liberal Democrat opinion and wish to end the coalition. Similarly, if any precious

Liberal Democrat ideals are abandoned, they, too, may wish to leave and put the government in jeopardy.

Source: Original material

(a) From the source, what is meant by the term 'coalition government' as referred to in the article? (5 marks)

AO1 marks for correctly describing coalition government as a situation where more than one party shares in government, where cabinet posts are divided between the parties and where a set of policies is agreed between the parties.

(b) From the source and your own knowledge, what problems might arise if a cabinet contained members of both the Conservative and Liberal Democrat parties? (10 marks)

AO1 marks for material from the sources. This should include the fact that the coalition parties had previously been criticising each other's policies, that there will be stresses and strains over future policies and there is the problem of how to distribute seats in government. Material from 'own knowledge' might include such issues as collective responsibility, how to deal with Parliament and the possibility of resignations on issues of principle. There is also the problem of what happens if the coalition collapses.

AO2 marks would be awarded for analysis of why problems arise with a coalition that would not arise under single-party government.

(c) What factors might a prime minister take into account in forming a new cabinet? (25 marks)

AO1 marks for such factual knowledge and understanding as the qualities required of ministers and the different ways in which a prime minister would attempt to balance the cabinet. A good number of examples should be used.

AO2 marks for analysis of why these issues are important, for evaluation of the more important from the less important issues and the reasons for different kinds of cabinet and why various individuals might be used. There might be analysis of why such selection is so important.

AO3 marks for appropriate vocabulary such as 'patronage', 'collective responsibility' or 'ideological unity', together with a logical structure, distinguishing between examples of individual appointments and the building of the cabinet as a collective entity.

The assessment objective marks for essay questions in Section B of Unit 2 are allocated thus:

AO1   20 marks

AO2   12 marks

AO3   8 marks

Total   40 marks

Note that the marks for essay questions are biased towards knowledge and understanding, accounting for half the total. This means there needs to be more emphasis on the use of illustrations and examples as well as general factual evidence to support conclusions.

Question 3 (40 marks)

Analyse the main distinctions between the role and importance of the House of Commons and the House of Lords.

AO1 marks will include the practical differences between the Lords and the Commons. This means the differences in formal powers, the differences in status – Commons is the senior house; explain why – and importance, i.e. what different roles they tend to play and what are the most important roles. There should be examples of the work of each House and illustrations of how they have been important. Key incidents and developments should be included. Answers should be as up to date as possible.

AO2 marks can be gained first through analysis. For example, why the Commons is seen as more important, why the Lords can be more independent, why there may be more expertise in the Lords, but why the Commons has more democratic legitimacy. Second, these marks are gained through evaluation. This will involve distinguishing the more important from the less important factors. Evaluation also means assessing the importance of the Commons against that of the Lords. What are the decisive differences? Are there any changes taking place in the relationship?

AO3 will be partly for structure. A good structure will include an introduction, which should discuss what role and importance mean. The content should be logical, demonstrating the various aspects of the distinctions between the two. Each distinction should be clearly drawn out. A conclusion is needed, containing an overall comparison between the two chambers.

Question 4 (40 marks)

Why is the independence of the judiciary so important and how is it maintained in the UK?

AO1 marks will be gained by describing effectively the various aspects of the term 'independence', together with the practical ways in which independence is maintained. There should also be examples of how independence is indicated in practice, probably using important cases to illustrate this importance.

AO2 marks will be gained largely by addressing the 'why' part of the question. There should be an analysis of the relationship between independence and the role of the senior judiciary in terms of protecting rights and liberties, maintaining the rule of law and controlling the arbitrary power of the executive and other public bodies. Here, again, examples of cases should be used to illustrate the analysis. This analysis should also be related to key concepts such as justice, rights and the separation of powers.

AO3 marks will depend largely upon structure and the appropriate use of political vocabulary. The logical structure might be an explanation of independence followed by a description of how it is maintained. The main content should describe in analytical terms the relationships between independence and the roles of the judiciary. A conclusion should draw out the key issues and contain a summary of why this is such an important feature of government. Appropriate vocabulary might include such phrases as 'separation of powers', 'rule of law', 'arbitrary power' and 'civil liberties'.

Index